Sensuous Thoughts:
Essays on the Work of
Donald Judd

Richard Shiff

In memory of

VERNON FAULCONER

ARLENE DAYTON

WILLIAM JORDAN

Sensuous Thoughts: Essays on the Work of Donald Judd

Richard Shiff

MARFA BOOKS

HATJE CANTZ

Contents

6 Editors' Note

10 There Is No Meaning

16 Donald Judd: Fast Thinking

48 A Space of One to One

76 Judd Through Oldenburg

92 Specificity

106 To Stop the Heart

116 Projection, Projection

126 What Judd Knows

154 Every Shiny Object Wants An Infant Who Will Love It

184 As It Feels

202 Sensuous Thoughts

248 Plates

290 Credits

Editors' Note

We would like to to begin by thanking Richard Shiff for his work on this project. As these essays demonstrate, Shiff's contributions to the critical understanding of Donald Judd's work are among the most insightful and thoroughly conceived in this time. We are grateful to him for this work and for allowing us to publish it.

We are especially indebted to Richard Shiff for providing such a rich art historical and philosophical grounding for Judd's work. It is a body of work that, as Judd suggested, calls us to a sensuous experience in which thought and feeling coincide. It's worth noting that this same work sustains, and even produces, consideration from multiple viewpoints, under a variety of conditions. In this way, Shiff's recurrent emphasis on the sensuous quality of thought, present throughout these essays but changing as the occasion demands, makes this book a work in variations consonant with the subject itself.

We have retained Shiff's original footnotes because they are extensive and indicate his thinking and the sources available at the time of each essay. Minor changes have been made for stylistic or typographic consistency and where new research requires an update for clarity; we have also updated references to Dr. Shiff's own essays which are included in this volume. Recent publications gather many of Donald Judd's notes, interviews and essays. Of particular significance are the volumes, *Donald Judd Writings* and *Donald Judd Interviews* co-edited by Flavin Judd and Caitlin Murray and published by Judd Foundation and David Zwirner Books; and *Donald Judd*, written by David Raskin and published by Yale University Press.

We have incorporated black and white images throughout the text which function as visual notes to the essays. Color plates are included at the back of the book. Image attributions and provenance information can be found with the credits that accompany each plate.

We would like to thank Flavin Judd and Rainer Judd at Judd Foundation for their generous support of this project. Additionally, we'd like to thank the artists and their studios and foundations: Lee Bontecou, Mark Bradford, Claes Oldenburg, Bridget Riley and Frank Stella; Josef and Anni Albers Foundation, The Barnett Newman Foundation, The Chinati Foundation, The Pollock-Krasner Foundation and The Willem de Kooning Foundation. We'd also like to thank the following galleries for technical assistance: David Zwirner Gallery, PACE, and Paula Cooper Gallery.

Several individuals have provided essential support to this publication. In particular, we'd like to thank our designer, Rutger Fuchs, and our copy-editor, David Tompkins. We're also grateful to Tim Crowley and the staff of the Marfa Book Company.

There Is No Meaning

[2019]

There must have been a moment during the late 1960s when the art of Donald Judd interrupted me, as I first recognized that it compelled my attention. *Compelled* is the right word, for Judd's art affects me by occupying the totality of my sensations and thoughts. The American pragmatist Charles Sanders Peirce linked the experience of compulsion to the nature of experience itself: "Consciousness of the action of a new feeling in destroying the old feeling is what I call an *experience*. Experience generally is what the course of life has *compelled* me to think."[1]

During the mid-1970s, while teaching at the University of Chicago, I occasionally met my graduate seminars at the Art Institute. In one of the galleries, facing a Judd "stack," I could demonstrate the tension between a concept already known and an experience in the course of its being lived. The experience compelled far more reaction than the concept. Each unit in the vertical of a Judd stack—an array of eight, ten, or twelve prismatic elements—is in concept and measurement identical to the others. But as sensory experience, each differs due to its unique existential situation vis-à-vis a viewer. In 1975 or 1976, this realization accorded conveniently with poststructuralist theories of identity and difference, a fashionable currency among academics at the time. Yet Judd's identities and differences were physically actual, as opposed to being linguistically hypothetical. His attitude was pragmatic, like that of Peirce or William James, not speculative, like that of Gilles Deleuze or Jean-François Lyotard. To me, American pragmatism and French poststructuralism held equal intellectual appeal; but the former related to a decidedly bodily art like Judd's, with its affinity to phenomenological description, while the latter, despite its recourse to bodily metaphors, seemed excessively cerebral. In any event, for Judd, sensation was hardly removed from cognition. Each of his art objects derived from feeling and thought, compelling his thought and feeling in return, as much as the thoughts and feelings of others.

This volume represents a selection of my published essays (plus one lecture) devoted to Judd's art and thought. Several closely related items have been excluded for various reasons, most evidently "Donald Judd, Safe from Birds," a contribution to the widely distributed catalogue of the artist's 2004 retrospective at Tate Modern, London. It followed my writings for two exhibitions at Pace Gallery, New York

1 Charles Sanders Peirce, letter to Lady Victoria Welby, 12 October 1904, *Collected Papers*, ed. Charles Hartshorne, Paul Weiss, and Arthur W. Burks, 8 vols. (Cambridge, MA: Harvard University Press, 1958–1960), 8:222–23 (original emphasis).

(then PaceWildenstein): "Donald Judd: Fast Thinking," 2000, and "A Space of One to One," 2002. Initially, Tate planned to reprint the essay of 2000. Because of a delay in scheduling the exhibition, I had in the meantime published the essay of 2002. My writing for the retrospective developed into something of a synthesis, following the main points of the preceding essays while eliminating passages of secondary analysis. The present collection also excludes essays having a narrow focus, as well as those that capitalize on Judd's art to address, with a broad scope, a general issue in modern practice or contemporary thought.[2]

Some of Judd's remarks—published or unpublished, from his articles, art criticism, lectures, interviews, or private notes—capture both his reasoning and his feeling so well that I found it advantageous to return to them, essay to essay. The same applies to certain thoughts and concepts from Peirce, used to ground Judd's philosophical and moral orientation. I could have cited other figures from the pragmatist tradition, for Judd knew all of them; but I find Peirce's complexity analogous to Judd's own and his rhetorical style especially appealing, an aesthetic preference on my part. Given the instances of repetition, a unique set of concerns nevertheless motivates each essay. In each case, my discussion of specific works of art or writings reflects an orientation to the context (such as an exhibition or symposium), including the prospective readership for the text. Collectively, the essays represent my extended learning process, as I returned to works previously considered, sometimes with new sources of documentation in hand or new witness accounts.[3] For this publication, a few of the original illustrations in "Donald Judd: Fast Thinking" and "A Space of One to One" proved impossible to access. I have substituted analogous examples where the illustration served a general point or have slightly modified the text to accommodate an absence of visual reference. Despite the occasional sentence that annoys me, I have not otherwise altered the texts as initially presented, except to correct my error in transcribing a line of Judd's handwriting in his private note of 18 November 1990, unpublished at the time (see "As It Feels," 2014).

Judd's notes, like Nietzsche's aphorisms, are monuments to the human mind. Some project a thought by graphic or diagrammatic means (see "What Judd Knows," 2011); others are verbal, like the ruminations jotted down on 3 December

2 See, for example, Richard Shiff, "Space Is Made," *Donald Judd: Single Stacks 1964–1969* (New York: Van de Weghe Fine Art, 2006), 8–13; *Doubt* (New York: Routledge, 2008), 49–56; "On Knowing an Object," *Byzantine Things in the World*, ed. Glenn Peers (Houston: Menil Collection, 2013), 128–39.

3 For example, in "Donald Judd: Fast Thinking" (2000), I referred to an untitled work of 1964, alluding to its significance as the first application of Judd's way of radically projecting an object from a wall. A more complete account of this work and its relation to another plausible candidate for "first," created in 1963, would come in "What Judd Knows" (2011). There I elaborated on my initial argument, aided by a drawing that I had not yet seen in 2000 (as a precedent, William C. Agee had made a case for the work of 1963 in "Unit, Series, Site: A Judd Lexicon," *Art in America* 63/3 [May-June 1975]: 44). One of Judd's relevant statements (published long after Agee's account) strongly favors the 1964 work; his other remarks on this matter are ambivalent. The difference between the work of 1963 and the work of 1964 hinges on the distinction between a volume for which the projective depth is equal to the height (1963) and one for which the depth is greater than the height (1964).

1986. Judd was recalling the autumn just past in far West Texas: "The desert was spare, as usual, but very green and beautiful." Challenging his habits of judgment, he wondered what distinction the category of beauty might meaningfully entail:

> I realized that the land [itself] and presumably the rabbits, quail, lizards, and bugs didn't know that this was beautiful. Only I knew it, or we, since such observations are assumed to be held in common by everyone ... But then I realized that the observation is only ours, the same as the lizard's opinion of the bug [of interest only to the lizard]. The observation has no relevance, no validity, no objectivity, and so the land was not beautiful—who's to say. It simply exists.... But when I realize that our [human] appreciation is really only mine or anyone's, with nothing wider, that the appreciation exists as everything does, that's it. There is no meaning. Except that it exists.... It's important to remember that the large and natural reaction [that the land is beautiful] is natural, at least one thing among others.[4]

"There is no meaning" because there is no alternative, no counterargument. An A means nothing without the differential introduced by a B. Judd's meditation severs cultural meaning from unmediated experience, severs it from the animal sense that is specifically human, the source of all sensation and thought, including the sense that our natural environment is "beautiful." To invoke this term represents more of an application of instinct than of analytical judgment. Or rather, it is instinct disguising itself as judgment in the hubristic belief, so widespread among intellectuals, that we cultivated humans construct all value, including that of the "natural" and the "beautiful."[5] As neither modernist nor postmodernist, Judd denied the prevailing doxa of his contemporaries, which attributed virtually all judgments of sense to social identities and cultural ideologies. He recognized in himself an emotional response to the land, which, in turn, identified him as the human *animal*. He appreciated the land as the lizard appreciates the bug, his animality providing the ground for his humanity—a condition that lacks cultural significance because it cannot be otherwise. Philosophical concepts of beauty sustain the drift of intellectual argument but leave little or no trace on experience.

[4] Judd, "3 December 1986," *Donald Judd Writings*, ed. Flavin Judd and Caitlin Murray (New York: Judd Foundation and David Zwirner Books, 2016), 444–45.

[5] Compare Maurice Merleau-Ponty, "An Unpublished Text by Maurice Merleau-Ponty: *A Prospectus of His Work*," trans. Arleen B. Dallery, *The Primacy of Perception*, ed. James M. Edie (Evanston: Northwestern University Press, 1964), 7: "Through its 'sensory fields' and its whole organization the body is, so to speak, predestined to model itself on the natural aspects of the world. But as an active body capable of gestures, of expression, and finally of language, it turns back on the world to signify it." So-called beauty is a signification, not a truth.

Judd created his art from materials that remained largely as they existed in their relative neutrality, whether natural (the mud and straw of adobe, the gravel and sand of concrete) or industrial (sheets of steel, aluminum, copper, plywood, and Plexiglas). Like the land, wild or cultivated, all was "beautiful." His works became beautiful as their default position, when they succeeded in avoiding the distraction of connotative meaning; they were specific with respect to sensation, non-specific with respect to culture. Aided by technical fabricators, Judd used various industrial materials to fashion objects to be seen, not to be interpreted. References to the industrial revolution and its capitalist economy were beside the point, as were the inflections of a post-industrial culture. Yet materials, like words, cannot interminably escape the connotative minefield that human history establishes. And a physical art like Judd's has the limitation (also the opportunity) that it must rely on *some* material. The artist's trick is to stave off the invocation of cultural cliché as a suitably valid response, long enough for the lizard-brain instinct for beauty to arise.

Judd's constructs aimed at being "intelligent without being ordered."[6] He favored the simplest ratios, so that the intelligence of the work could be perceived along with its direct sensation—a polar composite of beauty, no decipherment required. Much of his art plays on proportions of one to two, divisions by halves, and direct oppositions of monochrome surfaces, one to one. These fundamental formal abstractions become objects of immediate perception, appreciated by an animal intelligence equally sensitive to the beautiful organicism of land.

■■■

Thanks are due to many individuals who have aided my research into Donald Judd over the years, and I apologize in advance to those I may inadvertently omit. Tim Johnson and Caitlin Murray proposed our book project and spurred this slow-to-react academic to do something about it. Rutger Fuchs volunteered his extraordinary genius for design. Friends and colleagues at the Judd Foundation and the Chinati Foundation, past and present, have been immensely helpful in supplying first-hand information, as well as access to works of art and primary documentation. Judd Foundation has been especially generous in their support of this project by providing access to their image archive. Marianne Stockebrand and Rob Weiner of

6 Judd, "Note, 1965," *Donald Judd Writings*, 160.

the Chinati Foundation, accomplished scholars themselves, first suggested (during the 1990s) that I commit some of my interest in Judd to publication. For many years, Marianne and Rob have been quick to apply their expertise to my diverse queries. Rainer Judd, Flavin Judd, and Julie Finch have afforded me insight into aspects of Judd's style of life and politics that would have been impossible to grasp without their willingness to relate their personal experience so openly. Peter Ballantine, Ellie Meyer, and Douglas Baxter have been endless sources of information concerning Judd's design process and management of his professional career. My academic colleagues, most prominently David Raskin and Adrian Kohn, have generously shared their independent archives of research in a collective spirit of honoring Judd's achievement. To much the same collective end, I have been aided by James Lawrence, Matthew Simms, Gail Hastings, William Agee, Fredericka Hunter, Brooke Alexander, Brydon Smith, the late William Jordan, Nicholas Serota, Jenny Moore, and Ann Temkin. Deep thanks to Nina Serebrennikov for her forbearance as we devoted European travel to tracking Judd installations; it interfered with her research on Pieter Bruegel, Judd's worthy rival for aesthetic attention.

Donald Judd: Fast Thinking

[2000]

Hypothesis: "a little speed"

Unfortunately for me, I encountered Donald Judd only once. It was an appropriate occasion, however—a symposium on Barnett Newman held at Harvard University in 1992. Judd had known Newman, been inspired by him, and written insightfully on his art during the 1960s.[1] It's clear that Newman represented an important precedent for Judd's thinking and practice. Judd regarded him, along with Jackson Pollock, Mark Rothko, and Clyfford Still, as having gone far toward liberating painting from its "European" compositional hierarchies and conventional illusionism. These Americans had succeeded in producing material *objects* that held specific "interest" (an important word for Judd), as opposed to creating *pictures* that referred to traditional, generalized artistic content, whether drawn from aesthetic or political practice.[2] Judd's early comments on Newman remain for me among the most astute critical statements of the 1960s, all the more impressive

1 "I was with [Judd] when he got the call that Barney Newman had died. He was devastated"; Larry Bell, statement in *Artforum* 32 (Summer 1994): 73.

ACKNOWLEDGMENTS
For help in many ways, thanks are due to Tommy and Sherry Jacks, Alexander Dumbadze, and Eileen Costello in Austin; Marianne Stockebrand, Rob Weiner, Craig Rember, and the Donald Judd Estate in Marfa; Douglas Baxter, Peter Ballantine, and Nan Rosenthal in New York; James Cuno in Cambridge; David Raskin in Chicago; and Charlie Wright in Seattle.

2 On the constellation of Pollock, Still, Rothko, and Newman (especially the latter three), compare Clement Greenberg, "'American-Type' Painting" (1955), "After Abstract Expressionism" (1962), in John O'Brian, ed., *Clement Greenberg: The Collected Essays and Criticism*, 4 vols. (Chicago: University of Chicago Press, 1986–1993), 3:217–36, 4:121–34. In art reviews from the 1940s on, Greenberg had been commenting on how the modern public's materialistic, positivistic, and scientistic values corresponded to the increasing desire among artists to found their expression in a self-contained, specific materiality; this would be opposed to an art consciously directed at the representation of generalized cultural themes, social relations, and ideological values. The parallels between Greenberg and Judd on this issue have been studied from a number of historical and critical perspectives. For my own views and citations to other relevant sources, see Richard Shiff, "Breath of Modernism (Metonymic Drift)," in Terry Smith, ed., *In Visible Touch: Modernism and Masculinity* (Chicago: University of Chicago Press, 1997), 184–213; "Autonomy, Actuality, Mangold," in Richard Shiff, Robert Storr, Arthur Danto, Nancy Princenthal, and Sylvia Plimack Mangold, *Robert Mangold* (London: Phaidon, 2000), 21-73.

"Interest" and "interesting," as Judd used these terms, imply an intensity of thought and feeling: "The thing as a whole, its quality as a whole, is what is interesting"; Donald Judd, "Specific Objects" (1964–65), *Complete Writings 1959–1975* (Halifax: Nova Scotia College of Art and Design, 1975), 187. Such a statement is double-edged because the work's qualities and their "wholeness" (another key word for Judd) both solicit and retain the viewer's interest (as a complex of intellectual and emotional predispositions), while also enhancing that interest in the way that sensation can be intensified when stimulated. Michael Fried's misconstrual or belittling of Judd's sense of "interest" (commentary appearing first in "Shape As Form: Frank Stella's New Paintings," *Artforum* 5 [November 1966]: 27, n. 8) led Judd to focus on the concept of interest in interviews (unpublished interview by Margot Willett, 1968) and writings ("Complaints: Part I" [1969], *Complete Writings 1959–1975*, 198). Frances Colpitt in 1980, and later James Meyer in 1991, questioned Judd on this issue in connection with their dissertations on Minimalism; Judd referred them to Ralph Barton Perry's philosophical discussion of interest in his *General Theory of Value* (see Frances Colpitt, *Minimal Art: The Critical Perspective* [Ann Arbor: UMI Research Press, 1990], 120–28; James Sampson Meyer, "The Genealogy of Minimalism: Carl Andre, Dan Flavin, Donald Judd, Sol LeWitt and Robert Morris," unpublished dissertation, The Johns Hopkins University, Baltimore, 1995, 182–85). On Judd's philosophical formation, see also Rainer Crone, "Symmetry and Order: Formal Logic in the Sculptures of Donald Judd," in Rudi Fuchs, ed., *Donald Judd*, exh. cat. (Eindhoven: Stedelijk Van Abbemuseum, 1987), 61–75. The most comprehensive account of Judd's educational background and its relevance to his later philosophical and political positions has been developed in David Barry Raskin, "Donald Judd's Skepticism," unpublished dissertation, the University of Texas at Austin, Austin, 1999. I am indebted to Raskin's study for its precise mapping of the intellectual world Judd inhabited.

because they derive so directly from his sensory engagement with the works of art. This isn't to claim that in his approach to Newman Judd lacked "interests" of his own, but rather that his interpretive descriptions seem utterly straightforward and honest. I'm induced to suspend my belief that all writing is a matter of rhetorical effect. Judd's writing—its thought—*feels* honest.

So much of Newman, and of Judd as well, is contained in Judd's early remarks on Newman's paint application. In 1964 he made a particularly significant observation concerning Newman's use of masking tape in *Shining Forth (to George)*, 1961 [fig. 1], a large work which actually contains very little paint: "Newman sometimes leaves brushstrokes along [a taped] area, since that is the way the paint was applied."[3] Here, by Judd's reckoning, paint is allowed to be paint; its appearance isn't of illusion, expression, or gesture, but merely traces the artist's process of manufacture.[4] The paint does what it does and doesn't refer to anything else; it doesn't picture anything. Judd's own favored materials—industrial sheet metals (sometimes enameled), Plexiglas, plywood (sometimes painted, monochromatically)—are versatile like paint from tubes and cans, but with a more pronounced identity. They exist in standardized sizes and meet graded quality standards not necessarily linked to surface appearance; they're rigid and can be shaped only in certain ways. Such materials are far less likely than paint to produce an image of something different from themselves.[5]

Whenever possible, Judd preferred to leave the surfaces of these materials as they were, without superfluous layers of beautification or the enhancements of metaphoric association. Surface was surface, "something itself."[6] The common culture thought differently, as Judd indicated caustically the same year as his Harvard talk: "An imitation wooden surface of plastic is the symbol of the century. All classes love it."[7] Traditionally, the advantage of applying paint, especially oil paint, lay in its capacity to assume illusionistic disguises, just like a plastic veneer. In contrast, Judd's new art of boxes, tubes, "stacks," "progressions," and so forth, whether involving painted surfaces or not, was as non-illusionistic as he could make it. He saw the same attempt in Newman's *Shining Forth*, despite the artist's choice of oil paint. When questioned in 1971 about its "brushiness," Judd once more came to Newman's defense: "It's not used to make air or illusionistic space. It's used as the nature of the edge, the process of making the edge. That has to do with brushwork as contrasted with making space." The brushwork was

3 Judd, "Barnett Newman" (1964-1970), *Complete Writings 1959–1975*, 202.

4 Of Pollock, Judd wrote: "The dripped paint ... is dripped paint. It's that sensation, completely immediate and specific, and nothing modifies it ... It's not something else that alludes to dripped paint" ("Jackson Pollock" [1967], *Complete Writings 1959–1975*, 195).

5 As Judd was aware, a number of other artists attempted to use paint in the way that he came to use sheet metal and the like: "I began to wonder how I could use paint merely as material, as an industrial found object: I did not want to use it to make something else, to create an illusion"; Richard Serra, interview by Alfred Pacquement (1983), *Writings / Interviews* (Chicago: University of Chicago Press, 1994), 158. Serra was referring to his student years, the early 1960s; like Judd, he would turn from painting to three-dimensional work.

6 Judd, "Statement" (1968), *Complete Writings 1959–1975*, 196: "A shape, a volume, a color, a surface is something itself. It shouldn't be concealed as part of a fairly different whole." For Judd's views on the colors of materials, see Jochen Poetter, ed., "Back to Clarity: Interview with Donald Judd," in *Donald Judd*, exh. cat. (Baden-Baden: Staatliche Kunsthalle Baden-Baden, 1989), 94–95; Angeli Janhsen, ed., "Discussion with Donald Judd," in *Donald Judd*, exh. cat. (St. Gallen: Kunstverein St. Gallen, 1990), 54.

7 Donald Judd, "Art and Internationalism: Prolegomena" (1992), *Donald Judd*, exh. cat. (Osaka: Gallery Yamaguchi, 1992), 8.

1
Barnett Newman
Shining Forth (To George), 1961
Oil on canvas
114 × 174 inches
(290 × 442 cm)

just brushwork. Finally, however, Judd had to say that all painting, even Newman's, was "spatially illusionistic."[8] But this was no longer his own worry; he had given up painting in 1962.

The Harvard symposium took place thirty years afterward. With Newman as the focus, Judd gave a historical account of the mid-century golden years of American painting, including off-the-cuff allusions to the general inferiority of the painting of the 1990s. He chose to read from an essay on Abstract Expressionism he had composed for a 1983 BBC Open University course. Given the pedagogical intent, Judd took it upon himself to begin at the beginning and explain everything. "It's a general history, and it's a little bit of philosophy about Newman and Pollock," he commented by way of introducing the Harvard version. (I quote this remark and others from a tape recording of the event; why Judd's presentation included Pollock along with Newman will become clear.) As a foil for modern art, Judd invoked Bernini's Baroque and its official, institutional patronage. Modern art, an emblem of individualism, was motivated by a "desire to escape the institutions and the conventions and to start over with new and personal work [involving] basic elements."[9] Judd touched briefly on Courbet, Cézanne, Cubism, Russian Constructivism, Mondrian, Matisse, and Miró, before approaching Newman and the Abstract Expressionists.

This historical run-through might have been somewhat inappropriate before the audience of specialists at Harvard, but there was nevertheless a specificity to Judd's account, a certain idiosyncrasy. For one thing, he departed from his text to interject the kind of no-nonsense evaluations he had made as

[8] Donald Judd, statement in Jeanne Siegel, "Around Barnett Newman," *Art News* 70 (October 1971): 60. Perhaps Judd would allow the painting of Kasimir Malevich as an exception because of its strictly "matter-of-fact" manner ("Malevich: Independent Form, Color, Surface" [1974], *Complete Writings 1959–1975*, 212). This was the effect he had sought to create by his own hand, before he began to employ fabricators: "None of the three-dimensional work is meant to look handmade [gestural, expressive], including the wooden ones [from 1962–64] which I made in as matter-of-fact a way as I could"; Judd, in John Coplans, "An Interview with Don Judd," *Artforum* 9 (June 1971): 45. See also Donald Judd, *Josef Albers*, exh. cat. (Marfa: The Chinati Foundation, 1991), 14.

[9] Donald Judd, "Abstract Expressionism" (1983), *Complete Writings 1975–1986* (Eindhoven: Van Abbemuseum, 1987), 38. Greenberg had put a similar emphasis on "factual, empirical reality," the reluctance "to admit illusion and fiction," and the guidance of the "personal" in modern art ("The New Sculpture" [1949], "Modernist Painting" [1960], *Clement Greenberg: The Collected Essays and Criticism*, 2:314, 4:91). Reading before the Harvard audience, Judd eliminated certain paragraphs of his essay that dealt with Newman's contemporaries, but the general historical introduction remained as it had been. James Cuno kindly supplied the tape recording of Judd's lecture, which occurred on 14 May 1992.

a reviewer for *Arts Magazine* during the 1960s: "Bradley Walker Tomlin ... a nice painter." For another, his language was his own. He spoke of Mondrian's having "restore[d] to art the wholeness which is necessary to it."[10] What did he mean by "wholeness"? In the discussion that followed, Judd said "there's nothing rational or irrational about wholeness"; he wanted to eliminate all such dichotomies and referential categories.[11] It was as if he had figured out the history of art by himself, as well as its philosophical underpinnings, and this was it, the only history he knew. I was impressed by his assurance, his measured firmness, the precision of his words. He may have learned much of what he understood of philosophy and art, the Baroque, and even the modern from the books housed in his large libraries in New York and Marfa; and no doubt there was a residue of his Columbia University education (he was a fan of Rudolf Wittkower's work on Bernini).[12] Nevertheless, it all assumed a Judd-like quality. And it was convincing. Judd gave the impression of speaking from direct, personal experience and insight.

In fact, the principle of working from personal experience was what Judd attributed to Newman, as he quoted from Newman's 1948 essay, "The Sublime Is Now": "We are making [art] out of ourselves, out of our own feelings." Of Newman and his cohorts, Judd said: "The first two necessities ... were to create a new reality and a new wholeness. The only thing they could claim to be whole was themselves. A person thinking, feeling and perceiving, which occurs all at once, is whole."[13] "Which occurs all at once": again, a very Judd-like notion, another kind of "wholeness," psychological and temporal rather than material and spatial.[14] As for Newman, if he as a person was whole, then by his own estimation he transferred that wholeness to his art: "My paintings ... are not a construction ... the wholeness has no parts."[15] The psychological and temporal whole becomes a material and spatial whole. Both exist. Judd often evoked the same relationship between the quality of his experience (his existence) and the quality of his three-dimensional objects.[16] Although constructed, the objects had no "parts," at least not in the sense of parts of a similar nature being arranged to form a whole.[17] If there were parts, they remained separate and *dissimilar*, despite the sensation of combined wholeness. Such elements aren't "parts" because they aren't subordinate to whatever the whole is. Their dissimilarity preserves the identity of their distinct qualities within the wholeness. [18] In his last published writing, Judd referred to the juxtaposition of red and

[10] Judd, "Abstract Expressionism," *Complete Writings 1975–1986*, 39.

[11] Analogously, Judd had spoken of using "a simple form that doesn't look like either order or disorder"; in Bruce Glaser, "Questions to Stella and Judd" (1964–1965), ed. Lucy R. Lippard, *Art News* 65 (September 1966): 58; also Judd, "Statement" (1977), *Complete Writings 1975–1986*, 7. On eliminating dichotomies, see Judd, *Josef Albers*, 11.

[12] On Wittkower, see Judd, "Jackson Pollock," *Complete Writings 1959–1975*, 195.

[13] Judd, "Abstract Expressionism," 41-42; Barnett Newman, "The Sublime Is Now" (1948), in John P. O'Neill, ed., *Barnett Newman: Selected Writings and Interviews* (New York: Knopf, 1990), 173.

[14] Judd argued that time and space are abstractions or generalities, made real only through a person's specific actions: "Time and space don't exist; they are made by events and positions" ("On Russian Art and Its Relation to My Work" [1981], *Complete Writings 1975–1986*, 17).

[15] Newman, supplemental statement (1965) to "Interview with David Sylvester" (1965–72), in O'Neill, *Barnett Newman: Selected Writings and Interviews*, 254.

[16] It may be quixotic, but I will avoid calling Judd's work sculpture. Asked if he was a sculptor, he replied, "No, it means carving to me ... I never had a word; I don't know"; Katharina Winnekes, "Interview mit Donald Judd," *Kunst und Kirche*, April 1993, 136.

[17] Judd defined conventional painting in terms of "the quality of the parts [being] like the quality of the whole" ("Jackson Pollock," *Complete Writings 1959–1975*, 195.)

black panels as a familiar "two-color monochrome."[19] The specific dissimilarity of the two colors is conjoined in a wholeness that, Judd might say, "occurs all at once."

This is a thought difficult to grasp, yet it can be approached from several directions. It's a problem for those like myself, who (when I'm thinking slowly) perceive difference, division, and delay within psychological and phenomenological fields that our culture strives to keep integrated and coherent. These battlegrounds of division and integration include not only the individual's perspective on the external world, but a person's sense of self, the (illusory?) healthy ego. Judd's case is complex because he rejected the traditional forms of integration and totalization founded on hierarchical systems and compositional harmonies of subordinate parts, yet he still accepted wholeness as a reality, or at least an ethical aim.[20] As I've said, his was a wholeness of dissimilars, not likenesses. Bear in mind that Judd was a great skeptic, who (like a skeptic) had faith in his senses and in all things he could perceive, things that were definite. He was also a champion of individual agency.[21] Art need only point in the direction of a better world; it needn't achieve the ultimate. A few local successes, by whoever could do it, would be enough.

It may be that difficult combinations (dissimilar elements and qualities) define who Judd was and what he did. For instance, it was characteristic of him to mix pragmatic, skeptical philosophy with dry, skeptical wit. This combination made him an assured but flexible critic and contributed to the force of conviction one senses in his art. In both areas he relied on what he knew from experience, what he could see and judge for himself. One of his common themes, especially in his later writings, was the need to integrate thought with feeling. We've already seen the evidence in the way Judd articulated his appreciation of the personal origin of Newman's art ("a person thinking, feeling and perceiving ... all at once"). Judd understood experience as thought and feeling together:

> I've always considered the distinction between thought and feeling as, at the least, exaggerated ... Emotion or feeling is simply a quick summation of experience, some of which is thought, necessarily quick so that we can act quickly ... Otherwise we could never get from A to Z, barely to C, since B would have to be always rechecked. It's a short life and a little speed is necessary.[22]

[18] Judd used the word "quality" to encompass factors of both thought and feeling, which he did not regard as distinct, dichotomous categories; see Janhsen, "Discussion with Donald Judd," 55.

[19] Donald Judd, "Some Aspects of Color in General and Red and Black in Particular," *Artforum* 32 (Summer 1994): 113. On the monochromatic effect of dissimilar colors, see also Judd, "Malevich: Independent Form, Color, Surface," *Complete Writings 1959–1975*, 214. Possibly, a "two-color monochrome" of contrasting hues would depend on an equivalence of saturation value.

[20] "The artist is trying to make a totality": Janhsen, "Discussion with Donald Judd," 55.

[21] "One of the many destructive assumptions now [the 1980s and '90s] is that all ideas have no originators; they are mutations in the public domain. The use and meaning of the ideas are vague. But someone invents ideas"; Judd, "Some Aspects of Color in General and Red and Black in Particular," 75. Judd seems to have used "invention" in its strong modern sense, as opposed to its traditional sense of a new combination of old material.

[22] Judd, "Art and Architecture" (1983), *Complete Writings 1975–1986*, 30.

We have to "act quickly," Judd says. He means relatively quickly, of course, given the number of considerations that must somehow be taken into account with efficiency. To reach a goal, we take chances with our reasoning; we guess, letting thought be guided by feeling. If we don't take chances, we get no further than "B," which is hardly anywhere. What we can't prove to be correct, we can *feel* to be correct; and feeling, Judd implies, should be considered a valid cause of action. In fact, feeling is thinking of a certain sort—thinking that's too fast to be "thought," or rational analysis. "Insight" and "intuition" are other words for fast thinking: an immediate apprehension of an object or a situation by either the mind or the senses. With such immediacy, the distinction between mind and sense, thought and feeling breaks down. Judd merely asks us to accept this fact and profit from what it allows—"a little speed."

Is quickness consistent with the fundamentals of Judd's practice? One wouldn't think so, given the delay between the designing, sketching, looking, thinking, pondering ... and the eventual execution of a work by fabricators. (After 1964, Judd no longer crafted works himself but employed artisans and manufacturers with highly specialized skills and knowledge.) A piece wasn't complete until Judd had seen it, experienced it, thought-felt it in its material specificity after fabrication: "Even if you can plan the thing completely ahead of time, you still don't know what it looks like until it's right there ... One thing I want is to be able to see what I've done ... Art is something you look at."[23] Judd's waiting to see might have been slow, but quickness can be a psychological phenomenon, a certain feeling that accompanies a certain thought, perhaps occurring both before and after the relatively slow fabrication of a work.

Charles Sanders Peirce, the great American pragmatist—as such, one of the heads of Judd's intellectual lineage[24]—stressed the factor of speed in thinking. If a scientist were to use a system to test all possible hypotheses concerning a single problem, Peirce argued, he would be unlikely to reach a solution during "the whole time that has elapsed since the earth was solidified."[25] The choice of a hypothesis that actually proves true, winning the bet with chance, faces infinitely unfavorable odds. Yet, to a statistician's surprise, our choices, our guesses, are sometimes correct—"wrong oftener than right, yet the relative frequency with which [we are] right is on the whole the most wonderful thing in our constitution."[26] If we can guess or intuit the correct hypothesis rather than working through the

[23] Judd, in Glaser, "Questions to Stella and Judd," 60–61.

[24] On the details of Judd's education and the origins of his empiricism and pragmatism, see Raskin, "Donald Judd's Skepticism." Judd quoted a passage from Peirce at the conclusion of his "A Long Discussion Not About Master-pieces But Why There are So Few of Them, Part II" (1984), *Complete Writings 1975–1986*, 85–86.

[25] Charles Sanders Peirce, "Lectures on Pragmatism" (1903), *Collected Papers of Charles Sanders Peirce*, ed. Charles Hartshorne and Paul Weiss, 6 vols. (Cambridge: Harvard University Press, 1960), 5:106.

[26] Peirce, "Lectures on Pragmatism," 5:106–07.

entire system, we radically increase our speed of intellectual production.

"Everything which happens is infinitely improbable."[27] This is one of Peirce's characteristically odd statements and rather Judd-like. Its validity lies in the realization that "everything which happens" has an infinite number of opportunities to happen otherwise—in principle, not to happen at all. Something of the sort may be what Judd was thinking when he wrote, "Things that exist exist, and everything is on their side ... Everything is equal, just existing, and the values and interests they have are only adventitious."[28] By existing, the things that exist have already beaten the odds. The generalized values and pictorial references of traditional art would be "adventitious" additions to any object brought into existence by an artist. Existence alone is sufficient to develop a personal interest on the part of the viewer, especially when the qualities of the object are specific, escaping familiar categories, making *this* existence "interesting."

Works of art enter the world as hypotheses, attempts at meaningful integrations of thought and feeling. Thought without feeling would not have the force of hypothesis, which is a premature or guessed conclusion; in many of his writings, Peirce called hypothetical guesswork by a technical term, "abduction." Like an aesthetic judgment, hypothesis or abduction feels correct but can't be proven: "No reason whatsoever can be given for it," wrote Peirce, "and it needs no reason, since it merely offers suggestions."[29] As both critic and artist, Judd operated within this realm of suggestiveness that also entailed a certainty: "It's not possible to prove a proposition about the world [as opposed to a logical proposition]. One can only assert, point and list characteristics. The proof of a high level of [artistic] resolution, of high quality, falls into this familiar quandary."[30] A work by Judd is a hypothesis materialized, an aesthetic proposition. It's relevant that Peirce described the act of hypothetical inference not only as thought but as emotion—"a single feeling of greater intensity ... belonging to the act of thinking the hypothetic conclusion ... Hypothesis produces the *sensuous* element of thought."[31]

Judd the pragmatist-empiricist never followed systems of idealized, rational analysis. Results would come too slowly without the shortcut of insight. This doesn't mean that Judd came to his artistic decisions quickly, but that the process would involve a certain mental speed, or at least the

27 C. S. Peirce, "Illustrations of the Logic of Science: Deduction, Induction, and Hypothesis," *Popular Science Monthly* 13 (May/October 1878): 481.
28 Judd, "Black, White, and Gray" (1964), *Complete Writings 1959–1975*, 117.
29 Peirce, "Lectures on Pragmatism," 5:106. In summation, Peirce wrote: "Deduction proves that something *must* be; Induction shows that something *actually is* operative; Abduction merely suggests that something *may be*" (original emphasis).
30 Judd, "Abstract Expressionism," *Complete Writings 1975–1986*, 39–40. Compare Clement Greenberg, "The Bennington College Seminars" (1971), *Homemade Esthetics: Observations on Art and Taste* (New York: Oxford University Press, 1999), 99: "You 'intuit' quality. But you can't analyze it."
31 Peirce, "Illustrations of the Logic of Science: Deduction, Induction, and Hypothesis," 481–82 (original emphasis).

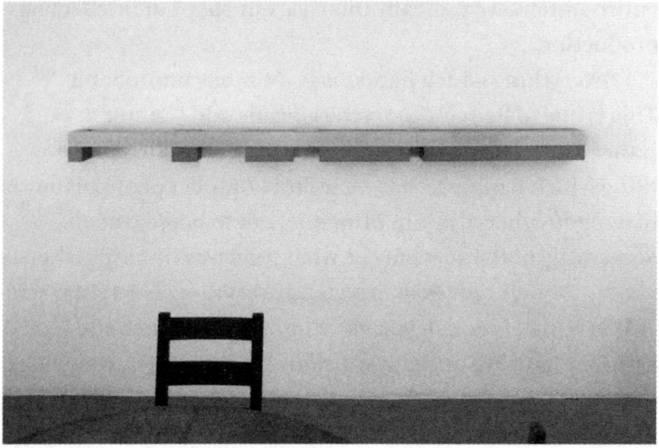

2
Donald Judd
Untitled, 1987
Anodized aluminum
6 × 110¾ × 6 inches
(15.2 × 281.3 × 15.2 cm)

sensation of it, as, from time to time, he experienced that Peircean "single feeling of greater intensity," the sensuous satisfaction of reaching a hypothetical conclusion. From a mass of material information—sketches, notes, calculations, books, illustrations, samples of materials, and perhaps most importantly, the presence of his own artworks—Judd would conceive of a new possibility, a proposition. It might be a variation on an existing type, or it might be a new structure. According to Peter Ballantine, who began fabricating plywood and other wooden works for Judd in 1969, the artist needed to keep all his creative resources as visible as possible in his various library and studio spaces.[32] The drafting tables and writing desks he designed typically had shelving and open compartments rather than drawers, so nothing would disappear from sight. I assume that this practice of spreading out and leaving things visually available facilitated Judd's return to any material and any idea at any time. It would also increase the likelihood of a chance association between one bit of sensory data and another. Judd's working environment was one of "wholeness," where feelings quickly stimulated thoughts and thoughts just as readily passed into feelings.

Richard Serra, who joined Judd in addressing Newman's art at the Harvard symposium, wrote in a memorial to his colleague: "Judd's work is to be looked at, first and foremost. The experience is always rooted in perception."[33] For Judd, as for Newman and Serra too, looking was a form of feeling, a sensory and emotional experience, therefore a kind of fast thinking. When asked in 1990 whether his viewer should "understand something" or "just look," Judd answered:

32 Peter Ballantine, conversation with the author, 6 September 2000.
33 Richard Serra, statement in *Artforum* 32 (Summer 1994): 114.

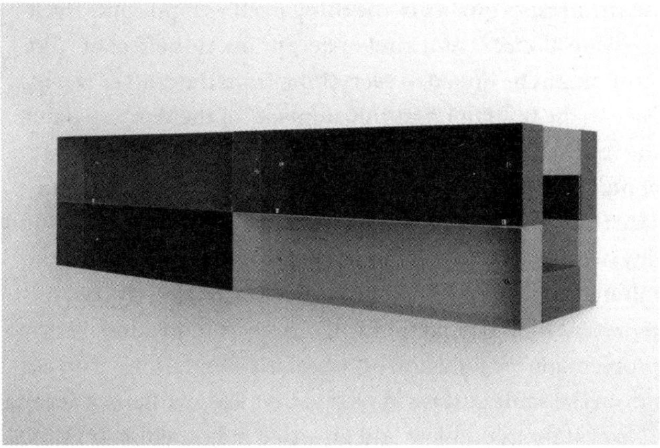

3
Donald Judd
Untitled, 1987
Painted aluminum
30 × 120 × 30 cm
(11¾ × 47¼ × 11¾ inches)

> That's the division between thought and feeling. You have to do it [think and feel] all at once. You have to look and understand, both. In looking you understand; it's more than you can describe. You look and think, and look and think, until it makes sense, becomes interesting.[34]

Illusion

When Judd said "Things that exist exist and everything is on their side," he was taking the side of sensory specifics as opposed to conceptual generalities. He was looking at things, feeling something, thinking ("in looking you understand"). Critics, however, often think first, before feeling. They think in order to understand how to look. Thinking by way of their medium of written language, they drift into disembodied generalities: words suggest other words; metaphors and metonymies are tempting; ideas expand; the concrete specifics become conceptual abstractions. Consider what's happened to the issue of illusion and illusionism in relation to Judd's art.

It's often been argued that the complex optical qualities of Judd's three-dimensional works contradict his indictment of illusionism in painting. Rosalind Krauss initiated this line of commentary in 1966 when she noted, astutely, how deceptive the experience of an object by Judd was likely to be. Frontal and perspectival views of one and the same work did not readily predict each other and were difficult to relate logically. (Think, for example, of Judd's progressions [fig. 2] and later, his multicolored bent aluminum pieces [fig. 3], where what appears to be a solid bar-like construction proves to be a hollow tube.) Krauss concluded that Judd's art was "play[ing]

[34] Judd, in Janhsen, "Discussion with Donald Judd," 54.

off the illusory quality of the thing itself as it presents itself to vision alone."[35] As a kind of deception, this effect of "illusion" might be linked to everything from the craft of *trompe l'oeil* to the fundamental "illusionism" of the Western painting tradition. Illusionism is the effect of a certain cultural conditioning, determining that we see any rectangular surface through the space and perspective of a window view, and any two juxtaposed colors as situated on different representational planes.[36] Such ubiquitous "illusionism," linked to representational depiction and orderly composition, became problematic for Judd and others of his generation: "Two colors on the same surface almost always lie on different depths ... Except for a complete and unvaried field of color or marks, anything spaced in a rectangle or on a plane suggests something in its surround, which suggests an object or figure in its space, in which these are clearer instances of a similar world—that's the main purpose of painting."[37] In the context of his early discussion of Newman, Judd offered a variant formulation of the problem: "Ordinary abstract painting and expressionistic painting ... [have] a residual naturalism ... They are still pictures."[38] And pictures are illusionistic.

Over the years, as Judd's constructions evolved and viewers became conscious of an increasing complexity of optical and coloristic effects, critics frequently noted an apparent split between Judd the artist and Judd the critic-theorist-polemicist. The terms "illusion" and "illusionism" were used loosely in this discussion (which continues), sometimes with the acknowledgment, but often not, that they invoke two distinct categories of phenomena: illusion as a natural condition of vision, a physiological fact; illusionism as a constructed effect for the pictorially indoctrinated.[39] Because the words overlap, suggesting similarity where it may not exist, it isn't easy to keep the referential fields apart. The problem was initially present in Yve-Alain Bois's commentary of 1991, but he quickly corrected it: "I detected a contradiction between Judd's anti-compositional position ... and the voluptuous luxuriance of his materials ... I saw it as a lapse into the very illusionism that Judd, to his credit, had always strongly opposed." The correction—or rather adjustment, for Bois was merely recounting a series of his impressions—came in a note to the text: "From the seventies on, in his many interviews, Judd was at pains to distinguish between the spatial illusionism proper to painting ... and all other forms of illusion."[40]

35 Rosalind Krauss, "Allusion and Illusion in Donald Judd," *Artforum* 4 (May 1966): 26.

36 With conventional sculpture, a similar illusionism results from the fact that any three-dimensional object set on a base evokes a figure in space.

37 Judd, "Specific Objects," *Complete Writings 1959–1975*, 182.

38 Judd, "Barnett Newman," *Complete Writings 1959–1975*, 202.

39 Judd himself doesn't seem to confuse these two terms; see his repeated references to illusionism in "Specific Objects," *Complete Writings 1959–1975*, 181–89.

40 YveAlain Bois, "The Inflection," *Donald Judd: New Sculpture*, exh. cat. (New York: Pace Gallery, 1991), n.p. For other references to the contradiction of Judd's "illusionism," see Prudence Carlson, "Donald Judd's Equivocal Objects," *Art in America* 72 (January 1984): 117; William C. Agee, "Donald Judd and the Endless Possibilities of Color," in Dietmar Elger, ed., *Donald Judd Colorist* (Ostfildern: Hatje Cantz, 2000), 44; Martin Engler, "Specific Objects—The Illusion of Factuality," *Donald Judd Colorist*, 58, 73. William Agee's observation that Judd "seemed uncharacteristically quiet or even perplexed" by the problem of lighting conditions and reflections is especially provocative; see William C. Agee, "Donald Judd in Retrospect: An Appreciation," *Donald Judd: Sculpture*, exh. cat. (New York: PaceWildenstein, 1994), 13–14.

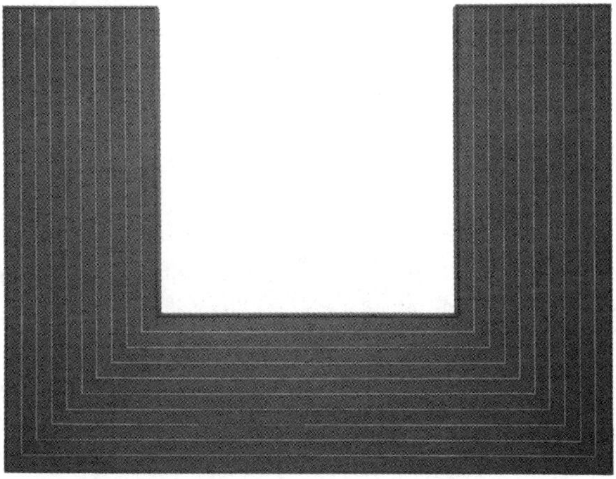

4
Frank Stella
Lake City (second version), 1963-64
Copper oil paint on canvas
82½ × 110¼ inches
(209.6 × 280 cm)

Indeed, Judd did take pains, going so far as to point out that, among all the subjective psychological experiences people have, optical illusions (such as chromatic afterimages) are "absolutely objective."[41] Everyone sees optical illusions in the same places, at the same times. Such illusions are not only objective but real—real illusions.[42] They have little to do with illusionism. The "illusions" of illusionism are images called up by the use of paint or other materials, effects neither physiologically nor phenomenologically inherent in the direct apprehension of an object. Illusion is the way things are. Illusionism is the way things aren't.

Judd's critical reviews indicate that he regarded optical illusion as one of a number of proper *material* features of painting, as much a fact or quality of the medium as color and shape. Illusion factored into his appreciation of the early Frank Stella, whose work he considered the only true rival of Pollock's "drip" paintings with respect to escaping pictorial reference and illusionism; even Newman didn't quite make the cut.[43] Here is Judd's concisely detailed description of Stella's U-shaped canvas *Lake City*, 1960-61 [fig. 4], supplemented by me for emphasis:

> The geometric field initially appears rigid, objective and somewhat oppressive. The successive angles at the two turns align into diagonals. That [phenomenon], the greater distance between the lines [along the diagonal, as they turn] and the paint reflecting differently [from one side of the right-angle turn to the other] cause the surface surrounding the angles to borrow the diagonal direction.

[41] Judd, "Some Aspects of Color in General and Red and Black in Particular," 77.

[42] In 1975, William Agee, responding to "a striking illusion of receding shapes" in Judd's large floor pieces, made the correct distinction: "the illusionism is real—a physical consequence of the structure of the work, not depicted or suggested as in painting"; William C. Agee, "Unit, Series, Site: A Judd Lexicon," *Art in America* 63 (May–June 1975): 46. Other examples of "real" illusion would be the dramatic and somewhat confusing effects of shadow cast at various times of the day on the outdoor concrete works by Judd in Marfa, or any number of effects seen in Dan Flavin's works, which Judd so much admired: "I can't think of a way to describe it," he once wrote of Flavin's art ("In the Galleries: Dan Flavin" [1964], *Complete Writings 1959–1975*, 125).

[43] Judd, "Jackson Pollock," *Complete Writings 1959–1975*, 195.

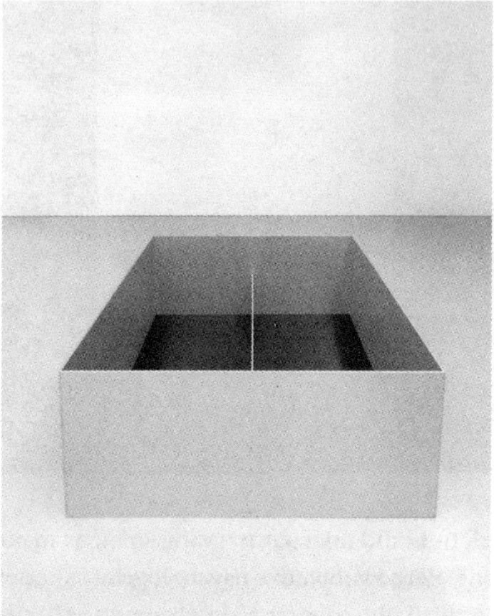

5
Donald Judd
Untitled, 1989
Clear anodized aluminum with blue acrylic sheet
100 × 200 × 200 cm
(39.3 × 78.7 × 78.7 inches)

> The sensation is optical and definite. [This is what we would call, in another context, an optical illusion.] The [illusory] diagonals are free and electric in a static field. The [painting is] both objective, like geometric work, and truculently subjective, unlike that.[44]

"Optical" (that is, illusory) and "definite," "electric" (that is, moving) and "static," "subjective" and "objective": these improbable pairings depend largely on the play of light against the grain of Stella's paint. At the angles, light produces a difference in perceived color while the physical layer of pigment remains uninflected; the viewer also perceives a diagonal where Stella never drew one. These illusory but real and inescapable effects join other material qualities to secure for Stella's art "the absence of illusionistic space."[45] There's so much to see precisely as it is that nothing drifts off into illusionism. When interviewed along with Judd in 1964, Stella said (famously) that his painting was "based on the fact that only what can be seen there *is* there ... What you see is what you see."[46] For Judd at least, illusion was an accepted feature of "what you see."[47]

When Judd prepared sketches and instructions for fabricators, he was careful to specify whether an application of paint should be glossy or flat; from the 1960s, he used both kinds of paint finish just as he used both shiny and matte metals.[48] Reflectiveness, along with all the illusions and complex

44 Judd, "In the Galleries: Frank Stella" (1962), *Complete Writings 1959–1975*, 58 (paragraphing suppressed).

45 Judd, "In the Galleries: Frank Stella," *Complete Writings 1959–1975*, 57.

46 Stella, in Glaser, "Questions to Stella and Judd," 58-59 (original emphasis).

47 Accordingly, Judd tended to treat Op artists of the 1960s favorably, describing illusory features such as afterimages; see "In the Galleries: Tadasky" (1965), *Complete Writings 1959–1975*, 162–63.

48 See Judd's notations to his 1965 drawings, illustrated in Walter Hopps, ed., *United States of America: VIII Sao Paulo Biennial*, exh. cat. (Pasadena: Pasadena Art Museum, 1965), 31.

6
Donald Judd
Untitled, 1981
Brushed aluminum with blue acrylic sheets
4 units, each 50 × 100 × 50 cm (19⅝ × 39⅜ × 19⅝ inches)

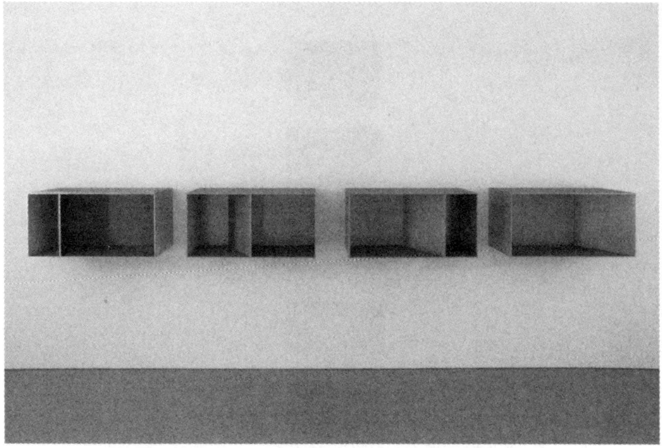

chromatic effects it might generate, was a fundamental consideration; it could be featured or suppressed. A work might revel in it, such as certain types of floor boxes Judd created during the 1970s and '80s (for example, *Untitled*, 1989 [fig. 5]). From within the polished brass or aluminum sides of these open boxes, an atmosphere of blue, red, or amber light emanates. The color itself belongs to the surface of an interior base, a transversal panel, or both, which may be made of either Plexiglas or painted metal. The immaterial, vaporous effect results from a complicated play of reflection. This is an optical effect of the same general type that Judd appreciated in Stella—an illusion, which, because it refers to nothing outside itself, is not illusionistic.[49]

Judd's floor and wall boxes (both vertical stacks and horizontal works) exploit many other optical effects we might be tempted to call illusions—forms seen in various kinds of perspective, partly obscured, multiple in their wholeness, presenting visual contradictions. These intriguing, but disconcerting phenomena are so conspicuously at the center of our experience of the work that we're likely to judge them "real." Or at least to regard them, as Judd did, as the real alternative to the illusionism of all other art.

Consider the wall piece, *Untitled*, 1981 [fig. 6]. It consists of four brushed aluminum box units with blue Plexiglas back panels and internal aluminum panels. Each unit is a horizontal double square along the front plane and a single square at the sides (50 × 100 × 50 cm). Think of its volume as defined by a double cube. The dimension of the basic square (50 cm) is used to space the four individual units. The internal planes

49 Of course, like "interest," references can be *brought* to a work by its audience. On the knotty problem of reference in nonreferential art, see my "Autonomy, Actuality, Mangold." Although illusory effects of light and color were for Judd nonreferential, the suggestion of weight was another matter: "I wanted to avoid any sensation of weight. This goes back to the business of representation. I think that most of the European tradition of art represented weight"; Judd, interview by David Batchelor, "A Small Kind of Order," *Artscribe International*, November/December 1989, 64. Needless to say, Judd also discouraged metaphorical and iconographic references of the type customarily developed by critics and historians; hence his belief in "the necessity for a work to maintain 'silence' in the face of speech" (David Rabinowitch, statement in *Artforum* 32 [Summer 1994]: 78).

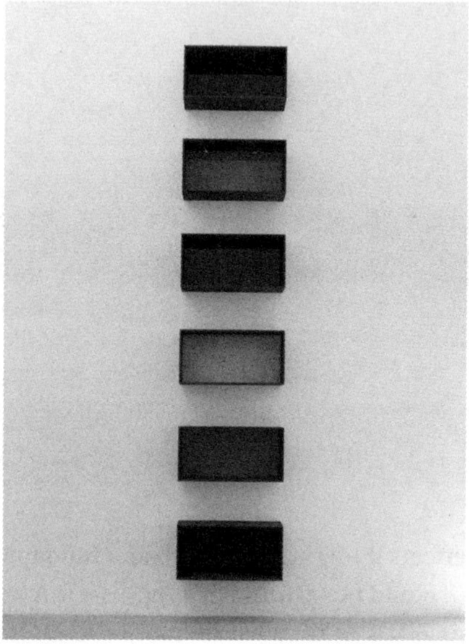

7
Donald Judd
Untitled, 1989
Cor-Ten steel with green, yellow, purple, ivory, orange, and black acrylic sheets
6 units, each 50 × 100 × 50 cm
19⅝ × 39⁵⁄₁₆ × 19⅝ in.

establish a conceptually simple pattern of variation, easy enough to analyze; yet the visual effect is unrelentingly complex. The interiors of the boxes exhibit varying degrees of illumination, color, reflection, openness, occlusion. Here, feeling is on the side of visual immediacy, mere existence; thinking analytically about the underlying pattern won't reproduce the feeling.[50] But fast thinking will. The essence of the feeling can be derived (more quickly?) from simpler variants on Judd's wall-box format, such as his six unit works of 1989, constructed of Cor-Ten steel with Plexiglas back panels (see *Untitled*, 1989 [fig. 7]. These wall boxes lack the complexities of internal panels, but a full range of optical elements still enters into play, including a curiously compelling sense of perspective, much more like that of architecture than sculpture.[51]

Judd's wall boxes appear as neither low nor high relief in relation to the wall. They avoid relating to the wall as a ground plane, which would be a conventional sculptural effect, a situation analogous to paint within a rectangle set against its fictive ground plane or "background," illusionistically.[52] The space of Judd's boxes is their own, not some pictorial space that appears larger than the actual space of the art. We see Judd's boxes at their true size, neither larger nor smaller than they are, regardless of the viewing position. Although the size of the installation room may affect the placement of a work, it

50 The pattern: All internal planes measure one half meter square. An internal plane is set parallel to the side one quarter meter from the left; this remains a constant in all six boxes. Planes parallel to the front in the three boxes to the left of center abut the right side. Planes parallel to the front in the three boxes to the right of center are centered in relation to the width of the box (and therefore abut the internal plane parallel to the side). Each subset of three boxes has the following sequence of planes parallel to the front: one, flush with the front; one, halfway back; two, one front and one halfway back.

51 Judd's architectural works have many of the features of his three-dimensional art. When he redesigned two artillery sheds at Marfa to house his group of mill aluminum floor works of 1980–84, he created buildings that appear closed and solid from their entrance ends, yet entirely open and spatial from their elongated sides—a variation on the usual effect of Judd's many box-like and tube-like structures.

52 In connection with work in relief, Judd mentions three artists whom he had praised repeatedly during his years as an art critic—Claes Oldenburg, Lee Bontecou, and John Chamberlain; Judd, "Some Aspects of Color in General and Red and Black in Particular," 75.

8
Donald Judd
Untitled, 1964
Red lacquer on wood
4 13/16 × 25 1/2 × 8 3/8 inches
(12.2 × 64.8 × 21.3 cm)

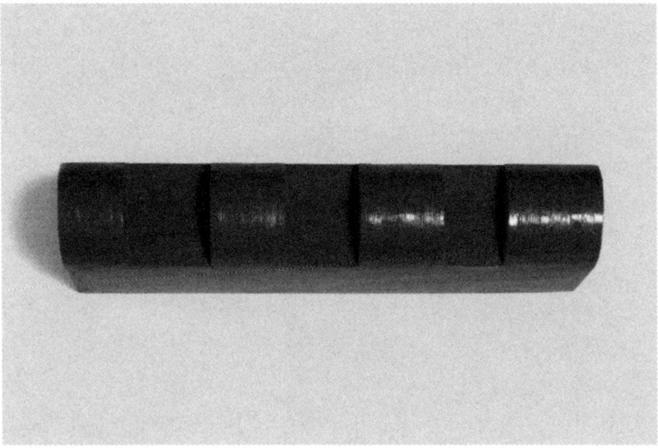

will not affect the perception of true size. "Don thought of scale as fundamentally inherent in an object," the sculptor David Rabinowitch recalled; "I saw it as a function of conditions of observation."[53]

Most people would agree with Rabinowitch. "Inherent scale" is one of those strange Juddisms, one of his counterintuitive intuitions. Sometimes it benefits us to suspend what seems like the sophisticated notion—"a function of conditions of observation"—in order to test out, hypothetically, what seems like the naive one—"inherent scale," or things as they are. Judd provided an explanation of his insight in his last essay, albeit cryptically. With regard to the degree of projection from the wall, he stated that this dimension should be "at least as much as [the object's] height [or] width" (*Untitled*, 1981 [see fig. 6], projects 50 cm, its height; *Untitled*, 1989 [see fig. 7], projects 50 cm, which, again, is its height). With this provision, "the work [would] not be flattened, low or high, to the wall, whether it be small or large." The first work to materialize this insight was *Untitled*, 1964 [fig. 8], which should probably also be regarded as the first progression; it was "made of left-over plywood semicircles, and it projected further than its height." Judd took pride in his scheme for securing or stabilizing "inherent scale" and believed it continued to escape his superficial imitators: "This invention [of 1964] is still not understood [thirty years later], or rather it is completely lost. Derivations are everywhere, but are always low or high relief, new in appearance only."[54]

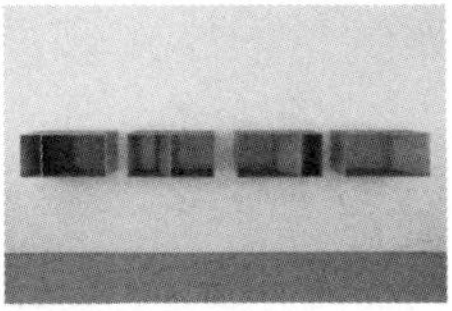

6 see page 252

Given Judd's hypothetical conclusion concerning the degree of projection from the wall, I think at least two other

53 Rabinowitch, in *Artforum*, 117.
54 Judd, "Some Aspects of Color in General and Red and Black in Particular," 75–76.

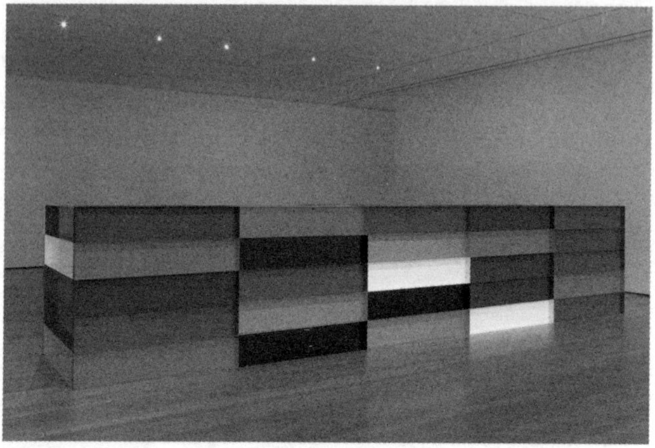

9
Donald Judd
Untitled, 1991
Enameled aluminum
150 × 750 × 165 cm
(59 × 247 ¼ × 65 inches)

factors were involved in creating the distinctive "look" of his work. First, the viewing angle dictated by his instructions for hanging. Judd set the height of most of his horizontally oriented wall pieces so that the top edge would be approximately 59 to 63 inches above the floor (also a height used for many floor boxes, including some large single-unit works in concrete, and for large free-standing versions of the multicolored pieces [fig. 9]).[55] This means that the typical viewer looks slightly over the top and perceives the depth both frontally (glimpsing the top) and laterally (glimpsing the sides), with the result that the formal structure seems to regulate and reveal itself, even though elements (sometimes unexpected ones) remain wholly or partly hidden from any particular position. Viewing the work entails moments of surprise (a pragmatic, empirical experience) but no mystery (a metaphysical element, outside real time and space). In certain other works, such as the late series of plywood wall boxes containing cylindrical plywood tubes, the hanging height is set at 68 ¾ inches (see *Untitled*, 1993 [fig. 10]). This positioning results in the most natural view being directed entirely within the box, all *interior* planes being revealed, including the inside top. Again, the effect is to render the appearance of the form intensely specific, as if its orthogonals could belong to no grid but its own, terminating at the back panel (which is sometimes layered with transparent Plexiglas).

Many of Judd's works have so much more width than height that they appear panoramic relative to normal viewing distance, when one stands close enough to perceive surface quality and details of construction. Judd's horizontal

55 In 1971, Judd stated that "the viewer is meant to see a little of the tops of the boxes, but the ceiling height doesn't matter. They should be hung at either 62 or 63 inches. The choice of the height is meant to avoid flattening the boxes when they are on the wall" (Coplans, "An Interview with Don Judd," 49).

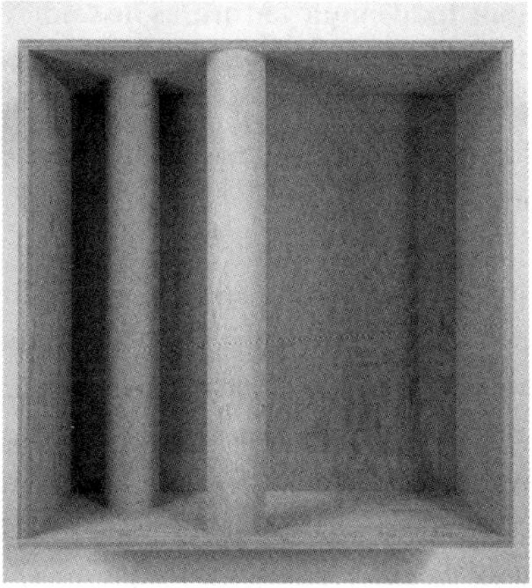

10
Donald Judd
Untitled, 1993
Plywood and yellow acrylic sheet
100 × 100 × 50 cm
(39 5/16 × 39 5/16 × 19 5/8 inches)

The work in reference has a single cylinder that is 1/3 the width of the box, the work pictured here has two cylinders.

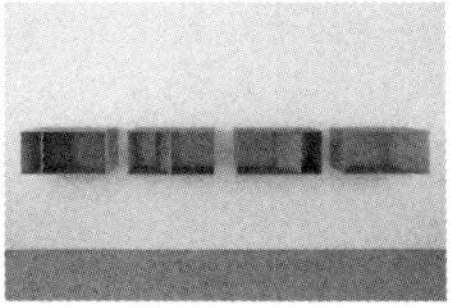

6 see page 252

multiple-unit pieces such as *Untitled*, 1981 [see fig. 6], belong to this category, as do his elongated single-unit pieces, including most members of the multicolored series. These works exaggerate the multiplicity and simultaneity of perspective associated with the hanging height of just below eye level. I assume that Judd intended his works to be perceived from near enough not to cancel out the effect I've described; he commented favorably on Newman's similar concern in his Harvard talk: "[Newman] wanted [his large] paintings to be seen at the usual distance, not fifty feet back reducing them to pictures."[56] The "usual distance" causes Judd's horizontal works to be viewed both frontally and laterally "all at once."[57] This is wholeness of a very complex sort. There's no single position that eliminates this complexity and assures a defining, encompassing shape or a rhythmic, unifying order for all the boxes and all their proportioned divisions. This remains so despite the fact that in a great many cases the simplest of orders, the ratio of 1:2, is articulating the structure.

The second of the two additional factors in manifesting "inherent scale" has just been broached: internal proportions. In Judd's art, proportion is simple but bears complex results. Perhaps either the simplicity or the complexity is illusory and could be unmasked by a critic's rational thought applied to Judd's fast thinking. But I regard each of Judd's works as an ad hoc hypothesis that converts oppositional sensations (simplicity and complexity) into wholeness of experience. Judd approved of complexity, which for him could be consistent with wholeness, and often sought it by simple means; he tolerated no unnecessary complication.[58] It's interesting that the

[56] Judd, "Abstract Expressionism," *Complete Writings 1975–1986*, 47. Compare Newman's statement of 1951 in O'Neill, *Barnett Newman: Selected Writings and Interviews*, 178.

[57] The analogous argument for the vertical stacks is obvious; there one sees from above and below simultaneously.

[58] See Judd, "On Furniture" (1986), *Complete Writings 1975–1986*, 107; Agee, "Donald Judd and the Endless Possibilities of Color," 34.

simple relations Judd employed are, as he said, "complicated to explain"; Peirce, we remember, believed of hypothesis that "no reason whatsoever can be given for it."[59]

Note Judd's wording as he answers an interviewer's question about proportion:

> My idea of proportion is simpler than [something like the Golden Section], although it's rather complicated to explain. My first work was developed by looking. Then I figured out that many things [that I constructed] were very close to even proportions [such as 1:2]. And slowly I made the proportions even. I think what you see [in the ordinary experience of looking] are just the simple ones, 1:2 and 2:3 and 3:4.[60]

What Judd has described is the process of hypothetical inference, or thinking-feeling, that is, fast thinking. After a period of "looking," he realizes he's been approaching a hypothetical rule, the use of a 1:2 ratio. He decides to use that ratio without ever having proven systematically that it generates the best results. "No reason whatsoever can be given for it"; it simply looks right. There's no theory, even though there's both thought and feeling underlying Judd's perception. Judd's simple ratios, such as 1:2 and 1:2:4, dominate his late works. They, not the wall, hold his objects in place. A more complicated, nuanced, or irregular set of proportions would approach the compositional rhythms, hierarchies, and subordination of parts that Judd always associated with "European" art. A more complicated relief would require the support wall to orient, stabilize, and ground its fictive movements. It would have no "inherent scale" to keep it fixed in its own space and time.[61]

The following is speculation, a guess. It's clear that Judd didn't always retain his hypothetical principle of having a wall piece project outward by at least the dimension of the height or width of the box. (After all, if each work has the feel of a hypothesis materialized, any other work can exemplify a different hypothesis. Each work is its own rule.) *Untitled*, 1991 (Douglas fir plywood with Plexiglas, six units), *Untitled*, 1991 (Cor-Ten steel with painted yellow back, four units [fig. 11]), and *Untitled*, 1991 (Douglas fir plywood, one unit) each project to only 50 centimeters while their other dimensions measure 100 centimeters. Despite this relative shallowness (by Judd's standards), I think these works still succeed in escaping association

59 Judd, in Winnekes, "Interview mit Donald Judd," 135; Peirce, "Lectures on Pragmatism," 5:106.

60 On the ratio 1:2, see also Judd, "Art and Architecture," "Abstract Expressionism," *Complete Writings 1975–1986*, 33–34, 47.

61 Judd, "Statement" (1968), *Complete Writings 1959–1975*, 196: "The shapes and materials shouldn't be altered by their context."

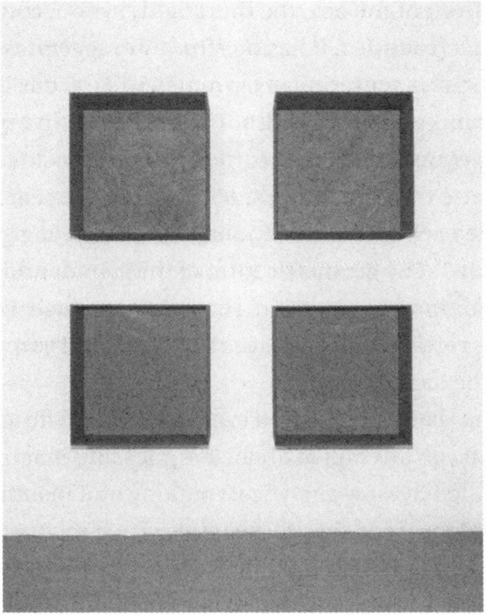

11
Donald Judd
Untitled, 1991
Cor-ten steel with painted yellow back
4 units, each 100 × 100 × 50 cm
(39⅜ × 39⅜ × 19⅝ inches)

with traditional relief.[62] The effect—unusual in painting or sculpture, perhaps much more common in architecture and design—depends on factors of viewpoint and proportion.

The three works in question employ the 1:2 ratio; we might regard it as self-affirming because people are remarkably accurate in judging halves by eye. Furthermore, each work reveals a total, specific structure, despite the presence of dissimilar elements (such as a cylindrical tube within an open box). The multiple-unit work in plywood and Plexiglas (*Untitled*, 1991) and the one in Cor-Ten steel (*Untitled*, 1991 [fig. 11]) are sets of boxes arranged in two tiers. Eye level lies between the upper and lower tiers, with the upper edge of the lower units set at approximately 59 inches above the floor. This causes the units of these works to be seen simultaneously looking inside the lower boxes from above, and inside the upper boxes from below. The impression is of seeing all possible views of a complex, multiple object, as it presents itself to objective inspection. Such an arrangement renders scale definite—like a ratio of 1:2, as obvious and available to vision as can be.

The situation of the plywood box with the cylindrical tube is related. We look into the box's relatively shallow depth, judging its scale by the play of the relatively broad cylinder within it. The fact that the box is only half as deep as it is wide and high is dramatized by the presence of the cylinder, one-third the width of the box and therefore two-thirds its depth. When viewed

62 In many cases, especially with Cor-Ten steel, an increase in one of the dimensions might conceivably add sufficient weight to cause Judd's usual devices for wall attachment to fail. Although this and other practical matters were always concerns, I assume they would never be allowed to have a negative impact on what Judd regarded as the essential visual qualities of particular works.

from the front of the box, the thoroughly symmetrical form of the cylinder (rounded, it has no "front") exaggerates the somewhat surprising sensation of asymmetry in the box by "filling" the depth more than the width. This relationship becomes especially complex when discerned from the normative frontal view because the containing sides of the box appear to recede toward the back precipitously, since they're set at right angles to the front.[63] The geometric form of the cylinder doesn't itself suggest this kind of recession, yet somehow, flush with the front, this vertical tube manages to occupy and compress the space of the back.

This has been a belabored explanation, and no doubt incomplete, an attempt at abductive guessing that may have been derailed by slow analytical thinking and insufficient feeling. Judd warned that even simple visual relations were "complicated to explain." He had a far more eloquent way of addressing the issues that have concerned me. He referred to "polarization" and "polarity"—extreme dissimilarity. Thinking fast, he realized that polarization can be consistent with wholeness. It's not the most likely thought to have. I needed Judd for that.

"Power lies in a polarization"

If Judd's pronouncements challenge the understanding, so do Peirce's. I've been quoting Peirce here and there because he reminds me of Judd: a pithy, penetrating thinker who often referred to intuition and the way that situations, things, and even thoughts feel; who also, somewhat paradoxically, inclined toward exhaustive observational detail, directing it toward surprising ends. Perhaps it's fair to say that Peirce and Judd shared a capacity for concrete abstraction. A final reference to Peirce's discussion of hypothesis and abduction (guesswork that tends to prove correct) helps to illuminate Judd's notion of polarization. Peirce wrote that "hypothesis infers from facts of one kind to facts of another"; to hypothesize is to connect dissimilarities rather than derive "similar facts" from given ones.[64] Hypothesis operates outside conventional association.

On his part, Judd argued that the pictorial illusionism he sought to escape had been engineered to extend familiar domains of similarity.[65] His own claim to inventiveness rested on his having created paradigms for works that would define space and time without becoming part of a synthetic

63 Because the rear planes of Judd's wall boxes need to be slightly recessed to accommodate brackets for hanging, the space between the cylindrical tube and the rear plane is correspondingly less than it "should" be, were the piece to be realized in ideal dimensions. This type of irregularity escapes ordinary visual inspection, yet an idealist (not Judd) would be concerned that the variation could be measured, even if otherwise passing unnoticed. For Judd, only what a viewer might actually be inclined to look at will matter. In a similar way, Judd tolerated a certain degree of scratching, abrading, and staining of polished metal, especially if caused by the tools used in its customary manufacture (this is the opinion of Peter Ballantine and Rob Weiner, both of whom worked with the artist [conversations with the author, August–September 2000]). But Judd objected to such marking when it resolved into an independent pattern, becoming a perceptual distraction and destroying the wholeness of the aesthetic experience.

64 Peirce, "Illustrations of the Logic of Science: Deduction, Induction, and Hypothesis," 481.

65 Judd, "Specific Objects," *Complete Writings 1959–1975*, 182.

environment of metaphor and anthropomorphism: "I developed space as a main aspect of art."[66] He said "*a* main aspect," not "*the* main aspect." He meant that the space of his works, instead of becoming a general field encompassing all other features, was a distinct quality to be sensed among those others, neither greater nor lesser, like shape, color, light, or the simple proportion 1:2. Space became an active element rather than a passive container. It was no longer a homogenizing background. Judd's art therefore developed its wholeness while it maintained its fundamental internal difference, a quality not to be confused with mere fragmentation.[67] Judd realized that critical analysis posed a threat to sensations of wholeness as well as to the kind of separateness he linked to wholeness. With his own style of criticism, he attempted to break from rationalist methods and generalities, offering instead his distinctive lapidary observations: "Things that exist exist and everything is on their side." Judd's statement is more hypothesis than deduction, more sensation than analysis. It leaves sensation to be.

Reviewing the tape of Judd's Harvard lecture, I was struck by his word "polarity." In common usage, it refers to some obvious opposition, such as right and left, up and down, red and black, one against two. In the Harvard context, he was applying the term appreciatively to paintings by Pollock; checking back, I saw that he had made virtually the same observations in the 1967 essay he devoted to this artist.[68] So "polarity" was a value of long standing, stated in 1967, restated in 1983 and 1992. (In 1983, it was incorporated into the essay "Art and Architecture" as well as into "Abstract Expressionism.")[69] Judd clearly identified with Pollock's art as much as with Newman's. But there were differences: on the one hand, he had known Newman personally and could observe directly his integration of "thinking, feeling, and perceiving"; on the other hand, although Pollock's oeuvre was less consistent than Newman's, Judd ranked Pollock's achievement somewhat higher, at least in his assessment of 1967.[70] At Harvard in 1992, for whatever reasons, Judd resisted addressing Newman's art without also addressing Pollock's. Reworking his "Abstract Expressionism" essay, he was willing to jettison much of his discussion of de Kooning, Still, and Rothko—"Rothko's fine," he explained, "this isn't a criticism"—whereas he kept most of his Pollock material.[71] It's possible that by referring to Pollock's art as opposed to

66 Judd, "Some Aspects of Color in General and Red and Black in Particular," 72.

67 "Fragmentation" was a pejorative term in Judd's lexicon; see his negative judgment of Cubism in "Abstract Expressionism," *Complete Writings 1975–1986*, 38–39.

68 Judd, "Jackson Pollock," *Complete Writings 1959–1975*, 195. Early in 1961, a number of years before writing his "Jackson Pollock" essay, Judd reviewed Bryan Robertson's book on Pollock sufficiently negatively that the review was editorially "killed." Despite his otherwise low opinion of the book, Judd concurred with Robertson's view that Pollock had to overcome "fragmentation" in modern art; Judd, "*Jackson Pollock* by Bryan Robertson" (1961), *Complete Writings 1959–1975*, 31.

69 Judd, "Art and Architecture," "Abstract Expressionism," *Complete Writings 1975–1986*, 34, 45.

70 Judd, "Abstract Expressionism," *Complete Writings 1975–1986*, 42, 44; "Jackson Pollock," *Complete Writings 1959–1975*, 195.

71 For example, he eliminated four long paragraphs on Rothko and Still found in "Abstract Expressionism," *Complete Writings 1975–1986*, 42–44. Material omitted from his discussion of Pollock is found on p. 46.

Newman's, Judd found a handier explanation of how wholeness might be created in a painting, a rare feat. He was also very concerned with who did what first, and believed that Pollock had been somewhat ahead of Newman, Rothko, and Still as this group of American "Abstract Expressionists" liberated their art from European traditions and methods.[72]

Collecting Judd's various references from 1967 to 1992 about polarity in Pollock helps clarify what the term might have meant to him. He spoke of two primary, "main" factors: the sensation of "dripped paint" (Pollock's materiality) and the sensation of the whole composition. In Pollock, these features were "further apart in quality than is usual."[73] Here, as nearly always with Judd, "quality" refers to character, not value or level of attainment (but the two can be linked). This separateness or internal difference led Judd to realize that the whole of a Pollock could never be inferred from a "fragment"—a most interesting notion in the light of Peirce, who defined "hypothesis" in just such a manner, because its elements were dissimilar and its conclusion might appear to have arrived from nowhere. Hypothetical reasoning never moves from like to like. Indeed, Judd implicitly countered the common opinion that any one part of Pollock's "allover" surface would predict the general character of any other part. To the contrary, Pollock's marks each retained a distinct quality, as the artist developed what Judd called an "extension of extremes." "Most paintings by other artists," he argued, "seem harmonious in comparison" and have a "moderated a priori generality." Harmony and moderation either produce or are produced by similarity, not dissimilarity. A "moderated generality" is a lot of like things gathered together. But Judd's interest was in the unlike.[74] Hence, his conclusion: "The level of quality of a work [the power or strength of its character] can usually be established by the extent of the polarity between its generality [the whole composition] and its particularity [Pollock's materialized marks]." Proportion is especially notable, Judd cleverly perceived, because it represents "both extremes at once"—extreme generality in the mathematical ratio, extreme particularity in *this* sensory instance of it. Reaching still further, Judd stated: "The greater the polarity of the elements in a work, the greater the work's comprehension of space, time and existence."[75] With an art of polarity, not only the space but the very "existence" of the work would become large, commodious, powerful.

72 "Pollock seems to have been involved in the problem of this [new] scale first": Judd, "Barnett Newman," *Complete Writings 1959–1975*, 202.

73 Judd's observation here is analogous to the one I stressed at the beginning of this essay: in 1964, he remarked on Newman's having let paint look "the way [it] was applied."

74 Of his color, Judd wrote: "I especially didn't want the combinations to be harmonious ... or to be inharmonious in reaction ... I didn't want [the color] to combine. I wanted a multiplicity all at once that I had not known before"; "Some Aspects of Color in General and Red and Black in Particular," 113.

75 Quotations from "Jackson Pollock," *Complete Writings 1959–1975*, 195; "Art and Architecture," "Abstract Expressionism," *Complete Writings 1975–1986*, 34, 45. Compare Judd, "Specific Objects," *Complete Writings 1959–1975*, 187: "In the new work [of the type Judd approves] ... there aren't any neutral or moderate areas or parts, any connections or transitional areas."

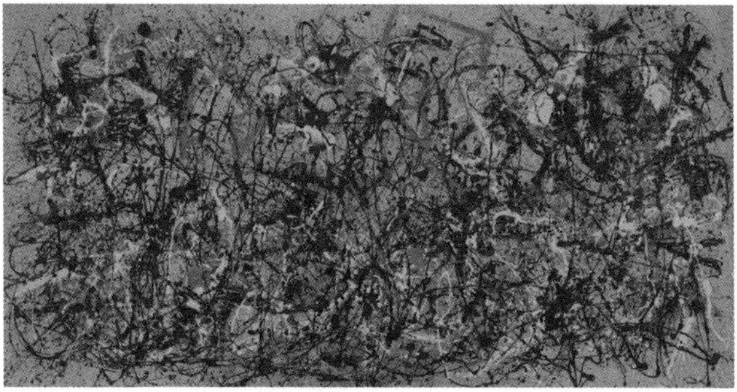

12
Jackson Pollock
Autumn Rhythm (Number 30), 1950
Enamel on canvas
105 × 207 inches
(266.7 × 525.8 cm)

Judd's primary examples from Pollock were *Echo*, 1951, and *Autumn Rhythm*, 1950 [fig. 12]. In the case of *Echo*, he remarked on Pollock's having developed "positive and negative areas [which] seldom overlap or are ambiguous." I assume Judd was referring to the clustering of marks ("positive") that leave relatively open spaces ("negative") between them. The negatives do not constitute a field to set off the positives but are something in themselves, equivalent, not subordinate. *Echo* becomes a painting of "extremes." In the case of *Autumn Rhythm*, Judd stressed its near 1:2 proportion, as if Pollock intuited the ratio as a way of ensuring his work's specificity. (Judd stated in discussion at Harvard that it's natural to see in the art of others what interests you in your own. Proportion in Pollock would be a case in point. He added that the more exhaustively you detail your study, the closer you can come to the other's position. Perhaps this principle underlay Judd's practice of providing long descriptions of the "qualities" of individual works.)

Judd's logic of Peircean abduction, his intuitive guesswork that beats the odds against existence, generates its proper share of surprise. Before reading his collected writings in sequence, I had no inkling that he had applied his notion of Pollock's polarization to the sculpture of Lee Bontecou. In Peircean terms, this is an instance of inference from "facts of one kind to facts of another": the works of the two artists are dissimilar—two qualitatively different sets of facts—if only because of the difference in medium. If Judd did direct his thinking from one of these artists to the other, it was Bontecou whose "facts" must have borne upon Pollock, at

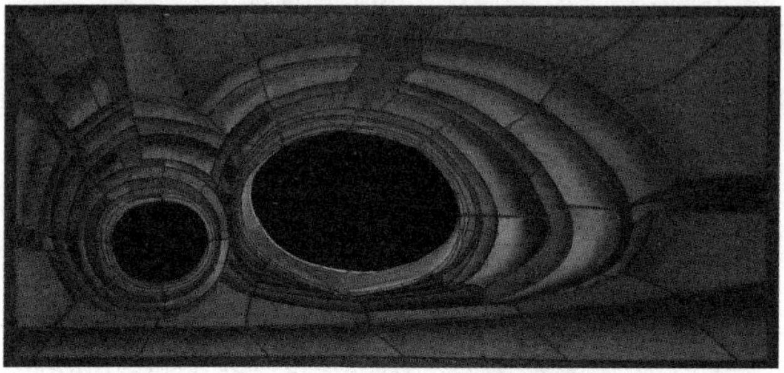

13
Lee Bontecou
Untitled, 1960
Steel, canvas, parchment, and plastic
54½ × 120 × 26 inches
(138.4 × 304.8 × 66.4 cm)

least according to the chronological record of the published criticism, where Judd articulated his developing theory of art.

He first reviewed Bontecou's works at the end of 1960. Clearly, Judd noticed she was constructing her wall pieces with an unusual degree of projection outward; *Untitled*, 1960 [fig. 13], extends forward from the support wall by 26 inches, nearly half the height of the sculpture. Judd resorted to metaphor to meet this critical challenge: "Bontecou's constructions stand out from the wall like contoured volcanoes. Their craters are voids but exceedingly aggressive ones ... threateningly concrete holes to be among."[76] "Concrete," another term for "definite" or "self-defining," is the prescient figure in this context, despite Judd's strongly connoted allusions to aggression, threat, and a sexualized topography. Two years later, in early 1963, he made what to my mind is one of his most important statements:

> The quality of Bontecou's reliefs is exceptionally single. *Often power lies in a polarization of elements and qualities or at least a combination of dissimilar ones*. The four obvious aspects of the reliefs—the broad scale, the total shape, the structure and the image—combine exponentially into an explicit quality and are the aspects of a single form [Judd would later call this "wholeness"]. The new scale excludes everything but the positive elements: there is no field in which the structure or the image occurs; there is no supporting context [hence, no "illusionism"]. The entire shape, the structure and the image are coextensive.[77]

[76] Judd, "In the Galleries: Lee Bontecou" (1960), *Complete Writings 1959–1975*, 27.

[77] Judd, "In the Galleries: Lee Bontecou" (1963), *Complete Writings 1959–1975*, 65 (emphasis added). At the end of the same year, in an essay on Chamberlain, Judd linked Pollock to his developing thoughts on polarity: "The polarity of [Pollock's] work, greater than that of Chamberlain's, is based on corresponding extremes of form. A point of sensation, the immediacy of the dripped paint, is opposed to a volume of structural and imagistic forms" ("Chamberlain: Another View" [1963], *Complete Writings 1959–1975*, 108). It remains possible that Judd formulated his notion of "polarity" around his experience of Pollock, even though he articulated it first through writings on Bontecou, and secondarily through Chamberlain. The material factor in Chamberlain's art, like that in Pollock's and Bontecou's, achieved "an independent power" because it was never subordinated to illusionistic likeness or compositional hierarchy ("Chamberlain: Another View," 110; see also Raskin, "Donald Judd's Skepticism," 56–59). As in the case of "illusion," Judd's sense of "power" has been misconstrued because of the generalized preconceptions of many of his readers. Discussing Judd in an essay on "Minimalism and the Rhetoric of Power," Anna Chave ignores his statements on Bontecou and confuses his concern for the "power" of separate qualities in a work of art with a more traditional interest in creating a "singular, coherent totality" ("Minimalism and the Rhetoric of Power," *Arts Magazine* 64 [January 1990]: 56). Judd insisted that the "qualities" retain their power independent of the power of wholeness.

Judd repeated these same observations when he authored a feature article on Bontecou in 1965, adding: "The black hole does not allude to a black hole; it is one."[78] Yet, as always in Bontecou's case, he admitted a certain allusiveness in the work, which suggested at least two channels of interpretation, one regarding the "image" and the other the politics of art. In Judd's account, politics came at the end, but let me present it first; it casts his objection to "European" composition in the historical and political light under which Newman, too, had seen it:

> The explicit power which displaces generalizations is a new and stronger form of individuality. Bontecou's work has an individuality equaled in the work of only a few artists. These are mostly Americans. The various American hierarchies [social and political] are bad enough, but apparently those elsewhere are worse.[79]

More evident than Bontecou's implicit "American" politics was the "image" in her work. In his writings on the artist, Judd called upon a number of metaphors, not just the "volcano" of 1960. The problem he had to negotiate was this: although Bontecou's "black hole" was decidedly a black hole, it also became a complex of cultural and psychological allusions extending "from something as social as war to something as private as sex ... from bellicosity ... to invitation."[80] In other words, the thing that merely was what it was, a certain concrete particularity, also encompassed a set of metaphorically linked generalities. Availing ourselves of the language Judd applied to Pollock, we would say that Bontecou had developed an "extension of extremes."

Although Judd let little if anything of "image" into his own art, he was such a flexible critic that he could appreciate imagistic features in others, so long as the "image" remained a distinct quality.[81] This explains not only why he could accept simultaneous sensations of sex and war in Bontecou's work, but also why he remained a lifelong admirer of Claes Oldenburg, another creator of "sexy," and therefore seemingly referential, art. Judd's 1962 review of Wayne Thiebaud hints at what will come: "Oldenburg [unlike Thiebaud] makes his cakes and pies and other foods and articles actual objects, which is different epistemologically from illustration."[82] An Oldenburg pie is like a Bontecou black hole (or like paint by

78 Judd, "Lee Bontecou" (1965), *Complete Writings 1959–1975*, 178.

79 Judd, "Lee Bontecou," *Complete Writings 1959–1975*, 179–80. On the related perspective of Newman, see my introduction to O'Neill, *Barnett Newman: Selected Writings and Interviews*, xiii-xxviii.

80 Judd, "Lee Bontecou," *Complete Writings 1959–1975*, 179. It's interesting that whatever else he said of Bontecou, Judd avoided describing her work as mysterious, which others did (see, for example, Gerald Nordland, "West Coast in Review," *Arts Magazine* 36 [December 1961]: 64). Like Judd, the majority of critics appear to have called Bontecou's work "powerful" and "strong."

81 The directness of Judd's language leaves many readers with the impression that he was dogmatic. To the contrary, far more than most critics, he appears to have allowed his thinking process to be affected by immediate sensations as he responded in ways that may have surprised even him. In his criticism, to the extent that language would license it, there was little distinction between thought and feeling.

82 Judd, "In the Galleries: Wayne Thiebaud" (1962), *Complete Writings 1959–1975*, 60.

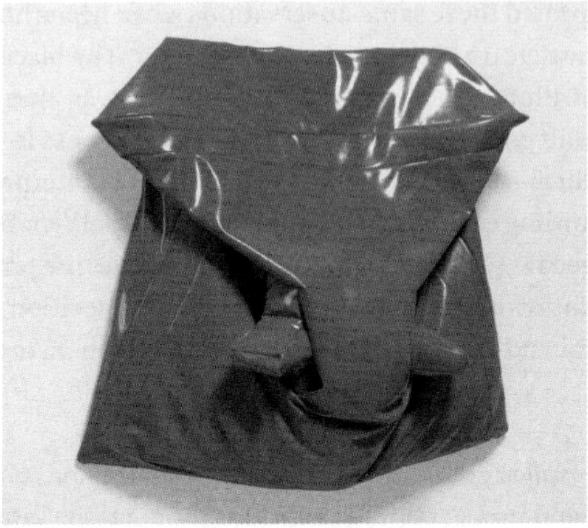

14
Claes Oldenburg
Soft Light Switches, 1964
Vinyl filled with Dacron
47 × 47 × 3⅝ inches
(119.4 × 119.4 × 9.2 cm)

Stella): it is what it is. According to Judd, Oldenburg's materials were themselves "objective."[83] They *looked* like what they were—vinyl was slick, canvas was matte, both were flaccid. The materials didn't necessarily match the sensory qualities of the things to which the image might be alluding. ("Objective" was the term Judd would later apply to optical illusions, another category of sensory quality that remained true to itself, referring materially nowhere else.[84] Illusionism refers. Illusion is. And so *is* Oldenburg's art.)

If a work by Oldenburg calls up a range of emotion while conveying its own material look, this too is independent of its imagistic references. The point Judd made is easy to miss, unless we engage in fast thinking:

> Oldenburg's pieces have nothing to do with the objects they're *like* ... The pieces have only the emotion read into [such] objects ... The grossness of the scale, simplicity and surface make it obvious that it's the interest in the object that is the main thing, not the object itself ... [Oldenburg has] made the emotive form, with him basic and biopsychological, the same as the shape of [a new] object, and by blatancy subverted the idea of the natural presence of human qualities in all things.[85]

By 1966, this was Judd's way of saying that the emotional content belonged specifically to what could be seen and felt in Oldenburg's art; it didn't derive from thinking through a chain of metaphoric associations. Oldenburg took the emotion that cultural associations might attach to an everyday

83 Judd, "Specific Objects," *Complete Writings 1959–1975*, 187.
84 Judd, "Some Aspects of Color in General and Red and Black in Particular," 77.
85 Judd, "Specific Objects," "Claes Oldenburg" (1966), *Complete Writings 1959–1975*, 189, 191 (emphasis added).

object and literalized or actualized that feeling in an object of his own creation, to which he gave an appropriate form, in some respect an exaggeration or distillation of an ordinary quality. The new object became specific to the feeling, and the feeling to the object. Oldenburg thus converted fictive "anthropomorphism" into "biopsychological" fact—a movement that would parallel the conversion of illusionism or illusionistic effects into "real" (optical) illusions.[86] To the typical, literal-minded critic, Oldenburg appeared intent on evoking consumer objects in the everyday world. Judd, with his greater concentration on sensation, saw that Oldenburg was creating a parallel world from his own materials, where outside references would became unnecessary and even irrelevant to understanding.

If I read Judd on Oldenburg correctly, taking his commentary on Bontecou as a precedent, it seems that Oldenburg represented a case of the convergence of thought and feeling.[87] With extreme concision (which I supplement) Judd wrote:

> The sense of objects occurs with forms that are near some simple, basic, profound forms you feel [each of which is a "particularity"]. These disappear when you try to make them into imaginable visual or tactile forms [by applying the generalities of illusionism]. The reference to objects gives them [that is, the basic emotive forms] a way to occur. The reference [a kind of thinking] and the basic form [which is sensed or felt] as one thing is Oldenburg's main idea [a kind of wholeness].[88]

As an example, Judd proposes one of Oldenburg's soft switches made of coral-colored stuffed vinyl, which he relates to nipples—but not to real nipples, rather, to the "feeling" or emotion of nipples (compare *Soft Switches (Version 2)*, 1964-69 [fig. 14):

> The whole switch is big and soft and the nipples [the toggle elements of the switch] are enormous—the main things ... The two switches aren't separate from the rectangle; the three physically separable parts [two switches, one rectangle] don't, visually, add up to the whole. They're made as a whole. They're the same material and it bulges and sags the same throughout.[89]

86 Judd linked anthropomorphism to illusionism and a generalized rationalism in essays such as "Specific Objects" (p. 189) and "Claes Oldenburg" (p. 191), as well as elsewhere in his writings. He didn't insist that Oldenburg had eliminated anthropomorphism, but instead was transforming it; compare his remarks in "In the Galleries: Claes Oldenburg" (1964), *Complete Writings 1959–1975*, 133.

87 The Bontecou-Oldenburg connection is especially apparent when Judd writes that "Oldenburg's objects involve an analogy between psychological, erotic and otherwise profound forms, on the one hand, and pieces of food and clothing on the other. The two kinds of form are coexistensive [*sic*], but with different references" ("Local History" [1964], *Complete Writings 1959–1975*, 153). Oldenburg's commingling of eroticism and consumerism parallels Bontecou's sex and war.

88 Judd, "Claes Oldenburg," *Complete Writings 1959–1975*, 192.

89 Judd, "Claes Oldenburg," *Complete Writings 1959–1975*, 193.

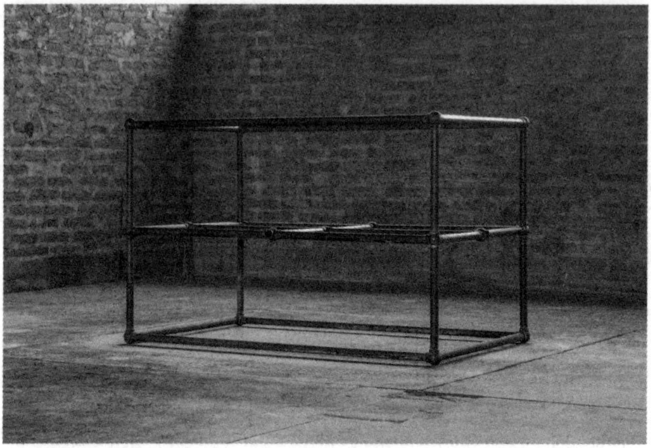

15
Donald Judd
To Dave Shackman, 1964
Iron pipe and fittings
54¾ × 88 × 54¾ inches
(139.1 × 223.5 × 139.1 cm)

One feeling, one thought, perhaps even one physicality that "bulges and sags the same throughout"—but a polarity of references to nipples and switches.

■■■

I'll end this discussion of Judd's artistic and critical hypotheses, his feeling and fast thinking, by referring to three of his typically complex works that are simple in structure.

To Dave Shackman, 1964 [fig. 15]: a rectilinear frame in three dimensions, made of pipes joined by pipe fittings and therefore somewhat accentuated at the nodal joints.[90] It rests directly on the floor.[91] From the front, the structure is a golden rectangle with a ratio of 5:8, which belongs to the "natural" Fibonacci series. From the side, the work is a square, approximately 4 ½ feet high. The height of the square is halved by pipes that establish a plane parallel to the top and bottom of the structure. This straightforward, self-revealing configuration has a "polarity" built into it: because the horizontal plane at the middle has two crossbars set at right angles, it appears relatively dense; this in turn creates a firm distinction between an inside and an outside, a thick plane and a number of thinner ones. It's almost as if the middle plane were opaque in relation to the transparency of the outer box, or were constituted by a different material. Yet every structural element is what it is, a pipe or a fitting. Appropriating the words of the later Judd, it seems that *To Dave Shackman* "develop[s] space [or volume] as a main aspect of art."[92] This work articulates space subtly yet also dramatically, without resorting to illusionistic means of any kind.

90 *To Dave Shackman* is one of only two works (to my knowledge) that have a dedicatory title instead of the generic *Untitled*. Dave Shackman was a part-time plumber who fabricated the object; he died in 1968, and Judd then titled the work; see Brydon Smith, ed., *Donald Judd* (Ottawa: The National Gallery of Canada, 1975), 118.

91 Judd claimed this type of direct relationship to the floor as one of his artistic innovations; "Some Aspects of Color in General and Red and Black in Particular," 73, 75.

92 Judd, "Some Aspects of Color in General and Red and Black in Particular," 72.

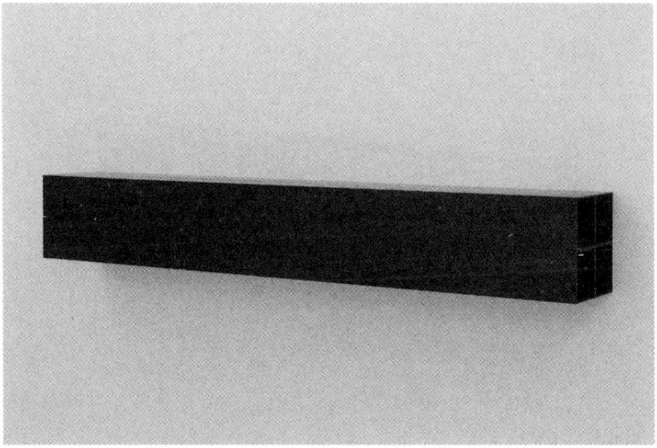

16
Donald Judd
Untitled, 1990
Anodized aluminum
30 × 210 × 30 cm
(11¾ × 82⅝ × 11¾ inches)

Note that the work in reference has one clear anodized tube and three blue anodized tubes, not four black tubes as pictured here

(The perspective recession of the rectilinear planes is a "real" illusion, not illusionism.) Judd never sold this work; he kept it available in one of his studios, an object for contemplation. It repays the looking.

Untitled, 1990 [fig. 16]: four square, elongated tubes of anodized aluminum, joined together to form a larger square and hung as a wall piece just below eye level. Initially, the work impresses because of its restraint, its spareness. Fundamental polarities again. From the front, a solid bar of clear, silvery anodized aluminum sits above a solid bar of dark blue anodized aluminum, although a hint of blue at the back also enters the view (a typical Juddism). From the side, the work reveals its compound four-square structure as well as its hollowness. From front to side, the structure and volume shift. In an analogous but ultimately arbitrary and independent way, the color also shifts—from the frontal view of half light and half dark, to the side view of one quarter light and three quarters dark. This simultaneous difference in the proportional distribution of the two colors yields complexity despite the simplicity of the ratios. We see the complexity, experience it, because the work projects far enough from the wall to render the side view as essential as the front view. From most positions, we see front, side, and top "all at once." My thinking and writing about this work can't catch up with my feeling or sensing it, with the fast thinking the work induces . But one thing can be said easily enough: each of the four aluminum tubes, despite a polar contrast of color, holds its position in the structure and the space, its thoroughly separate identity—no moderation, no harmoniousness, no hierarchy.

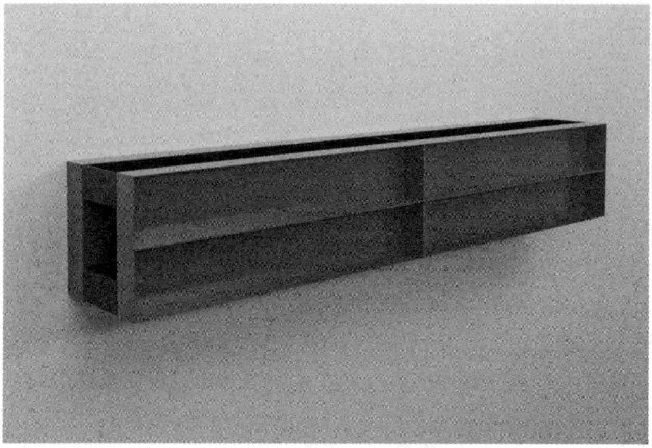

17
Donald Judd
Untitled, 1989
Painted aluminum
30 × 180 × 30 cm
(11¾ × 70 13/16 × 11¾ in.)

Untitled, 1989 [fig. 17]: a relatively small variant of the multicolored series of enameled bent aluminum wall pieces. Despite its modest size, it has impressive scale, a matter of internal oppositions. When seen from the front, there are four red panels; when seen from the side, there are four red and two black, extended between the reds. The form of the basic panel units ensures that the color appears at its greatest intensity, as it reflects back on itself from the somewhat shallow depth of its recessed surfaces. Judd's sense of "polarization" is evident in the compound structure of this work, which, like other multicolored wall pieces, creates a square tube. This interior space is a "full" hollowness by comparison to the "half" hollowness of each constitutive panel facing the exterior. By a "half" hollowness, I refer to the fact that the dimensions of the square orifice at the interior of the multicolored "tube" are double the depth of an individual panel unit, each of which opens to the outside, not the inside. So, in terms of ratios, each individual bent aluminum panel bears a 1:2 relationship to the central channel of the tube and to its hollow structure. The quality of "half" hollowness refers to a second fact as well: each individual panel of the work merely creates a recessed coffer, not a true channel open to either end. Here, by working with his simple 1:2 ratio, Judd succeeded in creating strange oppositions of space—the differentiated channels, hollows, and recesses. They maintain their difference as instances of idiosyncratic polarity in a structured wholeness. As for the color in *Untitled*, 1989—the red and the black—it neither combines, nor moderates, nor harmonizes. Red and black are like half and full hollowness: distinctly different.[93] Or are

93 With regard to the larger versions of the multicolored series, including floor pieces, Judd wrote of wanting "all of the colors to be present at once. I didn't want them to combine"; "Some Aspects of Color in General and Red and Black in Particular," 113.

they? There's no need to elaborate on Judd's hypothesis, an instance of his fast thinking already cited: "In a way, side by side, the red and the black become one color. They become a two-color monochrome."[94]

For those who care enough about Judd to perceive the ethical and political implications of his art, each of his works, from pipes and square tubes to two-color monochromes, can be an emblem of localized democracy—a case of polarity in wholeness.[95] Like Newman and Pollock, Judd was very "American."

[94] Judd, "Some Aspects of Color in General and Red and Black in Particular," 113; see also above, note 19. In 1962, Judd had looked favorably on Roy Lichtenstein's range of "red-black" color effects, which he considered "unusual"; "In the Galleries: Roy Lichtenstein" (1962), *Complete Writings 1959–1975*, 49. During the same year, he used red-black combinations in works of his own. The case of Lichtenstein, like the case of Oldenburg and also the painter John Wesley, indicates that Judd had no objection to representational imagery so long as its material, sensory "qualities" were of interest.

[95] Compare Raskin, "Donald Judd's Skepticism," 96-98; Judd, "Imperialism, Nationalism and Regionalism" (1975), *Complete Writings 1959–1975*, 220-23.

A Space of One to One

[2002]

"Actual space"

They had "not written and talked enough," Donald Judd regretted in 1984.[1] He was referring to his generation of the 1960s, and he included himself. They had conversed with each other but had insufficiently addressed the public. Yet Judd produced a book's worth of reviews and essays during the 1960s. The great respect these forthright statements have always commanded, now as much as when they first appeared, renders his mid-career self-criticism surprising.

"Specific Objects," an assessment of painting and sculpture published in 1965 and repeatedly anthologized, remains one of the most frequently cited documents of its era. It certainly was provocative enough. There Judd advocated an art of the real, as opposed to realism: "Actual space is intrinsically more powerful and specific than paint on a flat surface." He wasn't signaling the death of painting for the sake of a sculptural rival; if anything, it was sculpture he considered "finished." Whatever the medium, a certain European tradition of making art had, he believed, or should have, ended.[2] Judd imagined new ways of using color to create space, and not necessarily with paint. He would construct objects to project "actual space" (not fictive, illusionistic space) from walls (painting's support) and floors (sculpture's support).[3] Neither painting nor sculpture had an exclusive purchase on space. In "Specific Objects," Judd designated the alternative he envisioned "three-dimensional work." It wasn't sculpture as he knew it. It wasn't painting as he knew it. He might have called it "space work."

In 1984 Judd was aware that his written message had found an audience. But he also realized that many of his ideas were being misconstrued, which is why he concluded that he and a few like-minded colleagues hadn't "written and talked enough." Perhaps the cause of the problem was Judd's bluntly assertive rhetorical style, which, like his visual style, hadn't conformed to fashions of the 1970s and 1980s. Other forces had intervened to shape reception and sensibility between the 1960s—the period shared by Minimalism, Pop Art, and late Abstract Expressionism—and 1984, a very different cultural moment. An academicized style of criticism had developed, weighted with semiotic and psychoanalytic theory; its prolix discourse was far from Judd's terse pronouncements ("A painting isn't an image," he wrote).[4] In architecture, self-consciously "postmodern" design took advantage of new veneer-like materials to clad structures with complex, often gratuitous

1 Donald Judd, "A Long Discussion Not About Master-pieces But Why There Are So Few of Them, Part II," *Art in America* 72 (October 1984): 11.

ACKNOWLEDGMENTS
For help with diverse aspects of research, I thank James Lawrence, Mette Gieskes, and Sherry Smith in Austin; Douglas Baxter, Peter Ballantine, Eileen Costello, and Alexander Dumbadze in New York; Marianne Stockebrand, Rob Weiner, and Craig Rember in Marfa; David Raskin in Chicago; and Robert Murray in West Grove, Pennsylvania.

2 Donald Judd, "Specific Objects" (1964–65), *Complete Writings 1959–1975* (Halifax: Nova Scotia College of Art and Design, 1975), 184, 187. "I'm totally uninterested in European art and I think it's over with": Donald Judd, "Questions to Stella and Judd" (interview by Bruce Glaser, edited by Lucy R. Lippard; discussion recorded 15 February 1964 for WBAI-FM radio, New York; additions by Judd, December 1965), *Artnews* 65 (September 1966): 57.

3 Judd did sometimes call the medium of painting—*flat* painting—"finished," as in 1993, when he remembered 1965: "I didn't think when I said thirty years ago that painting was finished that it would be so thoroughly finished ... [that it] could continue no further on a flat surface"; Donald Judd, "Some Aspects of Color in General and Red and Black in Particular" (1993), *Artforum* 32 (Summer 1994): 113. Judd wrote this essay in 1993 for the Sikkens Foundation in the Netherlands, which honored him that year with an award.

4 Judd, "Specific Objects," 184. Judd meant by this remark that a successful painting can be a disparate collection of elements; it need not (in fact, in the context of 1965, should not) resolve into a unified image arranged from a hierarchy of parts.

referentiality; Judd's spare objects lacked apparent references. Consistent with the two phenomena, the new criticism and the new postmodernism, art "made to be direct" (Judd's description) was being "pilfered for art … made to be indirect." In 1984 Judd understood that these recent trends—"fifteen years of banality," "pedantry," "insincerity"—gave him a lot to complain about, so much that he may have felt his past performance as critic of the critics had been inadequate.[5] He needed a forum to register new, stronger complaints.

As *Studio International* had done in 1969 and *Arts Magazine* in 1973, *Art in America* in 1984 provided Judd with space to exorcise the failings of art, artists, architecture, architects, art critics, and art institutions in his time. He summarized his "sorry recitation" by observing that art during the 1970s had been integrated into "industrial [and] bureaucratic society."[6] Against such bureaucracy, Judd, the radical democrat, endorsed local independence: "The opposition can't be an institution but must be lots of diverse and educated people arguing and objecting." To the contrary, artists, architects, and their critics had become part of an encompassing commercial system. As a result, they suffered the same cultural blindness as their less contemplative peers, like the "guy in Tucson with the Spanish-Colonial TV set [who] bulldozed the adobe houses in the old part of town." In Judd's darkly ironic view, artworld trends paralleled the mindless conversion of American towns into "strip" cities: the strip developed "before [its] present developers … [It wasn't] considered or wanted by anyone, like most great changes." Things were happening and the changes were visible, but few who noticed were thoughtful about it, and no one was supervising. If the cultural environment was bleak and the situation of the artist out of control, good work nevertheless continued during the 1970s and 1980s, even if to little effect in the face of the postmodernism vogue and an attitude on the part of critics "that art should be democratic."[7] It was a position that might be nobly motivated, however misguided; but all too often, like other politicized aesthetic stances, it was merely opportunistic.

"Politics alone should be democratic," Judd objected: "Art is intrinsically a matter of quality." He uttered that final word shamelessly at a time when quality was under particular attack as an undemocratic notion.[8] Judd didn't hesitate to identify critics of "whose mediocrity [he was] sufficiently sure" and a painter who was "the ultimate in vapidity." He named as well a

5 Donald Judd, "A Long Discussion Not About Master-pieces But Why There Are So Few of Them, Part I," *Art in America* 72 (September 1984): 11, 13. See also Judd's account of a West Texas town occupied by a tourist class of people who "slowly remake the town into what their scanty and sentimental knowledge makes them think a town of the Old West should look like" ("Some Aspects," 78). Judd's dismissal of postmodernism may seem severe in view of the serious theoretical work and social analysis conducted in its name, much of it more properly "poststructuralist," as opposed to "postmodernist." He was justifiably reacting to the superficial *reference* to a postmodern (or late modern) culture that was already a fact, a reference that appeared in the work of artists and architects. In Judd's view, the certainty of theory was guiding the hypothetical aesthetics of practice, a situation unfavorable for inventors and makers of things. He lodged his harshest complaints against the likes of architects Philip Johnson, Robert Venturi, and Michael Graves, appropriationist painters such as David Salle, and linguistically oriented conceptualists such as Joseph Kosuth. Often in the guise of performing a critique, such figures were deepening the cultural problem rather than contributing to a solution.

6 Judd, "A Long Discussion, Part II," 15.

7 Judd, "A Long Discussion, Part I," 10, 15.

8 The various arguments against "quality" assumed (justifiably) that any such judgment implied a hierarchy of lesser and greater quality, reflecting an arbitrary set of culturally conditioned values, predispositions, and sensibilities. The specifically political argument against "quality" had two further premises: first, that a judgment of quality would rest on a codifiable order of preestablished criteria; second, that a dominant social class would institute such an order

number of contemporaries whom he admired—among them, Richard Serra, Dan Flavin, Claes Oldenburg, Carl Andre, David Rabinowitch.[9] These judgments pro and con aren't sacred, but it's significant that Judd was willing to exercise judgment against the fashionable grain. He was a true critic, astute, prescient.

By quoting the philosopher Charles Sanders Peirce, Judd introduced a paradigm of intellectual quality to match his sense of artistic quality: "I used for myself to collect my ideas under the designation *fallibilism*; and indeed the first step toward *finding out* is to acknowledge [that] you do not satisfactorily know already."[10] Aligned with Peirce, Judd wrote, "uncertainty ... is nearly everything"; in any situation most things remain to be "found out." Included would be the knowledge that conventional artists take for granted. Appropriately enough, Peirce had made his statement in response to being criticized for expressing uncertainty about what he should have been sure of—his own philosophical arguments. He understood, however, that uncertainty motivates a person to continue to investigate and discover. Peirce applied logic as tightly as any philosophical competitor, yet he reasoned that the greatest intellectual advances often depend on enlightened guesswork, which he called "abduction." A guess can be wrong, and is at the very least uncertain. The remarkable thing, according to Peirce, is that guesses sometimes beat the odds and turn out to be correct, at least as far as anyone can determine; and this happens more often than statistical science predicts it should. An intelligent guess saves the time and trouble of working systematically through all possible solutions

as a universal norm, effectively imposing its sense of quality on all other groups or individuals, to the detriment of the expression of any alternative set of values. Whatever the merits of the general political argument, the application of such a grand abstraction to the relatively small world of the critique of a specialized art quickly becomes absurd; followed relentlessly, the principle inhibits any responsible judgment whatever, as Judd realized. Clement Greenberg's critical writings became the canonical target of the argument against quality in art because he had been the dominant art critic during the 1950s and 1960s. Dominance, however, is not a condition an individual establishes, but one that others grant. Judd himself did not grant it. He complained about Greenberg's establishment of a "mainstream" in modern painting and offered a number of alternative "mainstreams," some that had as yet found no critical support ("A Long Discussion, Part II," 10). Nevertheless, Greenberg was in principle as opposed to preestablished criteria as were his detractors; he intended his critical judgment to be pragmatic and experiential. Like Judd after him and Peirce before him, Greenberg sought to overcome the traditional separation of thought and feeling, which he recognized as specific to modern Euroamerican culture: "The truth [conventionally] is not what is *felt* but what [is logical] ... This schizophrenia is part of the discomfort of our civilization"; Clement Greenberg, "Religion and the Intellectuals" (1950), in John O'Brian, ed., *Clement Greenberg: The Collected Essays and Criticism*, 4 vols. (Chicago: University of Chicago Press, 1986–1993), 3:40 (original emphasis). Greenberg wanted feeling to guide his reasoned evaluation: "You intuit quality. But you can't analyze it"; Clement Greenberg, "The Bennington College Seminars" (1971), *Homemade Esthetics: Observations on Art and Taste* (New York: Oxford University Press, 1999), 99. On the importance of overcoming the separation of thought and feeling, intellect and emotion, compare Judd's statements in Angeli Janhsen, ed., "Discussion with Donald Judd," *Donald Judd*, (St. Gallen: Kunstverein St. Gallen, 1990), 54–55; C. S. Peirce, "Illustrations of the Logic of Science: Deduction, Induction, and Hypothesis," *Popular Science Monthly* 13 (May–October 1878): 481–82. On thought and feeling, see Richard Shiff, "Donald Judd: Fast Thinking," *Donald Judd: Late Work* (New York: PaceWildenstein, 2000), 6–8.

9 Judd, "A Long Discussion, Part I," 10, 13; "Part II," 11.

10 Charles Sanders Peirce, "Concerning the Author" (c. 1897), quoted by Judd, "A Long Discussion, Part II," 10 (original emphasis). Judd's probable source is Justus Buchler, ed., *Philosophical Writings of Peirce* (New York: Dover, 1955 [orig. ed., 1940]), 4. I detect some of Judd's pragmatic humor in another passage of the Peirce essay (among many to similar effect): "In those sciences of measurement which are the least subject to error ... no man of self-respect ever now states his result, without affixing to it its *probable error*; and if this practice is not followed in other sciences it is because in those the probable errors are too vast to be estimated." Peirce follows immediately with: "I am a man of whom critics have never found anything good to say" ("Concerning the Author," in Buchler, 3 [original emphasis]).

to a problem.[11] For the artist who thrives on sensory and intellectual risk, as opposed to dreams and fantasies (which have no factor of error, hence no risk), Peircean abduction is the inspired method.

Judd the writer expressed his views with great assurance. Did he merely guess, but with more than his fair share of correctness? He was comfortable pronouncing on the truth of "great changes"—usually negative: town into strip city, political democracy into aesthetic democracy—as if he understood the principle behind all such transformative events. In their entirety, his writings are a source of pragmatic wisdom, a folk art in the philosophical domain. Many find Judd's aggressive wit annoying. Yet he was pointing out, as Peirce had, the conditions of his own fallibility: the "great changes" happen by chance. He wasn't claiming predictive power or absolute knowledge. Chance made that impossible. A sensitive guess would do as well as academic theory and systematic analysis. Judd realized that the broad cultural changes he was often observing satisfied no single person's desire (and certainly not his); rather, desire would typically accommodate itself to change in the cultural environment after the fact. Any individual remains free to resist this resultant, collective desire, a self-induced cultural fashion. But few choose to resist. If a greater number would, there would be no fashion.

Judd abhorred the strip city, the Spanish-Colonial television set, the "imitation wooden surface of plastic." This final commodity represented aesthetic democracy brought to its lowest level: "All classes love it," he said.[12] Such changes in the design of the human environment were products of anonymous commerce.[13] The changes Judd himself initiated were far less pervasive and remained largely imperceptible to others. He had invented "space" in art, he claimed, presumably a transformative event. But space in art had "no history": "There is no context; there are no terms; there are not any theories. There is only the visible work invisible." That last sentence is tricky. Judd's space was "invisible" because no one understood it. It was also invisible because space lacks material substance, doesn't reflect light, therefore can't be seen.[14] Nevertheless, Judd's new space had its physical effects.

"Space is so unknown"

Isn't space already here and hardly in need of invention? Not according to Judd, who argued that "space is made ... not found

11 See the discussion of Peirce in relation to Judd in this volume: "Donald Judd: Fast Thinking," 18, 32.

12 Donald Judd, "Art and Internationalism: Prolegomena" (1992), *Donald Judd* (Osaka: Gallery Yamaguchi, 1992), 8.

13 Judd, "Some Aspects," 78.

14 Judd, "Some Aspects," 70. Both references seem present at a later point in Judd's essay: "[Space] is the primary aspect in the work of the few very good younger artists, who, since space is invisible, are insufficiently recognized" ("Some Aspects," 72).

and packaged." During the early 1960s, he gradually realized that his objects should "not be flattened, low or high," to either floor or wall. Flatness had prevented the development of space in sculptural art. Yet, since sculpture is rarely flat and usually varies with the angle of view, what could Judd have meant? Given the context, a synonym for "flattened" is "pictorial," that is, an arrangement of form that gives the appearance of being placed within or against a ground, like a stage set that remains intelligible when seen from a great distance, in effect, projected onto a flat surface as a picture.[15] A cinematic scene is "flattened" even before being filmed for subsequent projection, since it has already been conceived in relief, as a succession of planes with perspectival and temporal continuity. Space as an independent quality is lacking. Traditional sculpture in low or high relief exists "in relief" against something, its pictorial ground. Whether the object is attached to the wall or standing or lying on the floor matters little; the pictorial grounding of an object and its structural, architectural support are different considerations. Michelangelo's *David* is high relief in relation to the floor, which both establishes its pictorial ground and bears its physical weight. Judd sought to relate his objects to the architecture of floor and wall in new ways. There would be no relief, therefore no "sculpture."[16]

High relief can be as pictorial as low relief and just as "flat." "Low and high relief are basically painting," Judd wrote.[17] Both systems of representation treat space as conventional painting does, as if space were a familiar void to be filled with things, whether real or imaginary. An implied progression from front to back within the pictorial space of relief constitutes the essence of its "illusionism."[18] Internal compositional relationships secure that pictorial quality: the eye moves from part to part, following familiar patterns of differentiation, such as passages from advancing to receding elements or from large to small features in the assemblage.[19] Once interpreted, such

15 Judd tended to associate pictorial effects with the tradition of representing nature: "[With traditional sculpture,] the resulting space is primarily negative, which is inherent in representation; the space is pictorial"; Donald Judd, "21 February 93," *Donald Judd: Large-scale Works* (New York: The Pace Gallery, 1993), 9. The term "pictorial" can also refer to a modernist opposition to "natural" effects; see Richard Shiff, "Expression: Natural, Personal, Pictorial," in Paul Smith and Carolyn Wilde, eds., *A Companion to Art Theory* (Oxford: Blackwell, 2002), 159–71.

16 Judd, "Specific Objects," 184: "Since sculpture isn't so general a form [as painting], it can probably be only what it is now—which means that if it changes a great deal it will be something else; so it is finished." During the early 1960s, Judd was particularly fascinated by the three-dimensional art of Lee Bontecou, which seemed to have brought sculpture to an end in just this sense: "There is no field [or ground] in which the structure or the image occurs; there is no supporting context" (Judd, "In the Galleries: Lee Bontecou" [1963], *Complete Writings 1959–1975*, 65; compare Shiff, "Donald Judd: Fast Thinking," 36–37). Judd's objection to pictorial effects would have been reinforced by Barnett Newman, with whom he conversed regularly during the late 1960s. Discussing Newman's art, Judd noted that large Abstract Expressionist paintings should be appreciated for their specific material qualities, including their actual largeness; they should be seen close up, "not fifty feet back reducing them to pictures" ("Abstract Expressionism," [1983], *Complete Writings 1975–1986* [Eindhoven: Van Abbemuseum, 1987], 47). In the opinion of Robert Murray, who assisted Newman with his sculptural projects, "Don patterned himself on Barney more than any other artist" (statement to author, 11 September 2002).

17 Judd, "Some Aspects," 5.

18 "Illusionism" should not be confused with illusion, which Judd regarded as a natural, physiological fact of human perception. For example, when a red is next to a green, both colors appear brighter along their common border; everyone sees this as clearly as they see the border itself. Unlike illusion, "illusionism," as the suffix implies, is a secondary quality, a fabricated effect specific to a cultural practice, which Judd believed had lost its usefulness and credibility for the art of his time; see Shiff, "Donald Judd: Fast Thinking," 21-32.

19 "Most sculpture is made part by part, by addition, composed": Judd, "Specific Objects," 183. Newman, among others, had "a dislike for the old part-by-part composition" (Judd, "Abstract Expressionism," *Complete Writings 1975–1986*, 47).

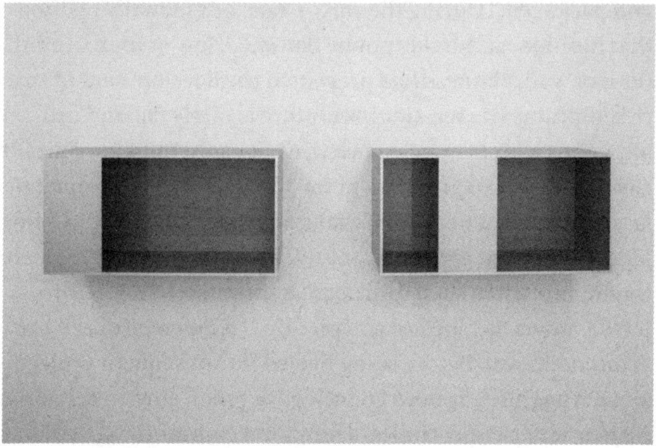

18
Donald Judd
Untitled, 1988
Anodized aluminum with brown acrylic sheets
2 units, each 50 × 100 × 50 cm
(19⅝ × 39 5/16 × 19⅝ inches)

patterns create the pictorial effect, hence the flatness—again, like a stage set or a movie (my analogy, not Judd's). This is contrary to the usual association of pictorial construction with fictive depth. With Judd's sense of flatness, we encounter a terminological paradox, because the illusionistic effect constitutes virtual depth while the physical structure of relief, low or high, exists in real depth. How can this double depth also result in flatness? Perhaps some tacit recognition of the paradox spurred Judd to discover an alternative to the conventional forms of low and high sculptural-pictorial relief. He sought a way of creating objects with sensually and psychologically active space—real space, not projective, illusionistic space. Judd, like a good architect, wrested space from nature's void.

Does the argument seem odd? That would not surprise Judd. "Space is so unknown," he complained as late as 1993, "that the only comparison is to the beliefs of the past."[20] He perceived that his invention of space during the early 1960s was "still not understood, or rather it is completely lost. Derivations are everywhere, but are always low or high relief, new in appearance only." Judd must have been thinking of the fashion in new modes of installation, with eccentric objects attached to the wall or resting on the floor of a gallery space; he referred to "the use of the whole room, which is now called an installation, which basically I began."[21] In the hands of his imitators, the result was clutter, not space. If the foundation of Judd's new sense of space had gone undetected, while the look of his innovative mode of presentation was being adopted, perhaps this had happened because the typical artist, like the

20 Judd, "Some Aspects," 70. According to Judd, what typically must follow from comparison with the past is a judgment that the present condition of things is degenerative and reductive: "If changes in art are compared backwards, there always seems to be a reduction, since only old attributes are counted and these are always fewer. But obviously new things are more" ("Specific Objects," 189). The implication is that the new things go unrecognized, and therefore uncounted. This is as good an explanation of a cultural critic's charge of reductiveness as we are likely to get. Concerning his own art, Judd said: "If my work is reductionist it's because it doesn't have the elements that people thought should be there. But it has other elements that I like" ("Questions to Stella and Judd," 60).

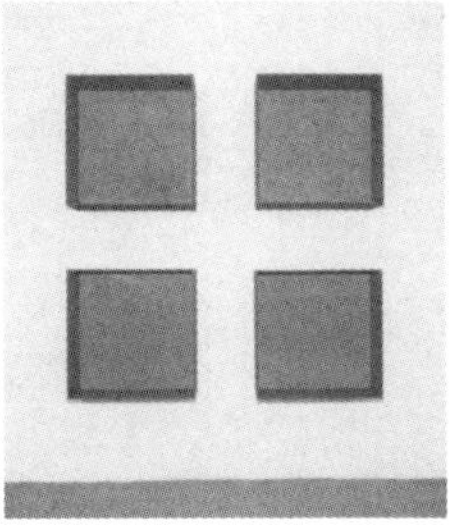

11 see page 257

typical "everyone else," assumes too much knowledge to begin with. Some Peircean fallibilism would help.

In Judd's words, the principle he developed, which others might have perceived once he gave it form (no doubt, some did), was this: an object should project from the wall "at least as much as its height and width."[22] The individual rectangular prisms that constitute Judd's multi-unit wall "stacks" are often quite close to following this intuitive order, with the projective depth being nearly equal to the width of the unit and much greater than its height (a typical set of measurements is 6 × 27 × 24 inches). In practice, it seems that Judd intended something less restrictive, less severe—the object would project at least as much as *either* the height *or* the width.[23] The wall pieces he produced from the late 1970s onward, with metric dimensions of 50 × 100 × 50 are of this type [see fig. 18], as deep as they are high, but not as deep as they are wide.[24] Works with the dimensions 100 × 100 × 50 are a further derivation [see fig. 11]. Their straight-on projection from the wall, more or less at eye level, amounts to only half of the height or width; but if judged by traditional standards, these objects nevertheless extend forward to an unusual degree.[25] The forward projection is so abrupt that the space of the work registers as independent of any ground; the object, with its rectilinear exterior, establishes no transition or other concession to the flatness of the wall. To this end, the hanging height of the object is quite specific, as Judd explained at an earlier date: "The viewer is meant to see a little of the tops of the boxes ... They should be hung at either 62 or 63 inches ... to avoid flattening the boxes when they are on the wall."[26]

When a Judd box projects from the wall, its space becomes distinct. When the projection opens to the eye, whether completely or incompletely, to reveal an inside play of light and color, space is enhanced by a potential for ambiguity and indefiniteness. Judd worked with a great variety of materials. A wall box might be constructed of a metal with a standard industrial finish, matte or shiny, presented in its conventional color (aluminum looking silvery, brass looking golden); or a metal could be colored by an anodizing process. Judd's works in plywood introduce the inherent color and grain of the wood, and sometimes an interior plywood element would be painted. In addition, Judd often set panels of luminous Plexiglas into his boxes, whether of metal or wood. He might choose a transparent color or an opaque one; occasionally he

21 Judd, "Some Aspects," 75–76.
22 Judd, "Some Aspects," 75.
23 This was my assumption in 2000; see Shiff, "Donald Judd: Fast Thinking," 27–30. Given the example that Judd indicates—a work of 1964 that "projected further than its height" but not further than its width ("Some Aspects," 76; "Donald Judd: Fast Thinking," 28, fig. 8)—there remains the possibility that he simply miswrote the statement of his principle. However, he also gave the example of what he called the "minimum, which would be a cube," an object that would project from the wall at a depth precisely equal to both its height and its width ("Some Aspects," 75). It should be emphasized that, no matter what the proportional dimensions, Judd's new type of object was not to appear "flattened, low or high, to the wall, whether it be small or large" ("Some Aspects," 76).
24 In fact, Judd may never have constructed any wall pieces in which the depth equaled or exceeded the width.
25 In the design of Judd's works, there were always practical, structural considerations. Materials of relatively light weight allowed greater cantilever projection from the wall than did heavier ones.
26 Donald Judd, in John Coplans, "An Interview with Don Judd," *Artforum* 9 (June 1971): 49.

doubled the Plexiglas, layering one sheet over another to create a compound hue. He spoke of analogous effects in works on the floor in which "the outside is definite and rigorous [while] the inside is indefinite."[27] This sense of contrast or clear differentiation is essential to Judd's aesthetic. Neither of the two spatial qualities should yield to the other. Together they constitute the work, not as a harmonious or hierarchical order, but as separate and equal aspects forming a composite whole. Each of the two spaces, definite and indefinite, is an invention of an artist, spaces that are "made," just as Judd claimed.[28]

So Judd invented space and produced a type of art never seen before. This was what he had intended. During the 1970s and 1980s, it was common for academics, and a certain number of artists too, to insist that intention was a fantasy, that what seemed to be inventive ideas were mere "mutations in the public domain" (Judd's phrasing in 1993, his gloss on the postmodernist annihilation of individual agency).[29] The no-agency notion attracted critics and theorists who remained free to exercise personal creativity without claiming to invent anything; as interpreters, their intellectual fulfillment could come in identifying the network of relations from which the anonymous cultural configurations were emerging. A critical mind might even tackle the very same Spanish-Colonial television model that so offended Judd's ethics and aesthetics; it was a suitable example for a study of the structural dynamics of popular culture, including an analysis of its web of connotations, correlated with the attitudes of the various social classes within its consumer base. Judd was no formalist (few artists were or are), and he held no absolutist ideas that would contradict the cultural relativism of his more academic contemporaries. Nature conveyed no ready-made meaning; Judd believed that people made meaning.[30] But when academics extended the notion of "mutations in the public domain" to include all works of art, this could only rankle someone consciously intending to create a new kind of object rather than belaboring an old idea. Judd conceded that "the use and meaning of the ideas are vague." "But," he insisted, "someone invents ideas."[31]

Judd himself must be held responsible for some of the vagueness, for he applied his inventions rather inventively. As I've noted, he violated his own intuited system by producing works with significant projection, but of an extent less than both the height and width of the object (boxes with dimensions of 100 × 100 × 50 cm, for example). He understood that his

27 Judd, in Coplans, 50. With these effects, color was always a factor: "It never occurred to me to make a three-dimensional work without color.... Color and space occur together.... All materials ... are colored" (Judd, "Some Aspects," 110).

28 "Space is made by an artist or architect": Judd, "Some Aspects," 70.

29 Judd, "Some Aspects," 75.

30 "There is no neutral space, since space is made, indifferently or intentionally, and since meaning is made, ignorantly or knowledgeably": Judd, "21 February 93," 9. "No immediate feeling can be attributed to color. Nothing can be identified. If it seems otherwise, usually the association is cultural": Judd, "Some Aspects," 113.

31 Judd, "Some Aspects," 75.

principle wasn't a formula for success but only a suggestion, an insightful hypothesis that would need to be tested case by case. The hypothesis would remain open to adjustment, every individual work becoming an experiment, a guess.

"There is a limit to how much an artist can learn in advance," Judd wrote in 1993, in the same essay in which he discussed his several inventions in the area of space and color; this was the last piece of writing he completed. "An artist works only step by step into the unknown."[32] Judd may have been quirky, but he was consistent. He had expressed that same view three decades earlier as he explained that the European art tradition suffered from being "based on systems built beforehand." In that instance, he admitted that there was a strong element of the systematic in his own practice, whether thinking things through while fabrication proceeded or conceiving of the entire object beforehand. Either way, his system was local, applied only to the "smaller" realm of actual construction: "Geometry and mathematics are human inventions. I use a small simple portion in my work for my purposes. Four units in a row are only that." Guesses would need to be verified empirically: "Even if you can plan the thing completely ahead of time, you still don't know what it looks like until it's right there."[33] In any event, the larger meaning or purpose of Judd's art could not be contained within a system. He was so decidedly apart from the usual institutions, hierarchies, and ideologies that it would be entirely wrong to call him subversive; a subversive works within. Like his philosophical model Peirce, Judd worked his way "into the unknown."[34]

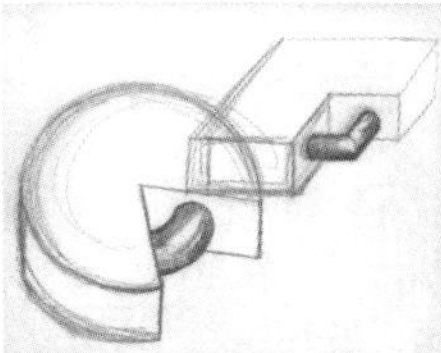

19
Donald Judd
Drawing from sketchbook, 1964-65
Pencil on paper
11 × 14 inches
(27.9 × 35.6 cm)

"Intelligent without being ordered"

Around 1964-65, Judd sketched on a single sheet two related objects in perspective: a narrow rectangular prism, probably intended to have a height and width of equal dimension so that it would appear as a square when viewed from its side; and a cylindrical disk, which, when seen from its side, would appear as a circle [fig. 19]. My description is incomplete, however—or rather, it's overly complete—because Judd conceived each object with a section removed. The prism appears to be missing its upper right quadrant, while the disk is missing a wedge in the analogous position, perhaps amounting to a quarter of its volume. In his conceptualization of the two objects, Judd inserted a right-angled segment of pipe into the missing quadrant of the prism (right angle echoing right angle) and fit

[32] Judd, "Some Aspects," 76.
[33] Judd, "Questions to Stella and Judd," 56, 60; "Some Aspects," 110.
[34] Judd cited Peirce among others in the pragmatist tradition that Peirce had initiated. He was probably more intimately familiar with some of the later pragmatists such as Ralph Barton Perry. On Judd's involvement with philosophy, see David Barry Raskin, "Donald Judd's Skepticism," unpublished dissertation, The University of Texas at Austin, Austin, 1999; "Specific Opposition: Judd's Art and Politics," *Art History* 24 (November 2001): 682-706. See also, Thomas Kellein, "The Whole Space: The Early Work of Donald Judd," *Donald Judd: Early Work 1955-1968* (Bielefeld: Kunsthalle Bielefeld, 2002), 13-48.

a circular segment of pipe into the corresponding area of the disk (curvilinearity echoing curvilinearity). A viewer is called on to imagine contrasting materials, wood and metal, that relate to each other by exhibiting analogous formal features, angle or curve as the case may be.

These two sketched images evoke a similar, somewhat earlier work that Judd executed in 1962, for which he later provided an extensive description. To understand the focus of that description, it helps to read first Judd's generic account of the kind of sculpture he had already abandoned:

> Most sculpture is made part by part, by addition, composed. The main parts ... and the small parts are a collection of variations, slight through great.... Wood and metal are the usual materials, either alone or together, and if together it is without much of a contrast. There is seldom any color.[35]

Now, Judd's description of *Untitled,* 1962 [fig. 20]:

> I made a right angle of wood [painted red] placed directly on the floor.... The size of the right angle is determined by the right angle of a black pipe, whose two open ends are the centers of the outer planes of the right angle ... The right angle doesn't stand or sit ... There is scarcely an inside and an outside, only the space within the angle and the space beyond the angle. The only enclosed space is inside the pipe. This slight linear space determines the dimensions of the broad [wood] planes. The [metal] shell of this narrow space passes through the breadth of the inner angle, a definite space through a general space.[36]

"The right angle doesn't stand or sit": notice Judd's concern that his object should escape the illusionistic, anthropomorphic effects associated with pictorialism. The human body either resists or yields to gravity; Judd designed his object to do neither, at least in appearance.[37] Although vertical, it cannot be a "figure" and it occupies no "ground." Unlike conventional sculpture, it has no hierarchy of "variations, slight through great"; rather, it has "slight," the pipe, and "great," the boards, with nothing between. Its internal contrast, red against black, can hardly be considered "part by part" composition, whether with respect to value or hue. As for space, this object

35 Judd, "Specific Objects," 183.

36 Judd, "Some Aspects," 73. A link between the 1964–65 drawing and the 1962 object has been noted de facto by Thomas Kellein, who juxtaposed illustrations of these works in his catalogue for the recent exhibition in Bielefeld (Kellein, *Donald Judd: Early Work 1955–1968,* 104–05).

37 Judd commented to similar effect about a wall piece of 1964 in which he extended five vertical elements below a horizontal brass bar. He noted that the verticals "both support the brass and pend from it" ("Questions to Stella and Judd," 58). This was tantamount to saying that the verticals neither supported the bar nor were hanging from it, since the ambiguity negated any definite relationship. Here and elsewhere, a larger issue was at stake: "I wanted to avoid any sensation of weight. This goes back to the business of representation. I think that most of the European tradition of art represented weight"; Donald Judd, interview by David Batchelor, "A Small Kind of Order," *Artscribe International* (November–December 1989): 64.

20
Donald Judd
Untitled, 1962
Cadmium red light oil on wood
and black enameled metal pipe
48 × 32½ × 21¼ inches
(121.9 × 82.6 × 54 cm)

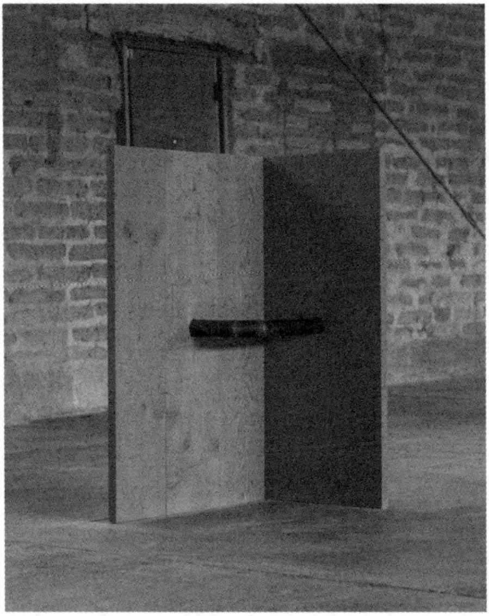

generates its own, from the inside out, in two contrasting ways (as Judd's wall boxes would do at a later date): first, through a precisely defined container, the pipe, which amounts to a shaped, linear volume; second, through an imprecisely defined enclosure, the angle, which creates a graduated space reaching its greatest density or intensity where the two wooden panels join in a concentration of redness. (With the later wall boxes, it's often the case that the exterior structure creates a definite space, while the interior planes, divisions, and color create an indefinite space.)

By Judd's account, the given piece of metal pipe determined the angle and the dimensions of the wood panels. In principle the reverse could also have been true: the pipe could have been cut to fit the boards. Curiously, Judd ignored the actual shape of the pipe, which doesn't bend at a right angle, but follows a more complicated vector. It has not two but three segments, bending twice in order to accomplish its right-angle turn. This seems to have been the condition in which Judd found his material when he decided to use it.[38] It functions as a right angle for all practical purposes—a good guess at "rightness"—just as his somewhat battered wooden panels, also found material, stand in for unblemished rectilinear planes.

Are the imagined objects in the 1964–65 drawing an improvement? With a drawing, an artist escapes pragmatic problems of construction. As Judd drew them, his sections

[38] See Roberta Smith, "Donald Judd," in Brydon Smith, ed., *Donald Judd* (Ottawa: National Gallery of Canada, 1975), 21.

[39] I say "pragmatic" perfection because Judd didn't wish the nature of the fabrication process, whether by manual or machine finish, to be projected as a refinement for its own sake: "I don't like the quality of craft. I want my work to be well made, but not in that [referential, value-laden] sense. There's a certain preciousness if a work is made too conspicuously well by hand. I don't want handwork to show at all" (interview by Batchelor, "A Small Kind of Order," 63).

of pipe became a perfect right angle and a perfect segment of a circle. The actual drawing has a freehand look to it, but a viewer nevertheless imagines or intuits the potential perfection. Presumably, the two objects could have been fabricated; with sufficient effort and expense, they might have attained pragmatic perfection.[39] Yet, to my knowledge, the drawn forms were never realized in three dimensions; or, if they were, the works failed in some respect and Judd rejected them. I suspect that Judd may have seen a certain issue emerge from these two designs, which (despite its structural irregularities, and perhaps because of them) his 1962 right-angle object avoided. In each of the imagined works, a small form is generated within a gap in an analogous large form. At just about the time of the drawing, 1964-65, Judd wrote that with conventional sculpture, "the main parts ... and the small parts are a collection of variations, slight through great." Judd would not have intended it, but this could well express the principle of the two imagined objects, which imply an external regulative system and manifest an internal hierarchy, a stepped set of relations (antithetical to what Judd was already calling "polarity," to be discussed below). Given the rectilinear and circular versions of the type of structure he conceived on paper, it becomes possible to imagine an entire geometric series of corresponding forms. They might be progressively difficult to build, but each would be predictable in conception. There would be a triangular prism with one of the angles removed, replaced by a section of pipe bent at an equal angle.

"The first step toward finding out is to acknowledge [that] you do not satisfactorily know already": Peirce had said it, and Judd quoted it in approval. The problem is not to recognize *what* you don't understand, but *that* you don't understand. This problem is comprehensive; and any solution can only be local and partial, that is, specific. Judd's two sketched objects project not only space but also knowledge, perhaps too much knowledge. In advance of any concrete experience, they imply a logical order of objects yet to be made. In 1965 Judd wrote a note to the effect that form and color should be "intelligent without being ordered," that is, rational and intuitive without requiring the support of a logic.[40] Yet the two objects he drew around that same time had a logic and occupied a general, conceptual space, not a specific, experiential space. Judd "invented" space for the purpose of having specific alternatives to generality. His two objects are best left on paper, drawn as

[40] Judd quoted his 1965 note in 1993; "Some Aspects," 113.

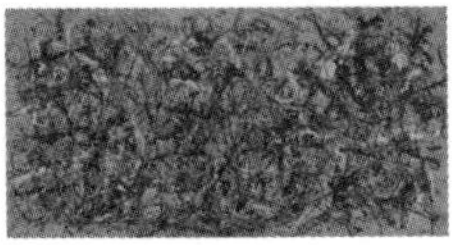

12 see page 39

they are, pictures in convincing generalized perspective. Were they to enter the specific space that Judd invented, they would fall back out.

"The extension of extremes"

In February 1964, when Judd, Frank Stella, and Dan Flavin taped an interview for a radio broadcast, the conversation turned several times to the geometric forms of Victor Vasarely, then a figure of major reputation, whom the three younger artists nevertheless treated dismissively. At one point Judd contrasted the European Vasarely to the American Morris Louis with respect to different ways of painting diagonals: "No one [in Europe] ever used as direct a diagonal as, say, Louis did.... When you make a diagonal clear across the whole thing—and [make it] the main thing—it's a pretty different thing." In contrast, Vasarely confined his use of the diagonal to compositional details that could hardly be considered "the main thing": "He has about three, four squares, one slanted, tilted inside the other, and they're all arranged."[41]

The idea of a "main thing," "main aspect," or "main fact" is a typical Juddism. Referring to his invention of space, Judd wrote: "I developed space as a main aspect of art."[42] In Judd's view, space can always be opposed to some other factor. It is "*a* main aspect," not *the* main aspect, an equal among equals, neither subordinate nor dominate. Space as Judd conceived it, isn't constituted of parts, nor is it ubiquitous and all-encompassing. Space in traditional sculpture had never been a main thing.

Judd acknowledged a number of contemporaries who paralleled his 1960s invention of space, each working independently. These included Claes Oldenburg, whose soft volumetric objects enclosed space dynamically, while his unique sense of scale enhanced spatial specificity; Larry Bell, whose transparent boxes contained spaces of evanescent color; and Dan Flavin and Robert Irwin, who activated the phenomenological space surrounding their depersonalized objects.[43] Lee Bontecou and John Chamberlain had moved in the direction of "actual space" somewhat earlier.[44] It was a significantly older artist, however, to whom Judd gave the most credit for anticipating his understanding of space: "This [main] aspect [of space] was begun by Pollock in his specific use of color and material" [see fig. 12].[45] From the cool, anonymous look of Flavin and Irwin back to Jackson Pollock's

[41] Judd, statement in "New Nihilism or New Art?" (discussion by Dan Flavin, Donald Judd, and Frank Stella, moderated by Bruce Glaser, 15 February 1964; broadcast on WBAI-FM radio, New York, March 1964), Pacifica Radio Archive, audiotape. The published version of this discussion (see above, note 2) was edited and recomposed; it differs significantly from the audiotape version.

[42] Judd, "Some Aspects," 72. The phrase "main fact" occurs within Judd's discussion of color ("Some Aspects," 113).

[43] For details of Judd's appreciation of Oldenburg, see Shiff, "Donald Judd: Fast Thinking," 37–39.

[44] On Bontecou and Chamberlain, see Shiff, "Donald Judd: Fast Thinking," 36 and 38, n. 77, respectively. When I referred to the order of publication of Judd's thoughts on Bontecou, Chamberlain, and Pollock in "Donald Judd: Fast Thinking," I did not consider Judd's review of Helen Frankenthaler, important for his sense of Pollock; see the discussion below.

[45] Judd, "Some Aspects, " 72.

extremes of gestural expression—how was Judd making the connection?

Judd had experienced his central intuition, or at least presented it, in the course of reviewing Helen Frankenthaler's new work in 1960; but it did not involve Frankenthaler directly. Her abstract painting established a "progression" of similar elements "near in quality to each other and to the total result." In Judd's estimation, Frankenthaler's "total result" was "valid" as painting, but represented the kind of pictorial harmony he would soon associate with "flatness" and a lack of "actual space." Rather than Frankenthaler, his intuition pertained to Pollock, who achieved the antithesis of pictorial progression. This was no mere negation or reduction of progression and harmony but something separate, self-sufficient, and new:

> [His] marks and bare canvas are equally positive, almost in competition for frontality ... Pollock achieves generality by establishing an extreme polarity between the simple, immediate perception of paint and canvas, a reduction to unexpandable sensation, and the complexity and overtones of his imagery and articulated structure. Such diverse elements combined under tension produce a totality much greater [than] and unlike any of the parts.[46]

In 1967, Judd made analogous observations in an essay devoted to Pollock exclusively: "The elements and aspects of Pollock's paintings are polarized rather than amalgamated ... Everything is fairly independent and specific."[47] He restated the idea in two essays of 1983, and yet again at a symposium in 1992.[48] In 1993, he concluded that after Pollock "the century's development of color could continue no further on a flat surface."[49] Judd regarded Pollock's "polarization" as a formal device (or better, an anti-formal device) that would assure the independence of every feature from every other, hence their specificity to their own existence. No one part would depend on any other part for its effect. With polarization, parts don't become elements of a motif, rhythm, or harmony. Nevertheless, they are parts of a whole that has polarization as *its* proper characteristic. Judd's right-angle floor piece of 1962 was in this sense "polarized": it gave a single sensation of two materials (metal, wood), two forms (narrow and tubular, broad and planar), two kinds of space (definite, indefinite), two colors (black, red). In the spirit of polarization, Judd would later call black and red a

46 Judd, "In the Galleries: Helen Frankenthaler" (1960), *Complete Writings 1959–1975*, 13-14. Roberta Smith long ago recognized the significance of this early, brief review by Judd (see Smith, "Donald Judd," 13); it was independently brought to my attention by Alexander Dumbadze.

47 Judd, "Jackson Pollock" (1967), *Complete Writings 1959–1975*, 195.

48 Judd, "Art and Architecture" (1983), "Abstract Expressionism," *Complete Writings 1975–1986*, 34–35, 45; contribution to Barnett Newman symposium, Harvard University, 14 May 1992, audiotape, Harvard University Art Museums. On Pollock, see also Judd, "Chamberlain: Another View" (1963), *Complete Writings 1959–1975*, 108.

49 Judd, "Some Aspects," 113. Here and in a number of other instances, Judd included Barnett Newman, Mark Rothko, and Clyfford Still as significant contributors to the situation, but clearly Pollock was the prime mover in his estimation.

"two-color monochrome." With the equal familiarity, intensity, and self-identity of the two colors, not to mention their absolute opposition, the juxtaposition of black and red creates a condition where parts and whole exist both apart and as one, at once.[50]

Linked together, Judd's various references to polarity or polarization in Pollock, from 1960 to 1993, further expand what the notion meant to him. He spoke of two "main" factors: the sensation of "dripped paint" and the sensation of the whole composition. In Pollock, these features were "further apart in quality than is usual." (In this instance, "quality" signifies the particular character of the effect, not its degree of excellence or value.) Judd compared Pollock's manner to that of Willem de Kooning, for whom a fragment would imply more of a similarity to the whole than a difference, because (as Judd reasoned) de Kooning was guided by a constant emotion as opposed to a multiplicity of specific sensations. This meant that de Kooning was the more pictorial of the two artists. His paintings, Judd implied, were additive and without specific dimension, like the spatial void they filled; there could always be more of de Kooning's marks, all similar, as if the marks themselves extended not only through a generalized space but within a generalized time. To the contrary, each of Pollock's marks retained its distinctness as he developed "the extension of extremes."[51] Judd realized an appropriately far-reaching conclusion: "The level of quality [the value] of a work can usually be established by the extent of the polarity between its generality and its particularity. ... The greater the polarity of the elements in a work, the greater the work's comprehension of [specifics of] space, time and existence."[52] In Pollock's case the generality was the entire composition and the particularity was its constituent features, both the marks and the areas of bare canvas, a source of polarity within polarity. This internal polarization counteracted any incipient pictorialism or hierarchy, the generator of both "flatness" and deep, illusionistic space (no contradiction). Polarity keeps things as they really are, existing in "actual space," neither falsely flat nor falsely deep.

Judd had a clever way of casting the situation: "You don't have to mimic chance ... Pollock and those people [Barnett Newman, Mark Rothko, Clyfford Still] represent actual chance."[53] Things happen, Judd believed, and chance is the way things are. In a world of chance and of many local orders, as opposed to one totalizing order, only the immediate specificity

50 Judd, "Some Aspects," 113. See also Judd, "Malevich: Independent Form, Color, Surface" (1974), *Complete Writings 1959–1975*, 214.

51 "Jackson Pollock," *Complete Writings 1959–1975*, 195; "Abstract Expressionism," *Complete Writings 1975–1986*, 45. Judd categorized de Kooning, although a "very good artist," as an "old-fashioned" expressionist: "The fragmentation, the distortion of nature and the comparatively deep space are a continuation of the expressionism of Soutine, Kokoschka and Kirchner, which is the old picture of nature distorted by the artists' feelings" ("Abstract Expressionism," 40).

52 Judd, "Art and Architecture," "Abstract Expressionism," *Complete Writings 1975–1986*, 34, 45.

53 Judd, "Questions to Stella and Judd," 58 (order of phrases reversed).

of a guess, an intuition, can match conditions. Intuition generates a work and suggests other works, but establishes no precise formula for the future. The intuited reality of Pollock's art, and also Newman's, was the specific "way the paint was applied." In Newman, "the few parts, all equally primary, comprise the quality [now, both character and value] of a painting." By way of contrast, Judd introduced Piet Mondrian, whose "lines are dominant and the white is secondary, volume and space once removed"—pictorial, not polarized.[54]

When artists use gestural strokes self-consciously to imitate what convention dictates as the *look* of chance, they distance themselves from the specific reality of the mark and its color. Instead, Judd advised, "use a simple form that doesn't look like either order or disorder," one that looks like what it is.[55] Judd argued that Newman's work was "concomitant with chance and one person's knowledge [derived from direct experience] ... It doesn't claim more than anyone can know [a very Peircean thought]; it doesn't imply a social order.... The color, areas, and stripes are not obscured or diluted by a hierarchy of composition and a range of associations." Newman's way of painting gave an artist a chance in a world of tragic failure: "What is good is not necessarily perfect," Newman himself wrote around the time Judd, in turn, was writing about him.[56] In the type of work Judd called "ordinary" abstraction and expressionism, "forms run off the edges to imply a continuum, [and] the painting is a segment of that continuum." In Newman's paintings, to the contrary, "everything is specifically where it is." In short, according to Judd, a painting by Newman is never a "picture."[57] Order, completion, perfection—none of this was at issue in either Newman or Pollock.

A certain history supports Judd's view of the significance of the aesthetic attitude Pollock and Newman adopted. Beginning in the early nineteenth century and continuing into the twentieth, critics increasingly acknowledged that material features of a painting sufficiently prominent to draw attention to themselves interfere with illusionistic representation and its totalizing "picture." Accentuated materiality nevertheless had its distinct advantages: it stimulated sensation (not only the viewer's but also the artist's) and asserted the act or presence of the individual maker. But the extreme specificity of an artist's accentuated mark threatened to terminate the process of cultural association, disabling interpretive commentary.

[54] Judd, "Barnett Newman," *Complete Writings 1959–1975*, 202. See also Shiff, "Donald Judd: Fast Thinking," 13–18.
[55] Judd, "Questions to Stella and Judd," 58.
[56] Barnett Newman, manuscript notes appended to an edited transcript of an interview of Newman by David Sylvester, 1965, Barnett Newman Foundation archives, New York.
[57] Judd, "Barnett Newman," *Complete Writings 1959–1975*, 202.

Canonical modernist paintings, such as Paul Cézanne's, often displayed aggressive, repetitive strokes and irregular figuration. Material interference characterized Cézanne's works as much as anything else. His paintings and many like them divided appreciative critics between those who would attend to "painting for itself" (medium and form) and those who would struggle to decipher the eccentric depiction (image and content).[58] A polarization in viewing developed—provocative, but not necessarily beneficial.

Critics also acknowledged that the intellectual abstractions associated with artistic "content" or subject matter were cultural constructions linked to massive ideological generalizations. Judd said of Newman that his art "didn't claim more than anyone [any one person] can know." To assert one person's individual liberty, an artist could stress working from immediate experience; the imagery of experience would be inherently opposed to the cultural ideology of the powerful and their fixed pictorial conventions. Within a nineteenth-century context, this type of resistant, liberated art shifted its focus from thematic subject matter to immediate, sensory aspects of nature, a realm of experience that could be appropriated by individuals. In the early twentieth century, artists gave ever more attention to the actual materials and devices used to render naturalistic effects, a practice many critics of the time believed they had discerned already in Cézanne.[59] Turning inward in this physical rather than intellectual sense—to concentrate on paint, graphite, canvas, paper, wood, or metal—artists evaded the obvious ideological clichés. They found individual expression by engaging with ordinary physical matter as directly as possible.

The knowledge a cliché imparts, however, isn't inherently untruthful; the issue is whether to accept or resist the order the cliché implies or the attitude it induces—you purchase the Spanish-Colonial television console or you don't. When Judd warned against mimicking chance, he was rejecting what had become one of his generation's clichéd signs of their own rejection of culture—a hyperactive, personalized brush. Judd occupied a rather skewed position in relation to the long modernist tradition. He worried that residual elements of representational illusionism, thematic allusion, and idealist utopias—and even the modest intent to express an emotion or a personal identity—would interfere with the chance sensuous reality of art.[60]

58 Compare Emile Bernard's early response to Cézanne: "He opened to art this amazing door: painting for itself ... The more he works, the more his work removes itself from the external view [and] the more he abstracts the picture" ("Paul Cézanne," *Les hommes d'aujourd'hui* 8, no. 387 [February–March 1891]: n.p.; "Paul Cézanne," *L'Occident* 6 [July 1904]: 21 [my translations]).

59 See Richard Shiff, "Mark, Motif, Materiality: The Cézanne Effect in the Twentieth Century," in Felix Bauman, Evelyn Benesch, Walter Feilchenfeldt, and Klaus Albrecht Schröder, eds., *Cézanne: Finished—Unfinished* (Ostfildern-Ruit: Hatje Cantz, 2000), 99–123.

60 Because it became an element of polarization in Bontecou and Oldenburg, Judd accepted emotional content in their work, but not in de Kooning's. On de Kooning, see Judd, "Jackson Pollock," *Complete Writings 1959–1975*, 195; on Bontecou and Oldenburg, see Shiff, "Donald Judd: Fast Thinking," 36–43.

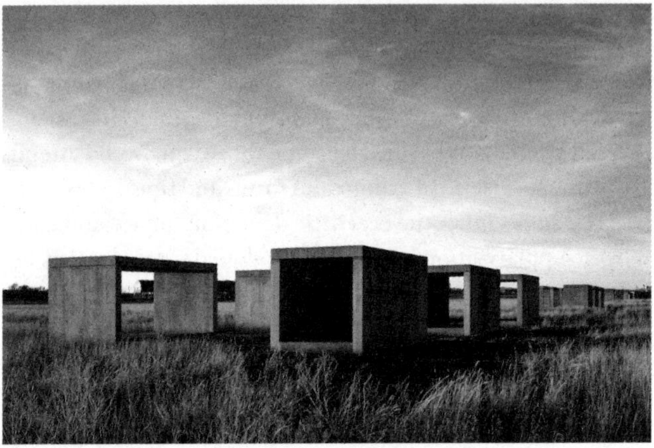

21
Donald Judd
15 untitled works in concrete, 1980-1984
Chinati Foundation, Marfa, Texas

> *"Space is made"*
> There is no neutral space, since space is made ... [My] smallest, simplest work creates space around it, since there is so much space within. This is new in art, not in architecture of course. All old sculpture, great as it is, from any civilization, is monolithic; it is the stone [that you kick,] not the glass that you pick up.... A Greek sculpture is the stone; the building that it was in is space.... Space is new in art and is still not a concern of more than a few artists.... There is no vocabulary for [its] discussion.[61]

Judd made sculpture ("three-dimensional work") that was more like the building and the glass than like the stone. This may be easiest to grasp in his large outdoor pieces, such as the group of fifteen works in concrete, set into a kilometer of land at Marfa (*Untitled,* 1982 [fig. 21]). Each unit within each work belonging to the group is massive yet hollow, like a box or a channel ample enough to be walked into (the units measure 8 ft. 2 in. × 16 ft. 5 in. × 8 ft. 2 in.). Describing the work in this manner, however, I may be conceiving of architectural space, as well as the volumetric human body that enters it, too conventionally. "Space is new in *art*," Judd says, "not in architecture." Space is a thing to be perceived, like a solid not a void, but also like a simple proportion. Good architecture already has these elements. Art that features them is new.

It's likely that in all of his large outdoor works Judd sought to establish a polarity of space in relation to the land. This is certainly the case with a number of works consisting of a pair of concentric wall-like structures, usually rectilinear and

[61] Judd, "21 February 93," 9, 13. Judd thought that the last good sculpture of the old type was David Smith's, "the last of the stone in the field." Concerning lexical inadequacy, he noted that "somewhat new work is usually described with the words that have been used to describe old work"; Judd, "Statement" (for *Perspecta,* 1968), *Complete Writings 1959–1975,* 196.

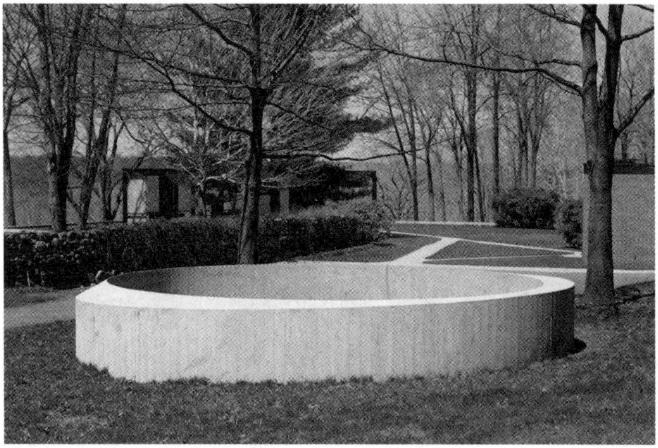

22
Donald Judd
Untitled, 1971
Concrete
36 to 48 inches × 300 exterior diameter × 18 inches
(91.4 to 121.9 cm × 762 × 45.7 cm)

closely positioned, such as a square within another square of only slightly greater dimension; Judd described this condition as an "enclosed narrow space enclosing a large space."[62] These works have an additional polarizing feature: the top edge of one wall-like plane parallels the natural slope or contour of the land, while the top edge of the other remains level. In the case of *Untitled,* 1971 [fig. 22], a single circular ring of concrete deploys both systems.[63] The inner surface remains level, while the outer parallels the ground, maintaining its height of four feet everywhere along the ring. The ring itself is eighteen inches thick and requires a complex bevel to accommodate the shifting difference between its inner and outer surfaces. Here a single (or whole) object in the land creates different spaces of different character inside and outside its bounded surfaces. At the same time, the oddly bilateral ring—its canted top surface appearing to perform two movements at once—is polarized like a Pollock painting. It is both two things and one thing, but not the usual sum of one and one. With Judd's ring, the condition of one against one, one apart from one, produces ... one. In its commodious wholeness, his concrete structure makes space of the land and also of itself.

His "smallest, simplest work creates space around it," Judd said, "since there is so much space within." We should expect his relatively small wall boxes of wood or metal—often called "meter boxes" because of their metric dimensions—to generate a quality of space (if not a quantity) analogous to that of a large concrete structure like the 1971 *Untitled*. Judd's large and small objects are similar in looking whole, while their parts or features look separate. The simplest type of wall box

62 Judd, "21 February 93," 12.
63 Compare Judd, "21 February 93," 12.

23
Donald Judd
Untitled, 1977
Copper and blue acrylic sheet
50 × 100 × 50 cm
(19⅝ × 39 5⁄16 × 19⅝ inches)

consists of a single unit. Among examples of this type, some lack the internal divisions Judd often employed as he set single or multiple panels parallel, perpendicular, or angled to the open front planes of the boxes.

Judd had a way of keeping perception complex while maintaining the greatest aesthetic simplicity as an "illusion" (if I may invoke that notion, which in his thinking refers to a very real sensation).[64] A work such as *Untitled,* 1977 [fig. 23] promises simplicity deceptively. If we are deceived, it is not because Judd has lied with his materials, but because we are inclined to correlate simple geometry and proportion with simple space (to most people, even artists, "space is invisible," Judd warned).[65] The work is a single copper box with no internal divisions and with external proportions of 1:2:1 (50 × 100 × 50 cm); it is twice as wide as it is either high or deep, a square at the sides, a double square at the front. A sheet of blue Plexiglas, rendered opaque by its placement, covers the back inside plane of this open box. (Typically, a small interval remains behind the Plexiglas to accommodate a bracketing system for hanging.)[66] The open area of the box, perceived as an undivided volume, is both a definite space that matches the double-square exterior and an indefinite space of diminishing illumination and changing color; reflections of bluishness play against the warm copper to varying degrees. Copper is itself a color as much as blue: "All materials, [even] gray and tan, are colored," Judd wrote.[67] Definite and indefinite spaces—which at times occupy the same volumetric position (the same "space"?)—form the wholeness of the box, its polarity. By Judd's standards, this is simple, basic, just a beginning, like thinking about the stone and the glass.

64 Compare Shiff, "Donald Judd: Fast Thinking," 21–27.
65 Judd, "Some Aspects," 72.
66 The actual dimensions or placement of an element of a work may be slightly at variance with what the official dimensions imply. In order to reserve space for a bracket to support box units intended to be hung on a wall, Judd typically projected the back plane of the rectilinear prism forward. This enables an unusually snug fit to the wall, but also means that the interior dimensions of the box fail to match the exterior dimensions, and that the positioning of modular units set within the box may lack absolute symmetry. This type of irregularity seems to escape ordinary visual inspection, yet an idealist (not Judd the pragmatist) would be concerned that the variation could be measured, even if otherwise undetectable. For Judd, only what a viewer is likely to notice matters.
67 Judd, "Some Aspects," 110.

24
Donald Judd
Untitled, 1989
Cor-ten steel with purple acrylic sheet
100 × 100 × 50 cm
(39 5/16 × 39 5/16 × 19 5/8 inches)

Another untitled work of 1977, a single-unit wall piece made entirely of red anodized aluminum, represents a near inversion of the copper box with blue Plexiglas; rather than being closed at the back, a slightly recessed plane closes the implied volume of the box at the front. The space left open from the front has a depth of only 6.7 cm and represents about 2/15 of the volume, not a proportion to be recognized by sight. This interior space is indefinite with respect to proportion, but perhaps quite definite in its color and light. Yet its shallowness or recessed quality contrasts with the definitive fullness of the exterior shape and space of the same 50 × 100 × 50 cm box. A 1977 work in stainless steel, also 50 × 100 × 50 cm, has a red Plexiglas panel set 24 cm back from its open front, a depth essentially half the total.[68] Here, the structure creates an indefinite space of color and light inside the box, but because the position of the Plexiglas is measurable by eye, a definiteness also develops, comparable to what the eye grasps regarding the exterior of the box in relation to its supporting wall.

Variations on these direct, but not so simple effects occur in any number of single-unit works—the play of exterior and interior spaces, of definite and indefinite space and proportion, of contrasts of hue and reflectivity. *Untitled,* 1979 sets a sheet of blue Plexiglas diagonally within a copper box. Likewise, *Untitled,* 1977 has an interior diagonal running front to back, bottom to top; but because this work is uniformly of brass, color contrast isn't a factor. In this instance, internal polarities of space, reflectivity, and color hinge on a dramatic narrowing of the volume from open front to closed back.

68 Interior dimensions of Judd's spaces will fail to match or measure half of an exterior dimension because of the actual physical thickness of the exterior and interior panels.

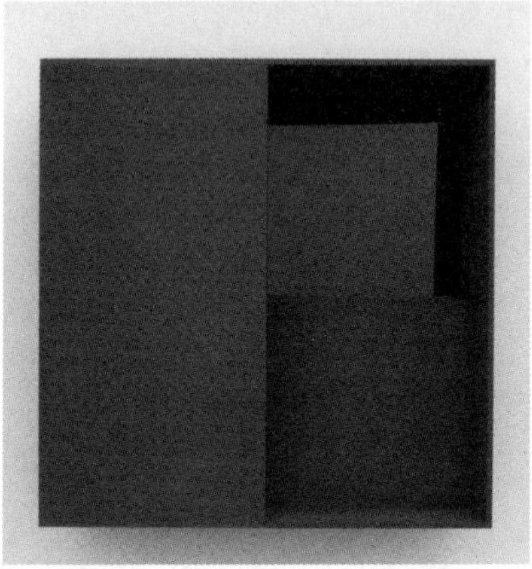

25
Donald Judd
Untitled, 1986
Cor-ten steel with purple acrylic sheet
100 × 100 × 50 cm
(39 5⁄16 × 39 5⁄16 × 19 5⁄8 inches)

If the transition here from one condition (open) to another (closed) is continuous, in other works Judd staged it discontinuously by halving, using the simplest of proportional systems. *Untitled,* 1989 [fig. 24], a 100 × 100 × 50 cm box of Cor-Ten steel, is half closed vertically at the front, which partially occludes its interior space and hence a viewer's access to the back panel of violet Plexiglas. The definite color of the Plexiglas fades from an area of relative illumination (unobstructed vision) to obscurity (complete obstruction), but the ratio of bright to dim space also changes, of course, in relation to the angle of view. This chameleonic space is in polar opposition to the fixed 1:2 and 1:1 proportions perceived or intuited at the exterior from virtually any position. Consider also three other works of different material composition (*Untitled,* 1987, *Untitled,* 1989, and *Untitled,* 1986, [fig. 25]) that share dimensions of 100 × 100 × 50 cm; they are variations on a single configuration involving the addition of a half-size interior plane, located halfway between front and back. Each of the three works is half-open, half-closed by a vertical plane at the front. This type of structure causes the color of the Plexiglas, located at the rear of the box, to diffuse through a maze of light and shadow, within open and closed volumes. Each of the three works generates an indefinite space by employing a set of definite proportional relationships of 1:2 and 1:1.

These are among the "simple" wall boxes. Related works are structurally more complex (as if the "simple" boxes were not already complex). And then there is the 1977 *Untitled* [fig. 26]. I hesitate to place it among either the simple or the complex. This 50 × 100 × 50 cm box has a stainless steel panel flush with its front plane, but separated from the exterior edges

26
Donald Judd
Untitled, 1977
Stainless steel
50 × 100 × 50 cm
(19 5/8 × 39 5/16 × 19 5/8 inches)

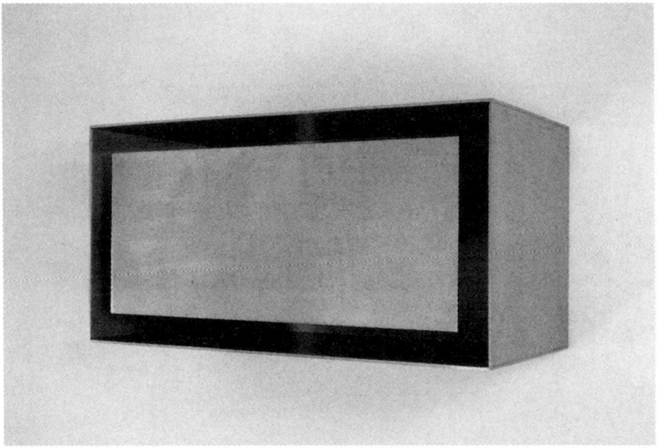

and therefore not entirely closing the volume; hidden brackets, canted to the rear of the box, support this panel. Strongly reflective, it appears to hover, while the interior space, both closed and open and itself bearing a degree of reflectivity, recedes into luminous obscurity. The exterior and interior of this box merge like a coat and its lining, perhaps because the box appears to have something inside it, its hovering panel, which is also outside it. Inside is to outside as one is to one.

Proportion is especially notable, Judd perceived, because it represents "both extremes" of the greatest polarity of all—the general and the particular. And these extremes appear "at once," that is, seen for what they are at a single moment in a single proportion.[69] Both conceptually and experientially, everyone recognizes unity, halving, and doubling—relationships of extreme generality. The same ratios of 1:1 and 1:2 involve extreme particularity whenever they appear in "actual space," because they induce a specific, memorable sensation: *this* (not that) perceived instance of 1:1 or 1:2. We don't measure 50 cm or 100 cm by eye; but we do see that the one plane or edge is a whole measure and the other a half, or the one is a unit and the other a double unit. Judd's recognition of the value of the simple ratios derived from his inspired guessing:

> My first work was developed by looking. Then I figured out that many things [that I constructed] were very close to even proportions [such as 1:2]. And slowly I made the proportions even. I think what you see [in the ordinary experience of looking] are just the simple ones, 1:2 and 2:3 and 3:4.[70]

[69] Judd, "Art and Architecture," *Complete Writings 1975–1986*, 34.
[70] Donald Judd, in Katharina Winnekes, "Interview mit Donald Judd," *Kunst und Kirche*, April 1993, 135. On the ratio 1:2, see also Judd, "Art and Architecture," "Abstract Expressionism," *Complete Writings 1975–1986*, 33–34, 47.

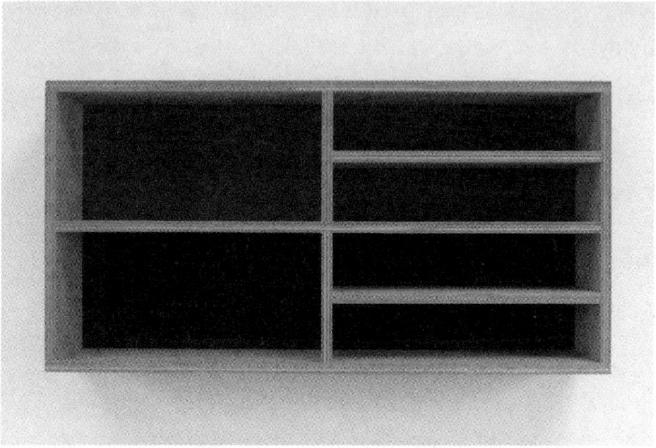

27
Donald Judd
Untitled, 1992
Plywood with blue and red acrylic sheets
50 × 100 × 25 cm
(19⅝ × 39 5/16 × 9 13/16 inches)

"1 to 2 is … as much its own quality," Judd wrote in 1983, "as red, or red and black," the two-color monochrome.[71] Fundamentally simple ratios, such as 1:2 and 1:2:4, predominate in Judd's late works. Red and black, two opposing colors of equal familiarity and force, if set beside each other as equal areas, become a 1:1 ratio of radically dissimilar elements. This and other color combinations, perhaps in other simple ratios that Judd employed, result in symmetrical asymmetry. A work becomes symmetrical because it manifests a stable, binary relationship of oppositional equivalence. It becomes asymmetrical, and radically so, because nothing mediates between the opposing pairs of colors or forms, nor dispels the fact that one side differs entirely from the other, the two relating as a polarity. The proportional relationship itself becomes a polarizing element because it remains so distinct from the color and other qualitative features. Accordingly, Judd concluded, "1 to 2 is … its own quality."

Many of Judd's wall boxes follow this order of dissimilar equals, whether as single units divided internally (half into dissimilar half), or as pairs of dissimilars. Note that Judd's dissimilars don't negate each other. A situation of that sort would be too predictable, with either of the two elements poised to determine the configuration of the other (recall the previous discussion of Judd's 1964-65 drawing). Instead, Judd presented his dissimilars as arbitrary, chance combinations: nothing more than one person could know from immediate experience, "nothing to do with either order or disorder in general."[72] *Untitled,* 1992 [fig. 27], a plywood box with dimensions of 50 × 100 × 25 cm, is a fitting example. To comprehend

71 Judd, "Art and Architecture," *Complete Writings 1975–1986*, 34.
72 Judd, "Statement," *Complete Writings 1959–1975*, 196.

its internal divisions, imagine that Judd halved the box vertically, then halved it horizontally, and then halved the two right quarters horizontally once again. This created left/right asymmetry both structurally and spatially. He also backed the top half of the interior with blue Plexiglas, while giving the bottom half red Plexiglas. This introduced top/bottom asymmetry. Just as 1 and 2 are different but equal in the ratio 1:2, so blue and red, which Judd called a "contrasting pair," form one of his two-color monochromes.[73] What results is a compound asymmetry that has neither hierarchy nor composition. One thing stands against another, against another, and so on, producing a visually complex version of the simple type of order Judd preferred: "one or four boxes in a row, any single thing or such a series, is local order, just an arrangement, barely order at all."[74]

When Judd used *pairs* of wall boxes as a single work, he created an analogous effect by representing two of a number of possible variations of a structural type, but without resorting to mirror-image combinations. In other words, Judd tested out arbitrary oppositions instead of using standard opposites [See fig. 6]. He guessed, and the guess was right. The result was symmetrical asymmetry. I can't determine with certainty that Judd never employed mirror-image combinations, but if he did, it would have been inconsistent with his notion of "local order." His pairs relate as one thing against another, not one thing as the reverse or inverse of another. With the latter possibility, I would suspect the imposition of a theory, rather than the immediacy of a guess—a guess "intelligent without being ordered."

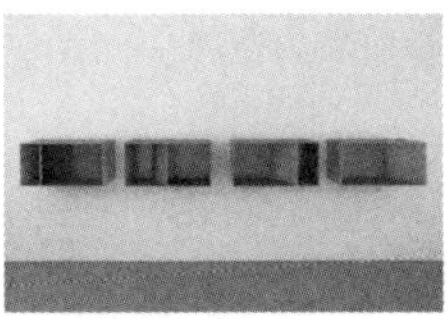

6 see page 252

Judd's wall boxes, as singles or pairs, are like his other objects, small or large, set against wall or floor, placed within architecture or in the land: they establish aesthetically intriguing combinations, striking in the independence of the parts, a separateness that occurs without loss of wholeness. For Judd, the polarization of the parts, as well as polarity between the quality of the parts and the quality of the whole, meant that "actual space" could be "made." He expressed his sense of space best in 1993, his thinking having benefited from three decades of work with objects. At that point he discussed the new kind of object and its space, and he also imagined a new "painting": "Someday, not soon, there will be another kind of painting, far from the easel, [and also] far from beyond the easel, since our environment indoors is four walls, usually flat. Color to continue [after Pollock] had to occur in space."[75]

73 Judd, "Some Aspects," 113.
74 Judd, "Statement," *Complete Writings 1959–1975*, 196.
75 Judd, "Some Aspects," 113.

In Judd's era, painting, an art of color, needed to project itself out from the wall, not *in* space (in the conventional sculptural sense), but *as* space, with its own three dimensions. This was Judd's way, *as a painter*, of making "three-dimensional work," "specific objects." "Someday, not soon," he speculated, an art would emerge that was more obviously painting; it would be neither easel painting nor anti-easel painting. Mere negations and mirrorings would be too predictable to represent the real change.

Donald Judd died in February 1994 at the height of his productivity. Had he "talked enough"? If his life's work failed to terminate the analysis of painting and sculpture as fundamentally distinct mediums, it was not for lack of effort and inventiveness on his part. Judd invented more than enough for one person; he never pretended to know more than one person can. He made space—not sculpture, not painting. We would do well to catch up with him. Space is still very new in art.

Judd Through Oldenburg

[2004]

Donald Judd and Claes Oldenburg had a good relationship—not only the personal friendship, which was strong, but the relationship figured through Judd's early critical writing. Virtually all of Judd's reviews are worth pondering, even now, decades after his career as an art critic. They remain fresh, presenting a critical model to follow rather than a historical document to be analyzed. Within this corpus I often consider that the commentaries on Oldenburg are the most stimulating and provocative. Yet every time I review my interpretation of Judd's interpretation of Oldenburg, I wonder whether readers will grasp my sense of Judd's insights.[1] Do my paraphrases take a reader closer to or farther from Judd's own targets?

Judd was a quirky writer, but I don't think the problem originates in his style or rhetorical manner. His rhetoric was sophisticated and may well have been adequate to his thinking and to Oldenburg's. That may be the problem. I suspect that Judd's thinking about Oldenburg was operating at the very limits of what words can convey coherently; accordingly, Judd had to take his rhetoric to extremes. My insecurity as an interpreter lies in the nature of Judd's creative vision of Oldenburg and in what Oldenburg himself accomplished, rather than in some failing of the expressive or expository style of either of them. I am reminded of Clement Greenberg's complaint (in 1967) concerning the term formalism. Too many critics, Greenberg argued, assume through their use of this term:

> That 'form' and 'content' in art can be adequately distinguished for the purposes of discourse. This implies in turn that discursive thought has solved just those problems of art upon whose imperviousness to discursive thinking the very possibility of art depends.... You know that a work has content because of its effect.[2]

Greenberg insisted that the best understanding is experiential and should not be limited by the interpreter's own preexisting discursive structures. Although this issue is endlessly debatable in theory, there may be little profit in the argument whenever decisions have to be made regarding elements of practice. Oriented toward what material practice could accomplish, Judd's position was similar to Greenberg's. In 1993, he flatly stated what for him was obvious: "There is a limit to how much an artist can learn in advance."[3] The same would apply to critics. They need to grasp the experience, not

1 See Richard Shiff in this volume, "Donald Judd: Fast Thinking"; "A Space of One to One"; and "Donald Judd, Safe From Birds", in Nicholas Serota (ed.), *Donald Judd*, (London: Tate Publishing, 2004), 28–61. In consultation with translator Jürgen Blasius, I slightly expanded my remarks on the Judd/Oldenburg issue for the German edition of "Donald Judd: Safe from Birds".

2 Clement Greenberg, "Complaints of an Art Critic" (1967), in John O'Brian (ed.), *Clement Greenberg: The Collected Essays and Criticism, 4 vols.*, (Chicago: University of Chicago Press, 1986–93), 4:269.

3 Judd, "Some Aspects of Color in General and Red and Black in Particular" (1993), in Serota 2004, 151.

some concept that either precedes, encompasses, or supersedes it.

Concerning his work of the 1960s, Oldenburg himself said: "I want the object to have its own existence" (a remark to which this essay must return).[4] As a critic of others' work, Judd was obligated to explain the effect an Oldenburg object produced, as opposed to restating the state it sought ("existence"). His evaluations did not come easily and reflected candid feeling as much as conceptual analysis. In 1964, he reviewed a group of objects that included a version of *Soft Switches* in vermilion vinyl (1964) [see fig. 14], commenting: "I think Oldenburg's work is profound. I think it's very hard to explain how."[5] After this bold admission, Judd noted something crucial: in significant ways, Oldenburg's representations failed to resemble the familiar objects they called to mind; they were not "descriptive, even abstractly." This is more hypothesis than fact, for who can say where the limits of descriptive abstraction might lie? When is a circle the sun, and when is it just a circle? Something about Oldenburg's objects was causing Judd to remove them from the category of sculpture and its mimeticism. We should not expect the logic to be self-evident. Hypothetical conclusions like Judd's tend to relate facts of one kind to facts of a very different kind. They never appear inevitable but are nevertheless convincing. Like good intuitions, they convince without offering compelling sets of reasons.

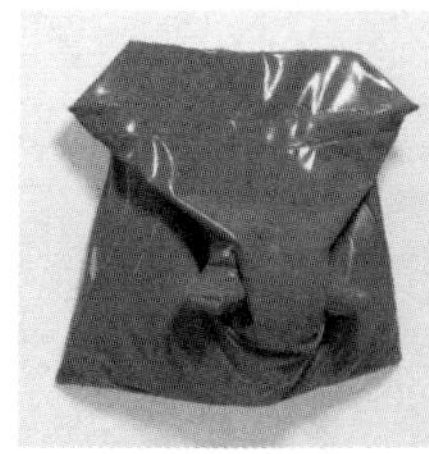

14 see page 42

Appropriately enough, Judd became a critic by happenstance—without compelling reasons. In 1959, he attended Meyer Schapiro's art history seminar at Columbia University where he encountered Thomas Hess as a guest speaker. Hess announced that his journal *Artnews* was looking for new writers for monthly reviews and asked whether any of the students were interested. Needing a source of income, Judd volunteered. He wrote for three issues of *Artnews* during the fall of 1959, but then moved to *Arts Magazine* fearing that Hess was going to dismiss him. As Judd recalled a decade later: "[Hess] didn't like it. He wanted [my writing] to be more poetic. He said I wasn't saying anything."[6] Yet from the very start, it seems that Judd had certain notions in mind, conditions of which he approved, specific qualities that he was probably seeking in his own art at the time, as it evolved from two dimensions into three.

Judd's earliest reviews contain elements of appreciative analysis that he would repeat in increasingly sophisticated form as he developed his thinking as writer and artist. On one

4 Claes Oldenburg, statement in Jan McDevitt, "The Object: Still Life", *Craft Horizons* 25, September 1965, 31.

5 Judd, "In the Galleries: Claes Oldenburg" (1964), *Complete Writings 1959–1975*, Nova Scotia College of Art and Design, Halifax, 1975, 133.

6 Donald Judd, interview by Lucy R. Lippard, New York, 10 April 1968, Lucy R. Lippard Papers, Archives of American Art.

7 Judd, "Reviews and Previews: Yoyoi Kusama" (1959), *Complete Writings 1959–1975*, 2.

of his first assignments, in October 1959, he reviewed Yayoi Kusama, characterizing her work as "both complex and simple."[7] Hess may have thought that this type of statement was a hopelessly vague generalization, if not a gratuitous contradiction; but it was actually a minor articulation of a major insight on Judd's part. In December 1959, reviewing Josef Albers, Judd said the same kind of thing with more specificity. He contrasted what he called the "rigidity" of Albers's geometry to the "ambiguity" of "unbounded" effects of his color.[8] In Kusama's case, art became complex and simple; in Albers's case, somewhat analogously, art became ambiguous and precise.

A few months later, Judd embedded some remarks on Jackson Pollock within a brief review of Helen Frankenthaler, to Frankenthaler's detriment: "Pollock achieves generality by establishing an extreme polarity between the simple, immediate perception of paint and canvas—a reduction to unexpandable sensation—and the complexity and overtones of his imagery and articulated structure."[9] He was claiming that Pollock attained a coherent, total image without obscuring any of the disparate marks of paint. Nor did the parts combine to create the whole. Rather, the parts and the whole existed as very different entities—in fact, so dissimilar (as Judd would explain in later statements on Pollock) that the appearance of the whole could not be predicted on the basis of the parts. This is why he used the word "polarity." A polar differential is the widest possible gap. He also used the phrase "extension of extremes" to the same purpose, as he moved toward his conclusion: "The level of quality of a work can usually be established by the extent of the polarity between its generality"—the total image—"and its particularity"—the individual marks.[10]

In 1963 and 1965, between the time of his earlier and later comments on Pollock, Judd approached the same principle through a consideration of the relief sculptures of Lee Bontecou [see fig. 28]: "Often power lies in a polarization of elements and qualities, or at least in a combination of dissimilar ones."[11] Some of his verbal playfulness appears as he elaborates on the features of Bontecou's reliefs, punning on whole and hole: "The image [of a volcano-like mound with a hole], all of the parts, and the whole shape are coextensive. The parts are either part of the hole or part of the mound which forms the hole. The hole and the mound are only two things [that is, they constitute a single opposition], which, after all, are the same thing [a polarized but integrated image]."[12] From the

8 Judd, "In the Galleries: Josef Albers" (1959), *Complete Writings 1959–1975, 6.*

9 Judd, "In the Galleries: Helen Frankenthaler" (1960), *Complete Writings 1959–1975*, 13.

10 Judd, "Jackson Pollock", *Complete Writings 1959–1975*, pp.195; Donald Judd, "Art and Architecture" (1983), "Abstract Expressionism" (1983), *Complete Writings 1975–1986* (Eindhoven : Van Abbemuseum, 1987), 34, 45.

11 Judd, "In the Galleries: Lee Bontecou" (1963), 'Lee Bontecou' (1965), *Complete Writings 1959–1975*, pp. 65, 178.

12 Judd, "Specific Objects" (1964–65), *Complete Writings 1959–1975*, 188 (punctuation altered for clarity). Judd associated Bontecou's "constructions" with "contoured volcanoes" in "In the Galleries: Lee Bontecou" (1960), *Complete Writings 1959–1975*, 27.

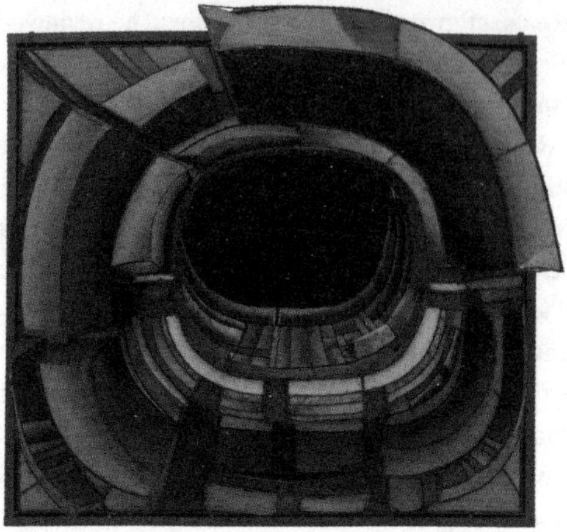

28
Lee Bontecou
Untitled, 1961
Welded steel, canvas, black fabric, copper wire, and soot
80¼ × 89 × 34¼ inches
(203.6 × 226 × 88 cm)

character of her art, Judd inferred Bontecou's political personality as someone immune to the usual dogmas: "Bontecou is obviously unimpressed ... by artistic generalizations.... [Her] reliefs are an assertion of herself, of what she feels and knows. Their primitive, oppressive and unmitigated individuality excludes grand interpretations."[13]

I think Judd wanted a certain lesson for life to emerge from his kind of critical writing. He seems to have recognized that when an artist sets the main aspects of a work in some kind of opposition, while also preventing the separate parts from being subordinated to a generalized harmony or composition, then the entirety of the work remains alive in the viewer's perceptual experience—every part, every sensory quality of it, and all the emotional and intellectual qualities as well. Every element (including the totality) becomes focused, as if art allowed its viewer to function on every level with equal acuity, never sacrificing one area of human potential for another. To understand the conditions of a life within a specific social and physical environment, Judd implies, a person needs to concentrate on what can be known through the most immediate forms of experience, resisting the generalizations of categories, clichés, and logical inferences. Yes, try to grasp the big picture (the "whole"); but don't allow it to rule over the independent significance of a detail (a "hole"). With this approach to life, Judd admired Barnett Newman just as he admired Bontecou: Newman's art "doesn't claim more than anyone [any one person] can know." Judd meant that every formal element in Newman's painting was no more than it appeared to be,

[13] Judd, "Lee Bontecou", *Complete Writings 1959–1975*, 179.
[14] Judd, "Barnett Newman" (1964–70), *Complete Writings 1959–1975*, 202.

and appearances were there to be experienced as something entirely real: "The color, areas, and stripes are not obscured or diluted by a hierarchy of composition and a range of associations."[14] This was an art that performed its own judgments, without referring to established belief and the common, acculturated forms of experience that people rarely investigate for themselves.

Newman's art "doesn't imply a social order," Judd reasoned; it offered no grounds for a generalized theory.[15] Perhaps, then, Newman was risking incoherence, or the sense of nonsense that might derive from simply setting one thing against another, pale cerulean blue against deep black, with the two barely relating, if at all. If such a thing were done for the sake of incoherence or nonsense itself, and merely intended to be provocative, it would be a new Dadism, rather than a critical skepticism. Newman, in fact, had denounced the Dada artists for their implicit claim to know what art was and what it was not.[16] However nonsensical, Dadaist actions were directed toward a conceptual goal; they reduced the experience of art to a philosophical principle, a kind of intellectual idealism. Such generalization could not be true to conditions at hand. On these matters, Newman and Judd were in complete agreement. So Judd had a least two admired models to follow from the Abstract Expressionist generation, Pollock and Newman (and he liked Mark Rothko as well). Artists of the New York School who practiced figuration, such as Willem de Kooning, brought about a different situation. Judd disliked the fact that de Kooning subordinated the materiality of the painter's mark to emotions associated with the experience of the body, even if that body were internalized as the artist's own. According to Judd, de Kooning displaced the specificity of sensation with emotional generalization: as a referential response to bodies and objects, the "expressive brushwork ... portrays immediate emotions. It doesn't involve immediate sensations."[17] Here I can't agree with Judd's conclusion that de Kooning fails to respond sufficiently to material circumstances, but his point is important for what follows.

In 1966, Judd participated in a symposium at the Jewish Museum, moderated by Barbara Rose. The transcript from the Rose archive differs from the one in the museum archive, which is quite rough. Apparently, the Rose version went through an editing process to restore its fluidity and also expand its scope. Additional sentences were most

15 Ibid.
16 Barnett Newman, "Remarks at the Fourth Annual Woodstock Art Conference" (1952), in John O'Neill (ed.), *Barnett Newman: Selected Writings and Interview* (Berkeley: University of California Press, 1992), 245.
17 Judd, "Jackson Pollock", *Complete Writings 1959–1975*, p.195. See also Judd, "Abstract Expressionism", *Complete Writings 1975–1986*, 40.
18 Donald Judd, edited transcript of "The New Sculpture: A Symposium on Primary Structures", Jewish Museum, New York, 2 May 1966, Barbara Rose Papers, Archives of American Art.

likely inserted by Judd to set the historical record straight. In these supplementary remarks, he emphasizes his affinity to Bontecou, John Chamberlain, and Oldenburg, three artists about whom he had already written in some detail. "One of the reasons I stopped painting," Judd tells Rose, "was that Oldenburg's work was much stronger than anything I could possibly make in a painting."[18] Why would Judd be so attracted to Oldenburg, who represented clothing, foodstuffs, household appliances and furnishings? Why would this practice not lead to de Kooning's kind of compromised expressionism—part figurational, part abstract—which Judd believed could only generate the shallowest emotions?

In 1968, this enigma troubles Lucy Lippard, an unusually astute critic, as she interviews Judd. Lippard was well aware that Judd had featured Oldenburg in his notorious article "Specific Objects," first composed in 1964. Initially, she objects to the anthropomorphism of Oldenburg's art, which seems to conflict with Judd's principles. Judd replies that Oldenburg is not "anthropomorphic quite."[19] A lot hangs on his appended word *quite*. Judd had already distinguished Oldenburg's anthropomorphism from the usual kind by calling his type "extreme" and "blatant"—so extreme that it did not seem comparable to what people identified as anthropomorphic.[20] Yet there was no other name for it. As a pragmatist, Judd knew that things tend to have more or less of a quality, only rarely all or nothing. Whether a person regards qualitative variance in a given characteristic as generating sameness or difference becomes a matter of perceptual attitude (in turn, perhaps instilled by temperament or emotional attitude). Judd preferred to use geometric forms in his art, as opposed to Oldenburg's organic forms; yet this distinction did not always make a difference, nor did it prevent other abstract art from being just as anthropomorphic as organic figuration. Abstract, constructed form—not abstraction *from* or *of* something else—was Judd's personal way of trying to avoid artistic clichés. With his dry humor, he imagined a condition potentially better for art than anyone had yet been able to achieve, including himself: "A form that's neither geometric nor organic," he wrote in 1967, "would be a great discovery."[21] He also wanted to escape the generalities known as "order" and "disorder."[22] Any concept that might categorise and contain his art, or even exclude it, was its inadequate antithesis.

19 Judd, interview by Lippard.

20 Judd, "In the Galleries: Claes Oldenburg" (1964), "Claes Oldenburg" (1966), *Complete Writings 1959–1975*, 133, 191.

21 Judd, "Statement" (from "Homage to the Square," 1967), *Complete Writings 1959–1975*, 193. As a further example of Judd's imagining his way out of dichotomies, compare his reference to "another kind of painting, far from the easel, [and also] far from beyond the easel" (Judd, "Some Aspects of Color in General and Red and Black in Particular," in Serota 2004, 157).

22 Judd, "Statement" (from 'Portfolio: 4 Sculptors', 1968), *Complete Writings 1959–1975*, 196.

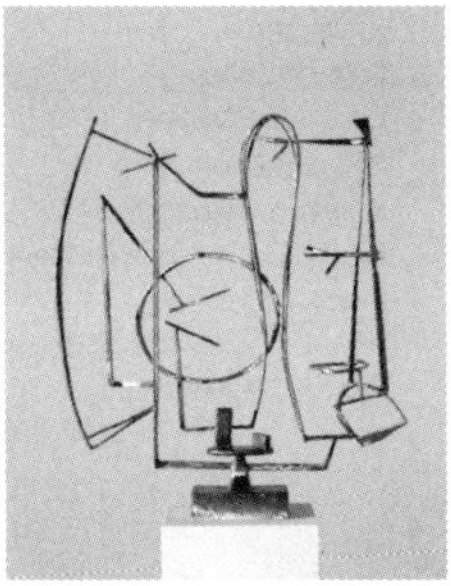

29
David Smith
Stainless Window, 1951
Stainless steel
31½ × 28¼ × 7¼ inches
(80 × 71.8 × 18.4 cm)

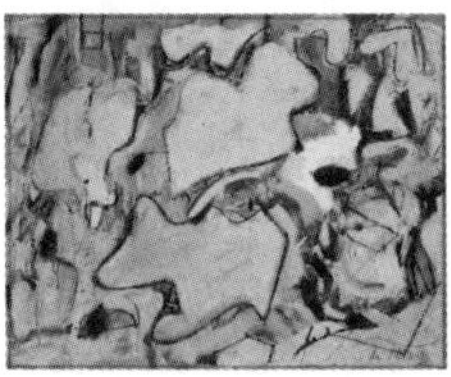

30
Willem de Kooning
Attic Study, 1949
Oil, enamel, and graphite on paperboard mounted on hardboard
18⅞ × 23⅞ inches
(47.9 × 60.6 cm)

Proceeding with his defense of Oldenburg, Judd raises the example of David Smith. He regards Smith's sculpture as the more anthropomorphic of the two, despite the fact that Smith was working in terms of abstraction, whereas Oldenburg was making expressive representations of real things in the human environment. One would think that Oldenburg already had two strikes against him when it came to anthropomorphism, for he created objects related to the human image as well as to human use. Judd understood that Lippard needed some kind of explanation: "Smith ... is seeing it [the anthropomorphic quality] out there and it's in the work, he's feeling it out there and it's in the work and it's beyond him." Like de Kooning, Smith seems to combine the anthropomorphism of his forms with the anthropomorphism of things he might observe—as Judd says, "it's in the work *and* it's beyond him." Although the example is not Judd's, perhaps we grasp his reservation about Smith through a sculpture such as *Stainless Window* (1951) [fig. 29]; it resembles de Kooning's "abstractions" of the late 1940s (see *Attic Study*, 1949 [fig. 30]), though in shallow relief. The tensile organicism of de Kooning's and Smith's imagery evokes human bodies and the physicality of familiar objects—whether the artists' forms are abstract or representational, whether set in a vertical or horizontal format, whether created of paint or metal, and whether or not the tensile factor might relate to those materials. With de Kooning and Smith, the general anthropomorphism is not merely set in opposition to a more specific material factor but (in Judd's view) dominates it.

Continuing to address Lippard, Judd elaborates on Oldenburg's difference: "Oldenburg is so far over the hill that it's only Oldenburg, you see, in which case it's sort of turned full circle and isn't really anthropomorphic in the old sense."[23] Oldenburg's works are "not really about the objects ... [Instead, they're] what Oldenburg feels.... It's Oldenburg's interest in these things. So there's really nothing about the ice cream cone as an ice cream cone" [see *Floor Cone*, 1962]. Here Lippard must object again, for Judd is seeing differences where there should be none: "I don't know how you really split that," she replies. "I can vaguely sense what you're talking about but I don't think that it makes any sense." I sympathize with Lippard; as close as she was to Judd's situation, she was having trouble comprehending his thinking. Judd wasn't daunted and replied in turn: "Look, you feel something about a certain object. It's obvious." But (I must comment) it isn't obvious, because Judd

[23] Judd, interview by Lippard.

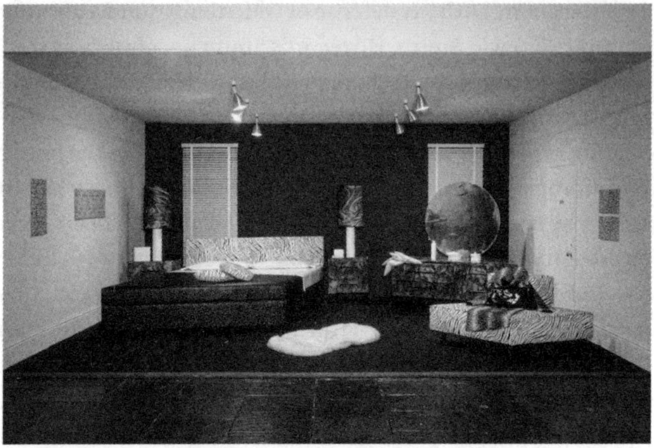

31
Claes Oldenburg
Bedroom Ensemble, 1963
Wood, Formica, vinyl, aluminum, paper, fake fur, muslin, Dacron, polyurethane foam, and lacquer
119¼ × 201½ × 255⅛ inches
(303 × 512 × 648 cm)

has already said, "[it's] not really about the objects." Perhaps "you feel something about [the] object," but when the feeling is strong, the object ceases to matter. The art object related to it becomes all feeling.

Judd reaches Lippard by distinguishing between attributed feelings and felt feelings: "You look at all the things you look at or deal with and you know you have feelings about them; it's pretty obvious. But the fact is that they have no feeling or meaning or anything in themselves." Like a good American pragmatist, Judd can extend this insight to almost anything: "All of European art is really involved in reading things into things. You look out there and somehow what you feel is supposed to be out there." Judd's problem with conventional art, including nearly all modern art, is that it accepts a preconceived notion of what an object signifies—matching feelings to things, and things to feelings. To the contrary, with Oldenburg (as Judd says), "it's only Oldenburg." If a specific feeling appears in the form of an Oldenburg art object, we feel it because the artist felt it, not because of some general correlation that results in a rule (such as: all toggle switches that come in pairs are breast-like). This is the same type of claim Judd was making for Newman's abstract paintings around the same time, 1964: Newman represents no more than his personal experience. Despite the representational quality of Oldenburg's work, Judd asserts that (like Newman's) it doesn't depend on outside objects. Oldenburg starts from an object but develops that thing in a chosen material according to his feelings for the material as much as for the form it assumes. The difference between what Oldenburg does and what (in

Judd's opinion) de Kooning and Smith do may seem to hinge on a very fine point, so fine that it can escape attention; yet, to Judd it was critical. In the end, there is no ice cream cone, no generalized cultural artifact, but something new that exists only because Oldenburg created it—"new" not in the sense of some radical originality, but new because it is a specific object with defining properties best understood through direct experience. To view an Oldenburg object is to acknowledge its specificity, not its deviation from a cultural template.

In his writings, Judd gave most of his attention to Oldenburg's soft sculptures and contrastingly hard *Bedroom Ensemble* (1963) [fig. 31]. Consider first what he says about objects such as *Floor Cone* and the various versions of *Soft Switches*: "The trees, figures, food or furniture in a painting have a shape or contain shapes that are emotive. Oldenburg has taken this anthropomorphism to an extreme and made the emotive form ... the same as the shape of [his sculptural] object, and by blatancy [he has] subverted the idea of the natural presence of human qualities in all things.... Oldenburg exaggerates the accepted or chosen form and turns it into one of his own."[24] In sum, Oldenburg divorces the conventional thematic form or image from its conventional emotional content. This is why his objects become his own, and as his own, they also become "objects as they're felt, not as they are.... They're exaggerated, as [personal] interest is, gross and overblown." Having mentioned that Oldenburg makes hard objects as well as soft ones, Judd inserts a sentence that may seem to come out of nowhere: "A girl said once that sometimes the corners of things would seem to be points pointing at her." In fact, this serves as an example of a specific emotion detached from a general image; the identity of the object does not matter as long as it has a corner. In the girl's eroticized emotional life, corners are exaggerated, blatant, extreme. Eventually, Judd concludes: "The reference to objects [in representational art] gives [the basic emotive forms—corners, for example,] a way to occur. The reference and the basic form as one thing is Oldenburg's main idea"—that is, the "main idea" for his new three-dimensional object.[25]

If this still puzzles (and I believe it does), imagine that Oldenburg is using organic representation to reach the point Judd might reach through geometric structure. It seems that Judd identifies Oldenburg's referential image as conventional and general, distinguishing it from the form developed

[24] Judd, "Specific Objects", *Complete Writings 1959–1975*, 189.
[25] Judd, "Claes Oldenburg", *Complete Writings 1959–1975*, 192.

through the artist's personal interest; and then Judd claims that Oldenburg's art combines these two disparate qualities—image and feeling—combines them as "one thing," his "main idea." This is the mysterious part, but we can see that it follows the pattern of Judd's appreciation of Pollock's abstractions, which oppose aggressively sensuous marks to a general, unified image that never reduces to the sum of its sensuous elements. Nor do the parts become subordinate to the whole.

Judd first addressed Oldenburg's *Soft Switches* in 1964, the year they were made. Here the generalized image was of functional switches, while the sensuous element, analogous to a painter's constitutive marks, became erotic—erotic because of the soft or flaccid nature of the canvas or vinyl as well as the structural allusion to nipples, and further, because those nipples evoke breasts. But perhaps they don't ... "quite." As Judd states, "there aren't two breasts, just two nipples. The two switches are too distinct to be breasts."[26] He means that they retain their identity as switches, yet their form describes neither switches nor breasts. Rhetorically, for what it may be worth, the dominant figure in Judd's writing is not metaphor. He doesn't relate toggle switches to human nipples by sensuous, metaphoric resemblance. Instead, he invokes the more troublesome figures of syllepsis and catachresis. With syllepsis, we understand the meaning of a term in two opposing directions, one of which usually appears more proper than the other. An example: Hope sank with the ship. Because ships are solid objects, we know they can sink. But does hope sink in the same sense, in the same direction? How do intangibles like hope and other emotions move at all? Hope cannot sink metaphorically because it bears no resemblance to a solid object, or even to heavy air. To describe it as moving somewhere is to enlist a different rhetorical figure—catachresis—an indication of cognitive desperation, a figure to be used when no other device is available. With catachresis, we borrow a term that applies elsewhere, and we extend it.

In rhetorical practice, both syllepsis and catachresis represent the kind of "extension of extremes" that Judd appreciated in art practice. Rather than operating like refined poetic devices, bringing nuance to existing images, these rhetorical figures force thought into unfamiliar realms. Although Judd sometimes resorted to metaphors—and who does not?—his writing is better characterized by catachresis and syllepsis. He took pleasure in pointing out that Jasper Johns's *Thermometer*

26 Judd, "In the Galleries: Claes Oldenburg", *Complete Writings 1959–1975*, 133.

(1959), as he wrote, "has one," that is, the painting with the title *Thermometer* also has the actual object, a thermometer.[27] This is an instance of syllepsis. Catachresis and syllepsis bring a strange quality of literalness to Judd's most figurative descriptions, as Thomas Hess must have intuited right at the beginning. I believe Hess knew that something disturbing was occurring in Judd's writing but couldn't characterize it. He just knew that he didn't like it, as Judd later recalled. To Hess, who packed his own writing with metaphors, Judd's reviews lacked style. One might expect this, because writers resort to syllepsis and catachresis when faced with a situation in which words fail them, when no more agreeable figure will work because the effect being described lies outside the range of all standard metaphors. Catachresis is the absence of style and stylistic eloquence. It strong-arms language. Yet, with catachresis, a writer discusses what otherwise can't be discussed.

A critic relying on a concept of metaphor to guide the evaluation of Oldenburg might well turn negative, having extinguished the specificity of the art by generalizing its features. Consider a statement by Max Kozloff, to which Judd appears to have objected: "[Oldenburg] strives for a metaphor, not of the motif itself [the object represented], but of particular attitudes toward it. His pastries are wreathed in an aura of glutinous ecstasy.... [He] doesn't lift a thumb that isn't satirical, and hence finally reportorial in intention. Ultimately, his pieces are in danger of becoming what they are parodying."[28] In Judd's view, parody and reportage were beside the point. If the emotion was ecstasy, then the object was an ecstatic object, not one merely referring to ecstasy: "Oldenburg, who has done something artistically new, as Max Kozloff in *Art International* says he [has] not, makes his cakes and pies and other foods and articles actual objects, which is different epistemologically from illustration."[29] Parody illustrates.

This is why Judd will state of Oldenburg, "the switch doesn't suggest this single, profound form [the archetype of a breast] but is it, or nearly it." Metaphor suggests; it creates evocative analogies. But catachresis says, no, this is no time for suggestion, no time for mere comparison and approximation; the situation *is* this way, even though we find no word for it. Metaphor generalizes; catachresis specifies.[30] Having committed himself to a hypothesis specific to Oldenburg's art, Judd could then explain it in general terms: "Ordinarily the figures and objects depicted in a painting or sculpture have a shape

[27] Judd, "In the Galleries: Jasper Johns" (1960), *Complete Writings 1959–1975*, 14.

[28] Max Kozloff, "New York Letter", *Art International* 6, 25 September 1962, 35.

[29] Judd, "In the Galleries: Wayne Thiebaud" (1962), *Complete Writings 1959–1975*, 60. Judd may have been replying to a comment by Kozloff that preceded the one I have quoted, for the two statements seem to have appeared during the same month, September 1962. Kozloff applied his metaphoric, comparative analysis—the type of critical observation Judd steadfastly resisted—to another of Judd's favorites in March 1962, elaborating on 'the great affinity [John] Chamberlain has with Bernini' (Max Kozloff, "New York Letter", *Art International* 6 [March 1962], 63).

[30] In a recent statement on the evolution of his drawing and sculpture, Oldenburg alludes to a shift from metaphoric illustration to a kind of catachrestic literalness: "I began by trying to represent things accurately. Gradually I became interested in representing different states of mind and feelings; then gesture and material became independent" (Claes Oldenburg, interview by Janie C. Lee, 29 May 2001, in Janie C. Lee, *Claes Oldenburg Drawings, 1959–1977, Claes Oldenburg with Coosje van Bruggen Drawings, 1992–1998, in the Whitney Museum of American Art* [New York: Whitney Museum of American Art, 2002] 18).

or contain shapes that are emotive. Oldenburg makes one of those subordinate shapes the whole form." The exaggerated form becomes distinct from the standard image of the object, because the object has been transformed in accord with the artist's interest. Perhaps now we grasp what Judd means when he says: "The reference and the basic form as one thing is Oldenburg's main idea."[31] We would not expect the reference and the basic form to exist together in this way (as opposed to forming a metaphoric comparison between them); but they are together, as they are nowhere else, both polarized and integrated.

For his *Bedroom Ensemble*, Oldenburg took a perspective drawing of a set of bedroom furniture, the kind of rendering found in newspaper advertisements for clearance sales, where the typical geometry would include trapeziums, rhomboids, rhombuses, and ellipsoids—rectangular and round figures skewed by imaginary angles of view.[32] He then built his own set of furniture in three dimensions, giving the pieces the forms they had as two-dimensional drawing. In his description, Judd calls the quadrilateral forms "parallelogrammatic"; this may be a clever use of catachresis to signify the appearance in art of forms as new and strange as Judd's own.[33] Where a right angle in a real three-dimensional bed might have translated into an acute angle in a perspective drawing, there is an acute angle in the bed Oldenburg created, as if he were following an interest in drawings as much as in bedrooms. The *Bedroom* that he designed put the accidental angularity of things seen in perspective on an equal footing with the rectilinear geometry of typical objects, objects idealized in our minds as if never subject to the illusions of perspective. For Judd and Oldenburg, idealization constitutes the fantasy, and perspectival illusion is the reality of any actual situation. This is precisely the kind of realization that comes through the rhetorical figure of catachresis, which establishes an accident of appearance as the normal or standard view. For example, we refer without hesitation to the legs, arms, and back of a chair, but hardly ever notice that chairs usually lack a head, which ought to disarm the metaphor—but it isn't one. "Arm of a chair" is a textbook example of catachresis. Here the word is entirely specific to the thing; the arm of a chair has no other name.

Oldenburg's reflections on his work are consistent with Judd's. In notes of 1976, he emphasized the disjunction of

[31] Judd, "In the Galleries: Claes Oldenburg", "Claes Oldenburg", *Complete Writings 1959–1975*, 133, 192. Referring to the entire class of "three-dimensional work" (as opposed to conventional sculpture), Judd states: "If there is a reference it is single and explicit. In any case the chief interests are obvious" ("Specific Objects", *Complete Writings 1959–1975*, 188).

[32] Oldenburg's notebook pages from 1963–64 contain such advertising images; see Claes Oldenburg, *Notes in Hand*, (New York: E. P. Dutton, 1971 plates 5, 6.

[33] Judd, "In the Galleries: Claes Oldenburg", *Complete Writings 1959–1975*, 133; also "Claes Oldenburg", *Complete Writings 1959–1975*, 193, where the word is "parallelogram".

the formal look of his installation objects from the concepts associated with their identification: "Geometry, abstraction, rationality—these are the themes that are expressed formally in *Bedroom*. The effect is intensified by choosing the softest room in the house and the one least associated with conscious thought.... Hard surfaces and sharp corners predominate.... [The] subject matter is not necessarily an obstacle to seeing 'pure' form and color."[34] Oldenburg understood that he had created a "pure" abstraction that was also purely representational; and he had done this without resorting to a hybrid expressionism as de Kooning or Smith did. Judd referred to *Bedroom Ensemble* as "grossly geometric," indicating that here the element of exaggeration was the geometry, the angularity, the rigidity of things as they are felt, not merely seen.[35] Around 1963, while Oldenburg with his *Bedroom Ensemble* was creating a hard version of a "soft" space, he was also translating the soft effects of painting into nominally "hard" sculptural form—a form that became soft not metaphorically but actually. In Oldenburg's objects, the fluidity of paint in two dimensions became the flaccidity of canvas or vinyl in three dimensions. As he said, he realized "the tendency of a hard material [sculptural form] actually to be soft, not look soft."[36] This would accentuate the emotional force of the created object, conveyed by its softness or hardness, whatever its representational identity. The polarity between emotional sensation and representational concept would exist in the hardness of *Bedroom Ensemble* as well as in the softness of *Floor Cone*. "Obviously what you feel and what things are aren't the same," Judd wrote in 1967.[37]

For both Judd and Oldenburg, the harsh angularity of *Bedroom Ensemble*—a formal element inspired by an interest in the feeling it generates—distanced the emotional impact of the object from its conventional, identifying image. Oldenburg noted that he had created a hard version of the softest room of a house, soft by conventional association. He wanted to:

> remove the object from context ... to individualize it ... to create an independent object which has its existence in a world outside of both the real world as we know it and the world of art.... The object will slip out of whatever definition it may be given.... My intention is to make an everyday object that eludes definition.... I want the object to have its own existence.[38]

[34] Claes Oldenburg, note on *Bedroom*, 1976, in Germano Celant (ed.), *Claes Oldenburg: An Anthology*, (New York: Guggenheim Museum, 1995), 204.
[35] Judd, "Claes Oldenburg", *Complete Writings 1959–1975*, 192.
[36] Oldenburg, note of 1963 (edited in 1995), in Celant, 192.
[37] Judd, "Jackson Pollock", *Complete Writings 1959–1975*, 195.
[38] Oldenburg, in McDevitt, 31.

I'm reminded of what Judd wrote in 1964, not as a reference to Oldenburg's work, but at more or less the same moment that he may have been pondering it: "Things that exist exist, and everything is on their side ... Everything is equal, just existing."[39] Merely by existing, the things that exist, like the accentuated brushstrokes of Pollock or the exaggerated qualities of an Oldenburg object, have already beaten the odds against the chances that their particular configurations would ever be actualized. Art can be made from very little, so long as the little things acquire a forceful, "interesting" existence.[40] Thinking of Oldenburg's *Floor Burger* (1962), Judd remarks: "Three fat layers with a small one on top are enough."[41]

Much more could be said concerning Judd's way of linking a writing style to an art style. Catachresis and syllepsis are not the ultimate keys to the puzzle but provide a pragmatic way of dealing with it. There are many other ways. I think Judd especially appreciated that Oldenburg's *Bedroom Ensemble* and a number of related works demonstrated the potential of perspective to be at once the most specific of sensory phenomena and the most generalizing of perceived concepts. This happens to be the way he thought of proportion—that it could be at one and the same time the most particular and the most general relationship that a work might exhibit. The ratios were general, but what an artist did with them was specific. If, in Oldenburg's *Floor Burger*, it was enough to have three big things and a little thing, Judd himself could work endlessly with the complexities of 1 to 1, or 1 to 2, or 1 to 3, maintaining a sense of generality that would lead right back to the specificity of the particular work. His boxes, both early and late, demonstrate that whatever theory of proportion might be considered and however simple it might be, actual practice brings surprises.

Judd's art, like Oldenburg's, faces the fact that we acknowledge general conditions at hand (social, cultural, emotional, material) while actively creating something specific from their situation. We need to keep the two realms separate and equal, understanding that neither the totality nor the detail eliminates its counterpart. We must resist becoming ideologues (totalizers), yet we need to see the whole. Works of art are modes of integration—integration without subordination of the parts.

Early in 1993, just about a year before he died, Judd wrote of space in a way that parallels his sense of emotion and perspective in Oldenburg: "There is no neutral space, since space

39 Judd, "Black, White, and Gray" (1964), *Complete Writings 1959–1975*, 117.
40 On 'interest', see David Raskin, "Judd's Moral Art", in Serota 2004, 82–5.
41 Judd, "Specific Objects", *Complete Writings 1959–1975*, 189.

is made.... My smallest, simplest work creates space around it, since there is so much space within.... Space is new in art and is still not a concern of more than a few artists.... There is no vocabulary for [its] discussion."[42] When no vocabulary exists, rhetoric resorts to syllepsis and catachresis, which create a vocabulary outside the usual poetry as well as outside the usual logic.

Did Judd have a rhetoric of three-dimensional form? Sylleptically, he combined what was given at hand with what he chose to do, making strangely integrated structures that move beyond familiar logics of form. His large, site-specific concrete ring of 1971 is a striking example [see fig. 22]. While the top edge of its inner surface remains level, the top edge of its outer surface parallels the ground, maintaining a height of four feet above that given feature of the land—an arbitrary measure, but calculated along with the inner, constant edge to allow the interior space of the ring to be seen. All is exposed. The ring itself is eighteen inches thick and requires a complex bevel to accommodate the shifting difference between its inner and outer surfaces. Here a single object set in the land creates different spaces of different character, inside and outside its bounded surfaces. Given Judd's understanding of Oldenburg's art, it may be that the outer surface was his way of dealing with representational reference, for it blatantly mimics an aspect of the land, whereas the inner surface is just as forcefully abstract in its escape from reference. The most obvious feature of the ring is its existence as a single unit. In his boxes, Judd called the effect of red and black a "two-color monochrome."[43] I suppose that by analogy—would he have objected to this one?—his concrete ring could be called a bilateral unilateral. Its complexly canted surface gestures toward the given land and toward Judd the willful artist, accomplishing these very separate actions as one.

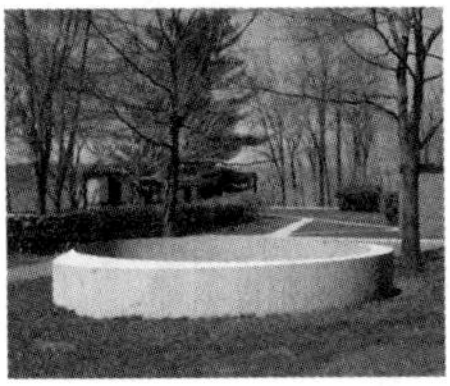

22 see page 67

[42] Donald Judd, "21 February 93", Donald Judd: Large-Scale Works (New York: Pace Gallery, 1993), 9, 13.

[43] Judd, "Some Aspects of Color in General and Red and Black in Particular," in Serota 2004, 158.

Specificity

[2009]

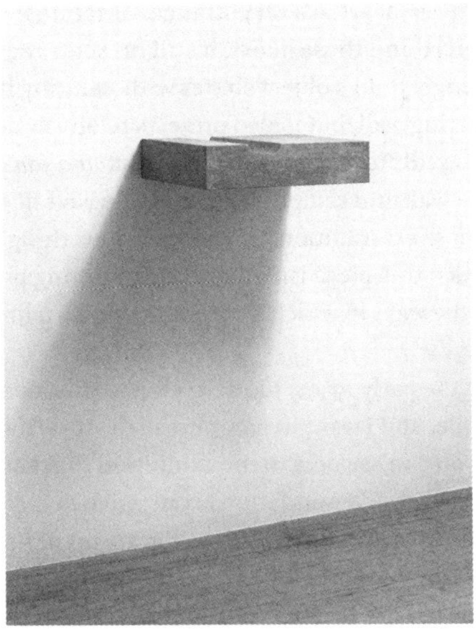

32
Donald Judd
Untitled, 1964
Red enamel on galvanized iron over wood
6 × 27 × 24 inches
(15.2 × 68.6 × 61 cm)

I'll start with one of Donald Judd's early wall pieces, which now tend to be called "single stacks"—objects that have the dimensions, more or less, of the units that would make up Judd's larger wall pieces. [fig. 32]. The larger ones consist of ten units similar to this one, but without the rounded element. I've chosen this example because it makes obvious the type of simple opposition that Judd would build into much of his three-dimensional work. This object has qualities of both curvature and rectilinearity, contrasting qualities that nevertheless exist as a structural whole without either of the two seeming to dominate the other. But even if this wall unit were flat on the front end, as most of the single stacks are, we would have a clear opposition of at least two elements. First, there would be the box-like form, a familiar shape that we recognize. Second, there would be the projection of this same form in space, which is certainly as noticeable as the form itself. I like this particular view of the work because it makes the projection all the more obvious. To the extent that the form itself is familiar, this kind of projection is not. Why not? Because we don't normally see objects extending straight out from a wall or facade in this manner, at least not "art" objects, that is to say, objects that don't belong to the class of things designed primarily for a recognizable function, like drawers that stick out of shelving units or marquees that stick out of the facades of movie houses. Judd's object is just something to look at, and,

EDITOR'S NOTE
"Specificity" is the transcript of a talk presented by Richard Shiff at "The Writings of Donald Judd," a symposium hosted by the Chinati Foundation, May 3-4, 2008.

as a work of visual art, it's very strange. As familiar as I am with this piece and those like it, it still presents me with a sensory challenge. Judd's object shares with painting its relation to a supporting wall, but it also projects relatively deep into space like a sculpture. This particular *combination* of painting-against-the-wall and sculpture-in-space doesn't fit easily into either of these art traditions, and the curious thing is that the ways in which this piece isn't like either painting or sculpture dominate the ways in which it might seem like painting or like sculpture.

During the early 1960s, Judd developed this idea in terms of a principle, and I want to paraphrase the text from a sketch page that you can see now in the exhibition that Valerie Breuvart at the Judd Foundation arranged to coincide with our symposium.[1] The exhibition shows the stages of Judd's composition of his "Specific Objects" essay. The relevant sketch sheet seems to have been produced earlier than the essay and is independent of it. But the essay inherits all of Judd's earlier thinking—his entire career, I think, is a single-minded development, ever expanded and ever refined both visually and intellectually. On the early sheet of notes there are drawings of boxes and an explanatory statement. Judd was writing a note to himself to the effect that the projected depth of his box-like constructions should equal or slightly exceed the height of the same form. Given the example, we might conclude that the projection does more than slightly exceed—it greatly exceeds. But, apparently, this degree of excess was not too much. Here I should simply read Judd's note, because I think that his words make the situation clear enough, despite his condensed syntax: he explains that the box needs "to project to not appear against wall[,] but no more." The projection takes the object away from or out of the wall, but only to a certain point. This quality of not being against the wall, but "no more," that is to say, not to project so much that the object would seem to belong in space rather than belong to the wall—this is what makes Judd's variation on a common box form so *specific.* Because the form projects from the wall so abruptly, it can't be seen as part of the wall like a painting or a relief sculpture. Yet it also doesn't project to the point that it would become a sculptural object in the space of the room, as if it were a traditional vertical monument set horizontally on its side. This not-painting, not-sculpture would qualify as what Judd came to call a "specific object."

1 *Donald Judd: The Writing of "Specific Objects,"* Judd Foundation, Marfa, TX, 2008; *The Writings of Donald Judd,* symposium hosted by the Chinati Foundation, May 3–4, 2008; Judd Foundation dates the sheet of notes 1963–64.

A moment ago I described Judd's single stack as "strange" in appearance. "Strange" is a word that he himself used in an early draft of the essay "Specific Objects." It occurs when he was explaining what was so unsatisfying about most of the contemporary practice of painting, painting tied to the tradition of using oil pigments on canvas. Judd had been impressed by the recent use of commercial and industrial paints in the work of Jackson Pollock, Frank Stella, and others. The draft contains the following passage, which is not found in the published text, although Judd retained the essential thought: "[Industrial paints] can be stronger and more specific than oil, which is interminably generalizing. Canvas is a quiet material. Many materials are more powerful, more strange." My word "interminably" must remain a guess, because I can't read Judd's handwriting at this point, and no one that I've consulted has been able to read this word either, whatever it is. But the more important word is "generalizing." Oil paint is "generalizing"; it isn't "specific." I think what Judd meant is that we are so used to seeing pictures created with oil paints that we hardly notice the paint. With oil paint, we can do anything we like—it's a one-size-fits-all kind of medium. We see only the image that this medium creates, not what constitutes the image. This makes canvas, as well as oil paint, a "quiet material," as Judd puts it. In contrast, many other materials—certain paints not associated with the painting tradition, such as the enamels that Pollock used, certain metals and plastics not associated with the sculptural tradition, such as the automotive steel that Chamberlain used, or the galvanized iron, the enameled aluminum, and the colored Plexiglas that Judd himself used—these were, as Judd says, "more powerful, more strange." In the published text, he put it this way: "Oil paint and canvas aren't as strong as commercial paints.... The quality is especially identified with art."[2] So what's wrong with being identified with art? The problem Judd perceived was that art was a category of object, and all categories set up expectations. You can't see the specific qualities of an object if you first identify it as art; you see only the qualities that art is supposed to possess.

Judd's own art as well as his writing gradually evolved. Working from his base of remarkable insights that he had during the early 1960s, the time of his most intensive critical writing, he kept getting better at being Donald Judd. Contrary to what many of my academic colleagues have often said about him, he was hardly fixed or dogmatic in his views. He may have

2 Donald Judd, "Specific Objects," *Arts Yearbook 8*, 1965, reprinted in *Complete Writings 1959–1975*, 181.

been passionate about advocating the good and condemning the bad, but he was also measured when he perceived that things were only relatively good or bad. Faced with a so-so situation, he could be quite funny about it. His brief review of Peter Saul's raucous, cartoon-like paintings, for a show early in 1963, begins with this line: "Saul is O.K., and no more."[3] So the sentence moves from the relatively good of "O.K." to the relatively bad of "no more." The self-undercutting character of this statement is typical of Judd's writing style, and we've already seen a benign version of it in his note to himself: "To project to not appear against wall[,] but no more." For me, there's something comical, but also deeply moral, about holding yourself responsible to the specificity of your own invention by keeping it from becoming more than it should be. I personally like Peter Saul's early art, but Judd objected to its overstatement, a judgment I have to respect. Saul's paintings are a case of overkill; they're loaded up with funny but obscene, scatological images. Judd could acknowledge the situation in three words: "Saul loves toilets."[4] The more important point was that too much of a bad thing was hardly different from too much of a good thing: both would slip from specificity into generality.

As an example of an early instance of Judd's critical flexibility, I'll refer to his view of an artist who plays only a minor role in "Specific Objects," but it's someone whom Judd considered carefully: Roy Lichtenstein. In the fall of 1963, a little over a year before Judd wrote the first drafts of "Specific Objects," he reviewed Lichtenstein's show at Leo Castelli's gallery. Judd's first sentence is this: "For one thing, I like Lichtenstein's work better than before, and for another, it has improved."[5] This is already a remarkably complex thought, one that may have to remain indeterminate for an interpreter like myself. Judd implies that he's correcting an incorrect judgment made on a previous occasion, yet he immediately introduces the possibility that his judgment is changing because Lichtenstein is changing. So which is it? Was the problem Judd's limited capacity to appreciate Lichtenstein, or Lichtenstein's improvements to his own areas of limitation? In fact, when Judd reviewed Lichtenstein at Castelli in the winter of 1962, there was already the same kind of ambiguity. At that time, he appreciated Lichtenstein's compositional skills but undercut this judgment with a comparison to Fernand Léger. I'll read just a few sentences, interjecting some responses as I go along: "There may be reasons as to the social meaning of comics and

3 Donald Judd, "In the Galleries: Peter Saul," *Arts Magazine*, March 1963, reprinted in *Complete Writings 1959–1975*, 79.
4 Ibid.
5 Donald Judd, "In the Galleries: Roy Lichtenstein," *Arts Magazine*, Nov. 1963, reprinted in *Complete Writings 1959–1975*, 100.

the aesthetic meaning of enlarging them, but these would be minor."[6] So this sentence already introduces the characteristic form of setting up a positive notion and then undercutting it with a negative one: Lichtenstein has his reasons, but they are minor. Judd continues: "It is not so unusual to appreciate the directness of comics; they look like Léger, as do [Lichtenstein's] versions of them. The commercial technique—non-art—is part of the jolt, but the schematic modeling, the black lines and the half-tones of Ben Day dots resemble Léger's localized modeling and black lines around flat colors. Lichtenstein is hardly as good as Léger, but is fairly good and has something on his own."[7] So, by the end of this passage, Lichtenstein has suffered from comparison with an older artist with a related look, and yet, as Judd admits, this painter "has something on his own." This something would be specific to the painter's interest, but it would not be until a later review that Judd would develop his appreciation of it. I'll read the relevant sentences:

> Lichtenstein's color is pretty straight and unharmonized. The printed quality [of the dots] and the paintings' nature as a representation of a representation are part of the same idea. This idea is related to questioning the method, the general way you deal with certain problems, in contrast to considering those singly. The paintings are dealing with an idea of something, rather than with something itself. They are twice removed. Similarly, they suggest metalinguistics, in which the indications of reality that a word seems to possess are not accepted as a basis for thought, but rather a word's usage is examined. [The word] "is" was once taken literally and discussed as if it were existence itself; now it is considered as a word, as a convention.[8]

So, Lichtenstein, according to Judd, was calling attention to his own graphic techniques and making them objects of specific interest.

Judd's insight into Lichtenstein becomes a single sentence in his essay "Specific Objects." Here it is, with what immediately precedes and what immediately follows: "Some things can only be done on a flat surface. Lichtenstein's representation of a representation is a good instance. But this work which is neither painting nor sculpture challenges both."[9] The work Judd refers to here is not Lichtenstein's but work with a not-this but not-more-than-this kind of quality to it—work like Judd's own

6 Donald Judd, "In the Galleries: Roy Lichtenstein," *Arts Magazine,* April 1962, reprinted in *Complete Writings 1959–1975,* 48–49.
7 Ibid.
8 Donald Judd, "In the Galleries: Roy Lichtenstein," *Arts Magazine,* Nov. 1963, reprinted in *Complete Writings 1959–1975,* 101.

single stacks, and also things with which they have a strong affinity. I'll put some Lee Bontecou on the screen because the affinity will be obvious [see fig. 28]. This is an installation shot of Bontecou's show at Castelli in 1960, which Judd reviewed very favorably. You can see that the Bontecou relief either satisfies Judd's principle in advance or comes very close to doing so: projection that should equal or exceed the height of the box.

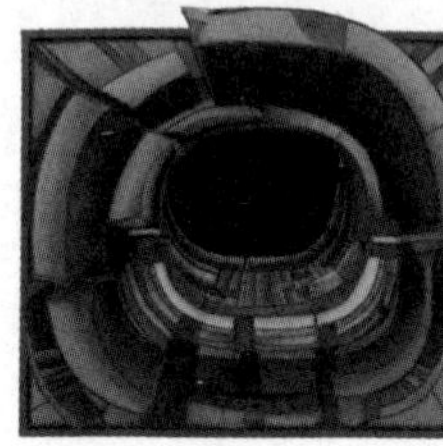

28 see page 80

I'll have more to say about Bontecou, but let me go back to the sentence that could be describing it: "This work which is neither painting nor sculpture challenges both." Judd's sentence represents a mild form of the syntactical compression that characterizes his writing style—a syntactical compression that may cause a slight delay in comprehension: "work which is neither painting nor sculpture challenges both." It may take an instant of time to connect the word "both" to the words "painting" and "sculpture." Perhaps this is the normal way to write a sentence of this type, but I've been struck by Judd's tendency to generate extreme forms of this kind of referential delay. If you read his sentences too quickly you lose the train of his thought. I'll read a sentence in which the word "thermometer" is italicized because it's the title of a painting by Jasper Johns: "*Thermometer* has one bisecting it with the number gauge running up either side as part of the abstract surface."[10] The essence of this sentence, the subject-verb-object part is this: "*Thermometer* has one." One what? One thermometer, obviously. But there's a certain mental switch that has to occur as we realize that the title of the painting isn't performing as a pictorial metaphor but as a literal description. So the title is entirely specific to the painting, not so much in identifying it by name but in naming what it is. The name switches from operating as a categorical abstraction or generalization to operating as a specific index. The title doesn't tell us about some thermometer that got represented, an instance of a thermometer; instead, it tells us of this specific thermometer, the one that Johns put into his painting, which may or may not resemble other things that go by the same name, "Thermometer." The name is not the thing; the *thing* is the thing.

Judd's habits as a reviewer, indicated by the pages of notes that remain in his archive, were the habits of a viewer. I suspect that he was much more of a viewer than most reviewers were or are. Generalized concepts ceased to guide him once he was facing a work in a gallery. He could have done less hard work as a critic than he did. His notes indicate that he assiduously

9 Donald Judd, "Specific Objects," *Arts Yearbook 8,* 1965, reprinted in *Complete Writings 1959–1975,* 181.

10 Donald Judd, "In the Galleries: Jasper Johns," *Arts,* March 1960, reprinted in *Complete Writings 1959–1975,* 14.

gathered information concerning the materials, the colors, and the measurements of the objects he considered—all the concrete, material data—a record of what the senses, not necessarily the mind, would have responded to in the work.

What about the mental, intellectual end of things? Among Judd's earlier writings, the essay "Specific Objects" stands out as a summary statement of views that had been developing since 1959, the year of his first experience as a critical writer of record in New York. Intellectually honest to a fault, he recognized the danger of articulating any position as a definitive one, even his own. Recording his personal views around the time "Specific Objects" appeared, he admitted that like anyone else, he found it "necessary to make general statements"—the normal use of language required it – "but it is impossible and not even desirable to believe most generalizations."[11] The generalities of conventional practice in painting and sculpture were, as he put it, no longer "credible." This may seem an exaggeration, but Judd knew from pragmatic experience that he had no compelling reason to believe in the principles and concepts associated with the traditional art media. There was nothing particularly interesting about seeing what you expected to see. As a writer, Judd could do no better than to say what he had to say with the best words available, while at the same time realizing that he needed to resist the full force of these words. He would reserve some doubt, wary of letting his own rhetoric convert half truths into whole truths. The formal conventions and the corresponding critical language of art were one thing—they were a set of generalities—whereas productive work in the material realm was something else. It extended beyond or simply lay outside the conventions. As a category apart, it was no proper category at all; the members of this class were each too specific to adhere to a category. In need of a new name for a non-category of work in sculpture—that is, work in three-dimensions—Judd tried the obvious: "three-dimensional work." And, in the one instance of the essay in question here, he used the term "specific objects." He had approached this verbal formulation previously—for instance, early in 1963, when he described a Bontecou relief sculpture as "actual and specific and ... experienced as an object."[12]

Judd stated that he first composed "Specific Objects" as long as a year before it saw publication, presumably in late 1964 as opposed to late 1965. He offered this information in 1975, when he reprinted the essay for a volume of his collected

11 Donald Judd, statement in Barbara Rose, "ABC Art," *Art in America*, October/November 1965, reprinted in *Complete Writings 1959–1975*, 181.

12 Donald Judd, "In the Galleries," *Arts Magazine*, January 1963, reprinted in *Complete Writings 1959–1975*, 65.

writings.[13] The second version, which is far better known than the first, changes the internal order without substantially affecting the argument. He shifted his penultimate paragraph on Chamberlain and his final one on Stella to a position closer to the middle of the essay. I can only speculate as to why he made this after-the-fact adjustment, which was unusual for him. Clearly, he cared enough about this essay to revisit it. At least part of the problem may have been the oddity of ending with a strong appeal to a new kind of painting when the topic was innovative sculpture. It's also the case that Judd had been unhappy with subsequent developments in Stella's work during the late 1960s and early 1970s, and perhaps he wished to diminish Stella's impact on his own essay.

A complete typescript draft reveals that Judd had restricted his point about painting—how it might escape generalization—to the single, quite special case at hand. With his characteristic directness, he wrote: "Stella's work isn't an image." We shouldn't confuse this position with a sense of finality—the question was still open to further thought. In works like *Marquis da Portago* (1960), the metallic paint and the geometric pattern cause the eye to see virtual diagonals that Stella never painted. This was a plus for Judd, not a minus, because you became all the more aware of the painting as a physical object with its own strange properties. If you look at how Stella painted his stripes, it's clear that he wasn't thinking of making the diagonals evident; his brushstrokes move around the corners of the pattern and actually curve a little. If anything, this would reduce the optical illusion of diagonals. So, in pictorial terms, Stella wasn't making an illusionistic image of diagonals in the way that a traditional landscape painter might make a diagonal recession seem to be part of reality of the scene. He was letting the form do what the form does. And he was making this clear and apparent.

Now, let's go back to Judd's sentence about Stella. In his final draft, he writes: "Stella's work isn't an image." Yet the printed version of this sentence is different. Judd appears to have exchanged his remark for a principle applicable beyond Stella alone: "A painting isn't an image."[14] This bold, somewhat cryptic pronouncement appeared close to the very end of the 1965 publication but at the mid-point in 1975. Either way, its implication was this: Stella's painting was the particular case that demonstrated the principle to be realized elsewhere. His works resisted being reduced to *mere* images

13 Donald Judd, "Introduction," *Complete Writings 1959–1975*, vii. A date of composition of late 1964 or early 1965 would suggest that Judd's introductory statement for an essay devoted to Bontecou, published in April 1965—"Lee Bontecou was one of the first to use a three-dimensional form that was neither painting nor sculpture"—may have followed from the position he had already established in "Specific Objects": "Half or more of the best new work in the last few years has been neither painting nor sculpture" (see "Lee Bontecou," reprinted in *Complete Writings 1959–1975*, 178). A preliminary draft of the Bontecou essay expands on ideas Judd developed in a previous review of her work but lacks the opening statement about "neither painting nor sculpture" (compare "In the Galleries," *Arts Magazine*, January 1963, reprinted in *Complete Writings 1959–1975*, 65).

14 Donald Judd, "Specific Objects," *Arts Yearbook 8*, 1965, reprinted in *Complete Writings 1959–1975*, 184.

within a world of illusionistic fantasies. Judd seems to have thought of images as belonging to a fictive space, in turn associated with the ill-defined pictorial field to which commentary on conventional painting reverted. It was as if these three conceptual abstractions—image, space, field—were in collusion, allowing critics to avoid acknowledging the dependence of art on concrete, physical objects. The sensory presence of Stella's painting—a result of its specific size, shape, color, reflectivity, and the like—was too insistent, too specific, to be exchanged for a mobile mental form devoid of physical matter. For a publication in 1964, Judd had already established that the distinguishing feature of Stella's art was its conversion of the painting format into a new kind of art object: "The projection [the unusual depth of Stella's stretched canvas], the absence of spatial effects and the close relation between the periphery and the stripes make the paintings seem like objects, and that does a lot to cause their amplified intensity."[15]

We do not meet our emotional match in an image but in a material object. Stella's paintings tipped a certain balance; Judd implied that they were objects more than they were "paintings" (in the sense of conventional "art"). They never became representations of things other than themselves—"the shapes, the unity, projection, order and color are specific, aggressive and powerful."[16]

As a counterexample to the integrated effect of Stella's painting-object, Judd might have referred to his previous account of one of Jacques Lipchitz's sculptures from the 1930s: "It looks best before you see that the broad, round forms are figures—and accurate, composed figures as well."[17] Judd was pointing out that in Lipchitz's art, material form and representational image were occupying separate realms of experience to the detriment of each. Stella's painting had the sensory and emotional integrity or wholeness that Lipchitz's sculpture lacked.

Yet, as Judd wrote of another of his group of favored artists, "Each of Bontecou's reliefs is an image."[18] What could he have meant? As plain as he was as a stylist, his argumentation sometimes became remarkably complex, easily misunderstood in a casual or rapid reading. His statement suggests that a Bontecou relief, projecting abruptly from the wall, object-like in a way characteristic of neither painting nor sculpture, nevertheless became an image as much as it remained an object. These examples of "three-dimensional work" projected

15 Donald Judd, "Local History," *Arts Yearbook* 7, 1964, reprinted in *Complete Writings 1959–1975*, 153.
16 Donald Judd, "Specific Objects," *Arts Yearbook 8*, 1965, reprinted in *Complete Writings 1959–1975*, 184.
17 Donald Judd, "Month in Review," *Arts Magazine*, October 1964, reprinted in *Complete Writings 1959–1975*, 137.
18 Donald Judd, "Specific Objects," *Arts Yearbook 8*, 1965, reprinted in *Complete Writings 1959–1975*, 188.

connotations of bellicosity and sexuality as well as their own material presence; the representational suggestiveness was integral to the felt effect, not merely supplemental: "The image is primarily a single emotive one ... explicit and aggressive."[19] Bontecou's "image" assumed emotive qualities not so different from those of Stella's painting, also "aggressive," also an "object." Invoking the case of Oldenburg, Judd drove the point home: "The emotive form [becomes] the same as the shape of an object."[20] Image, form, and object were sharing in a single emotion, a single feeling. The following year, for an essay devoted exclusively to Oldenburg, Judd put it this way: "His objects are objects as they're felt, not as they are"[21]—that is, not as we identify or name them. The name or category is a supplemental generalization, whereas the experience of sensory and emotional feeling is specific to the object.

A stray note jotted down in connection with "Specific Objects" alludes to Judd's desire to "have [the] whole without parts." This is to experience the emotion, the image, and the object all in one, inseparable—a fair enough description of Judd's own art, which becomes a meeting of extremes. He avoided generalized categories by allowing his concepts to become so inclusive that any particular thing could be a specific variation of any other thing. This condition would force the evaluating critic to recognize that the general categories were arbitrary and only the specific points of description mattered. In 1964, Judd had written of the aesthetics of bridges: "The forms of art and of non-art have always been connected.... It is better to consider art and non-art one thing and make the distinctions one of degree."[22] Did the topic of engineers' constructed bridges induce Judd to think straight through to this type of *conceptual* bridge, to an unnamable, comprehensive class of things created (neither art nor non-art)? The notion that one "bridge" might have led to the other seems far-fetched, yet I think Judd would have been amused by it, perhaps considering it seriously in retrospect. He knew that intuition operates with surprising independence and faster than we can follow it.

Occasionally Judd's pages of notes and manuscript drafts include fragments of drawing. It might be the sketch of a detail he wanted to remember—for example, the notch-like, right-angle turns in a Stella painting. A drawing might also represent the shaping of Judd's own thought, provoked by visual forms observed in the work of others. Just as his consideration of

19 Ibid.
20 Ibid.
21 Donald Judd, "Claes Oldenburg," written July 1966 for the Oldenburg retrospective at the Moderna Museet, Stockholm, unpublished at that time; in *Complete Writings 1959–1975*, 192.
22 Donald Judd, "Month in Review," *Arts Magazine*, October 1964, reprinted in *Complete Writings 1959–1975*, 138.

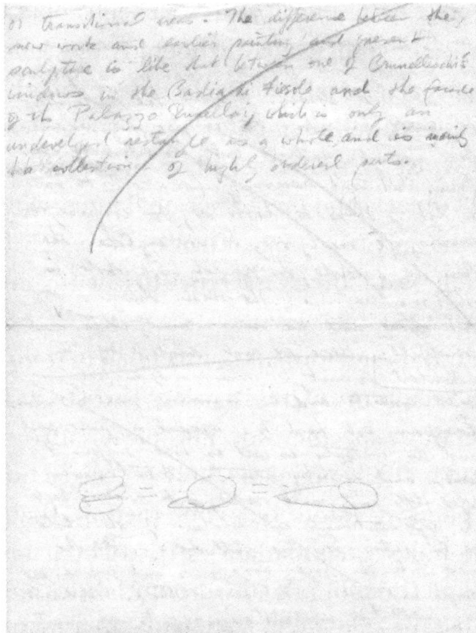
or transitional ones. The difference between the new work and earlier painting and present sculpture is like that between one of Brunelleschi's windows in the Badia Fiesole and the facade of the Palazzo Rucellai, which is only an undeveloped rectangle as a whole and is mainly a collection of highly ordered parts.

33
Donald Judd, Handwritten draft of "Specific Objects," 1964

bridges seems consistent with his sense that polar extremes can constitute a whole—"the forms of art and non-art have always been connected"[23]—his experience of Oldenburg's art seems to have expanded on this notion. One of the draft pages for "Specific Objects" contains a sketch that reads like a mathematical calculation or an exercise in philosophical logic. [fig. 33]. Judd rendered the form of Oldenburg's soft sculpture of a hamburger, then followed it to the right with an equal sign leading to an oval with a cone-like appendage, as if the hamburger were viewed from above or in a more schematic, reduced way, but completed by its cast shadow. Farther to the right, he drew another equal sign, now followed by the form of Oldenburg's soft sculpture of an ice cream cone. The ice cream cone could be the hamburger casting a longer shadow.

Judd's drawing, a kind of thought experiment, demonstrates that concepts such as "hamburger" and "ice cream cone" cannot contain the sensory and emotional significance of the forms that conventionally correspond to them. Just as a bridge can be seen as either art or non-art, each form is specific to its appearance under particular conditions. If you classify the hamburger-like form as "hamburger," you may not realize that with a change of perspective, it could become "ice cream cone"—or rather, ice-cream-cone-like: "Oldenburg exaggerates the accepted or chosen form and turns it into one of his own.... [His] pieces have nothing to do with the objects they're

[23] Donald Judd, "Month in Review," *Arts Magazine,* October 1964, reprinted in *Complete Writings 1959–1975,* 138.

like."[24] Beyond "hamburger" and "ice cream cone," the specifics become apparent when you liberate your senses from these conceptual generalities. By thinking through drawing, Judd could apply a certain mental logic—the generalizing force of the equal sign—and yet affirm the specific reality of Oldenburg's objects and their emotional force, which derived more from the particular appearance of these new forms than from their representational reference to existing forms they resembled or were "like."

New materials and formats contributed to transforming the painting and sculpture of Judd's favored artists, as their works became ever more specific: "specific objects." In Stella's shaped canvases and metallic pigments, Judd perceived novel conditions for painting. Bontecou's constructions that clustered around dark holes, Chamberlain's strips of bent automobile metal, and Oldenburg's soft, droopy fabrics and plastics demonstrated the changes in feeling that new materials could introduce. Judd acknowledged the interaction of format, material, and affect in the care he took to get his descriptive terms right. He was as verbally accurate as he was visually observant. A preliminary draft of "Specific Objects" contains this phrasing: "The plastic of Oldenburg's soft objects looks like it always does, slick, and a little disagreeable." A later draft reaches greater precision with regard to identifying the material and what might make it seem distasteful: "The vinyl of Oldenburg's soft objects looks the same as ever, slick, flaccid and a little disagreeable." Judd had used the word "flaccid" in this way once before.[25] It was just the term to fix the point about a particular kind of slickness—both visual and tactual—the physicality that characterizes vinyl. As always, Judd was specific.

[24] The first sentence is from "Specific Objects"; the second is from "Claes Oldenburg," *Complete Writings 1959–1975*, 191.

[25] See Donald Judd, "In the Galleries," *Arts Magazine*, September 1964, reprinted in *Complete Writings 1959–1975*, 133.

To Stop the Heart

[2010]

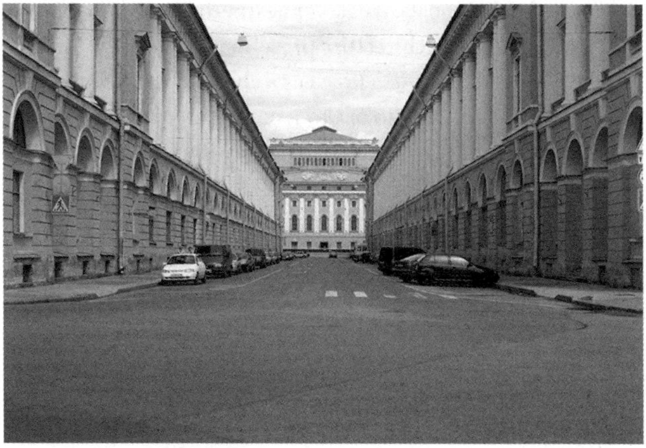

34
Ulitsa Zodchevo Rossi,
St. Petersburg

"The dimensions of the street are 22 m by 22 m by 220 m, numbers that stop your heart as some sights do." Donald Judd was referring to Ulitsa Zodchevo Rossi, the Street of Rossi the Architect in Leningrad (now St. Petersburg) [fig. 34].[1] He encountered this celebrated early nineteenth-century urban project while traveling in 1984. The effect—stopping the heart—was his retrospective metaphor. It could have been the literal fact, for a street or building will transfix a person thoroughly attuned to its proportions. Numbers were perceptible qualities for Judd, not ciphers to be counted. To those with senses anesthetized by habit, the numerical measure of a space is a conceptual abstraction. But Judd felt dimensions as physical.

During the 1970s, Judd was already creating comparably forceful spaces in Marfa, aspects of a building practice that stops the heart in moments of whole-mind, whole-body sensation. Dimensions themselves do this, even if belonging to less than brilliant architecture. Judd remembered the Rossi buildings as "derivative but ... homogeneous and not bad"—entities modest enough to yield to the power of the grander scheme of the street.[2] They were silently symmetrical because no specific function demanded otherwise.[3] The urban environment they formed had the potential to alter life by intensifying the character of everyday experience. The numbers 22, 22, 220 are catalytic: this order of unit proportions with its phantom decimal, this ratio of 1 to 1 to 10, remains in equilibrium as it moves the observer. The concepts of unit measure and decimal division are not what affects the human soul so profoundly but the realization of a comprehensive geometric figure. Its wholeness

1 Donald Judd, "Horti conclusi," *Donald Judd Architektur*, ed. Marianne Stockebrand (Münster: Westfälischen Kunstverein Münster, 1989), 41. The location is also known as Teatralnaya Street. Carlo di Giovanni Rossi (1775–1849) was a Russian architect of Italian origin who completed numerous commissions in St. Petersburg.

2 Ibid.

3 "Art, for myself, and architecture for everyone, should always be symmetrical except for a good reason.... Just realigning the doors and windows, if possible, of old buildings so as to be opposite one another or on axis, is a great improvement": Judd, "Symmetry" (1985), *Donald Judd Architektur*, 190, 192.

dampens, even cancels, whatever aesthetic noise and distraction a fragmented architecture presents.

Judd viewed the Ulitsa Rossi as a channel-like volume; its cross-section, with a ratio of 1 to 1, constituted a square. To perceive this hardly required aesthetic refinement. The street was no passive reserve for urban activity; it was constructed space already thickened with human feeling: "There is no neutral space, since space is made," Judd insisted.[4] And "nothing is architecture," he wrote, not even at a mediocre level, "unless the interior volume is evident."[5] A structure otherwise becomes a mere object of indeterminate scale. The open volume of the Ulitsa Rossi, edged uniformly by buildings of a height equal to the width of the passage, acquired the experiential presence of a commodious interior. If you stand in this street as Judd did, you know that you are *somewhere*, existing in dynamic relation to a specific place, affected by the local conditions.

The Leningrad dimensions "only show as intelligence," Judd remarked.[6] His statement implies what the dimensions did *not* show as: a template for interminable variations or an acknowledged motif referring elsewhere, whether to an ideal of the past or a paradigm for the future. "Most things happen by accident and continue by convention": Judd accepted the former, resisted the latter.[7] The heart-stopping dimensions, however rational and reproducible, did not *feel* formulaic or conventional. As Judd perceived them, they became his own single-minded intuition. Whatever embodies a simple intelligence appeals directly to the intellect and is likely to occupy it. Such a thought or feeling is self-sufficient, demanding no identification with a source or tradition. Simple geometry is direct in this way—a collective property, a common sense. Like an emotion shared by those who share an experience, we assimilate any sufficiently direct thought, any such intelligence, feeling it as much as reasoning it.

The emotion conveyed by the rational plan of the Ulitsa Rossi confirms Judd's fundamental claim: thought and feeling become one to the extent that we release our experience from cultural convention and ideological constraint. "Emotion or feeling is simply a quick summation of experience, some of which is thought, necessarily quick so that we can act quickly. ... It's a short life and a little speed is necessary.... You have to do it [think and feel] all at once."[8] Judd dedicated innumerable hours of thinking to his art and architecture; his thoughts, just

4 Donald Judd, "21 February 93," *Donald Judd: Large-scale Works* (New York: Pace Gallery, 1993), 9.

5 Judd, "Horti conclusi," *Donald Judd Architektur*, 40.

6 Judd, "Horti conclusi," *Donald Judd Architektur*, 41.

7 Donald Judd, "A Long Discussion Not About Master-pieces But Why There Are So Few of Them, Part II" (1984), *Complete Writings 1975–1986* (Eindhoven: VanAbbemuseum, 1987), 79.

8 For the first two sentences, see Judd, "Art and Architecture" (1983), *Complete Writings 1975–1986*, 30; for the final sentence, see Angeli Janhsen, ed., "Discussion with Donald Judd," in *Donald Judd* (St. Gallen: Kunstverein St. Gallen, 1990), 54.

as his choices of phrasing as he wrote, were feelings. The sum of his working hours should not be estimated chronometrically but experientially. He felt his works as he imagined, planned, and constructed them. Art and architecture worthy of the title are—or, it is embarrassing to have to add, ought to be—emotional. Serious thinking, too, is emotional.

Along these lines, Judd had stated (in a note to himself in 1965) that form and color should be "intelligent without being ordered."[9] Where do we find intelligence despite the lack of analytical order? Judd's description of his three-dimensional art implies an answer: "One or four boxes in a row, any single thing or such a series, is local order, just an arrangement, barely order at all."[10] The 22 meter square implied by the street in Leningrad, even when extended to the length of a 220 meter rectangular prism, was a "local order," a one-time experience. It established nothing more than the way this frame of buildings existed, simply existing. It was neither a reference to history nor to any similar configuration. A square or rectilinear construction by Judd would be an equally straightforward arrangement, though different. "There are a lot of rectangles in the world and one that I have made exists as one of them. The idea of a rectangle exists only as an idea, which is easy for rectangles and difficult for most ideas."[11]

Most ideas are more complicated than a rectangle and hard to realize either conceptually or materially. To reflect on Judd's art of box-like prisms and his rectilinear architecture is to recognize the advantage offered by these relatively simple geometric forms. We think through these forms with immediacy. They appear as—they are—intuitions. This is thinking that can be felt, thinking tantamount to feeling ("You have to do it all at once": thinking and feeling). Feeling distinguishes Judd's forms from the formal motifs developed—in fact, hyper-developed—in so much of the art and architecture of his time laying claim to avant-garde status. The new architectural forms were hybrids to be comprehended only through other conceptual abstractions. They were either unnecessarily complicated or engaged in what Judd considered cultural and aesthetic pilfering. Around the time of his Leningrad experience, he wrote that the new postmodernism exemplified "the tendency in this century for art to collapse into fragmented representation or into the literary. Art that was made to be direct is pilfered for art that is made to be indirect."[12] When the indirect feeds on the direct, the gain associated with this superfluity of thought

[9] Donald Judd, "Some Aspects of Color in General and Red and Black in Particular" (1993), *Artforum* 32 (Summer 1994): 113.
[10] Donald Judd, "Statement" (1968), *Complete Writings 1959–1975* (Halifax: Press of the Nova Scotia College of Art and Design, 1975), 196.
[11] Judd, "Some Aspects of Color in General and Red and Black in Particular," 156–57.
[12] Judd, "A Long Discussion Not About Master-pieces But Why There Are So Few of Them, Part I" (1984), *Complete Writings 1975–1986*, 59.

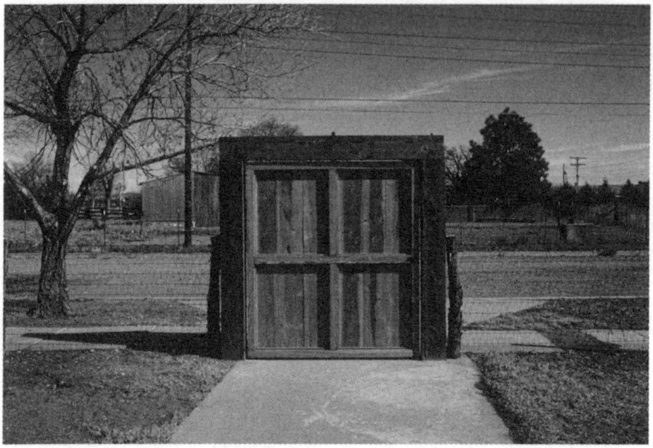

35
Pivoting doors at the Arena, Chinati Foundation, Marfa, Texas

translates into a loss in the intensity of feeling. An excess of reference demanding an indeterminate amount of analysis never stopped a heart. But proportions have.

By feel, Judd arrived at what he would have discovered by reason. Feeling is faster: "My first work was developed by looking. Then I figured out that many [of my] things were very close to even proportions [such as 1:2]. And slowly I made the proportions even. I think what you see [in the ordinary experience of looking] are just the simple ones, 1:2 and 2:3 and 3:4."[13] The simplest proportions correspond to the square, 1:1, and to the double square, 1:2. A double square doubled can form a square once again, as in the swiveling doors Judd designed for the Arena [fig. 35]. Architecturally, a double square extends a structure vertically or horizontally while maintaining its aesthetic integrity, for, as Judd observed, "1 to 2 is ... its own quality."[14] We recognize the most basic proportions for what they are: "Proportion is crucial; we see simple proportions. Much of the quality of a structure lies in these. The scale results from these."[15] This principle is not theoretical but experiential and pragmatic.

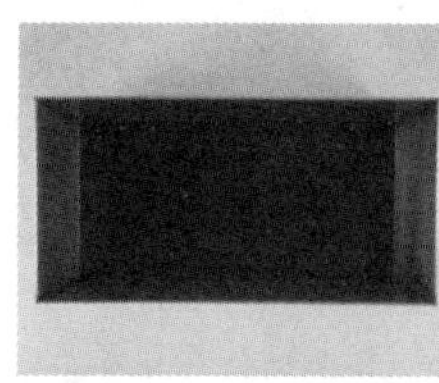

23 see page 262

Judd used the double square as the dimensions of many of his wall-oriented box units, hung either singly or in series—proportions of 1 to 2 to 1 (height to width to depth) [see fig. 23]. When dividing boxes internally, he used halves, thirds, fourths, or fifths.[16] Certain blunt oppositions of color, such as red and black or black and white, bear a corresponding potential for immediate recognition. We are hardly provoked to feel that a third color is needed to balance or integrate the initial two. "Side by side, the red and the black become one color. They

13 Judd, in Katharina Winnekes, "Interview mit Donald Judd," *Kunst und Kirche*, April 1993, 135.
14 Judd, "Art and Architecture" (1983), *Complete Writings 1975–1986*, 34.
15 Judd, "Art and Architecture, 1987," *Donald Judd Architektur*, 198.
16 See Judd, "Symmetry," *Donald Judd Architektur*, 190–92.
17 Judd, "Some Aspects of Color in General and Red and Black in Particular," 113.

36
Facade of Artillery Shed, the Chinati Foundation, Marfa, Texas

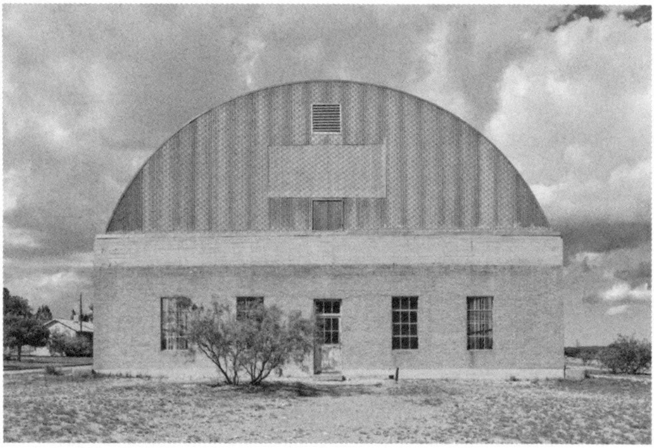

become a two-color monochrome."[17] This notion of a two-color monochrome butts against reason. Puzzled, we have an incentive to test reason against feeling. Take a moment to sense red and black together. Then Judd's thought becomes a feeling, and it will feel right.

When Judd considered improving the existing artillery sheds at Chinati, the buildings he selected to house his mill-aluminum floor objects, he decided to replace a flat roof with a barrel vault [fig. 36].[18] He calculated the profile of the vault so that it doubled the height of the building. This meant that the two fundamental structural elements, the flat façade and the arching roof, would each have a 1:2 ratio with respect to the totality – "1:2 is ... its own quality." These proportions brought clarity to a building otherwise indistinct in its happenstance vagueness. Judd converted accidental circumstances into art without slipping into convention. His plan had the virtue of economy; he applied only so much "design" as required to resolve the issues at hand, instead of designing further, which would amount to decorating what needed none. Decoration generalizes a work of art or architecture by applying elements of design that could be applied equally well elsewhere and anywhere—a "misuse of history."[19] Arbitrary decoration, such as rustic stonework on a modern highway bridge, obscures the distinctiveness of a structure that couples a specific response to a specific demand.[20]

In addition to the artillery sheds, Judd planned a set of ten new concrete buildings to house the remainder of the works in metal intended for Chinati. These structures had clarity from inception. Judd designed three building types to

[18] See Judd, "Artillery Sheds," *Donald Judd Architektur*, 72–74.
[19] Judd, "A Long Discussion Not About Master-pieces But Why There Are So Few of Them, Part I," *Complete Writings 1975–1986*, 63.
[20] See Judd, "Month in Review" (1964), *Complete Writings 1959–1975*, 137.

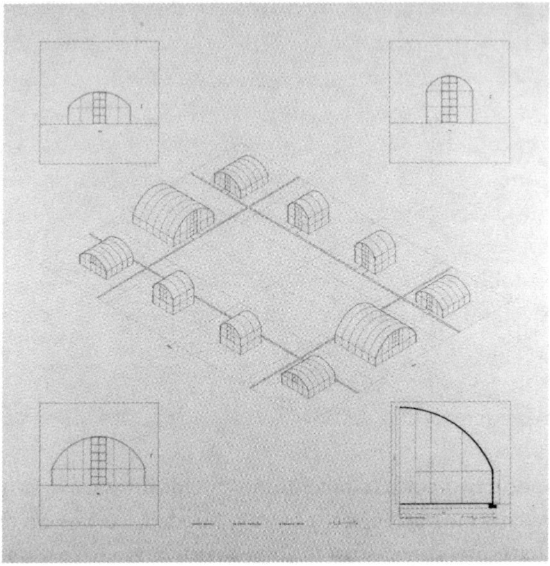

37
Donald Judd
Drawing by Claude Armstrong and Donna Cohen Axonometric drawing for concrete buildings at the Chinati Foundation, 1987
Ink on tracing paper
42 × 42 inches
(106.7 × 106.7 cm)

correspond to the dimensions and orientations of the works of art. In plan, each building is a square set into a grid of squares constituting the site. In elevation, the concrete structures resemble the modified artillery sheds, having a flat façade topped by a vaulted roof. The roof height is either equal to the façade height (1:1) or half this height (1:2) [fig. 37]. The overall proportions of the three building types are 1:1:1, 1:2:2, and 1:3:3—numbers that stop the heart.[21]

We would be wrong to argue that Judd's significance hinges on his use of such proportional relationships. What these ratios actually provided or facilitated is the crux. To put it Judd's way, the numbers produced space—a space to be lived. They brought sensory, intellectual experience into the present and held it there. Using simple ratios directly and obviously, Judd avoided the indirectness that he understood as having undermined so much contemporary practice. "In art and architecture," he wrote, "it's impossible to use forms from the past. They become symbols."[22] Symbols are indirect—multiple traces of intellectual and emotional pilfering. Indirectness generates ineffectiveness, a reductive proposition.

Regarding the vanity of symbols, Judd had a precedent in Barnett Newman, whom he deeply admired. In 1949, Newman had encountered his own Ulitsa Rossi. It was in Ohio, where he visited several sites of ancient Native American mound structures. He experienced an epiphany: "Surrounded by these

[21] See Judd, "Concrete Buildings," *Donald Judd Architektur*, 88–89.
[22] Judd, "A Long Discussion Not About Master-pieces But Why There Are So Few of Them, Part I," *Complete Writings 1975–1986*, 56.

simple walls made of mud ... somehow the Egyptian pyramid by comparison is nothing but an ornament." Newman realized that a viewer's experience of the pyramid was non-specific and exchangeable, because its proportions, in relation to each of its many sites, seemed arbitrary in every instance. The pyramidal monument could be any size, because its generic form reduced it to a symbol, a mere image. Losing any effective proportion, it lost its scale: "What difference if the shape is on a table, a pedestal, or lies immense on a desert?" This was not architecture but decoration, a kind of picture-making, as if photographs of the pyramidal form would provide as satisfying an experience as viewing it physically, precisely located. The space of the Indian mounds was otherwise. Open to the environment like a street, the mound complex nevertheless projected the sense of an interior architectural volume: "Somehow one is looking out as if inside a picture rather than outside contemplating any specific nature."[23] The pyramid, an object that had become a symbol, had become art history. The Indian mounds, ancient like pyramids, nevertheless remained alive as art—true architecture.

"The substitution of art history for art is a strange occurrence," Judd observed: "If you take an elementary course in art at a university, it is a survey of the history of art."[24] The history of art is to art as the pyramid is to the Indian mound: the making of history refers to the making of art by producing an amalgam or a distillation of qualities that might be called art-in-general. Museums construct and display the history of art—a little of this and of that, not too much, just the amount to catch commonalities while suppressing particularities. With regard to Marfa, Judd wanted to reuse old buildings as much as possible, often improving them by regularizing needlessly irregular features, yet leaving their vernacular character evident as serviceable architecture: "It's basically a cattle town of a certain period, and you don't want it to become a cattle town museum."[25] He guarded Marfa against its conversion to a symbol of its own type.

Historical symbol or living art: Judd often alluded to this distinction, which hardly pertains to chronology. Many old constructions remain alive; many new constructions are history at the outset. Judd referred to the irony of a worker who by day bulldozes old adobe houses and by night sits before a television set encased in a Spanish Colonial console.[26] Such a person passively prefers the dead historical symbol to the

23 Barnett Newman, "Ohio, 1949," *Selected Writings and Interviews*, ed. John P. O'Neill (Berkeley: University of California Press, 1992), 174–75.

24 Judd, "Kansas City Report" (1963), *Complete Writings 1959–1975*, 103.

25 Judd, "Donald Judd in Conversation with Regina Wyrwoll" (1993), *Chinati Foundation Newsletter* 14 (2009): 15.

26 Judd, "A Long Discussion Not About Master-pieces But Why There Are So Few of Them, Part I," *Complete Writings 1975–1986*, 54.

living reality of the corresponding art, which he unwittingly participates in destroying. With the contemporary use of plastic came an analogous irony. Architects and designers, Judd remarked, "even manage to make plastic look fake when plastic is already fake. Plastic can be made to look like plastic and therefore relatively real."[27] The fake variant, like the Spanish Colonial TV, was proving more attractive than the genuine item. Judd observed that a local consumer fetish was operating as if it were a universal cultural symbol: "Texas is paved with plastic walnut paneling, whose connotation isn't precise: all classes love it."[28] Plastic—"fake" plastic—had transcended social and economic difference, an accomplishment that the tradition of aesthetic theory associated with the noblest forms of art. Judd was living in a culture turned upside-down.

"All classes love it": when a symbolic manifestation of culture has been broadly accepted, whether the pyramid worldwide or plastic paneling across Texas, it becomes increasingly nonspecific, ever vaguer in both sensory effect and signification—weak in feeling, weak in thinking. Judd was particularly impressed by those of his contemporaries who managed to reverse this degenerative process. Claes Oldenburg had risen to the challenge during the early 1960s, producing art that "made the emotive form ... the same as the shape of an object."[29] Oldenburg developed emotive singularity by manipulating sensory elements of shape, scale, surface, and the like, with the result that generic items from the urban and domestic inventory acquired an eccentric physicality, incongruent with their accepted symbolic profile. The cultural identity of an Oldenburg-inflected product remained legible; but it no longer defused the emotional charge specific to its manifestation as an object made of a certain material, located in a certain place, existing at a certain moment. In terms of artistic technique, directness was key. To create Oldenburg's *Floor Burger*, Judd wrote, "three fat layers with a small one on top are enough."[30] This supersize version of the standard configuration shared the structure of layering with its consumer referent (bottom bun, burger, top bun, pickle). Exaggerating this feature, Oldenburg interfered with the customary comprehension of the cultural icon. An observer is as likely to empathize with the weight, pressure, and expansive scale of the layering as to muse on comfort food. Here, singularity overrules convention—a reversal of the historical process. This is what Judd had observed: the shape was now emotive rather than symbolic;

27 Judd, "Donald Judd in Conversation with Regina Wyrwoll," 14.

28 Judd, "Mansana de Chinati," *Donald Judd Architektur*, 48.

29 Judd, "Specific Objects" (1965), *Complete Writings 1959–1975*, 189.

30 Ibid.

the object was to be seen for itself, not merely recognized for its type. Retrieving the structure of the "burger" from cultural history, Oldenburg restored this form to the sensuality of art.

At Chinati, Judd let the art of his generation remain art in its immediate sensory appeal. He wanted no museum of art history. "The installation of my work and of others is contemporary with its creation. The work is not disembodied spatially, socially, temporally, as in most museums.... Visual, spatial art cannot be reduced to performance"—limited appearances in museum galleries, helter-skelter.[31] Judd aimed "to be able to live with the work and think about it, and also to see the work placed as it should be."[32] He would preserve the creativity of his generation in the specific form of its thinking and feeling, apart from what the critics and historians were establishing as its generalized symbols. This work needed to be seen in quantity, in all its variety, not isolated as a few representatives. Judd sought to keep the art of his passing generation alive so it might stop the hearts of other generations. "The high quality and the nature of an artist or of several artists occur in time and will not come again.... Here and now is little and short."[33]

[31] Judd, "In Defense of My Work" (also known as "The Austin Street Foundation," 1977), *Complete Writings 1975–1986*, 9.
[32] Judd, "On Installation" (1982), *Complete Writings 1975–1986*, 19.
[33] Donald Judd, "Una stanza per Panza, Part I," *Kunst Intern*, no. 4 (May 1990), 5 (order of sentences reversed).

Projection, Projection

[2010]

This essay was written upon the retirement of Marianne Stockebrand, Director Emeritus at the Chinati Foundation. To celebrate Marianne and her eminent career as scholar-curator, it seemed to me that a focus on Donald Judd's integration of feeling and thought would suit the occasion. This is but one of the qualities of Judd's art that Marianne's writings and curatorial projects have conveyed so well. It may have been Judd's most elusive aspect. Many commentators who rightfully perceive the rationality of his practice as well as its polemical elements, appear not to respond to its emotionality, always present. Marianne is the one who has been able to represent and interpret the whole, and to succeed in the case of other artists also (Dan Flavin, Carl Andre, Richard Serra, David Rabinowitch, John Chamberlain—and the list continues). In my brief essay to follow, I refer to how "the direct presentation of Judd's forms allowed a complex of sensations to shine through." This is a lesson I learn from the example of Marianne's precise description that magically evokes the poetry of the art. I dedicate the following thoughts and feelings to Marianne in anticipation of the products of her thoughtful, sensitive looking, still to come.

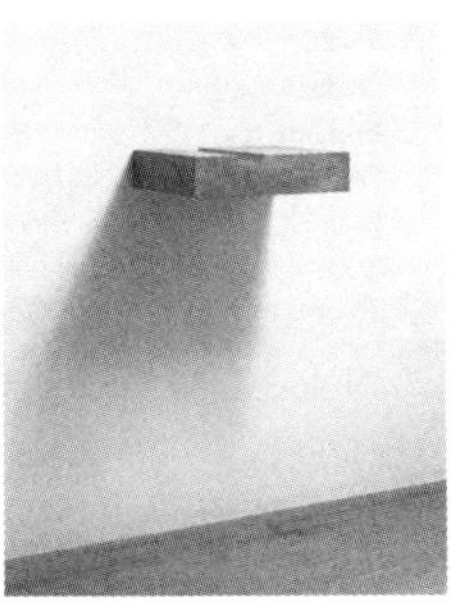

32 see page 265

“There is no neutral space, since space is made,” Donald Judd stated in 1993; “[my] smallest, simplest work creates space around it, since there is so much space within. This is new in art.”[1] If Judd were living now, he would probably conclude that significant space, activated space, still appears only rarely in art production, despite the longstanding example of *his* space. He first established “space as a main aspect of art” in 1962, setting constructed objects in a radically direct relation to the plane of the floor.[2] By the 1990s, because it had become “common for work to be placed anywhere in a room” (as in installation art), it had also become “impossible for people to understand that placement on the floor and the absence of a pedestal were inventions.” “I invented them,” Judd reminded the critics, referring to this combination of placement and absence (the lack of transitional elements).[3] He had produced a space with the autonomy of an object.

Another way of saying this: Judd’s objects existed in a space of their own making in which no anthropomorphic metaphors applied. Such extraneous language would set a readymade interpretive scheme—an order of cultural clichés—between the viewer’s experience of an object and its actual space, deflecting contact. In the case of Judd’s art, to the contrary, the usual metaphors are ineffectual; they come up empty. A physical body made of wood or metal remains so; it doesn’t morph into the image of a human body made of flesh. We sense Judd’s art, we feel it, without needing to convert it into something like ourselves. His forms appear neither to rise nor to fall, neither to stand nor to recline.[4] And just as the aesthetic object remains a material body (not an image, not a metaphorized presence), so does the space. To describe Judd’s art in terms of bodies of space is to use *body* merely as a generic reference to physical extension.

In 1964, having already made works relating matter-of-factly to the floor, Judd followed with an analogous invention: objects projecting abruptly from the wall (no transitional planes, nothing that would correspond to a frame or a base). His wall-oriented objects include the so-called single stacks. These are rectilinear, prismatic forms—typically 6 inches high, 27 inches wide, and 24 inches deep—sometimes with the addition of concave or convex elements, which slightly alter the standard dimensions [see fig. 32] The strictly rectilinear examples appear morphologically identical to isolated units of the “stacks” of ten (and sometimes twelve) that Judd began

1 Donald Judd, “21 February 93,” *Donald Judd: Large-scale Works* (New York: The Pace Gallery, 1993), 9. The following argument revises my essay of 2006, “Space Is Made,” published for the exhibition “Donald Judd: Single Stacks 1964–1969” at Van de Weghe Fine Art, New York.

2 Donald Judd, “Some Aspects of Color in General and Red and Black in Particular” (1993), in Nicholas Serota, ed., *Donald Judd* (London: Tate Publishing, 2004), 147–48.

3 Ibid., 148.

4 Referring to one of his works of 1964 (*Untitled* [DSS 55]), Judd stated that “the piece with the brass and the five verticals is above all that shape” (Donald Judd, in Bruce Glaser, “Questions to Stella and Judd,” ed. Lucy Lippard, *Artnews* 65 [September 1966]: 58). Glaser’s initial interview occurred 15 February 1964 and included Dan Flavin; this segment of Judd’s commentary was added by Judd and Glaser in December 1965. Judd was insisting that his work presented no definitive ordering of parts, nor was it formless. Because of their size, color and surface, the vertical elements appeared neither to support nor to be hung from the horizontal bar. This made them resistant to being transformed by anthropomorphic anecdote, the projection of feelings not derived directly from the object.

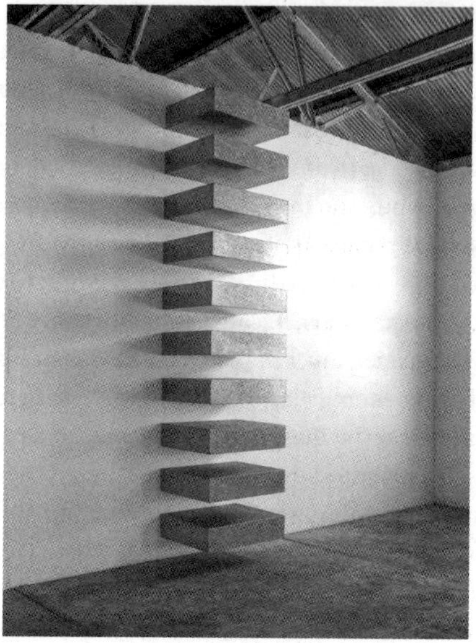

38
Donald Judd
Untitled, 1966
Galvanized iron
10 units, each 9 × 40 × 31 inches
(22.9 × 101.6 × 78.7 cm)

to produce in 1965 [fig. 38]: hence, the somewhat contradictory designation "single" stacks. The full stacks and the single stacks address a viewer in very different ways, if only because a full stack of 6-inch units extends from the floor up the wall to a height of 10 feet (each unit separated from the next by a measure equal to itself).[5]

With good reason, Judd regarded his single stacks as self-sufficient: he realized that these relatively modest forms were enough to divert the customary course of vision and revolutionize sculptural practice. Yet *revolutionize* isn't the correct term, for the revolution that ought to have occurred never happened. Judd explained: "The necessary difference [from conventional sculpture] was that the work not be flattened, low or high, to the wall, whether it be small or large. This invention is still not understood, or rather it is completely lost. Derivations are everywhere ... new in appearance only."[6] It might seem obvious that low relief would physically flatten the imaginary space of a work, causing it to appear low to the wall, drained of nearly all actual space. But how does a fully volumetric sculpture become "flattened *high*" to the wall? It helps to be aware that Judd prefaced his commentary with this proviso: "Low and high relief are basically painting."[7] Virtually all wall-oriented sculpture produced before the 1960s, Judd believed, shared the limitations and failings of painting, which, of course, would customarily hang on a wall.

5 On the various sizes of the "stacks" and their architectural impact, see Marianne Stockebrand, "Catalogue," in Serota, *Donald Judd*, 191.
6 Judd, "Some Aspects of Color in General and Red and Black in Particular," 150.
7 Ibid., 149.

Given the context, a synonym for *flattened* (as an adjective) is *pictorial*, a term referring to an arrangement of form integrated by a background. Pictorial composition is analogous to the theatrical staging of live actors in a space designed to remain intelligible from various angles and distances, resembling a coherent picture even as the actors move. To the contrary, Judd argued that space should be "made" independently, not found as the passive ground or base for pictorial action. Art did not enter an existing space such as the volume of an architectural structure or the expanse of a planar field; it *made* the space and its dimensions. Such a space would not be a container of objects of interest; it was itself an object of interest. In this respect, although transparent, the space was the equal of an opaque surface or the structural material forming the (open) boundaries of the very same space.

Judd's differentiation of made space from "neutral" or found space applies to film, although in an inverse way. Film is a medium of projection. A conventional cinematic scene is "flattened"—rendered as, projected as, pictorial—even before being recorded by the camera. Its appearance as filmic projection must be preconceived as a mental projection. A filmic scene will be staged in either low or high relief as a succession of planes with continuous perspective and narrative logic. According to Judd's understanding of the Western tradition of art, it was as if this entire history had been filmed—art history was its own BBC or PBS program in advance of itself—setting itself at a remove from reality through its pictorial organization. In a word, it was *flattened*. Or, to introduce an alternative description (as I've already slipped into doing), it was *projected*. This type of projection doesn't refer to extending physically into space or creating space by extension. Rather, it's projection that converts the existing physicality of space into an image and an imaginary order, an order that may no longer respond to changes in the physical position of the viewer.

"A painting isn't an image," Judd wrote in connection with the early art of Frank Stella. This is to say, a painting need not and *ought not* be an image—a visualization of a thought. Stella's painting was more singular than this. It didn't reduce to a verbal concept that might be illustrated or exemplified by various other means. Judd's remark appears as the penultimate sentence in the original publication of his canonical essay, "Specific Objects" (1964-65). It refers to the fact that Stella had taken painting out of the realm of image projection and into the (real) world of "continuity, one thing after another"—each thing separate and distinct, although factors of an integrated experience. The result was material form, the stuff of painting, perceived as "specific, aggressive and powerful."[8]

Judd wanted the space of his art to be actual. People would experience it physically, bodily, not merely intellectually as a point of reason or imagination. Hierarchical, compositional order drains physical space from the imagery it projects, whether presented as the low relief of wall sculpture or the high relief of floor sculpture. Judd considered all traditional standing sculpture, including David Smith's modernist abstractions, as high relief, whereas painting amounted to low relief (*very* low relief). Both mediums were pictorial and similarly compromised. Their imagery and range of cultural associations dominated their actual physical presence; Smith's abstractions were "figures," Judd said.[9] He implied that pictorial, "flattened" imagery would present no challenge to the position of the viewer's body. This is the sense in which it was analogous to cinematic projection: it was dematerialized even though dependent on a material medium. In the case of Smith's sculptural constructions, projection as physical extension devolved into projection as image. The latter projection provokes no significant emotional response other than the stock emotions to be associated with the site of a codified thematic: the "natural," the "surreal," the "sublime," the "desublimated," the "utopic," the "dystopic," the "uncanny," "desire," "grace," "beauty," and on and on. The existing tradition of painting and sculpture had long been setting sensation aside in favor of such interpretive clichés (the imaginaries of the prevailing cultural discourse, whether oriented toward furthering the dominant ideological drift or resisting it—no difference). I too resort to some of these categories and tropes, but their intellectual familiarity troubles me. The less we rely on them, the more we meet the challenge of Judd's art.

For Judd, the mere presence of volumetric form would not counteract thematic and compositional flatness: "It was necessary for the work to project sufficiently"—that is, to extend into physical space, not into mental space or hyperspace.[10] Judd used physical projection to inhibit—but then, ultimately, to stimulate—mental projection. The space within and around the single stacks becomes dynamic and arresting because the work projects abruptly at right angles to the wall, extending forward from a depth four times the height of the frontal

[8] Donald Judd, "Specific Objects," *Arts Yearbook* 8 (1965): 82. Judd later stated that space "is made by thought," a remark that can mislead. He did not mean that space was a matter of conceptualization, but was instead arguing that we should be wary of regarding it as pre-existing and natural. It was a product of an artist's conscious application of mental effort: "Space is made by an artist or architect; it is not found and packaged"; Judd, "Some Aspects of Color in General and Red and Black in Particular," 145.

[9] Judd, "Some Aspects of Color in General and Red and Black in Particular," 148.

[10] Ibid., 150.

rectilinear surface. Judd attached his box-like prisms to the wall with their projection at eye level: "The viewer is meant to see a little of the tops of the boxes.... They should be hung at either 62 or 63 inches [above the floor] ... to avoid flattening the boxes when they are on the wall."[11] "Space is new in art," he asserted in 1993, "and is still not a concern of more than a few artists."[12]

"Specific Objects," Judd's most cited statement on the demise of traditional painting and sculpture, appeared late in 1965, but he probably composed it about a year earlier.[13] If so, "Specific Objects" corresponds to the remarkably inventive period when Judd first developed the form and installation of the single stacks. These were his own "specific objects": relatively uninflected and quietly box-like, yet generating space aggressively. They were not "sculpture," not as Judd used the word: "Since sculpture isn't so general a form [as painting], it can probably be only what it is now—which means that if it changes a great deal it will be something else; so it is finished."[14] It was finished because it was indeed changing: as Judd wrote this, his three-dimensional work had already transformed the sculptural medium. His objects provoked perception because viewers knew no categories that would contain the range of sensations and responses these forms were inducing. Judd's work in materials corresponded to the philosophical position he attributed to his generation: "There is a breakdown in universal and general values. I don't think that the artist believes in them."[15]

"Use a simple form that doesn't look like either order or disorder," Judd recommended during an interview in 1964.[16] By rejecting the look of order, he abandoned the established Western pictorial tradition: its painting, its sculpture, and the convenient philosophical dichotomies and socio-political divisions that had been accompanying traditional art.[17] By refusing the alternative of disorder, he avoided the trap of transgression, of substituting counter-cultural behavior for invention—merely resisting order rather than breaking out of the ideological syndrome: order-disorder. These antithetical notions constitute a single logic that furthers the conventional division between thought and feeling. Orderly thought rejects feeling, having determined that feeling lacks order. To eliminate thinking is not a wise retaliation on the part of advocates of feeling. This agonistic logic distances thinking from the beneficial immediacy of feeling and may well work

11 Donald Judd, in John Coplans, "An Interview with Don Judd," *Artforum* 9 (June 1971): 49.
12 Judd, "21 February 93," 13.
13 The better known version of the essay is the one that appeared as Donald Judd, "Specific Objects" (1964–65), *Complete Writings 1959-1975* (Halifax: Nova Scotia College of Art and Design, 1975), 181–89. On dating this essay, see Judd, "Introduction," *Complete Writings 1959–1975*, vii.
14 Judd, "Specific Objects," *Complete Writings*, 184. During the early 1960s, Judd particularly appreciated the three-dimensional art of Lee Bontecou, which seemed to have brought sculpture to the end he envisioned: "There is no field [or ground] in which the structure or the image occurs; there is no supporting context" (Judd, "In the Galleries: Lee Bontecou" [1963], *Complete Writings 1959–1975*, 65).
15 Donald Judd, quoted in "Vanity Fair: The New York Art Scene," *Newsweek*, 4 January 1965, 58.
16 Judd, in Glaser, "Questions to Stella and Judd," 58.
17 See Donald Judd, *Josef Albers* (Cologne: Distel, 1991), 11.

to stifle intuition, which is a mode of thought lacking apparent order. Yet, to regard intuition as subversive would be to misunderstand the nature of generative thinking. Intuition often provides the obvious solution to a problem, which, however obvious, may also feel elating and even transgressive (as if you were violating your own conceptual boundaries, outdoing yourself). When asked in 1990 whether his viewer should "understand something" or "just look," Judd answered as if the question frustrated him: "That's the division between thought and feeling. You have to do it all at once."[18] He wanted each work of art to be both whole and polarized within itself, that is, at once united and separated in its manifold qualities. Thought and feeling were distinct psychosomatic responses that could nevertheless unite in one sensation.[19] And a single stack, direct in its complexity, exemplified such experiential wholeness.

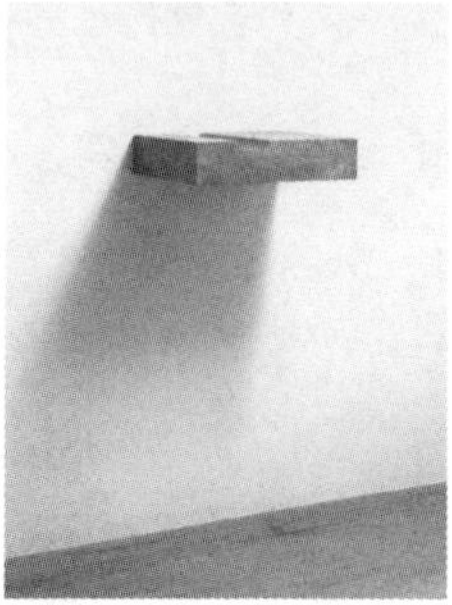

32 see page 265

In his interview of 1964, Judd had more to report on order and disorder: "The world is 90 per cent chance and accident. Earlier [art] was saying that there's more order in the scheme of things than we admit now, like Poussin saying order underlies nature.... Now there are no preconceived notions. Take a simple form—say a box—and it does have an order, but it's not so ordered that that's the dominant quality. The more parts a thing has, the more important order becomes, and finally order becomes more important than anything else."[20] This is why the simplicity and the direct presentation of Judd's forms allowed a complex of sensations to shine through. Neither order nor its antithesis was interfering. Order (up to a point) brings a work into line with Poussin and all of Western art, which, in Judd's view, was enervated, moribund.[21] Accordingly, his early box-like forms have no order of internal parts. We see both the parts and the whole each for what it is, rather than as parts designed to add up to a whole. When introducing an anomalous feature into a rectilinear structure—as in the case of the red lacquer channel inserted into the top plane of *Untitled*, 1964 (DSS 47) [see fig. 32]—Judd usually set it asymmetrically with no compensating counter-force, so that the opposing qualities (blue channel, flat copper surface) remain independent, at maximum sensory strength and without hierarchy. Similarly, when he used Plexiglas as the top and/or bottom plane of a single stack, not only its color but also its translucency would contrast with the opacity and reflectivity of the surrounding metal. Each material retains its inherent

[18] Angeli Janhsen, ed., "Discussion with Donald Judd," in *Donald Judd* (St. Gallen: Kunstverein St. Gallen, 1990), 54.
[19] See Richard Shiff, "Donald Judd, Safe from Birds," in Serota, *Donald Judd*, 35–40.
[20] Judd, in Glaser, "Questions to Stella and Judd," 58.
[21] "I'm totally uninterested in European art and I think it's over with": Judd, ibid., 57.

39
Donald Judd
Untitled, 1967
Galvanized iron and blue acrylic sheet
6 × 27 × 24 inches
(15.2 × 68.6 × 70 cm)

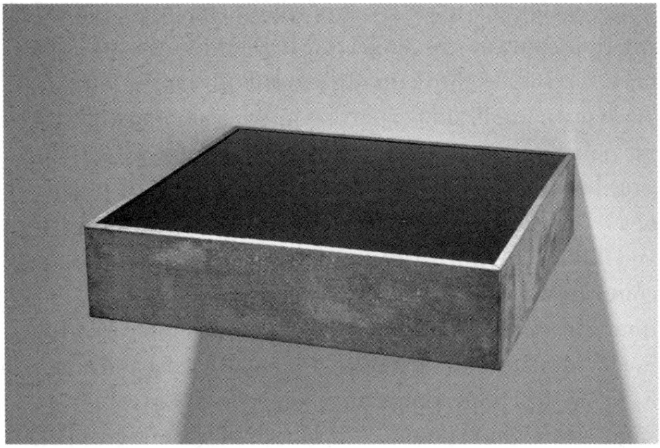

qualities without being affected by a pictorial harmony or compositional hierarchy.

Just as the single stacks eliminate pictorial effects and the "flattening" that accompanies pictorial relief, they seem to deregulate their implicit geometric regularity. Judd's boxlike forms do not have the readymade, generic space we expect from a sphere or a cube—spatial volumes so familiar that we need merely recognize them, not experience them. We can imagine these volumes in thought, without the feeling that accompanies physical proximity. Judd said that his space was new, that he was inventing it—materially. It was externalized. Affecting the lived space of the viewer, his rectangular prisms act physically. They become at times more cubic, at times less cubic, depending on the viewer's bodily orientation. The single stacks escape thoughts of geometrical classification. They aren't images.

Judd's forms—such as the single stack *Untitled*, 1967 [fig. 39] – are what they are; and this is surprisingly complex, in part because of the odd proportions, impossible to measure by eye. The ratio of the frontal dimension (width, 27 inches) to the projective dimension (depth, 24 inches) is 9 to 8, an uncommon, unstable relationship. At times, it may seem that the rectangle is a square; in fact, from a certain angled view, with both width and depth falling into perspective, the two dimensions appear equal. From certain other perspectives, the depth may seem greater than the width, even though measurement disproves this. The object lacks a conceptual presence strong enough to control its errantness in sensation, its apparent dimensions shifting with a viewer's induced movement.

Judd's art ignores many levels of cultural reference but offers multiple appearances. Projecting both unity and self-difference, it provokes the inattentive to attentiveness.

"I use a small, simple portion [of geometry] in my work for my purposes," Judd wrote: "There are a lot of rectangles in the world and one that I have made exists as one of them. The idea of a rectangle exists only as an idea, which is easy for rectangles and difficult for most ideas."[22] This is to say, most ideas, more complex than a rectangle, are hard to realize. Space is sometimes easier, although elusive. Judd demonstrated that space is not an idea but something real. He made it exist and activated it—a physical projection, not a mental one. His rectilinear single stacks don't produce the idea or image of a geometrical figure, much less that of a functional box. The material construction of each single stack produces physical space—charged first with sensation, with feeling.

[22] Judd, "Some Aspects of Color in General and Red and Black in Particular," 156–57.

What Judd Knows

[2011]

At some point one has to pass from explanation to mere description. What we call historical evidence points to the existence of the earth a long time before my birth—the opposite hypothesis has nothing on its side.

— Ludwig Wittgenstein, 1950-51[1]

Things that exist exist, and everything is on their side.

— Donald Judd, 1964[2]

The earth exists. Things exist. We exist. Donald Judd believed that human beings are at-one with everything else: "Things and us are part of the same world; factually speaking, we are one.... My simple objects encourage people to think about the nature of the world we live in."[3] What *is* this world? What do we know about it? How do we know what we know? Read Ludwig Wittgenstein's philosophical musings; possibly better, ask these questions of Judd's art.

Wittgenstein perceived that language mirrors nature and nature mirrors language—not much of a foundation for either but enough to generate a spectrum of belief. Under the circumstances, description of the world becomes tantamount to explanation. "At the foundation of well-founded belief," Wittgenstein concluded, "lies belief that is not founded."[4] Existence rests on our good faith in it. Things we do not question, such as the long duration of the earth, have no secure foundation other than appearing beyond doubt, a condition that makes what we take for granted secure enough.

As with Wittgenstein, Judd's sense of existence entails circularity. How we view the world is itself a feature of the nature we see, the only nature that exists: "There is no other world but this one."[5] When we encounter an object, we face an aspect of our existence. Perhaps the revelatory object will be one Judd himself created, because he produced each of his works to encourage us to notice it and by its example, to notice every other feature of the world. If seeing an object is knowing it, then to reflect on *how* we see is to ponder the structure of the world, which includes ourselves. This is to know our world at first hand, not by concept, principle, or acquired custom, but with the immediacy and intimacy of self-reflection.

Seeing, perceiving, reflecting: each is a function that involves both thought and feeling. If Judd had a moral precept guiding his art, it was to avoid analytical fragmentation.

1 Ludwig Wittgenstein, *On Certainty* (notes composed 1950–1951), ed. G. E. M. Anscombe and G. H. von Wright, trans. Denis Paul and G. E. M. Anscombe (New York: Harper and Row, 1972), 26e (emphasis eliminated; separation of successive notes eliminated). For essential aid in preparing this essay, I thank Rainer Judd, Flavin Judd, Craig Rember, and Caitlin Murray of the Judd Foundation; Alexandra Whitney, Lauren Knighton, Anna Gray, and the staff of the David Zwirner Gallery; scholars David Raskin, James Lawrence, and Adrian Kohn; and my research assistants in Austin, Jason A. Goldstein and Jessamine Batario.

2 Donald Judd, "Black, White, and Gray" (1964), *Complete Writings 1959–1975* (Halifax: Press of the Nova Scotia College of Art and Design, 1975), 117.

3 Judd, interview by Renée Steenbergen, "Ik ben niet zo onder de indruk van Plato," *NRC Handelsblad* 23 (30 April 1993): 178 (English version: unpaginated typescript, Judd Foundation archives; courtesy Caitlin Murray). "[Judd] wanted the gentle intimate precision of his art to change the people's perception": Rudi Fuchs, "Decent Beauty," in Brett Gorvy, ed., *Donald Judd: Selected Works from the Judd Foundation* (New York: Christie's, 2006), 22. The sense of being at-one links Judd to Barnett Newman, an older artist he much admired, who became a friend; on the social and political significance of being at-one, see Richard Shiff, "To Create Oneself," in Richard Shiff, Carol C. Mancusi-Ungaro, and Heidi Colsman-Freyberger, *Barnett Newman: A Catalogue Raisonné* (New Haven: Yale University Press, 2004), 46–49.

4 Wittgenstein, *On Certainty*, 33e.

5 Judd, "Ik ben niet zo onder de indruk van Plato," 178. I imply that Judd and Wittgenstein express similar attitudes toward experience, although their use of the verb *to know* is somewhat different. Judd's personal library includes ten books by Wittgenstein and one collection of scholarly essays on his thought. It does not contain *On Certainty* but does have *Zettel*, which presents closely related notes on consciousness and knowing, dated slightly earlier by the editors, 1945–1948; see Ludwig Wittgenstein, *Zettel*, ed. G. E. M. Anscombe and G. H. von Wright, trans. G. E. M. Anscombe (Berkeley: University of California Press, 1970), 71e–73e. On the philosophical heritage specific to Judd's education, see David Raskin, "Judd's Moral Art," in Nicholas Serota, ed., *Donald Judd* (London: Tate Publishing, 2004), 79–95; David Raskin, *Donald Judd* (New Haven and London: Yale University Press, 2010), 1–7. On Judd and philosophical parallels, see also Thomas Kellein, *Donald Judd: Early Work, 1955-1968*, trans. Fiona Elliott (Bielefeld: Kunsthalle Bielefeld, 2002), 14–17; Rainer Crone, "Symmetry and Order: Formal Logic in the Sculptures of Donald Judd," *Donald Judd* (Eindhoven: Stedelijk Van Abbemuseum, 1987), 61–75.

Never convert a source of new experience to the sum of available, familiar components—it will be less than the whole. Judd recognized that reduction was a common mode of response to any novel situation. Our tendency is to slight the most felt features of aesthetic experience: "If changes in art are compared backwards, there always seems to be a reduction, since only old attributes are counted and these are always fewer. But obviously new things are more."[6] Judd wanted something more, something new. He produced his art as a way of preserving a unity of thought and feeling, reason and sensation, the whole works. "Thinking is based upon feeling, it's all one," he insisted; "the feeling gets you off the ground fast."[7] Feeling operates with extraordinary efficiency: "Emotion or feeling is simply a quick summation of experience, some of which is thought, necessarily quick so that we can act quickly."[8] Regardless of intellectual doubt, when we feel at-one with the world, we act; we take a caring, intuitive guess at the right thing to do.

Our natural condition is to think what we feel and feel what we think; thinking is (or ought to be) a sensuous experience.[9] Psychologically—with respect to sensation, perception, and intuition—we are whole. Judd believed that any division of the human faculties must be the result of a cultural or philosophical failing. Among potential intellectual and emotional allies, he might have invoked Wittgenstein, who argued that the utterance "I know" has a genesis in sensation: "'I know' has a primitive meaning similar to and related to 'I see.'"[10] Seeing incorporates knowing; sense and intellect collaborate. Colloquially, the verb *to see* refers to understanding. When Judd was asked whether a viewer should "understand something" about his art or "just look," he answered as if he were frustrated by the question: "That's the division between thought and feeling. You have to do it all at once."[11]

Little and short

In early August 1989, Judd was interviewed in association with an exhibition of twelve large "floor boxes" in Baden-Baden, Germany, each measuring 100 cm in height, 200 cm in width, and 200 cm in depth (the particular focus of this essay). From the perspective of a well-established career, he alluded to his existential condition along with that of his art: "We are living in a very short time and a very small space in a very big situation. Basically we are living in a little point and everything is

6 Judd, "Specific Objects" (1964–65), *Complete Writings 1959–1975*, 189.

7 Judd, statement in Jochen Poetter, "Back to Clarity: Interview with Donald Judd" (7 August 1989), in Jochen Poetter, ed., *Donald Judd* (Baden-Baden: Staatliche Kunsthalle Baden-Baden, 1989), 91.

8 Donald Judd, "Art and Architecture" (1983), *Complete Writings 1975–1986* (Eindhoven: Van Abbemuseum, 1987), 30.

9 For this line of argument, with which Judd sympathized, see C. S. Peirce, "Illustrations of the Logic of Science: Deduction, Induction, and Hypothesis," *Popular Science Monthly* 13 (May–October 1878): 481–82.

10 Wittgenstein, *On Certainty*, 13e.

11 Angeli Janhsen, ed., "Discussion with Donald Judd," in *Donald Judd* (St. Gallen: Kunstverein St. Gallen, 1990), 54.

infinite in all directions."[12] Speaking extemporaneously, Judd presented his variant of a geometric figure often evoked by modern thinkers to picture an individual's place in the space and time of history (or, as some would put it, the order of creation). In 1810, Heinrich von Kleist had described the human condition using virtually the same image: "Two intersecting lines, converging on one side of a point, reappear on the other after their passage through infinity."[13] An individual lives at the nodal point of infinity, the limit of the converging lines or hyperbolic curve of history. At the node, here and now, the concentrated course of an artist's life feels both long and short—long in terms of an evolving creative experience, short in terms of the actual human lifespan and the currency of any particular form of art.

Flavin Judd recently described his father's sense of an artist's temporal dilemma. Even though time pressures aesthetic invention—better to work quickly than slowly—the course of an individual's creative activity need not follow what the culture establishes as signs of progress in art: "Time, while hanging over one's head, was simply to be lived in and not to determine what one should be doing."[14] We might paraphrase this insight, saying that current cultural fashion with its sense of "the times" limits the reach of an artist's effort only if the artist cedes this degree of control. Flavin Judd again: "Don slowly figured out how to make art that didn't (to him) require the symbolization of the society but instead, existed in real space."[15] Judd's aesthetic reality was reality, not an indirect symbol of the real. His effort was slow; it was time-consuming. But each of his inventions arrived untethered, at the flash point of an intuition.

The span of a life is short, and its ultimate significance may be little; but it faces the voids of its infinite past and infinite future, neither of which can be known in the animated way that its present can. Judd entertained no idealist fantasy that his art would appear in perpetuity just as it was appearing to him in his moment. If there was something permanent about art, it was its condition of persisting in a present tense: "Art is not a kind of utopia, because it really exists."[16] Like its creator, art had a life. If such life has no secure future, a turn to past history offers it nothing better. Judd had no interest in maintaining a tradition by extending the inventions of an admired predecessor, say, Jean Arp or David Smith. Yet—and this might seem contradictory—he sought space for the permanent

[12] Judd, in Poetter, "Back to Clarity: Interview with Donald Judd," *Donald Judd*, 92.
[13] Heinrich von Kleist, "On the Puppet Theater" (1810), *An Abyss Deep Enough: Letters of Heinrich von Kleist with a Selection of Essays and Anecdotes*, ed. and trans. Philip B. Miller (New York: Dutton, 1982), 216.
[14] Flavin Judd, lecture at Parsons School of Design, New York, 21 April 2011 (typescript courtesy Flavin Judd and the David Zwirner Gallery).
[15] Flavin Judd, lecture at Parsons School of Design.
[16] Judd, in Janhsen, "Discussion with Donald Judd," 56.

display of his creative effort as well as that of other members of his generation with whom he felt allied: "I wanted to install my own works for eternity."[17] In this case, eternity would not entail a future of increasing cultural significance but rather

the opposite—a resistance to cultural fashion, secured by a degree of isolation. Judd wanted to ensure that his work would not be distorted by involuntary participation in curatorial "performances" devoted to a succession of arbitrarily chosen themes. "The installation of my work and of others is contemporary with its creation. The work is not disembodied spatially, socially, temporally, as in most museums[,] reduced to performance."[18] Dan Flavin was one of those whose art would join Judd's in permanent display at the Chinati Foundation in Marfa, in remote West Texas.[19] Ironically, Flavin's dedication to the here and now of his being may have been still more extreme than Judd's: "Permanence ... There's no such thing. ... I would like to declare everything void at my death.... Only I think to know [my art] as it ought to be. All posthumous interpretations are less. I know this. So I would rather see it all disappear into the wind. Take it all away."[20]

Judd concurred with Flavin on the question of interpretation, whether informed or naive—it strays from a work rather than boring into it. An artist directing others toward the significance of his art also raises a problem; he reduces others' experience to his own formulation. Judd refused to anticipate a public response or play to it: "I'm not thinking about the public, so [my art is] not meant to have any effect on anybody, because that is an unknown matter.... It's one person's view and not the view of the rest of the world ... You don't know the public."[21] Art, Judd stated bluntly in an early interview, was not about perennial issues or even those of the day. These were the public's nominally "public" concerns—cultural matters, cultural clichés. The true province of art was "about what I know."[22] Judd never presumed to know more than what his singular experience indicated. Much later, he restated the position: "[Art] is both very personal and it's everything you know about the entire universe."[23] "You" remains one person—"what I know."

Judd's "what I know" is more "what I sense" or "what I feel is happening" than it is "what I can demonstrate, explain, or prove." The public's broad cultural consensus—the pattern of belief that a social psychologist, cultural historian, or art historian might discern in general terms—is what "people" (or

17 Judd, "Ik ben niet zo onder de indruk van Plato," 178. See also Judd, "In Defense of My Work" (1977; also known as "The Austin Street Foundation"), "On Installation" (1982), *Complete Writings 1975–1986*, 9, 19.

18 Judd, "In Defense of My Work," *Complete Writings 1975–1986*, 9.

19 On the Chinati Foundation and its collection, see Marianne Stockebrand, *Chinati: The Vision of Donald Judd* (New Haven: Yale University Press, 2010).

20 Dan Flavin, 13 July 1982, in Tiffany Bell, "Interview with Dan Flavin," *Chinati Foundation Newsletter* 5 (2000): 35.

21 Judd, statements in Janhsen, "Discussion with Donald Judd," 52–53. "There is no way you can know the public": Judd, in Poetter, "Back to Clarity: Interview with Donald Judd," *Donald Judd*, 88.

22 Judd, in John Coplans, "An Interview with Don Judd," *Artforum* 9 (June 1971): 44.

23 Judd, interviewed in David Batchelor, "A Small Kind of Order," *Artscribe* 78 (November/December 1989): 65.

"we," or the collective "you") know. This understanding exists apart from individual knowing, individual experience. Judd admired Barnett Newman for producing an art consistent with "one person's knowledge; the work doesn't suggest a great scheme of knowledge; it doesn't claim more than [any one person] can know; it doesn't imply a social order."[24] Here Judd was commenting on Newman in 1964, but the example of his predecessor remained ready to be invoked through the decades. Judd referred to Newman when arguing that a work of art had to be more than imagined, planned, or dreamed; it had to enter into material existence to assume its meaning. In actual experience, the feeling it provoked might be unexpected. When does an artist reliably know the situation of a work and its implications? "I have some idea of the quality I am after, but it's actually making the work of art that makes that clear. I'm sure Barney [Newman] was surprised too when he saw [his own] painting.... No one is going to know [a work] until a work actually exists, which is one reason to make art."[25] Once Judd could see his work in its physical presence, he knew it; and everything was on its side. In an analogous way, Wittgenstein knew color: "How do I know that this color is blue? If I don't trust *myself* here, why should I trust anyone else's judgment?"[26] Seeing something is a way of obliviating culture and public opinion; seeing is coming over to your own side.

Judd made the latter statement about Newman during a public discussion in Bochum, Germany, in February 1990, a few months after the close of his exhibition in Baden-Baden. One of his questioners at Bochum asked him to explain the function of mathematical order in his constructed objects—the repetition of units of equal volume and the repeated application of simple proportions, such as 1:2, the dominant ratio in the works for Baden-Baden and in most other late works. *Untitled,* 1988 (Menziken 88-27; fig. 40) is an example from the relevant period of Judd's career—a set of six anodized aluminum "wall boxes," each a horizontal but collectively arranged as a vertical column, with each unit having two types of transversal dividers as well as a plane of green Plexiglas visible at the back of the interior.[27] The external dimensions of each unit are 50 cm in height, 100 cm in width, and 50 cm in depth—a configuration that results in numerous instances of the ratios 1:1 and 1:2. Each unit has a vertical divider 25 cm to the left of the right side; this converts the spacing of the right end of the box to a double square, 50 cm in height by 25 cm in width, another ratio of 1:2. In the top

24 Judd, "Barnett Newman" (1964), *Complete Writings 1959–1975*, 202.

25 Judd, in Janhsen, "Discussion with Donald Judd," 55. "A big gap [lies] between thinking about [art] and figuring it all out [how to fabricate it] and finally seeing it. And usually I'm surprised": Judd, "Interview by Daniel De Wilde," 1979, Judd Foundation archives, quoted in Raskin, "Judd's Moral Art," in Serota, *Donald Judd*, 87. Richard Serra has similar thoughts: "Art is unexpected youth. It always takes a direction you could not have foreseen"; Serra, interview by Cristina Carrillo de Albornoz, "The Difference between Serra and Brancusi," *The Art Newspaper* 226 (July/August 2011): 41.

26 Wittgenstein, *On Certainty*, 22e (original emphasis).

27 With very few exceptions, Judd's works have no title but *Untitled*. I will identify them more precisely by their fabrication number (as here, "Menziken 88–27") or, in the case of early works, their Ottawa catalogue number (for example, "DSS 39"), which corresponds to the entries in Dudley Del Balso, Roberta Smith, and Brydon Smith, "Paintings and Objects, 1960–1974," in Brydon Smith, ed., *Donald Judd* (Ottawa: National Gallery of Canada, 1975), 91–280.

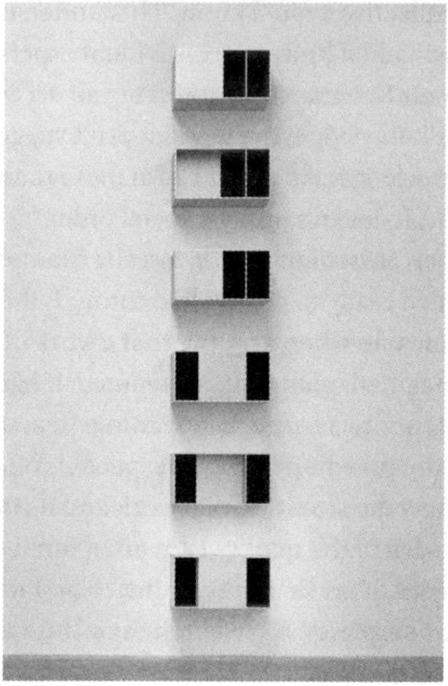

40
Donald Judd
Untitled, 1988
Clear anodized aluminum with green acrylic sheets
6 units, each 50 × 100 × 50 cm
(19⅝ × 39$^{5}/_{16}$ × 19⅝ inches)

three units, square transversal planes, 50 cm by 50 cm, occupy the left half of the box, whereas in the bottom three units, the same traversal planes occupy the center (25 cm from the left and 25 cm from the right). For each set of three units, the transversal planes are either flush with the front of the box, or half way back, or they double and occupy both positions. The result is a series of open and closed spaces in ratios of 1:1, 1:2, or, by another reckoning, 1:3—proportions readily comprehended at a glance.

The analytical description that I have just broached is hardly complete; yet it may already seem tedious, as if I were attempting to convert looking to verbal expression, lagging farther behind with every phrase. Our visual perception of the same situation feels immediate, whatever its potential complexities. To see simple proportions is, somehow, to think them. When Judd bisected a square, he arrived at two double-squares. The equation in words seems odd and may not lend itself to direct visualization: a single yields two doubles. To face the physical form, however, is to perceive the interchange of halves and doubles as obvious. *Untitled,* 1989 [fig. 41], one of the Baden-Baden series, is an apt example: in plan, it is a bisected square. We grasp ratios of 1:1 and, 1:2, as well as 1:3 and 1:4, as if they were an aspect of our nature. With a similar immediacy, we sense the play of silvery aluminum sheen and the greenish, reflective glow of Judd's Plexiglas in the six

41
Donald Judd
Untitled, 1989
Clear anodized aluminum
100 × 200 × 200 cm
(39.3 × 78.7 × 78.7 inches)

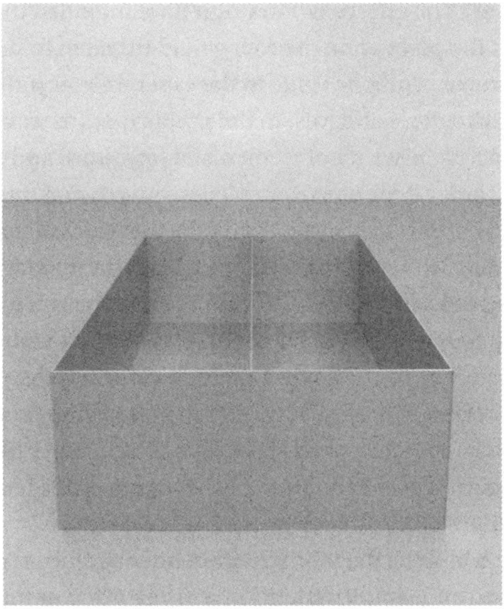

units of *Untitled,* 1988—one color against another, one quality of light against another—a combination of vagueness in coordinated opposition to the definitiveness of the proportions. "Proportion," Judd wrote in 1983, "is thought and feeling undivided.... 1 to 2 is just as particular, is—not 'has'—as much its own quality, as red, or red and black, or black and white, or a material."[28] He could just as well have added a reference to the metallic silver and translucent green of *Untitled,* 1988, the inherent colors of the materials in this instance. With these six internally divided box units, Judd was working his aesthetic magic by causing extremes of difference to cohere in wholeness. In 1963, a crucial year in the development of his thinking (or rather, his thinking-feeling), he recognized the essence of the condition he would develop: "Often power lies in a polarization of elements and qualities or at least a combination of dissimilar ones."[29] The "power" was the power of difference-in-wholeness, of being at-one. It was more of a feeling than a concept.

Is art a matter of ordering visual experience? This was the larger issue that the questioner in Bochum raised. Was mathematically precise order grounding the perception of each of Judd's objects in a set of definitive relationships? Did geometry offer a promise of "security" to the raw experience of a random viewer—a secure order that the public might grasp as a perennial cultural value, the type of meaning that Judd himself

[28] Judd, "Art and Architecture," *Complete Writings 1975–1986*, 34. Discussing the Baden-Baden works, Jochen Poetter refers to "proportions instantly recognizable"; Poetter, "Hermetic and Open—Precision and Beauty: Donald Judd at the Kunsthalle Baden-Baden," trans. Mary Fran Gilbert, in Poetter, *Donald Judd*, 35.

[29] Judd, "In the Galleries: Lee Bontecou" (1963), *Complete Writings 1959–1975*, 65. For details of Judd's development of this issue, see Richard Shiff in this volume, "Donald Judd: Fast Thinking."

dismissed? The questioner may not have intended the implication, but the perception of order would threaten to introduce a thematic or symbolic value to the experience of Judd's form, space, and color—and, yes, to the proportions as well. The artist replied: "I have a lot of elements in [my] work and perhaps what the order does most conspicuously is to make a relatively pragmatic order saying that this is the way something is, here and now, which I don't think is security, rather that it's given and it happens in the present. This is here, you can't say it isn't here." By Judd's account, his order does no more than assert a little clarity in a vague environment; it identifies the object in its particular wholeness. "The metal is often shiny and hard to pin down [because of its reflective surface]. But I think the order makes it perfectly clear ... It isn't a big order, it's only a small order."[30]

Judd had described the situation he sought in an earlier statement, and simple repetition was key: "One or four boxes in a row, any single thing or such a series, is local order, just an arrangement, barely order at all."[31] With the world's infinity compacted into a short time in a small space, a small order would suffice. Order is easily recognizable as order—it annihilates chaos—so encountering a little goes a long way. When provided with a bit more order than necessary, experience passes into a world of conceptualization; it risks rigidity. "Use a simple form that doesn't look like either order or disorder," was Judd's solution in 1964. Use order sparingly, to be sensed experientially but hardly acknowledged conceptually: "Take a simple form—say a box—and it does have an order, but it's not so ordered that that's the dominant quality." [32] Around 1963-1964, Judd decided to supplement the basic box in certain instances, introducing a second form equally orderly but in abrupt contrast to the first. He set either a semicircular trough or a circular length of pipe into the top plane of a number of painted wooden boxes, intended to rest directly on the floor; an example of the type is *Untitled,* 1963 [DSS 39; fig. 42]. This early box form, unlike later works such as *Untitled,* 1988, lacks precise ratios; its long side is almost a double square but not quite, and its short side is almost 2:3 but somewhat off. Judd later referred to the fact that, having used intuitive dimensions initially, he realized that they tended to whole-number ratios, "just the simple ones, 1:2 and 2:3 and 3:4."[33] He understood that these proportions arrived naturally enough to be non-signifying. They attracted no pointed attention to themselves,

30 Judd, in Janhsen, "Discussion with Donald Judd," 52.

31 Judd, "Statement" (1968), *Complete Writings 1959–1975*, 196. "[Repetition] is a small kind of order which I can deal with": Judd, in Batchelor, "A Small Kind of Order," 64.

32 Judd, "Questions to Stella and Judd" (interview by Bruce Glaser, edited by Lucy R. Lippard; discussion recorded 15 February 1964 for WBAI-FM radio, New York; additions by Judd, December 1965), *Artnews* 65 (September 1966): 58.

33 Judd, in Katharina Winnekes, "Interview mit Donald Judd," *Kunst und Kirche*, April 1993, 135.

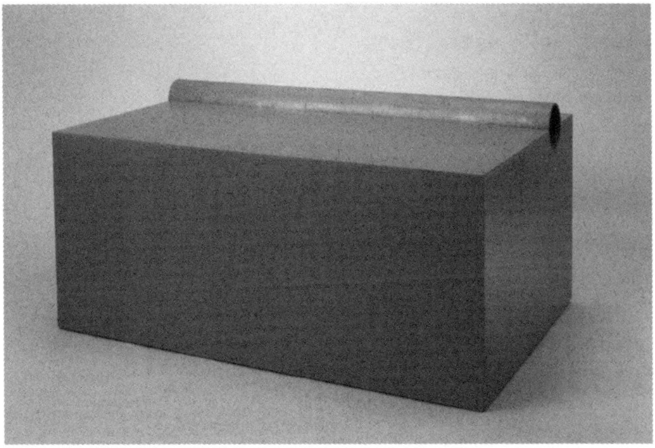

42
Donald Judd
Untitled, 1963
Cadmium red light oil on wood with iron pipe
22⅛ × 45⅜ × 30½ inches
(56.2 × 115.3 × 77.5 cm)

preserving the desired degree of order (or non-order): as he said, an order "not so ordered that that's the dominant quality."

Judd recalled how he determined a location for the inserted trough or pipe in works such as *Untitled,* 1963; he had struggled to find a position that would avoid introducing considerations of proportion or symmetry. If, for instance, he were to have set the length of pipe along the central axis of the plane, he would have reinforced symmetry already passively present in the geometry of the rectilinear prism, the box. A viewer would think that the order of the box had determined the location of the pipe, and Judd would have created a compositional hierarchy rather than a polarization of elements within the wholeness of the object: "I did a great deal of juggling to make it uncomposed."[34] The struggle had probably been necessary, yet, after the fact, unnecessary. Judd soon decided that a ratio of 1:1 or 1:2 was itself uncomposed—uncomposed enough.

An order that evokes the concept of order subordinates the authority of feeling to the authority of thought in a way that renders the two psychological forces dysfunctional. And a sense of order so severely violated that it screams disorder introduces the same reductive mechanism. Judd devised a type of aesthetic object that escaped this cultural syndrome—order-disorder, form-formlessness, composed-uncomposed—a logic of binary opposition that rends thought from feeling. Even as he structured line and shape geometrically, he allowed this nominally "pure" form to be "impure," but not in the sense of opposing the qualities of purity. Judd's impure geometry was to be simple and direct in an almost casual way, rather than refined and perfected. Frank Stella's

[34] Judd, in Coplans, "An Interview with Don Judd," 43. See also Marianne Stockebrand, "Catalogue," in Serota, *Donald Judd*, 178.

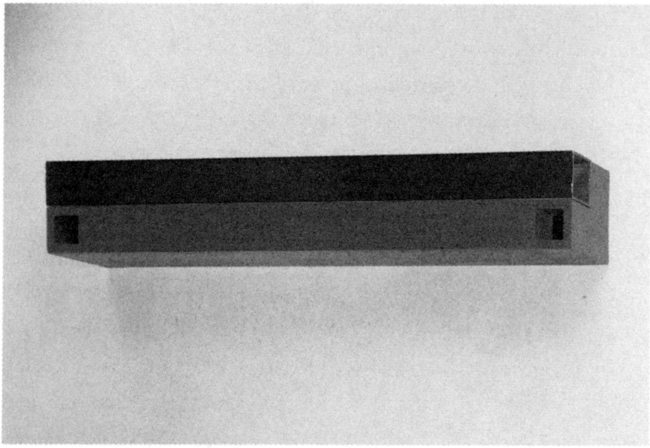

43
Donald Judd
Untitled, 1963
Purple lacquer on aluminum and cadmium red light oil on wood
5⅛ × 32⅝ × 5⅛ inches
(13 × 82.8 × 13 cm)

early art was a precedent. Judd described Stella's black paintings of 1959 as "an impure geometric art."[35] Stella had applied a geometric order, but only loosely, without insisting on a geometric statement. When he painted the individual stripes of *The Marriage of Reason and Squalor (second version)* 1959, he merely repeated the element until the canvas filled; it was as if the guiding external configuration exercised only the most passive control, a relatively silent partner in the operation.

Just as the order of Judd's rectilinear boxes was hardly a "dominant quality," so their internal geometric relationships were unexceptional—as with Stella's stripes. Judd's geometry was "matter-of-fact," a term he used to describe his attitude toward the craft of constructing his objects. While he tempered the logic of his geometry, he also "kept down the handicraft aspect"—this is evident in the relatively coarse construction of a work such as *Untitled,* 1963 (DSS 44; fig. 43).[36] Judd made no thematic fetish of precision, whether it pertained to the geometric refinement of his forms or his skill at building them. Were his objects to call attention to their degree of precision (or even its lack), they would introduce a long history of cultural debate regarding its significance, pro and con. They would cease to generate experiential phenomena, introducing instead an overt dialectics of concepts with no exit from a series of ideologically driven judgments.[37] These were distractions that the art process would do better without.

"I want my work well-made," Judd stated in 1971, a number of years after he had begun to rely on skilled fabricators; "but I don't necessarily want it made with a great deal of [industrial] precision.... A certain amount of variation doesn't detract from

[35] Judd, in Coplans, "An Interview with Don Judd," 40.

[36] Judd, in Coplans, "An Interview with Don Judd," 45.

[37] Despite his avoidance of points of obvious reference and standard, culturally sanctioned themes associated with various political orientations, Judd believed that his art, like any art, still implied a politics. He resented the inference that because his art was "acceptable as so-called abstraction, [it] had no political meaning. There is work in which the visual and the literary are differently emphasized—and to me the more visual the better—but there is no pure form" (Judd, "Art and Architecture," *Complete Writings 1975–1986*, 31). Presumably, the perception of a truly "pure" form would be politically inert. Such isolated purity would be inconsistent with Judd's desire to "encourage people to think about the nature of the world we live in," and to act on specifics rather than generalities, which is already a political position (Judd, "Ik ben niet zo onder de indruk van Plato," 178). Judd made a distinction between what was inherently political (his art) and what was overtly political (much traditional art): "I think it is bad for art when it's overtly political—or overtly scientific or technical for that matter. It becomes lop-sided.... In general I think the future of art lies in stressing phenomena more, but you can also make too much of that" (Judd, in Batchelor, "A Small Kind of Order," 65).

[a work].... I don't romanticize technology ... [It's] merely to suit one's purpose."[38] For the aluminum and Plexiglas objects to be shown in Baden-Baden, Judd contracted the Menziken company in Switzerland (Aluminium-Fabrik Menziken), anticipating a refined execution of his designs. He was by then accustomed to a very high standard for the fabrication of his art. Yet it would be wrong to think of precision—or, beyond precision, perfection—as a symbolic value to which Judd submitted his objects. The gallerist Gianfranco Verna, instrumental in establishing the relationship with Menziken in 1986, draws an important distinction: "The precision with which the material is processed is not an aesthetic strategy, but simply the standard of quality required and expected from a specialist operation."[39] We might say that precision in the engineering and fabrication of the works for Baden-Baden was, as always with Judd, a pragmatic factor as opposed to the realization of a cultural value. Judd had no interest in signifying quality in itself, for its own sake. The distinctions and decisions he made were delicate because he was working in a minefield of cultural connotation where nearly any action acquired symbolic resonances beyond its specific, immediate purpose. If he did not "romanticize technology," the culture would do it for him.

As a practical matter, certainly not a point of perfection, the aluminum sheet that forms the bottom panel of each Baden-Baden floor box (in certain examples, concealed by a sheet of Plexiglas) is much thinner and lighter than the side panels; floppy rather than rigid, its thickness is only 4 mm, approximately that of a common aluminum meter stick. This reduced physical state serves adequately because only the top surface of the panel, not its thin edges, will be visible in the presentation of the work. The situation of the remaining aluminum elements of the box is entirely different; each of these vertically oriented panels presents its top edge as a prominent feature of the visible design. In addition, the thickness of the central transversal divider in each unit serves a specific purpose in the engineering of the structure. While it acts as a rigidifying strut, it also stabilizes and hides a central join in the bottom panel, which consists of two thin sheets, each a double square (100 cm by 200 cm), as opposed to a single, larger square (200 cm by 200 cm).[40]

Beyond this specific function at the base, Judd manipulated the thickness of the aluminum panels used as transversal elements. *Untitled,* 1989 (Menziken 89-11) has an upper transversal

[38] Judd, in Coplans, "An Interview with Don Judd," 43, 45.
[39] Gianfranco Verna, *Donald Judd in der Schweiz* (Freiburg im Breisgau: Kunstraum Alexander Bürkle, 2007); English translation by Julia Thorson (typescript, courtesy Gianfranco Verna).
[40] I am grateful to Craig Rember for explaining this and many other inapparent features of the materials, engineering, and installation of the Baden-Baden works (communications with the author, 15 May through 9 August 2011). On certain details, see also Poetter, "Hermetic and Open—Precision and Beauty: Donald Judd at the Kunsthalle Baden-Baden," *Donald Judd*, 36.

30 mm (3 cm) in width, in contrast to the 20 mm width of the lower, central transversal, which bisects the box. This differential exaggerates the sense of perspective as a viewer approaches the open volumetric form, with both transversal panels coming increasingly into sight. So the relative thickness of an element can be an active feature of the perception of the work—a distinct, experiential quality that Judd was free to exploit. *Untitled,* 1989 (Menziken 89-5) has its lone transversal, the central divider, thickened—again, 30 mm as opposed to 20 mm. This element stands against a bottom of amber Plexiglas. Here Judd may have felt the need for a physically enhanced transversal because the bright amber would otherwise obliterate the effect of the thin silvery edge when viewed from directly above. To the contrary, *Untitled,* 1989 (Menziken 89-12), with a central divider of black anodized aluminum, establishes strong contrast against the surrounding environment of clear anodized surfaces, even at a thickness—a thinness—of 20 mm.

Given the severely reduced thickness of each bottom panel—a reduction to one-fifth of the prevailing standard, 4 mm as opposed to 20 mm, a differential that the structure renders invisible—this element contributes little to the stability of the engineered whole. Instead, a matrix of aluminum bars forms a substrate between each bottom sheet and the gallery floor. The hidden configuration supports the box above it while compensating for any irregularity in the plane of the floor below it. The design represents an economical, pragmatic response to immediate conditions, here and now. Judd's practice of varying the thickness of the transversal panels was also a matter of here and now but in a different respect: it affected—it affects—what there is to see, what there is to know, at the moment of experiential encounter. "The pragmatic, empirical attitude of paying attention to what is here and now: it's basic to science. It should be basic to art, too."[41]

In 1990, when Judd made this statement, he remained as convinced as ever that here and now should be the order of the day. History was not his idiom: "It's impossible to use forms from the past. They become symbols."[42] Art lives in the entirety of the present moment, with a wholeness that a person notices. Yet every moment passes: "Here and now is little and short.... The high quality and the nature of an artist or of several artists occur in time and will not happen again."[43] If its members apply themselves sincerely, each generation assumes a unique place in aesthetic history—an achievement that should be

41 Judd, in Janhsen, "Discussion with Donald Judd," 56.
42 Judd, "A Long Discussion Not About Master-pieces But Why There Are So Few of Them, Part I" (1984), *Complete Writings 1975–1986*, 56.
43 Donald Judd, "Una stanza per Panza, Part I," *Kunst Intern*, no. 4 (May 1990): 5.

ranked neither good nor bad by any absolute cultural standard, but merely different. It "will not happen again": this was why Judd needed to preserve the art of his generation at the Chinati Foundation. It would otherwise disappear, lost in the developmental currents that an official history of culture and art establishes. Judd's desire to do something new—"I wanted to do something of my own.... You want to make something which is a new thing itself"—was unrelated to earning a place in the permanence of art history.[44] He was not seeking originality but wanted to make objects from which he could learn. What the work of others had to teach, whatever was worth learning, were pragmatic truths to which he already had access. His concern for permanence was permanence of display, not of meaning. Meaning remains contingent: "Everything is equal, just existing, and the values and interests they have are only adventitious."[45] Meaning comes and goes. "The main thing is to find something new for yourself," Judd asserted at the time of the Baden-Baden exhibition: "I have a short life."[46]

Projection

The great majority of Judd's works are prismatic; his scale and mode of presentation ensures that a viewer sees more than one face of the prism, even when standing directly in front of it. The rapidly changing visual configuration of the Baden-Baden works—their change in experience, in knowing them—is a factor of their height, breadth, and openness, as well as their play of color and reflectivity. The concatenation of these qualities induces a viewer to ambulate, exploring a moving perspective. Perception is unlikely to convert such objects to a single pictorial image. The Baden-Baden works retain the complexity—the polarized power—of one aspect opposing another within the whole (at the very least, a frontal view contrasts and may even conflict with a top or lateral view).

Like Judd's other varieties of floor boxes, the Baden-Baden examples project abruptly upward toward a standing person's angle of view. Analogously, his wall boxes, such as *Untitled,* 1986 (Lippencott 86-9; [fig. 44]), project abruptly outward. From a thoroughly centered, frontal position, facing one of these objects or a stack of separate units [fig. 39], even if the sides of the prismatic form remain unseen, either a top or bottom plane is likely to be visible. At an early stage in the development of his three-dimensional art, Judd conceived of hanging single-unit works such as *Untitled,* 1963 (DSS 44; see fig. 43)

44 Judd, in Batchelor, "A Small Kind of Order," 63.
45 Judd, "Black, White, and Gray," *Complete Writings 1959–1975*, 117.
46 Judd, in Poetter, "Back to Clarity: Interview with Donald Judd," *Donald Judd*, 90.

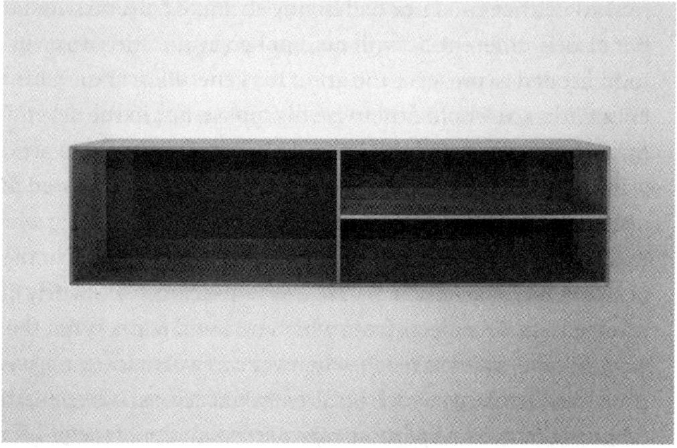

44
Donald Judd
Untitled, 1986
Aluminum with red acrylic sheet
10 × 40 × 10 inches
(25.4 × 101.6 × 25.4 cm)

at a height of 62 to 63 inches, a bit below the typical human sight line. "The viewer is meant to see a little of the tops," he explained, "to avoid flattening the boxes when they are on the wall."[47] Generating a similar effect, the Baden-Baden floor boxes, as large as they are, do not exceed 100 cm in height (just under 40 inches), so that even from a distance, a viewer notices their open interior spaces along with their exterior sides. The exterior planes block or deflect the line of sight as much as the visible interior surfaces and the spaces breathe it in. Exterior and interior constitute an active polarity.

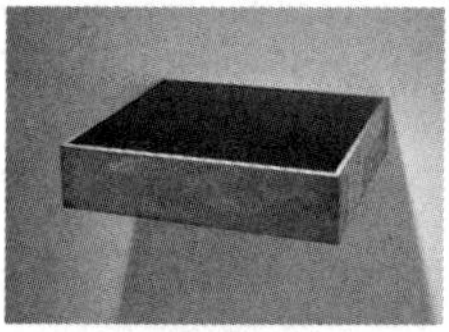

39 see page 267

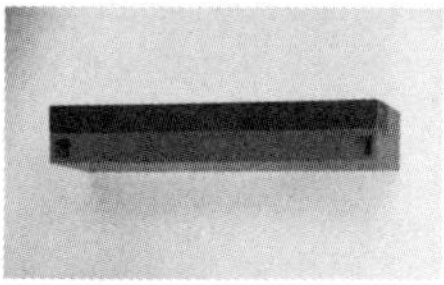

43 see page 270

The complex projective play evident in the Baden-Baden floor boxes has an extended history in Judd's practice. He had long before combined Plexiglas interiors with metallic exteriors: "While the outside is definite and rigorous, the inside is indefinite."[48] Bear in mind that Judd's abiding purpose was to make something new to his experience, not for the cultural value placed on novelty, but to provide instruction to himself, to push his here-and-now forward. The definite-indefinite polarity was new to sculptural practice; it was more than a mere variation on order-disorder, form-formlessness. Judd was producing a situation of incommensurables, whereas art that plays formlessness against form, or vice versa, generates a sliding scale of binary opposition. The indefiniteness of interior color is not the binary opposite of the definiteness of exterior geometry. When one of Judd's projecting boxes refused to flatten against the supporting wall, even from a distance—when it resembled neither painting nor traditional relief sculpture—this also went beyond any familiar binary logic.[49] It was not anti-painting. And it was new. Would an

47 Judd, in Coplans, "An Interview with Don Judd," 49.
48 Judd, in Coplans, "An Interview with Don Judd," 50.
49 "[Both] low and high relief are basically painting": Donald Judd, "Some Aspects of Color in General and Red and Black in Particular" (1993), in Serota, *Donald Judd*, 149.

analogous intuition apply to objects on a floor? Would a certain quality of projection remove a volumetric object from the traditional category of sculpture? This, too, would be new. I have already alluded to an aspect of the novel condition Judd created, as it appears in the Baden-Baden constructions: the interior appears as fully evident and compelling as the exterior. Judd transformed the traditional sense of sculptural surface, virtually turning sculpture inside-out. He was *surfacing space* rather than articulating the surface of a solid. This inversion gave him good cause not to regard his objects as "sculpture."[50]

Despite so much new, Judd had no linear trajectory, no master plan: "I don't have too great a sense of progress ... I like to work back and forth."[51] He could apply an insight derived from work on the floor to work on the wall, and then return it, modified, to the floor:

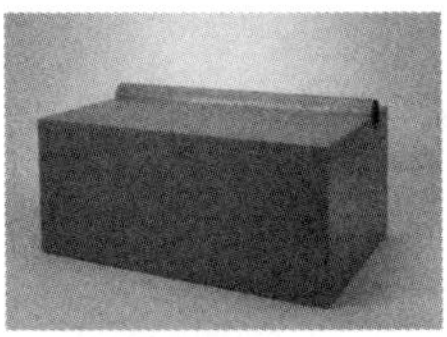

42 see page 269

> After I made the first works placed on the floor [among them, *Untitled,* 1963 (DSS 39; fig. 42)], knowing the new relationship to a surface, through at least 1963 I didn't think anything could be placed on the wall. Then I realized that the relationship to the wall could be the same as that to the floor. The work on the floor was not lying flat upon it, therefore it was not low relief on the floor, nor heaped upon it, therefore it was not high relief on the floor.... It was necessary for the work to project sufficiently ...[52]

This is Judd's explanatory recollection, part of a far-reaching statement on his career, first published in 1993. I have truncated the account in mid-sentence but will return to it. We have enough already to recognize Judd's strategy of avoiding known extremes (high relief versus low relief) while developing unknown extremes (polarities). He would explore the unknown effects from various material angles at different moments. Having combined a gray cylindrical iron pipe with a red rectilinear box in 1963 (see fig. 42), he was still investigating this intriguing polarity in 1991, but under altered sensory conditions, juxtaposing a silvery aluminum pipe with an unpainted blond plywood box (*Untitled,* 1991 [fig. 45]).

Judd was less focused but more detailed in an earlier version of his explanation of 1993, a segment of a lengthy interview conducted by John Coplans in 1971.[53] There he recalled how a sequence of radical wall objects came into being during

50 See Judd, in Winnekes, "Interview mit Donald Judd," 136.
51 Judd, in Coplans, "An Interview with Don Judd," 50.
52 Judd, "Some Aspects of Color in General and Red and Black in Particular," in Serota, *Donald Judd*, 149–50.
53 Judd's comments quoted in the paragraphs to follow are from Coplans, "An Interview with Don Judd," 43–47.

the mid-1960s. These material events liberated him from his culturally induced habit of interpreting forms seen against the ground of a wall as if they had the compacted perspective of painting. The medium of painting, regarded in terms of its most ingrained conventions of viewing, reduces actual depth (say, the thickness of a material mark) to apparent flatness; while from the *relative* flatness of its material surface of marks, it generates the boundlessness of fictive depth. By reconstructing the sequence of his phenomenologically oriented realizations, Judd was recounting how seeing becomes knowing. Rather than allowing knowing to generate more knowing—which might have produced a theory of painting and sculpture, but no more—Judd received some experience and generated some. In the various object-types that he invented, sensation and thought were converging. His replies to Coplans's questions capture his past moments of intuitive invention, what I sometimes call his "fast thinking"—thoughts occurring in instants of feeling.[54] "It's a short life," he commented later, "and a little speed is necessary."[55]

The relevant sequence of remarks begins with Judd's description of *Untitled,* 1963 (DSS 44; see fig. 43). He identifies this work as "a big shift, and though very small it's important. It's 5 by 32 by 5 inches, painted wood and an aluminum tube." On impulse perhaps, he had purchased the square tube from a hardware supplier on Canal Street, "to figure out what I could do with it."[56] Referring to late 1963, Judd sets the context: "I was tired of the whole relief idea against the wall and the rectilinear format, a painterly format." The drift of his account suggests that the innovation embodied in the work with the square tube came about in the production itself, unrelated to any initial notion inspiring his effort. As he speaks to Coplans, he fails to mention the laboriously pieced-together square holes or recesses at each end of the front plane of the wooden element (painted with red oil). From a transverse orientation, these two recesses echo the structure of the hollow square channel of the contrasting metal element above them (painted with purple lacquer). However much it may have demanded Judd's planning and attentive construction, this relationship of negative spaces seems not to have constituted the "big shift" of *Untitled,* 1963. "Most things happen by accident and continue by convention," he stated later, in a different context.[57] We are left to assume that the transformative moment arrived as a fortunate accident.

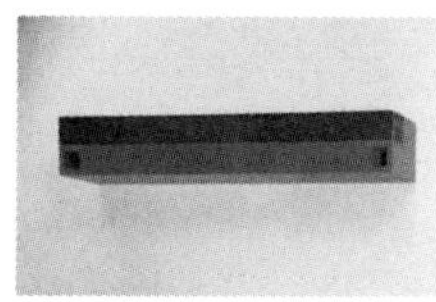

43 see page 270

[54] See Shiff in this volume, "Donald Judd: Fast Thinking."
[55] Judd, "Art and Architecture" (1983), *Complete Writings 1975–1986*, 30.
[56] In addition to the interview by Coplans, see Roberta Smith, "Donald Judd," in Brydon Smith, *Donald Judd*, 24.
[57] Judd, "A Long Discussion Not About Master-pieces But Why There are So Few of Them, Part II" (1984), *Complete Writings 1975–1986*, 79.

45
Donald Judd
Untitled, 1991
Plywood with aluminum found object
19½ × 45 × 30½ inches
(49.5 × 114.3 × 77.5 cm)

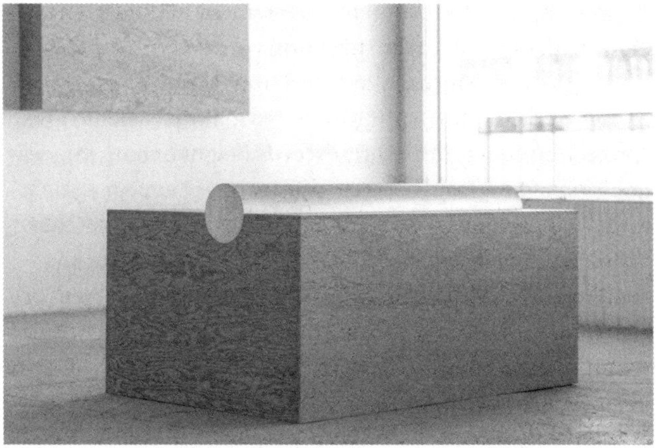

In the Coplans interview, Judd reveals the specific feature he had found worth repeating:

> At first it was just a casual thing ... but when I made the pipe and thought about it for a couple of months, it seemed to avoid all those things I didn't like. It wasn't rectangular [that is, it was too linear to have the familiar effect of a rectangle], it wasn't back against the wall—which was the main point—because it was long and because of its projection. It does not look like the extension of a canvas anymore. And it comes out as far as the height of the front [its depth equals its height]. The narrowness and horizontality keep it away from the whole idea of painting.... Afterwards it occurred to me that the idea would work if the pieces were projected, and that the painting situation would be completely avoided if they projected more than they were wide, top to bottom ... like a form cantilevered off the wall, as against a painting that clings to the wall.

Here, Judd recalls imagining a move beyond the initial step he took with the square-ended (5 by 5 inches) polarity of red wood and purple aluminum. He would project the object outward to an extent not equal to but greater than its height. This would further undermine a viewer's inclination to collapse the planes of an object *inward* toward a condition of pictorial depth coupled with physical flatness—the condition of painting.

On a sheet of notes, probably sketched in late 1963 or early 1964, Judd had recorded a version of his insight concerning projection. The sheet contains a statement in Judd's hand along with drawings of boxlike forms in perspective, which appear to extend abruptly outward from a wall. The text reads as follows, with punctuation added to make it easier to grasp: "projection equals or slightly exceeds height of box[,] anyway question of how far[:] needs to project to not appear against wall[,] but no more."[58] "To not appear against wall" rescues the object from painting and low relief. Why did Judd add "but no more"? As usual, he was sensitive to the problem of an effect becoming the symbol of itself, reduced to a cultural value that its presence would instill, contributing to the store of existing perceptual habits. If the projection were to become too evidently a demonstration of projection at the expense of everything else—no longer a polarization, but an epitome—then Judd's object would have conceptualized projection rather than provoked its sensation.

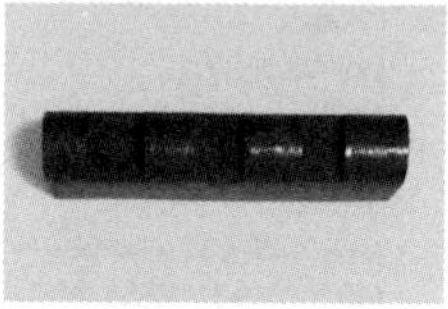

8 see page 254

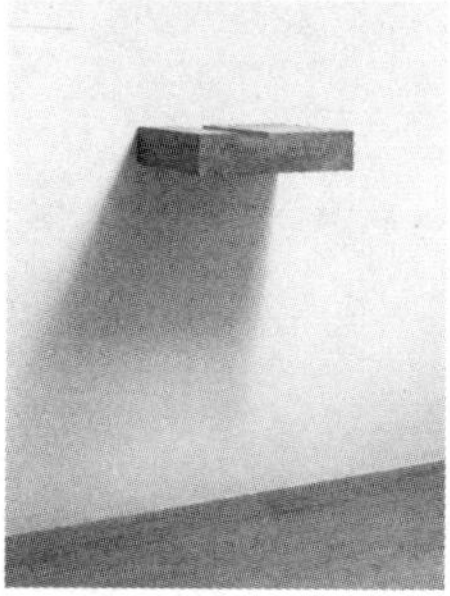

32 see page 265

The first work to project *more* than its height was *Untitled,* 1964 (DSS 45; see fig. 8): 5 inches high, 8 ½ inches deep. It was soon followed by *Untitled,* 1964 (DSS 47; see fig. 32), the first of the "single stacks." This object was of wood, which Judd somewhat later directed a fabricator to cover with sheet metal. Compared with what had preceded, its projection outward was far more pronounced—a depth of 24 inches in relation to a height of 6 inches—yet the effect was tempered by the familiar prismatic character of the form, and perhaps also by the presence of a trough set asymmetrically into the top plane, a polarizing element within the whole. "That box really projects and is the beginning of the idea for the stacks," Judd tells Coplans, who asks in return: "What determined the amount of projection?" The reply: "I didn't want to make too much of the cantilevering." Judd's factor of "but no more" reappears. To make too big an issue of the cantilevered projection would cause the work to be *about* cantilevering, even about the history of the cantilever, as opposed to being "about what I know," as Judd put it in the same interview. His "what I know" exists in the present as a matter of sensation, never a timeless concept: "The boxes just hang on the wall in a practical manner." This is matter-of-fact precision, matter-of-fact engineering, matter-of-fact projection.

Now, to return to Judd's later version of this early development, his account of 1993: I left his narrative just as he stated, "It was necessary for the work to project sufficiently ..." He continues:

58 I thank Craig Rember and Caitlin Murray for help in dating and deciphering Judd's note. Where I have inserted the colon, Judd has an odd graphic mark, which can be interpreted as a divider (a break in the thought) or possibly a variation on an ampersand.

... at least as much as its height and width. I never made this minimum, which would be a cube.[59] The first such work, in 1964, was horizontal, made of leftover plywood semi-circles, and it projected further than its height [fig. 8]. The same year a small work that projects was constructed by a nearby factory [see fig. 32 as the prototype]. ... The necessary difference was that the work not be flattened, low or high, to the wall, whether it be small or large.[60]

Given the context, a synonym for Judd's adjective *flattened* is *pictorial* (or, as he might say, "painterly"), a term referring to an arrangement of form fictively projected from a background plane, whether inwardly, as in Renaissance recession, or outwardly, as in analytical Cubism.[61] Projection is so commonly fictive—even in its Cubist invention, or, in a more ordinary way, in the projected imagery of films, or in our psychological projections, our fantasies—that the term itself connotes the unreal ("You're projecting"). Unreal projection is flattened projection: all image, no material substance. To the contrary, Judd's projections were real; they affected actual space. They converted space into a material. "Space is made," he insisted; "[my] smallest, simplest work creates space around it, since there is so much space within. This is new in art."[62]

Around and in and out

Do we experience something new, something from which to learn, something at least worth noticing, in the projection of Judd's Baden-Baden objects? Do they participate in the innovation he associated with his wall boxes of early 1964? As we know, the aluminum structures built by Menziken are large-scale works, two meters on a side, one meter in height. It may seem that any object this grand, placed on the floor within the space of a room, must project into its surroundings. But this is to conceive of the situation too passively, as if Judd were a variation on Bernini, Rodin, and David Smith, all sculptors who at times expanded their scale. "Space is made," Judd said. The boxes manipulate the space around them and contained by them, dividing it, coloring it, channeling it from light to dark and from out to in. Little before Judd's objects approached this degree of complexity-in-simplicity. His manipulation of space manipulates us as ambulatory viewers.

59 On this ambiguous statement, see Richard Shiff, "Donald Judd, Safe from Birds," in Serota, *Donald Judd*, 47, n. 62.
60 Judd, "Some Aspects of Color in General and Red and Black in Particular," in Serota, *Donald Judd*, 150.
61 "Painterly": Judd, in Coplans, "An Interview with Don Judd," 43.
62 Donald Judd, "21 February 93," *Donald Judd: Large-scale Works* (New York: The Pace Gallery, 1993), 9. See also Judd, "Some Aspects of Color in General and Red and Black in Particular," in Serota, *Donald Judd*, 145.

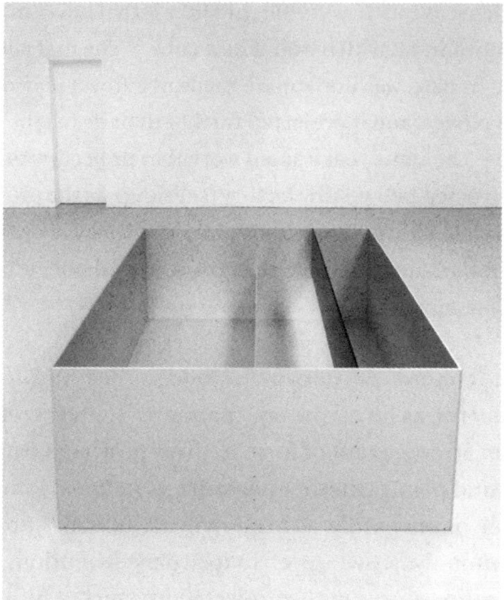

46
Donald Judd
Untitled, 1989
Clear anodized aluminum with black acrylic sheet
100 × 200 × 200 cm
(39.3 × 78.7 × 78.7 inches)

The twelve floor boxes originally displayed at Baden-Baden have a certain degree of geometrical symmetry but no phenomenological symmetry, no stable position at which their appearance and our view come to rest. Each outside perimeter is a symmetrical square, but the internal divisions span the rectilinear prism in a single direction. Within this specific group of twelve (several more units of this type exist), each work has at least one transversal, its central divider, which usually extends half way up from the bottom plane, though in two instances all the way up.[63] This central panel is clear anodized aluminum, except in *Untitled,* 1989 (Menziken 89-12), where black anodized aluminum appears. Any additional transversals—spanning an upper half of the height of the box, a lower half, or the full height—take the same privileged direction, converting the half length of a side panel into two quarter lengths.

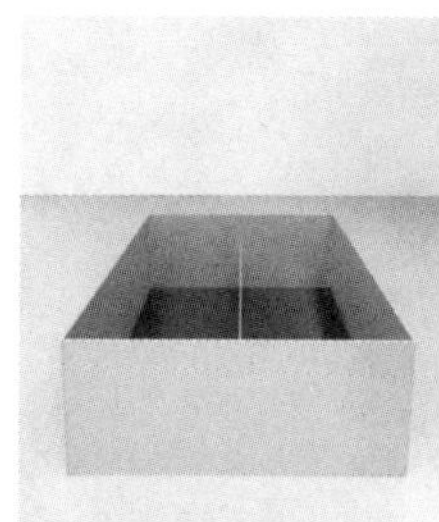

5 see page 251

Depending on our position, we are either facing one or more transversals, as if facing a barrier, or following their receding path. To sense the dynamics of the form, we need to turn at least one corner of the box. One turn may seem sufficient for perceiving *Untitled,* 1989 (Menziken 89-4; see fig. 5) because it has only the central transversal and a single blue Plexiglas plane, which covers the entire bottom. *Untitled,* 1989 (Menziken 89-11) complicates the situation by introducing an additional transversal to one side of the central divider; this element differs from the central transversal in having greater thickness

[63] See above, "Little and short," regarding the structural function of this element.

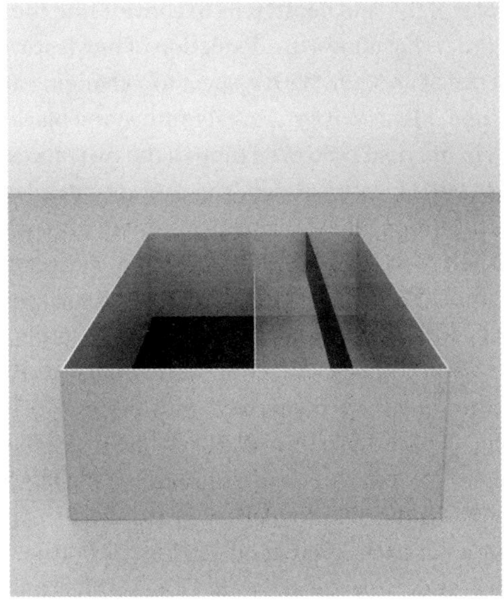

47
Donald Judd
Untitled, 1989
Clear and black anodized aluminum with amber and black acrylic sheets
100 × 200 × 200 cm
(39.3 × 78.7 × 78.7 inches)

(already mentioned above) and in extending half way down from the top while the central divider rises half way from the bottom (a set of conditions that generates numerous ratios of 1:2). The situation is similarly complicated in the case of *Untitled,* 1989 (Menziken 89-1; [fig. 46]), with the asymmetrical placement of a black anodized aluminum transversal; it introduces color contrast into the equation. The play of black anodized surfaces (one thin panel, two faces, recto and verso) against the surrounding clear anodized surfaces generates an asymmetrical pattern of reflections.

Some members of the Baden-Baden group introduce a second color contrast. *Untitled,* 1989 (Menziken 89-6), with its play of a blue anodized transversal against both a very different blue Plexiglas at the bottom and the several clear anodized surfaces, induces a viewer to turn at least two corners and preferably three. The view from one end differs radically from that at the opposite end (a polarity), and the remaining two views contrast in being mirror images of each other. Perhaps we learn that an *actual* mirror-view creates more sensory and situational variation than what the concept of mirroring might predict. Repeatedly, Judd's objects demonstrate that general concepts and specific perceptions hardly match.

With still more complex examples, such as *Untitled,* 1989 (Menziken 89-3; [fig. 47] and *Untitled,* 1989 (Menziken 89-10), a viewer is most unlikely to reach intellectual stabilization. The play of color, light, and depth fails to convert into the kind of rational order that allows the deduction of one feature from the presence of another. With respect to a changing ambulatory position, Menziken 89-3 reveals amber and black Plexiglas elements in unequal ratio even though the two pieces of material cover areas of identical size. The conceptual order of the design is one thing, its sensation in experience is something else. The half of this box with black Plexiglas at its bottom generates a gradual fade of reflected black up the surfaces of the sides. Amber Plexiglas covers the bottom of the other half, but the effect is not parallel. A black anodized transversal above tempers the amber reflections to varying degrees, depending on how much of this black panel fills the field of vision (aligning the point of view with the narrow edge of the black panel minimizes its influence). Menziken 89-10 introduces a third chromatic color to the clear anodized box; its bottom surfaces are of black and amber Plexiglas and it has a blue anodized transversal (as well as its central clear anodized divider). From different viewing positions, different combinations of colors and plays of reflection become visible because, as in all of the units, the one-meter depth of the box interferes with many available lines of sight. To approach this object is to be repeatedly exposed to the unexpected. It should go without saying that the unexpected appears in all of the Baden-Baden works, even the least complex examples. With Menziken 89-4, which has a single central divider and a bottom entirely of blue Plexiglas, or with Menziken 89-5, which has a similar configuration but with amber Plexiglas, to look from any position other than dead center is to realize that the two divided areas of Plexiglas never appear as the same size or quantity of chromatic color—not to mention the additional influence of the ambient or directed light of the room. Experience continually diverges from the order of the geometrical scheme.

As the dynamic structure of Judd's floor boxes stimulates our movement and then changes with it, we realize that projection in this instance is never projection into a void, into a neutral atmosphere or background. Each of the Baden-Baden works resembles a stable container, but what it contains alters its character. It is as if the very structure of a jar, not merely its appearance, were to change fundamentally according to whether it held amber oil or clear water—and perhaps Judd shows us that such changes are real, that appearances have physical consequences. Judd's boxes hold space, color, and light; they also project space, color, and light. Even in a relatively "pure" version of the Baden-Baden type—for example, *Untitled,* 1989 (Menziken 89-7), constructed entirely of clear anodized aluminum, with a base evenly divided in quarter segments by three identical transversals—even here, internal differences appear where we hardly anticipate them. The transversals create four segments of equal dimension, but the resultant spaces appear unequal because the first and the fourth each have one lateral bounding plane taller than those of the second and third. Even the mirror reversal that we perceive when viewing the second and third segments is a phenomenon to note. One segment shades to the left; the other shades to the right. The space makes the light, which makes the space. Effects of this kind surround us at every moment. Judd's art causes us to notice them.

Jochen Poetter, who curated the Baden-Baden exhibition, observed the circumstantial genesis of Judd's twelve objects, as opposed to the use of a system or conceptual order: "The variations which have been executed do not exhaust the theoretically given possibilities, but rather constitute a selection from among a variety of conceivable and workable possibilities."[64] If *all* possibilities of the Baden-Baden type existed, each member of the series might reduce to the derivative of a general formula: primary concept, secondary realization. It would seem unnecessary to view every variation. We would be satisfied imagining a repeat of the dominant features and inclined to ignore particularities. When questioned by Poetter, Judd himself indicated an intuitive, rather happenstance method: "It's not that I started with all the possibilities and picked twelve. I just started at one spot."[65] In experience, every specific situation has unlimited potential value. Art begins anywhere.

Color in the moment

Judd-like, I began this essay anywhere; "I just started at one spot." I took several statements from Wittgenstein's collection of notes on the problem of what a person knows, published posthumously (with unintended irony) as *On Certainty*. Wittgenstein's final note reads: "I cannot seriously suppose that I am at this moment dreaming. Someone who, dreaming, says 'I am dreaming,' even if he speaks audibly in doing so, is no more right than if he said in his dream 'it is raining,' while it was in fact raining. Even if his dream were actually connected with the noise of the rain."[66] During a dream, who is to

64 Poetter, "Hermetic and Open—Precision and Beauty: Donald Judd at the Kunsthalle Baden-Baden," *Donald Judd*, 35.
65 Judd, in Poetter, "Back to Clarity: Interview with Donald Judd," *Donald Judd*, 87.
66 Wittgenstein, *On Certainty*, 90e. This is not the entire note but its conclusion.

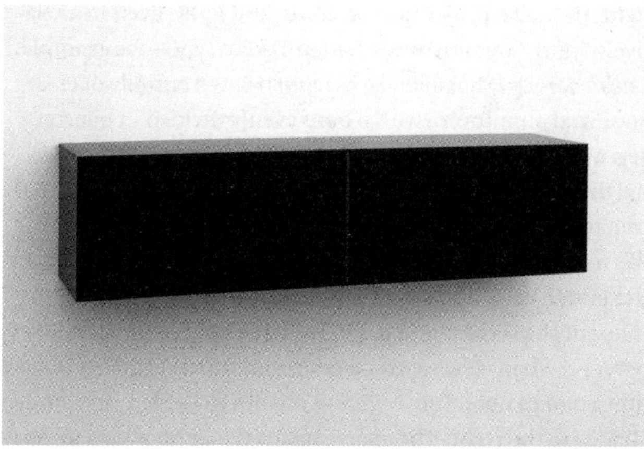

48
Donald Judd
Untitled, 1991
Clear and turquoise anodized aluminum and black acrylic sheet
25 × 100 × 25 cm
(9 13/16 × 39 5/16 × 9 13/16 inches)

believe the statements of the dreamer? What does a dreamer "know"? After the fact, a dreamer knows only of having experienced a dream-state. To assess the truth-value of a dream is to miss the point of dreaming, which connects feeling to thinking, even for those otherwise accustomed to dividing the faculties. We can consider a crude analogy: if we reduce a sensory array of color and light to its value as information, or to a set of cultural connotations, we miss the exploratory, experiential point of sensing. Judd's art is primarily a matter of sensing, not a method of cultural association. Arguments over its place within, or contribution to, the history of art are likely also to miss the point. There is no history of dreaming – dreams are for the dreamer. Judd did not dream his art, but it was personal. He made it for his experience, to know something. Even if not intended for the "public," it is now, as during his lifetime, for the experience of any other individual—to know something.

The space of Judd's floor boxes compares to that of his wall boxes, large or small: "There is so much space within," he said, an observation that applies to both types of object.[67] Where we might expect a void, color and light flow forth as if constituting a physical mass, at once nebulous and palpable. This happens even in a work like *Untitled,* 1991 (Menziken 91-44; [fig. 48]), which, by Judd's standards, is only modestly projective. The basic box, four times as wide as it is high and deep (25 × 100 × 25 cm), might initially appear understated and even recessive because of its relatively matte surface of black anodized aluminum. But the black modulates in the light, necessarily varied because of the structure of the box that both projects and captures illumination, unevenly reflecting it, unevenly absorbing

[67] Judd, "21 February 93," *Donald Judd: Large-scale Works*, 9.

it. A bright turquoise divider, extending only half way to the rear of the volumetric space, introduces a polar chromatic element and complicates the play of light. With its own version of a transversal panel, *Untitled,* 1991 amounts to a wall-oriented miniature variant of the Baden-Baden configuration. Each frontal half of this elongated box is a double square as is the turquoise divider itself and the space it leaves open. Black and turquoise, darkness and light, introduce a subtle indistinctness to be matched by the fully articulated, distinct proportions.

Color changes not only with the transient illumination of the hours of a specific day but also with the physiology and psychology of an individual observer. Color belongs to the object it colors, but just as much to the moment, the situation, the person. David Reed, a painter attuned to unusual effects of color, recalls his experience of *Untitled,* 1989 (Menziken 89-02; [see fig. 47]) as in part a play of phantom chroma—colors supplementing those directly identified with the anodized aluminum and Plexiglas surfaces of Judd's object. Viewing this work, Reed observed a reddish reflection resulting from the proximity of amber Plexiglas to clear anodized aluminum, and a greenish reflection resulting from the proximity of black Plexiglas to other surfaces of the same silvery aluminum. The complementary reflections, red and green, were enhancing or even generating each other in the existential confluence of *these* materials, in *this* configuration, at *this* moment, for *this* human subject. The transversal plane of blue anodized aluminum in the same work, perhaps to Reed's surprise, "seemed to increase these optical colors."[68] It might never happen again. Judd had said two decades previously: "Maybe with the large pieces in Baden-Baden, I know more about it." [69] "It" was how color behaves. He may also have been learning something about his behavior, his vision, his feeling.

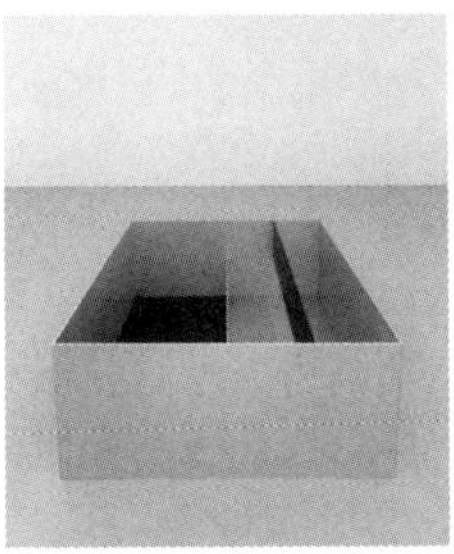

47 see page 274

My own sensation when viewing one of the Baden-Baden works or any other of Judd's objects is beyond my questioning it. As in a dream, I have whatever sensation I have. I can investigate its cause or significance but not the fact that it is my feeling, even my thought. Nor can I question the veracity of the colors that Reed observed, or the accuracy of his description, even if I myself see no more than amber, black, blue, and silver—no aura of red, no aura of green. I have my sensations; others have their sensations. Judd had his. Verbal description, which comes with a delay, is always at a disadvantage;

[68] David Reed, email to the author, 23 June 2011.
[69] Judd, in Janhsen, "Discussion with Donald Judd," 54.

little is on its side. The sensation, the experience of a moment, remains apart from its description and analysis. It has everything on its side.

Just as Judd's degree of involvement with either geometric precision or perfected craft never became so pronounced that it presented these factors as cultural values—they were never the "main thing," as he would say—so he believed that the purpose of color in art was never connotation. "Color is like material," he stated in 1993: "It is one way or another, but it obdurately exists. Its existence as it is is the main fact and not what it might mean, which may be nothing."[70] Judd's colors were material among his materials, chosen for their capacity to affect the senses, deflecting our ready urge to interpret. Like aluminum and Plexiglas, colors are not dispensable additives but "things that exist" – with real phenomenal presence—"and everything is on their side."[71] Whether color is inherent or applied, whether the source is a natural dye or a chemical compound—these were not pressing issues for Judd, though he was conscious of them. The genetics of a color mattered only if it began to interfere with a work by introducing a conceptual notion. His blue in the Baden-Baden group is neither the sea nor the sky. His amber is neither the sun nor the moon. His black is not the night. His silver is neither the cloud, nor the mist, nor the light. To repeat: color "is one way or the other, but it obdurately exists." "You want to make something [that] doesn't allude to something else," Judd explained in 1989: "It's not about referring to anything.... It's about itself and its own qualities."[72] These qualities—of color, of material, of space—Judd knew. They were his situation.

This essay has the title "What Judd Knows." Why the present tense? Why not "What Judd Knew"? Judd knew what he knew for the very reason that it was the present, *his* present. To extend the life of a work of art beyond the present by setting it into new contexts risks its degeneration into a series of cultural symbols; it loses its immediacy and specificity. What we know of a work of art does not apply forever. Like Wittgenstein's unfounded belief in the existence of the earth, what we know in the moment, nevertheless, may be worth repeating. We can turn to Judd's art whenever we, as individuals, seek the experience, the feeling, of knowing.

70 Judd, "Some Aspects of Color in General and Red and Black in Particular," in Serota, *Donald Judd*, 158. "Color [in my work] is always identical with a single surface": Judd, in Coplans, "An Interview with Don Judd," 50.

71 See note 2.

72 Judd, in Batchelor, "A Small Kind of Order," 63, 65; and, for the last sentence, in Poetter, "Back to Clarity: Interview with Donald Judd," *Donald Judd*, 96.

Every Shiny Object Wants an Infant Who Will Love It

[2011]

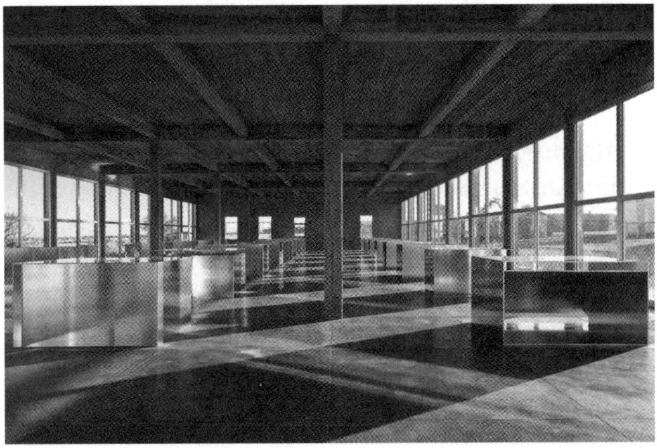

49
Donald Judd
100 untitled works in mill aluminum, 1982-1986
Chinati Foundation, Marfa, Texas

In Marfa, Texas during the 1980s, Donald Judd installed 100 box-like objects, each with the same exterior dimensions—41 inches high, with a base of 51 by 72 inches. Structural features of these objects vary, so that each is unique [fig. 49]. For example, a unit might be divided by an interior vertical plane or by an interior horizontal; and the division might occur in full or in part. Judd positioned the 100 units within two reconditioned artillery sheds, long rectangular structures fitted with glazing to either side. The volume of each unit, when viewed in isolation, relates readily to human scale [fig. 50]. It's easy to imagine your body inserted into any of the more open variations of the basic form. With less intrusiveness, you might peer into these box-like objects, especially in cases where Judd chose not to close off a side or the top. It wouldn't be voyeurism, for these objects beckon; they invite. You respond, approaching with respectful attention, as if knowing that the objects know you're there.

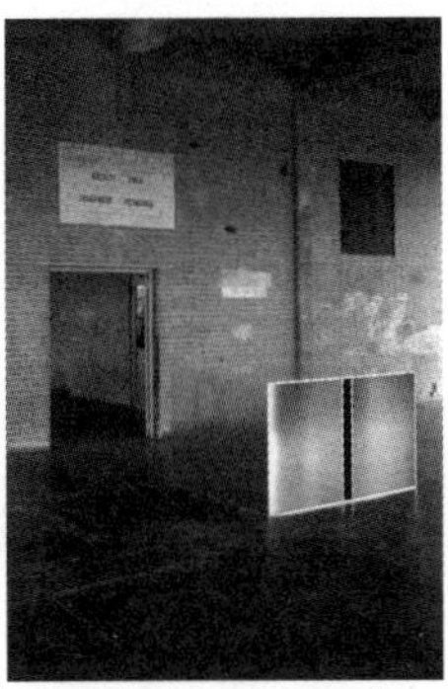

50
Donald Judd
100 untitled works in mill aluminum, 1982-1986
Chinati Foundation, Marfa, Texas

The material is mill aluminum, which has a shine. This attractive surface gloss or luster, somewhat muted, appears not only as shine but also as sheen. The reflected light becomes now an aggressive beam projecting, now a passive vapor rising. Such varied reflection is an inducement to keep looking. Within Judd's environment of aluminum objects, you may feel yourself shifting from observing material planes to observing immaterial light, or even shifting from one sense of illumination to another. And then you shift back again, experiencing any number of pairs of effects in tension.

Distinction, distraction

Critical analysis depends on familiar categorical oppositions of this very kind: material, immaterial; solid, void; closed, open; fixed object, ambient light; the formed, the unformed. For the analytical writer, Judd's art will evoke many of these abstract distinctions and the oppositional terminology of their paired-off qualities. The scene in Marfa, however, encourages active viewers to tolerate contradictions of convergence: solids evaporate in the light; the light in turn solidifies. The pairing is either degenerating in entropy or transcending itself in sublimity, depending on your attitude toward the situation. Rhetorically, to phrase the sensory effect in this manner—the solid form becomes light, the light becomes a solid—is to invoke chiasmic oxymoron. This provides the shell of an explanation, yet it's an empty one that explains nothing, at best deferring the problem. Although clever, the language remains inadequate to the feeling of Judd's forms and their environmental illumination. Surely, we already knew that this would be so. Language is always inadequate to sensory feeling and to emotions as well, even if we descend to expletive as a last resort. The experience of Judd's art makes this all the more evident to those loath to accept it. We are aware of the inadequacy, *and* we resist admitting it. Acknowledgment would undermine assertive argument and our professions of critical acumen, if not critical certainty. We bristle at realizing that our description and analysis goes nowhere.

As I've stated, each of Judd's 100 mill aluminum objects has structural uniqueness. But the distinctions we perceive are more than structural. As the abundant light within the artillery sheds changes during the day, it plays off the metallic planes with endless variation, not only because the source of illumination is moving (and so may be the viewer) but also because Judd's constructions face this light with a diverse array of directional surfaces. Exterior planes intersecting at right angles relate to the light in mutual opposition and dramatic contrast. Numerous other features may be present in any of the 100 variations of the structure: open interior partitions, closed interior volumes, recessed planes, double parallel planes, diagonal planes, and even canted diagonals (planes rotated around a primary diagonal axis). These secondary elements add degrees of nuance to the constant factor of extreme rectilinear contrast.

On my most recent visit to Marfa, I took particular interest in a canted diagonal panel that extended from just below

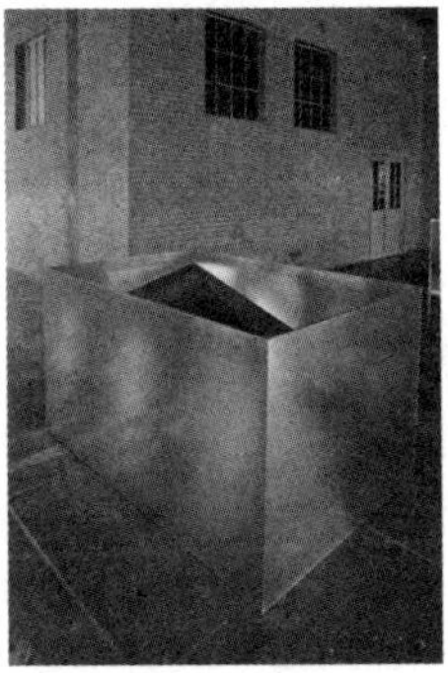

51
Donald Judd
100 untitled works in mill aluminum, 1982-1986
Chinati Foundation, Marfa, Texas

one upper corner of a box unit to a level somewhere above the opposite lower corner (*Untitled*, 1986 [fig. 51]). An element of this type introduces perceptual complexity, though not necessarily more of it than other elements generate. The effect was not new to me; I remembered this particular feature from previous observations. So I don't know why it drew my attention on this occasion—it just did. Perhaps what I remembered wasn't sufficiently specific, a distillation or averaging of effects. A memory of this kind would bear only indirect correspondence to past sensation (it is its own sensation). *This* occasion in Marfa was different. What was happening? The canted diagonal had a shine and reflected the light in its special way; but so did every other aluminum plane, each of them special. It may have been the time of day in combination with my specific position that seemed so new to me, and these existential coordinates were making a distinction I failed to perceive consciously but perceived nonetheless. To reflect on what happened, as I'm doing now, is to hypothesize, to theorize; it may approach, but won't recapture, the distinct experience.

Once you focus on the effect of a particular feature—particular in that it differs, in that it appears anomalous within its immediate context—then anything resembling or conceivably related to it will seem logical enough as its variation. Focusing on the exception causes it to become, at least in its moment, the standard against which all else will be judged. Even if this had been my first experience of the artillery shed installation and I had been unaware that Judd's rectilinear structures often incorporated interior divisions with a diagonal orientation—even without this knowledge—each element of the conceivable type would now seem anticipated, or nearly so. Granted, I wouldn't have imagined such features before a first encounter; yet, faced with an example, the type appears as familiar as not, as if the appropriate response would be, "Of course, this form makes sense in its context." Here, imagining or theorizing a general type merges with the belief instilled by the presence of the specific example. There is always a context, always a sense to be made, always a reasonable argument that will incorporate the moment's exception.

The concept of context is insidious. It may seem fluid but isn't. We tend to fix on a context as much as we fixate on a detail. My brief focus on the canted diagonal amounted to the initiation of a theoretical pattern, virtually a *habit* of looking—looking for the continuation of a possible scheme. Passive, wide-eyed seeing, receptive to shine, becomes active looking, assessing, ordering. In this instance, the prospective pattern was innocent of serious moral implications. The context was morally neutral: a use of diagonal planes and their variations set within the more constant form of a rectilinear container. But the pattern could be perceived as more of a directive or an imperative, especially given alternatives of description. Choice of language is determining. What if the diagonal plane were "resisting" or "refusing" the "enforced" regularity of the orthogonals? An interpreter might thematize the tension between diagonals and orthogonals—a *dia* culture confronts an *ortho* culture (imagine the connotative possibilities). Now the pattern suggests certain sets of values as well as, through their opposition, a potential for either conflict or mutual validation. In any case, once noticed, the arbitrary element (the canted diagonal plane) enters the field of expectations and becomes part of any number of prospective rational orders. It becomes its own justification—in context.

Everyday thinking is a process of either converting the arbitrary to the necessary or dismissing it as an insignificant accident. Yet, as I think about—well, as I sense or feel—what Judd did with his box-like configurations of shiny, metallic planes, it seems that the placement of diagonal elements within the fundamentally rectilinear structure was just arbitrary enough to be more willful than structural, more of an intuitive feeling on his part than his logical determination. He designed the units in one sequence, placed them in a different sequence.[1] Nothing appears to have determined the canted diagonal feature other than the fact of Judd's introducing it. It projects no cause either in my understanding of the order of nature, or in any logical order I imagine, or as a consequence of the inertial momentum of human history. The world could go on without this canted diagonal (but doesn't, because Judd's insinuation of it has occurred). As I stood within the configuration of Judd's installation I felt no order compelling me and was free to wander among the units. I was aimless, oblivious to external considerations. We would say, colloquially, that I was *in* the moment. If a reference to an other or an elsewhere were to emerge, I would be its cause, having passed *out* of the moment.

I stated that "I don't know why" my interest in the diagonally paneled box arose. Within its moment, this was how the experience felt: aimless, groundless. Retrospectively, however, I do know, must know, why the interest arose, for the business

1 See Marianne Stockebrand, *Chinati: The Vision of Donald Judd* (New Haven: Yale University Press, 2010), 287–89. I am grateful to Marianne Stockebrand, Rob Weiner, and Aurora Tang of the Chinati Foundation, as well as to Rutger Fuchs, for information and photography pertaining to Donald Judd's artillery shed installations, and to Susan May for help with photography of Mark Bradford's recent work. For essential aid in research, I thank Jason Goldstein and Sima Godfrey.

of retrospection is explanation. So here is the cause I imagine: something about the diagonal detail within the basic box structure remained unexpected for me, even though I had observed it several times previously. Strangely, it held inherent interest, provoking a set of observational perceptions from which I felt I was learning something new.

An interest piqued is a desire in need of satisfaction. As if to seize the opportunity and pass from unintended learning to a conscious intention to learn, I decided to compare Judd's various uses of diagonal planes as they appeared, helter-skelter, while I meandered through the installation. I was giving experience a purpose. But I found that I couldn't pursue my plan, not because I couldn't act on a whim, not because there wasn't some local order in place (perhaps there was), but because every example among the 100 metallic constructions—with or without diagonal planes—distracted me. To look was not to further the investigation but to be directed elsewhere. I became an infant in a sea of sheen and glance, seduced by each and every shiny object.[2]

Chiasmic oxymoron

Like anything else in the world that attracts notice, a work of art becomes a hypothesis-in-the-making, as if it were calling out, first, "Look at me, love me," then, "If you love me, explain me, put me in order, give me a lasting purpose." Why this, not that? Every object—especially an attractive object, an art object—amounts to the rudimentary presentation of a theory. Its shine of appearance tempts critic-theorists to elaborate. They rarely resist. But the shine may be a critic's own projection of an effect he or she presumes to admire, master, and possess—a case of perceptual narcissism.

Critical practice handles specifics by generalizing. "Most things happen by accident and continue by convention," Judd wrote.[3] Our tendency is to habit. We resort to accepting contradiction when we must, in order to reach a comfortable degree of generalization, allowing theorization to advance. Each of our cultural identities is a theory, a generalization that risks entailing a contradiction of specifics: "When I was younger I was a cowboy for a while," the Cherokee artist Jimmie Durham writes; "this other cowboy I knew said, 'You're an Indian *and* a cowboy? Be careful you don't kill yourself.'"[4]

Many works of art illustrate, report, or inform a situation or event already known, already debated, already in cultural

2 Common academic currency probably makes allusions to two writings inescapable, although I don't intend this essay as a commentary on either of them: the celebrated anecdote concerning the floating sardine can in Jacques Lacan, *The Four Fundamental Concepts of Psycho-Analysis*, ed. Jacques-Alain Miller, trans. Alan Sheridan (New York: W. W. Norton, 1981 [1973]), 95–96; and, especially because of its title, W. J. T. Mitchell, "What Do Pictures Want? An Idea of Visual Culture," in Terry Smith, ed., *In Visible Touch: Modernism and Masculinity* (Sydney: Power Publications, 1997), 215–32.

3 Donald Judd, "A Long Discussion Not About Master-pieces But Why There Are So Few of Them, Part II" (1984), *Complete Writings 1975–1986* (Eindhoven: VanAbbemuseum, 1987), 79.

4 Jimmie Durham, "Savage Attacks on White Women, As Usual" (1987), *A Certain Lack of Coherence: Writings on Art and Cultural Politics*, ed. Jean Fisher (London: Kala Press, 1993), 122 (emphasis added).

play, a locus of social or political interest. In the nineteenth century, it was common to illustrate social types within the contested terrain of bourgeois class identity. In the twentieth century, the presentation of ethnic, racial, and gender identity may have come to dominate association by socio-economic class, but the two types of category overlap. Whether by graphic means or bodily performance—by some primary appeal to the senses—artists who direct their efforts toward articulating social issues construct networks of secondary references to communicate their advocacy. They may be asking a viewer to absorb a political message by translating it into his or her preferred discourse, or they may be expecting the viewer to operate as a critical interpreter, reconfiguring the message and perhaps extending it. A different type of art presents a specific situation, avoiding—as best it can—any reference, cultural coding, or articulated message that would fix its context. Such art *is* the situation and needs no context. At least this is its pretense. But we shouldn't assume that all art must be one type or the other. Some works waver between informing the situation and being the situation.[5] For this and every other type of art—already generalized, already set out as elements in a classificatory system—a corresponding theory offers ever broader forms of generalization.

My preceding statements are themselves theoretical: they propose categories; they too generalize. Theory encompasses a situation, moving to manage its elements, reducing it to order. The theoretical gesture can be as direct as asserting that one thing is like another, even to say that art is like theory or theory is like art. Look for some respect in which this is so, and you will find one, probably more than one—despite, or to the detriment of, the differences. Theorization comes easily; it requires nothing more than imagination, fantasy. Myths are theories that have stiffened. To debunk a myth is to flex a counter-theory.

When a category applies to a situation or to the differentiation of elements, some likeness must exist to accompany the evident difference. Any two entities are alike in that a single concept is certain to apply to each of them even when they seem to take opposite sides. A ceiling compares to a floor: both are surfaces, and both are limits. Red and green, chromatic opposites, are alike in primary saturation. But enter within the specifics of sensation and the determinations become more difficult: "If, pointing to patches of various shades of red, you

5 An example would be the art of Marlene Dumas (also the art of Mark Bradford, discussed below).

asked a man 'What have these in common that makes you call them red?', he'd be inclined to answer 'Don't you see?'"[6] Having depleted our store of mediating, referential terms, we call on a common sense to save the day. We assume a tacit generalization.

To render distinct entities alike, generalization strips an object of at least some of its sensory qualities until it reaches common ground. This is its simplification or reduction. It also abstracts unique forces of agency, converting them to generalized semiotic functions. A work of art readily becomes an instantiation of a theory just as an individual becomes a subject or a subject-position. We often say that a work wants, needs, or demands a certain element for its expression or formal completion, as if it had motivation and consciousness independent of its maker. If I say that I'm in dialogue with the work as I make it, this too attributes to the object and its materials an agency similar to my own—another instance of critical projection.

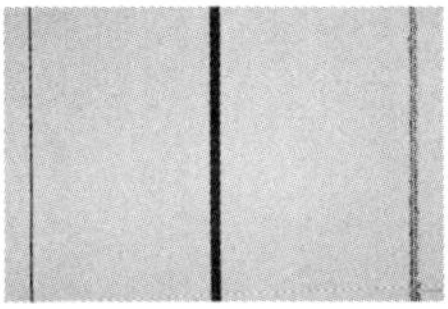

1 see page 19

Like many of his modernist colleagues, Barnett Newman let his work shine on him rather than assuming that he was the sole source of its light [see fig. 1]. With a certain (false?) modesty, he suppressed his mastery, projecting his position rhetorically: "It is as I work that the work itself begins to have an effect on me. Just as I affect the canvas, so does the canvas affect me."[7] Newman is to the art as the art is to Newman—a chiasmic configuration. He added a cerulean blue to the 18 feet of *Uriel* until the canvas indicated that he should take his blue, *its* blue, no farther. Newman said that he stretched this blue until "it broke."[8] He didn't break the color; *it* broke. It acted in cooperation and then in resistance to his effort at stretching. The painting indicated how the painter must respond in kind, bringing other colors to bear on the blue. *Uriel* shone on Newman—the title, coming after the fact, connotes light—and Newman loved *Uriel* in return, completing the work, a joint operation.

Each of us has desires and needs, but my *consciousness* of desire is limited to those needs that the rhetorical devices of my culture articulate. I become the pronoun *I* and can do only what it (an "I") does. I, "I," have no idea whether I, an "I," can have desires other than conscious ones. Introspectively and even publicly, *I* functions as if a generalized third-person singular (a mere infant with respect to receiving what the enabling culture offers). As far as theory is concerned, I am an *I* like any

6 Ludwig Wittgenstein, *The Blue and Brown Books*, ed. Rush Rhees (New York: Harper & Row, 1958), 131.

7 Barnett Newman, "The Fourteen Stations of the Cross, 1958–1966" (1966), *Selected Writings and Interviews*, ed. John P. O'Neill (Berkeley: University of California Press, 1992), 189.

8 Newman, quoted by Harold Cohen, introduction to "Barnett Newman Talks to David Sylvester," BBC radio broadcast, 17 November 1965, typescript, Barnett Newman Foundation, New York.

other—essentially an *it*, both a subject and an object, as much acted on as acting, given the rhetorical devices that take hold. I can't assert positions that the subjects of my culture aren't already in the habit of asserting.

When Newman inverted his subject position so that his work was configuring him rather than the other way around, he enlisted chiasmus, essentially a four-term analogy, A:B::B:A. Chiasmus enabled him to conceive of the conversion he believed—or wanted to believe—he was experiencing. His actual manner of painting was far more specific than his way of explaining what was happening. His chiasmus amounted to a critical cliché, a structural generalization. He was attempting to describe a "condition" that had long before been articulated by Heinrich von Kleist in his speculations on language—how language leads us to what we know and believe: "It is not *we* who 'know'; it is rather a certain condition, in which we happen to be, that 'knows.'"[9] The condition—for Newman, it might be *Uriel*—"knows" the artist. In other words, artists know no more than what the flow of their process allows them to know; the flow forms them. *A condition is more dynamic than a context*, in the sense that the flow of happenstance events is more dynamic than the theoretical history invoked to order those events. Artists respond to their captive "condition" within an environment of natural and cultural signs as if facing an object with an attractive shine. They don't resist. After all, the object of an art process is the artist's own creation. Why resist oneself? Well, artists may or may not think that the product is entirely theirs. One moment, yes; the next moment, no. They exercise aesthetic control, but they also experience aesthetic chance.

To be acted on even as you act, as if every action had immediate consequences, suffered by the actor—this is a mildly contradictory notion. Call it oxymoron, or note the frequency of chiasmic reversal in twentieth-century interpretive writing. When a quality (acting) and its inversion (being acted on) seem to apply equally well to an object or a situation, we describe it both ways, juggling the terms, indulging in a rhetoric of indeterminacy. This response satisfies the intellect, easing its friction with the senses. Finding the right phrasing brings relief from emotional insecurity—from not knowing what's what. To invoke indeterminacy, accepting both ends of a contradictory situation, is for modern thinkers a feel-smart, feel-good moment.

9 Heinrich von Kleist, "On the Gradual Fabrication of Thoughts While Speaking" (1805–06), *An Abyss Deep Enough: Letters of Heinrich von Kleist with a Selection of Essays and Anecdotes*, ed. and trans. Philip B. Miller (New York: Dutton, 1982), 222. I don't mean to imply that Kleist was the first to articulate this thought (especially given the topic of his essay: thoughts articulated only in the course of speaking). I do, however, find a certain historical significance in a member of Kleist's Romantic generation having entertained a principle later relevant to Newman's generation of modernist artists.

Consider an example from a collection of theoretical essays that approach the more shadowy reaches of art, Jean-Luc Nancy's *Les muses* (*The Muses*): "Man began in the calmly violent silence of a gesture ... At this, man trembled, and this trembling was him."[10] Such a radical beginning is something most art critics and historians would rather not discuss—too difficult to conceive, more appropriate to philosophical and theological speculation. The origin of man is difficult; the origin of art (the gesture) is nearly as much of a problem; both elicit complex thoughts. "Calmly violent" is oxymoron, and not very different in sense from *violently calm* when modifying *silence*. Oxymoron readily converts to chiasmus: imagine a calmly violent act that produces a violent calm. Is this sense or nonsense? "Man trembled ... this trembling was him" is chiasmus.[11] In French, the grammar is agreeable enough (*ce tremblement, c'était lui*), but not in English, where an experienced translator has allowed herself a mistake. It should of course be, "This trembling was he." The slip occurs because the existential verb *was* is improper in this context, mushing the thought. It establishes too strong an adequation; although metaphorical, it disguises this function (as metaphors often do) through the implied equivalence of the two reversible sides of the chiasmus. More accurate would be, "This trembling defined him," or "This trembling represented him," or even "This trembling trembled him." In this last sentence, we allow the intransitive verb to become transitive so that an emotional abstraction—an affect that generates a condition—might be attributed to a specific material body. To say that a shiny object "wants" our attention is a similar rhetorical fiction.

Nancy's translator senses that something is happening to "man," that there's an action or at least a change of state, so this "man" becomes "him," not "he," an object not a subject. Rhetoric is doing its work. It has its shine, seducing the writer as much as the reader, leading both on. Chiasmus suppresses a difficulty that often arises in assigning agency. Do you make the gesture, or does the gesture make you? To be more explicit: Do you make your gesture because of who you are, or does your gesture make *you* who you are? Did *Uriel* make Newman? The direction (sense) of the action would seem to make sense of (bring reason to) the situation, but the rhetorical form of chiasmus, because it plays relationships both ways, commits to nothing. Whether we've acquired an analytical habit or are physiologically hard-wired to the same end, our mental

10 Jean-Luc Nancy, "Painting in the Grotto" (1994), *The Muses*, trans. Peggy Kamuf (Stanford: Stanford University Press, 1996), 74. In French: "silence calmement violent ... L'homme en a tremblé: et ce tremblement, c'était lui"; Jean-Luc Nancy, *Les muses* (Paris: Galilée, 1994), 127.

11 Another example of chiasmus from the same writer: "Self outside of self, the outside standing for *self*, and [man] being surprised in face of self. Painting paints this surprise. This surprise is painting"; Nancy, "Painting in the Grotto," *The Muses*, 69 (emphasis original). In French: "La peinture peint cette surprise. Cette surprise est peinture"; *Les muses*, 121. "Peinture dans la grotte" first appeared in *La part de l'oeil* 10 (1994): 161–68, in an issue of this journal devoted to the aesthetics of Georges Bataille. Here, Nancy wrote only "La peinture peint cette surprise," without adding the chiasmic "Cette surprise est peinture." But the chiasmic supplement proved hard to resist.

practice of dividing the agent (noun) from the action (verb) causes intellectual blockage commensurate with whatever intellectual movement it enables. We insist that motivation must be in operation somewhere. When in doubt as to what motivates what, we reverse the questionable terms and have it both ways. This is chiasmus. Regard it as a statement of doubt rather than belief, even though the rhetorical form leaves an impression of assurance.

Why is the form of chiasmus, this nonsensical play in language, so satisfying? In mimesis, it may be that while A is imitating B, B is necessarily imitating A. Mimesis is a dance with a partner, or a combat, or a conversation, or a game, or Newman's process of art—all reciprocal actions. Reciprocity seems fair and just, whether returning a compliment with a compliment or an insult with an insult. It makes us feel that we're acting appropriately by acting in kind; we feel in sync with the order of the world, a structure to which we adjust rather than one we initiate. Because reciprocity makes it difficult to assign responsibility for any specific action, we become factors of a greater system. Actions clearly causal lose their identification with any particular motivation. Anything or anyone can be the cause of anything. Reciprocity offers the standard social excuse, "Everyone was doing it." A few like-minded, like-looking individuals—a subculture, even a sub-subculture—will be enough to provide mutual assurance in a mimetic relationship. "Everyone" can be a conspiracy of only two or three. The core of likeness might even be one's imaginary projection of oneself: megalomania, paranoia.

Cultural self, personal self

Historians are aware of a certain irony, by now an old one: the culture of modernity encouraged aesthetic self-expression, with each artist exemplifying his or her independence. But personally expressive art is likely to appear eccentric—ill-suited to function as an aesthetic model. By promoting artistic liberation from bourgeois norms, the culture of modernity fell into the self-defeating situation of advancing a counter-cultural standard that inhibited the promulgation of its own cultural position. If you followed this principle of self-formation, you would risk being dismissed as incoherent, incompetent, or regressively infantile. If too many people followed *you* in following this principle, you and they would become alike in collective, non-functional non-conformity, with the result that your art would implode along with its principle. This might be one way of viewing what happened to American and European art during the 1960s, '70s, and '80s. There was a collective race to distance aesthetic practice from both modernist and institutional values (many believed they were the same). Artists avoided identifiable styles unless manipulating them ironically. A situation of this kind quickly becomes ironical in itself. Because humans are predisposed to imitate each other, every critical gesture of either anonymity or appropriation—encouraged by prevailing theories of the context—was making its own small contribution to a mass movement.

A social critic might argue that the problem extends back to Romantic artists of the early nineteenth century. They responded to the conformist conditions of bourgeois life by stressing signs of cultural and social independence. But then they began to imitate each other. I nevertheless think that there may be a genuine counter-tradition within modernist art, and that certain artists of the nineteenth and twentieth centuries—if only by chance—operated outside the normative culture, even as it tacitly encouraged their eccentric activity. Here the term *eccentric* isn't adequate to the situation. It comes all too easily to critics and historians, with the sense that a culture has a privileged center, a disadvantaged, marginal periphery, and an outside, entirely excluded. Each of these positions, to the extent that it remains identifiable within the system, reinforces the stability of the entire order, which tolerates numerous forms of internal conflict. So perhaps there are two outsides. One "outside" remains a classification *within* the cultural system (in the way that the other is an aspect of you, that you are poor only to the extent that others are wealthy, you fail only to the extent that others succeed, and so forth). To preserve the prevailing cultural order, institutions act as flexibly as necessary, sometimes drawing the outside inside, adjusting categories: a police unit enlists a sociopath as a valued informer. But the second "outside" is decidedly different. It's experiential and has no classification. To fit or not to fit the culture is hardly its question.

When I return to some of the more ambitious art criticism written during the middle decades of the nineteenth century, I often see structural parallels to much later situations—exchange a few of the terms and the landscape and genre painting of the 1860s will resemble the photorealism of the 1960s or the postmodernist appropriations of the 1980s. Well, this is a kind of academic tic, to perceive and articulate parallels, a form of classification. Cultural critics and historians are predisposed to do this, and I should be wary of the habit. I'll limit my indulgence to invoking the politically engaged critic

Théophile Thoré. He made the following claim in 1847: "The represented subject [the theme, the referential content] does not matter at all in the arts.... The value of each work lies in the profound, unimpeachable, and in some way specific character that the artist has been able to impress on the creation."[12] "Character" shows in the sensory quality of the execution, not in the chosen theme, for themes are by nature generalities and subject to dogmatic hierarchies that blind both artist and public to the specifics of material expression. Thoré was democratic. As he conceived of it, force of character had no hierarchy of its own: "The soul of the proletarian is as divine as that of a Caesar."[13] Thoré wasn't suggesting that the completed pictorial, material work would be devoid of social, allegorical meaning or a differentiation of values. He meant only that a painter absorbed in practice was likely to remain unaware of the extensive range of potential referential meanings. An artist, Thoré wrote, engages in "an unreflective process, [and is] not obligated to be cognizant of its rationale."[14] As the artist senses, the critic thinks—a division of effort. The notion that the social or cultural meaning arises outside the conscious intention of the artist reappears in the writings of numerous later theorists, having become a cliché of modern criticism. Here is one of its many forms, more or less inverted: "Only by eliminating, or at least neutralizing in ourselves every operation of rational understanding, are we in the moment, without it slipping away."[15] A process of art, like a forceful emotion, remains "in the moment." Moments shine when you're in them. Whether the shine illuminates critical practice after the fact is another matter.

"Artists cannot abstract their personality," Thoré wrote; they cannot will away or extract their distinctive individuality merely by adhering to the conventions of a culture.[16] To the contrary, he praised landscape painters who attempted neither removal of the expressive personality (for the sake of adhering to institutional norms) nor exaggeration of this personality (for the sake of social recognition). He favored the landscapist "copying [a scene] straight on," without perspectival artifice or aestheticization.[17] No affectation: this would be the social remedy an individual could contribute without joining a mass

12 Thoré-Bürger (Théophile Thoré), "Salon de 1847," *Les Salons*, 3 vols. (Brussels: Lamertin, 1893), 1:447. Here and elsewhere, if not otherwise noted, author's translation.

13 Thoré, "Salon de 1847," *Les Salons*, 1:448.

14 Thoré, "Salon de 1845," *Les Salons*, 1:105.

15 Georges Bataille, *La part maudite: La souveraineté* (1954), *Oeuvres completes*, ed. Michel Foucault, 12 vols. (Paris: Gallimard, 1970–1988), 8:254.

16 Thoré, "Salon de 1847," *Les Salons*, 1:478.

17 Thoré, "Salon de 1845," *Les Salons*, 1:104.

mimetic movement. Paul Mantz, a younger, like-minded critic, took up Thoré's argument, insisting that the most naïve acts of representing nature might project a personal expressive force all the more; personality would "slip into" the picture even when, or especially when, this was no concern of the painter.[18]
So, just as Thoré disjoined allegorical meaning from conscious artistic intention, Mantz rendered expressive meaning involuntary. Their arguments worked to preserve the childlike innocence of the artist, his or her release from the grip of ideology. If, ultimately, social and cultural meaning developed—if, ultimately, the marks of paint became mere cultural *signs* of expressiveness—we should not blame the artist for the social consequences. The meaning of signs is the projection of those who consume them, not necessarily those who produce them.

Cimabue and a maelstrom

The Romantic critics' attitude persisted within an avant-garde modernist tradition. The aesthetic goal was sensory independence and immediacy, safeguards for the individual against the restrictions of his or her culture, its norms of conduct and thought. An effective aesthetic practice would let the shine shine through, as if the artist were more medium than master.

When the efforts of an artist fail to register with the sensibility of a critic—when the shine fails to transfer through the work to its viewer—it may be nothing more than the failure the critic thinks it is. But we might also credit the artist with having released the senses from the constraints of theoretical thinking, generating a condition that renders the work impervious to programmatic criticism. Certain artists, such as Willem de Kooning, have long remained at the edge of what critical thought has tolerated. Risking incoherence, de Kooning's art makes critics nervous, even now. His paintings challenged his contemporaries, whose commentary often went astray. Relying on rhetorical devices, their observation lapsed.

Manny Farber's response to de Kooning is an example of the phenomenon. He reviewed a Sidney Janis Gallery exhibition in autumn 1950, "Young Painters in the U.S. and France." Like many writers on art, Farber (revered today for commentary on film) was a painter himself—at the time, an abstractionist. He knew Jackson Pollock, Robert Motherwell, and others of the New York School, and understood materials and techniques. He restricted his account to the Americans in the Janis show, to whom he attributed a collective "speed fetish" according to the

18 Paul Mantz, *Salon de 1847* (Paris: Ferdinand Sartorious, 1847), 96.

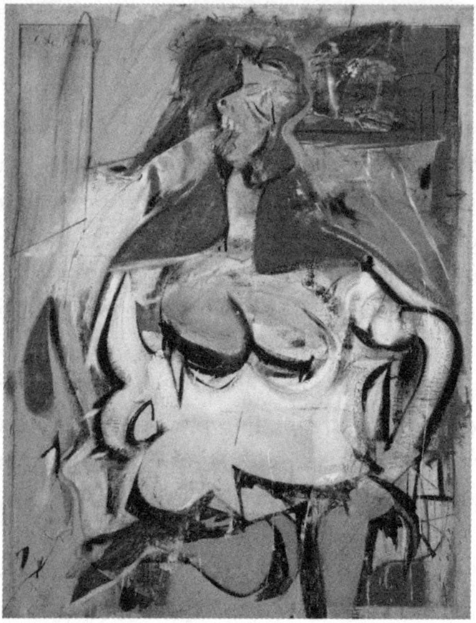

52
Willem de Kooning
Woman, 1949
Oil, enamel and charcoal on canvas
60½ × 47⅞ inches
(153.7 × 121.6 cm)

general look of their work. They would "use every line and color as a speed-up connection in an endlessly linked journey over anonymous terrain." Farber was interpreting marks of paint as cultural signs of expressiveness, intentionally manipulated and therefore (in Romantic terms) of questionable authenticity. Within the group of exhibiting painters, de Kooning was the first to whom the writer devoted an exclusive paragraph. He referred to a "maelstrom of black lines which lends a false excitement to a static, familiar composition."[19] He was accusing de Kooning of posturing, a charge that other critics would make in the years that followed, as they complained that the painter grafted his gesturing onto clichéd topics and formats. The detractors included Judd, who characterized de Kooning's manner as "basically old-fashioned expressionism enlarged and enlivened ... the old picture of nature distorted by the artists' feelings."[20]

For Farber, the specific painting at issue was *Woman*, 1949 [fig. 52]. He drew an initial analogy: de Kooning's frontal presentation of a female figure at majestic scale suggested the iconic style of the early Renaissance master Cimabue. With this comparison, Farber's vision was straying from the specific material character of de Kooning's surface. The critic linked his two visual observations causally, the one compensating for the other: de Kooning had added his "maelstrom of black lines" to resuscitate the "static, familiar composition" of his female

19 Manny Farber, "Art," *The Nation* 171 (11 November 1950): 445.

20 Judd, "Abstract Expressionism" (1983), *Complete Writings 1975–1986*, 40.

model. The compositional allusion to a Cimabue Madonna was an associative stretch to begin with, a generalization doing little more than demonstrating that Farber had an education in museum-grade art. But once it was in place, the "excitement" that de Kooning generated could only be "false" because Cimabue and a maelstrom constitute an improper mix.

Farber's suspicion that de Kooning had pulled a fast one—"too quick glib completion"—was self-induced. He experienced the de Kooning sensation and, in a flash, conceptualized it. I can't claim that sense ever remains free of conceptualization, that we can know a sensory or emotional feeling independent of intellectual habits already in place. But we should know from experience that our intuitions don't always pan out. De Kooning's black lines need not have been viewed through the generalizing metaphor of a maelstrom, nor did his straightforward presentation of a woman's image, vague in its representational details, need to conflict with these lines as something static against something agitated. Farber had a habit of perceiving forms in tension and opposition. He required more order—more of a play of forces in resolution—than de Kooning was providing. So he found this order in Cimabue, imposed Cimabue on de Kooning, and then noted the dereliction of Cimabue in de Kooning's black lines. This amounts to lazy critical writing: Farber terminated his observation too early in the process.

De Kooning was hardly a painter interested in resolving matters in quick completion. If he had a speed fetish, it applied to details, not the whole. Our collective habit is to distinguish the thematic subject—in this case, Woman—from the perceived character of its rendering. Farber described de Kooning's execution apart from a judgment as to how much of a subject was actually present: "split-second decisions and minimal torment ... startling swiftness ... replacing sensuality with shallow shock."[21] It seems that a habit of separating form from content turned Farber's commentary negative. De Kooning himself regarded such differentiation remarkably loosely. His iconic image of Woman was neither thematic representation nor formal abstraction. Paradoxically, this generic form became more of a specific concrete element, something to "get hold of," the painter said: "You have to start somewhere."[22] The Woman could be painted in any manner. Like de Kooning with his picture, Farber with his text needed something to "get hold of." To initiate his analysis, he invoked an

21 Farber, "Art," 445–446.

22 Quotations from de Kooning: see David Sylvester, "De Kooning's Women," *Sunday Times Magazine* (London), 8 December 1968, 52; and Elaine de Kooning's recollections, quoted in Harriet Janis and Rudi Blesh, *De Kooning* (New York: Grove Press, 1960), 17.

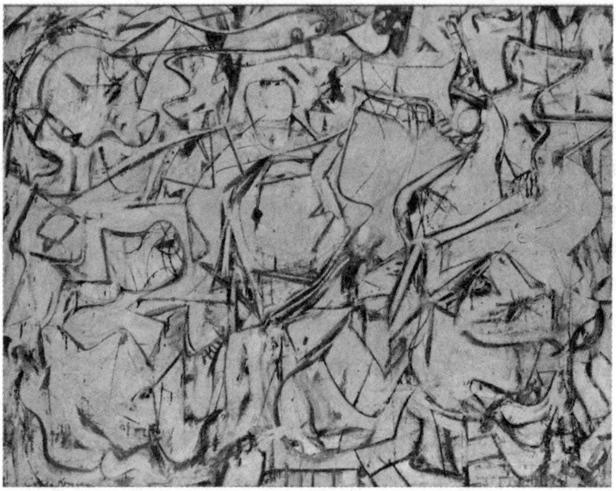

53
Willem de Kooning
Attic, 1949
Oil, enamel, and newspaper transfer on canvas
61 ⅞ × 81 inches
(157.2 × 205.7 cm)

early Italian compositional type, a standard against which de Kooning's new work did not appear new enough. (This type of complaint would follow de Kooning no matter what he did; as peculiar as his art might be, a significant number of critics demeaned it as never new enough to be new. It failed to fit the pertinent opposition: new, old. But novelty was never de Kooning's concern.)

Where in *Woman* is Farber's "maelstrom of black lines"? It must be the variety of marks defining the figure's torso and arms—a black-and-white abstraction within the predominantly brilliant hues of the full representation. De Kooning set these two modes of painting in abrupt juxtaposition, as if an effect of masking without use of paper or tape. When Farber hit on the metaphor of a maelstrom to describe these marks, he divorced them from the range of organic arm and hand movements to which they properly belong, attributing them to physical chaos—turbulence in water, in air, in particles of stuff. The critic may be thinking precipitously, as opposed to the artist painting too fast. "These lines," Farber wrote, "caught between illustration and ferocity, hide their glibness with an excess of shock and movement."[23] Speed was indeed the effect; and once Farber had perceived it, his own perception hardened his judgment. He had settled the question of subject by association: woman as static icon. Now he settled the question of technical presentation just as presumptively: a fetish for speed.

Appearances of speed can be deceiving. Appearances of anything are deceiving, as deceiving as shine and sheen, depending on what a viewer desires to see. Accounts by those who witnessed de Kooning, not only during the late 1940s but

23 Farber, "Art," 445.

during other periods as well, stressed his care and deliberation, even though quickness might characterize any single gesture of his brush. A visitor to his work on *Attic* in 1949, a nominal abstraction virtually contemporaneous with *Woman*, reported that the painter "would erase parts, redraw it.... It was not throwing his guts on the wall" [fig. 53].[24] Accidents were to be pondered. In 1955, de Kooning revealed his studio routine: "I spend most of the time sitting there, studying the picture, and trying to figure out what to do next."[25] No chiasmus, just conscious agency.

Most critics shortchanged the complexity of de Kooning's aesthetic experience and his working process. They received an impression of speed without the accompanying slowness. Farber objected not only to what he regarded as graphic histrionics but also to the fact of de Kooning's converting painting practice to drawing practice, "tending to skim color over shapes, stretching forms into directional lines"—composition made quick and easy.[26] Ironically, the situation of de Kooning's art proved offensive to both conventional and "advanced" taste. "To skim," as a movement, is "glib"—both Farber's verb and his adjective impute to de Kooning's results an absence of gravity, a lack of moral seriousness. The maelstrom encountered no resistance to its formless energy. Farber's account implied that the antithetical qualities evident in this art—now glib, now shocking—were remaining just as they were. This was the core of his objection: no dialectic, no synthesis. De Kooning was getting nowhere, though doing it fast. Farber looked for a dynamic play of opposing forces, a resolution of tension in mutual negation. Instead, the features of de Kooning's images drifted into an array of no consequence—a quality here, a quality there, abstraction there, representation here. Dark linear strokes at the left and right sides of *Woman* might be describing human arms or the arms of a chair. Curving strokes around the breasts and knees resemble phantom lettering. The marks amounted to little more than graphic effects for their own sake, one way or the other: "The painting never probes deeper than a hand-written declaration."[27]

Farber's brief review merits sustained attention because, to my reading at least, it is prodromal, the symptom of a coming cultural phenomenon—not so much a crisis in painting, more of an impasse in criticism. It demonstrates how difficult it was for critics to extract "critical," dialectical sense from de Kooning's art within its presumed context. His painting

24 Gus Falk, quoted in Mark Stevens and Annalyn Swan, *De Kooning: An American Master* (New York: Alfred A. Knopf, 2004), 294.

25 See Irving Sandler, *A Sweeper-Up After Artists: A Memoir* (New York: Thames & Hudson, 2003), 53.

26 Farber, "Art," 445.

27 Farber, "Art," 445. Perhaps Farber's restraint in his own practice of abstract painting prevented him from engaging more empathetically with de Kooning's sensory qualities. There seems to be no readily available visual record of Farber's work of around 1950, but it has been described as follows: "Thinner, stainlike paint application brings actual texture of support and material into finished product; abstract content suggests ribbons, flags, or targets"; Stephanie Hanor, ed., *Manny Farber: About Face* (San Diego: Museum of Contemporary Art, San Diego, 2003), 52.

failed to fit even a rather liberal discourse. The given categories hardly touched it: subject, subjectivity, medium, meaning, resistance, resolution. From de Kooning's perspective, it was beside the point whether he had reduced painting to drawing; by whatever means, he was obviating any transcendent composition of forms. With its evocation of illustration—cartoonish eyes, mouths, hands, shoes—his repeated image of Woman parodied the high drama of American popular culture, low culture, ordinary culture. The ordinary was de Kooning's true subject, the target of his imagistic trials. And if his subject was ordinary, so was its presentation—like Cimabue, straight-on like a billboard, no pretenses. This didn't constitute an advance in the form of aesthetic presentation; it explored the material fact of presentation.

Here was consistency of a sort, with neither a critical manifesto to announce it, nor back-up links to theories already in operation. De Kooning may have relished the ordinary, but he had no theory of the everyday, nor was he revealing a psychoanalytically determining factor to explain himself. Perhaps those within the circle of his avant-garde viewers—virtually all with greater intellectual pretension than he ever had—would have been helped by more of a verbal barrage: a bit of oxymoron, a bit of chiasmus. But this is cynicism on my part. By 1968, it was clear that de Kooning's pictures of Woman had "shocked the bourgeoisie through their violence [just as] they shocked the avant-garde through their commitment to a traditional subject."[28] Shocks don't amount to a theory, an interpretation, a meaning.

It may be that de Kooning—more than the neo-Dada artists of the 1950s, more than the Pop artists of the 1960s—eliminated any workable distinction between the emotional response of the bourgeoisie and that of the elite avant-garde, whoever might constitute the two groups, these generalized identities. Each theorization of these social classes had its points of failure. To those who paid attention, de Kooning's art made the failure of class differentiation all the more evident. Throughout the entire modern period, it seems that the majority of artists played some part in a cumulative cultural leveling, from the stress on individual sensation among the early European and American Romantics (very de Kooning-like), through to the ironic conformism of Andy Warhol (also very de Kooning-like). "I want everybody to think alike," Warhol said: "Everybody looks alike and acts alike, and we're getting more and more

[28] Anonymous, introduction to David Sylvester, "De Kooning's Women," *Sunday Times Magazine* (London), 6 December 1968, 44.

that way ... Millions of painters and [they're] all pretty good."[29] Warhol and de Kooning: art as ordinary. De Kooning understood that his vision of the ordinary was unique—in this respect, just like that of everyone else. It was as high as it was low. He accelerated a leveling process already in operation. When sophisticated observers viewed his paintings, their bourgeois sense of consistency (their sensitivity to its lack) appeared within their ranks. To criticize de Kooning for putting disorder into art would be analogous to criticizing Warhol for being repetitious. Each had an economy, making something of unpromising material, adding a gloss to what might otherwise seem dull.

As much as anyone else, avant-garde viewers were shocked by de Kooning's linear "maelstrom," his "violence." Although they were less likely than truly naïve viewers to succumb to attributing flesh wounds to brush marks (a version of the pathetic fallacy), they followed Farber in alluding to violence where they could have referred more judiciously to a play of aesthetic energy or a force of character. Clement Greenberg was well aware of the problem; he described works of the New York School in 1950 as "look[ing] too new—new beyond freshness, and therefore violent."[30] Aesthetic expressions of violence might have more than one cause. Because his work was largely abstract, Pollock, it was said, must possess a violent temperament; his violence was non-specific.[31] Because he often painted women, de Kooning, it was said, must harbor a violent misogyny. De Kooning received the more targeted of the two generalizations, yet it remains an arbitrary conclusion.[32] The response of most critics passed too quickly to verbal metaphors that hardly pertained to the materiality of painting, even as they recognized that the new generation of artists had been establishing "pure paint [as] their subject matter."[33] This last conceptual generality, quoted here from Farber's 1950 review, was common knowledge. The first serious notice de Kooning received already included a form of it: "The process of painting becomes the end."[34] This inversion still strikes us as an intelligent, historically relevant observation, despite having been a cliché even in 1948.[35] To paraphrase the notion: a process leads to an end, but here the end is the process. This is tacit chiasmus, and perhaps the sophisticated rhetorical structure accounts for the intelligence-effect of the statement. We remain suckers for chiasmus, intellectual infants drawn to its shine. But as explanation, it doesn't amount to much.

29 Andy Warhol, statement in "What Is Pop Art? Interviews by G. R. Swenson–Part I," *Art News* 62 (November 1963): 26.

30 Clement Greenberg, "The European View of American Art" (1950), *The Collected Essays and Criticism*, ed. John O'Brian, 4 vols. (Chicago: University of Chicago Press, 1986–1993), 3:62.

31 "Belligerence [toward] the subject, and you and me": Maude Riley, "Jackson Pollock," *Art Digest* 19 (1 April 1945): 59.

32 See Richard Shiff, *Doubt* (New York, Routledge, 2008), 76–92.

33 Farber, "Art," 445.

34 R[enée] A[rb], "Spotlight On: De Kooning," *Art News* 47 (April 1948): 33.

35 To cite only one earlier example, in 1945 Farber himself had made a similar point about Pollock, whose stylistic "individuality is in the way the medium is used rather than in the peculiarities of subject matter"; Manny Farber, "Jackson Pollock," *The New Republic* 112 (25 June 1945): 871.

With regard to the representation-abstraction divide, de Kooning was, so to speak, ambidextrous. The informed avant-garde felt his shock far more when responding to his nominal representations (*Woman*) than when engaging with his nominal abstractions (*Attic*). An abstraction could be "pure" in the way Farber noted that paint could be "pure": it could be itself, whereas a representation—always referential, always something other than itself—could not. For this reason, Greenberg preferred those of de Kooning's paintings that he perceived as abstractions, even though he reserved a deeper, unqualified love for representational art.[36] Around 1950, de Kooning's representational paintings shocked the majority of his avant-garde audience into bourgeois stupor. It wasn't only de Kooning who produced this effect, but also Newman, though by the alternate route: while de Kooning shocked through representation, Newman shocked through abstraction. And now it seems that I've generalized and theorized the two of them through a concept of shock. As I've implied, generalization of this kind may constitute criticism, but it explains—or rather exemplifies—little more than the attitude and method of the writer.

Feeling in oblivion

The likes of Newman and de Kooning wouldn't wish to be compared too closely to anyone. Yet there was a moment when Newman included de Kooning as his confrere in directness: "The distinction between what Bill and I were trying to do and what preceded us is the distinction between an art that is depictive and an art that is direct."[37] The more direct, the less in need of commentary, or rather, the less that commentary has any effect. Newman enjoyed talking about painting because the truth of it would never be touched by the discourse, so he could continue talking without fear of spoiling the experience of his art. A note to himself stated: "We should talk about only what you cannot talk about."[38] Here was contradiction in the service of directness: Newman the artist became his own critic and explained things as best he could but to little effect. He had both his talk (often as writing) and his art, and the two didn't interfere.

The lack of thematic depiction typical of the New York School artists made it that much more difficult for critics to find words of description suited to appearances and to an engaging narrative account. In 1948, Greenberg praised the expressiveness of de Kooning's art but without naming the

[36] One of many similar statements: "My prejudice is towards realistic [that is, representational] art"; Greenberg, as interviewed in "Clement Greenberg with Peter Fuller," ed. Linda Saunders, *Modern Painters* 4 (Winter 1991): 20.

[37] Newman, quoted in Douglas Davis, "After 10 Years, a One-Man Show by Mr. Newman," *The National Observer*, 14 April 1969, 20.

[38] Newman, undated manuscript note, inscribed on a Metropolitan Museum of Art lecture question card, Barnett Newman Foundation, New York.

subject or the effect: “You can’t specify what the emotion is, but are profoundly stirred nevertheless.”[39] He was referring to *Painting* of 1948, a nominally abstract work in black and white on paper mounted on canvas, where the artist cut or scraped away certain areas of the layered surface. De Kooning’s imagery seemed to prove a general point Greenberg had established a number of years previously: “Painting and sculpture ... *look* what they *do*. The picture or statue exhausts itself in the visual sensation it produces. There is nothing to identify, connect or think about, but everything to feel.”[40] “They *look* what they *do*”: the critic’s phrasing removed the word *like* from what we expect to hear. Instead of saying that modernist paintings look *like* what they do, Greenberg said that they *look* what they do. He imposed a more active verbal construction, abandoning the usual descriptive rhetoric of simile and metaphor, shifting to a rhetoric of fact—a direct language for a direct art. Yet his commentary assumed the form of a theory that might be applied indirectly in areas he hadn’t been considering.

In recent decades, numerous artists have been suspicious of theoretical generalization, if only because little separates generalization from ideology. Both involve abstractions, and abstractions morph into one another. A concept of social sacrifice can become a call to militarism. Abstract generalization follows from the use of signs and symbols. Established habit in the configuring of signs—what I’ve been designating as a pattern of critical cliché—is hard to resist because the pattern, once established, flows as naturally as the “condition” of our collective discourse. Habit, like pattern, intensifies. Strong concepts become too strong, and critical analysis degenerates into dogma. De Kooning tended to reverse himself whenever he felt that he was becoming too certain of his own thoughts. Newman was the most vociferous among mid-twentieth-century artists who formed a de facto community of the wary: those who either resolved to resist generalization or, regarding the issue from its other end, to pursue specificity. This was the basis of Judd’s deep admiration for Newman.[41]

Objects and concepts fashioned in resistance to ideological habit raise consciousness of the ideological presence, perhaps otherwise disguised. Yet acts confined to resistance and undoing fail to produce an alternative; they merely cast the existing condition negatively. They convert a good name to a bad name; but the name, the generality, remains. Each of two opposing political figures is likely to label the other as the fascist until

[39] Clement Greenberg, in Russell W. Davenport, ed., “A *Life* Round Table on Modern Art,” *Life* 25 (11 October 1948): 62.
[40] Greenberg, “Towards a Newer Laocoon” (1940), *The Collected Essays and Criticism*, 1:34 (original emphasis).
[41] See Donald Judd, “Barnett Newman” (1964-1970), *Complete Writings 1959–1975*, 200–02.

the concept becomes murky and no longer matters. The consequences of resistance, subversion, and counter-cultural activity are limited; a strategy of negativity is a stop-gap measure of short-term gain, easily resisted in turn.

Newman's directness was extreme. He didn't want his past experience to interfere with his present experience. Such a goal may be chimerical, but one can act on the desire. Accordingly, Newman once said that the last thing he wanted to do was to make "another Newman."[42] An affirmation of identity would have been his undoing. One generalization I can venture in "explanation" is that he and likeminded artists would regard a name as tantamount to a theory, because the identifying names for things are reductive generalizations. This holds even for the names of individual people, since we take the name as a predictor of how a person will act and what this individual's values are. I don't mean this in the very general sense that we often rely on a name to establish the class identity, ethnicity, and gender of a person, acting toward the individual with a corresponding bias, expressing either our respect or our disdain. I mean this in the more specific sense that a person's public record, or even their private record, signified by their name or whatever other sign represents their identity, is a prejudicial, limiting factor that affects not only others, but also this very same individual, who will feel responsible and obligated to be true to herself or himself, to protect or honor the name. You are a named cultural commodity, produced to a standard. You can be trapped by what you expect of yourself.

So your name controls you. And my name controls me. It is my theory of myself. De Kooning said: "It is disastrous to name ourselves."[43] To get outside a name, and outside all naming, it isn't enough to assume a new identity in an imaginative, dress-up, make-believe way. Going outside, truly outside, is riskier than this. Risk is at the other end of the attitude consistent with naming, categorizing, and identifying things. Outside there are no names, only feelings. Things produce feelings just as they produce shine. To what or to whom do the feelings belong? Objects reflect their shine—shine is a reflection—so perhaps they reflect feelings as well, deriving them from the people who receive them in (excuse the shiny rhetoric) chiasmic reciprocity. To allow objects and their feelings to remain nameless is to acknowledge their impermanence and instability. Because we cannot capture the effect in a category, it may direct us more than we direct it: we are infants captivated by the shine.

[42] Newman, "A Conversation: Barnett Newman and Thomas B. Hess" (1966), *Selected Writings and Interviews*, 282.

[43] Willem de Kooning, statement (23 April 1950) in Robert Goodnough, ed., "Artists' Sessions at Studio 35," *Modern Artists in America*, ed. Robert Motherwell and Ad Reinhardt (New York: Wittenborn, Schultz, 1951), 22.

By not naming a thing, by neglecting to provide this simple index, we obliviate the specific object or situation. Oblivion is where we consign most of material reality and its transient feeling, whereas all the named concepts and entities, along with our memories of them, become the cultural world of our fictions and fantasies. Oblivious objects and situations can't be reconstructed in imagination. Judd's installations in Marfa belong only where they are, only in experience apart from generalized memory. They exist in oblivion. Their shine must be sensed and felt where it is, as it is. An analogy would be the emotion in de Kooning: "You can't specify what the emotion is," Greenberg said. Oblivion is not necessarily a place of loss, for memory never does justice to feeling anyway. In oblivion, at least we *have* the feeling. It's just that we can't capture it within a concept; we can't store it in memory.

I assume that it would be impossible to live entirely in fantasy and its pictorial memories or entirely in sensory reality and its oblivion.[44] Culture is the fantasy; sense experience, its shine, is the reality. To live solely in culture would be stultifying; to live solely in sensation would be alienating. These polarities represent a false dichotomy; they belong together on a single continuum. Ideological and cultural fantasies, like the generalities we know as our names and social identities, give form to human communication. For an artist to pursue experiential specificity is to risk damaging these familiar theoretical totalities and cultural constructions. One doesn't want to move from everything to nothing. So artists oriented to the specific are selective about it—but not too selective. I think of the impulse to specificity as an attitude more extreme than the one we associate with a social avant-garde, which attempts to break through a certain number of restrictions set by a culture; it does so with a relatively narrow selectivity. Apart from this habitual avant-garde gesture of montage, of breaking and reordering the given elements, certain artists seem to be driven to get beyond themselves, to get outside the culturally formed self, to lose or forget the self and its cultural instruction.[45] A social avant-garde is a theory, a modern type, a historical function. An individual such as Newman or de Kooning or Judd lives a life, not a theory—or, accepting no more theory than necessary, such an individual *works* at living a life. A work of art is often the material evidence of this work of living.

Another artist-worker-individual: Bridget Riley. She became acquainted with Newman in 1965, a decade after his *Uriel*. In an

44 On culture as a conscious, memorable construction and reality as unconscious oblivion, we might loosely compare Lacan, *The Four Fundamental Concepts of Psycho-Analysis*, 107–08.

45 Among many others, T. W. Adorno addressed the notion of self-forgetting: "The most sublime lyric works ... are those in which the subject, without a trace of his material being, intones in language until the voice of language itself is heard. The subject's forgetting himself, his abandoning himself to language as if devoting himself completely to an object—this and the direct intimacy and spontaneity of his expression are the same.... When the speaking subject, the 'I' [of lyric poetry] forgets himself completely, he is yet entirely present"; Theodor W. Adorno, "Lyric Poetry and Society" (1957), trans. Bruce Mayo, *Telos* 20 (Summer 1974): 62.

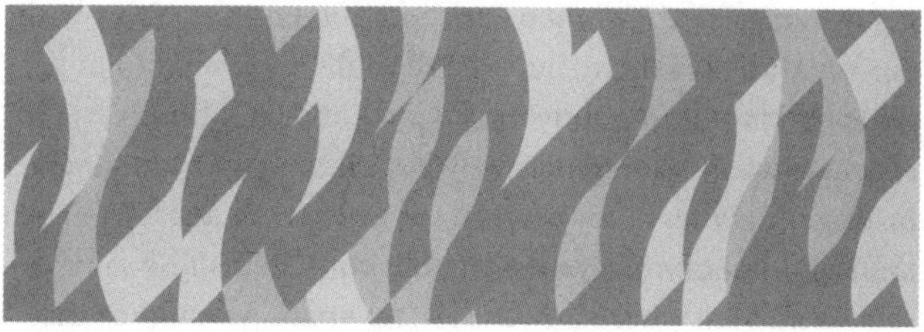

54
Bridget Riley
Evoë 3, 2003
Oil on linen
76 ¼ inches × 19 ft.
(193.7 × 579.8 cm)

interview of 2004, she spoke as he might have: "My main activity in the studio is the exercise of judgment—pure judgment.... Like pure color, such judgment is distinguished by having no referential role outside the work itself."[46] Riley's judgment has no standard to guide it; to feeling, it brings only feeling. Newman encouraged younger artists like Riley "to take risks," and his attitude impressed her.[47] But even before encountering him, she had been resisting the assimilation of her art to any style or program. Early in her career, she decided to hire assistants to paint the final versions of her images, so that her hand would never taint the work of sensation and judgment with personality. After all, personality isn't so personal; it evolves into a cultural product, a matter of semiosis and interpretation. To this day, Riley neither manipulates expressive style as many modernists do, nor exposes others' manipulation as many postmodernists do (as if it needed exposing: it exposes itself). With her impersonal look of anonymity, the sensation Riley projects can be individual without being coded as personal, without engaging in the generalizing cultural semiotics of expressiveness and personality.[48] "For quite a long time," she says, "I was embarrassed by using the word 'I,' the first person, in relation to my work."[49] Like the new Romantic artist that Thoré imagined, Riley neither inflated her personality nor reduced herself to a conventional subject-position.

Shortly after my recent visit to Judd's installation in Marfa, I viewed Riley's large, panoramic abstraction *Evoë 3*, 2003 [fig. 54]. As with Judd's box-like objects, the impression is of a simple system that produces a series of linked sensations, never exhausting itself. But is this "system" a system any more

46 Bridget Riley, "Bridget Riley in Conversation with Jenny Harper, April 2004," in Beat Wismer, ed., *Bridget Riley: Bilder und Zeichnungen 1959–2005* (Aarau: Aargauer Kunsthaus, 2005), 222.

47 Bridget Riley, statement to the author, 10 July 2001.

48 Traditional Western art tends to feature modes of production that involve the direct participation of an individual artist-producer. By convention, marks of the hand and similarly idiosyncratic features indicate this personalized process. Accordingly, some viewers hesitate to accept as art any products that lack such signs of personality: photographs, industrially fabricated sculptures like those of Judd, and also paintings like those of Riley.

49 Bridget Riley, "In Conversation with Robert Kudielka" (1972), *The Eye's Mind: Bridget Riley, Collected Writings 1965–1999*, ed. Robert Kudielka (London: Thames and Hudson, 1999), 84.

than Judd's is? His isn't. In *Evoë 3*, there are diagonals; and there are curves. There are edges that curve only to become diagonal and diagonals that become curves. If this is a system, it's so irregular that there's little point to invoking the concept. Riley's palette of four colors—pale orange, pale red-violet, medium blue, medium green—generates shifting rhythms of cool against warm and light against dark. A particular color associates first with one neighbor, then with another, to varying effect. I sensed the totality of *Evoë 3* but no logic in its parts. Its order was specific to its feeling, not exchangeable with any other order or feeling.

Evoë 3 is self-intensifying (its title alludes to a Bacchic cry). Rather than leading from sensation to a concept or a fully developed theory, the sensation stimulates still more sensation. The same might be said of Judd's play of shine and surface plane, or of Newman's stretch of cerulean in *Uriel*. The effect escapes generalization; it has no ready description, no name. It's felt instead as a singular concatenation of sensory qualities. One of Riley's trenchant observations is relevant: "For an artist those fleeting sensations which pass unrecognized by the intellect are just as important as those which become conscious."[50] This statement is theoretical—a generalization in support of specificity and its oblivion. "Fleeting sensations" occur in any situation at any moment. They manifest the present condition, provoking our emotional response to a specific environment that may resemble others in name or concept; yet the feeling is as different as the light on one of Judd's mill aluminum objects and the light on another. Feeling as feeling is difference; it differs from every other sense.

Like Judd, Newman, and Riley, Richard Serra produces works that affect viewers at an environmental scale beyond ordinary picture-making. He applies his hand throughout the process of completing large-scale drawings, covering sheets of linen or heavy paper with layers of black Paintstik, a dense oil crayon. The marks remain anonymous in character; they announce no particular temperament. As Riley might say, they "pass unrecognized by the intellect." Marks of Paintstik evoke the physical heaviness of the lead and steel typical of Serra's sculptural practice, as well as the weight we feel when we view his forms. This is a material and sensory weight, not the "weight" of an aritst's personality. In 1992, Serra stated: "I wanted ... to avoid the histories of existing styles, *even my own*. I wanted to free myself from my own ready-made handwriting....

50 Riley, "The Artist's Eye: Seurat" (1992), *The Eye's Mind*, 180.

I wanted the Paintstik mark to build up separately from its form-making capacity."[51] Through drawing, Serra was freeing himself from himself—from his past record and his anticipated future—at least for the time being. He was in the moment, immersed in his effort and absorbed by its dark shine.

Given his concern not to be bound to a style or a name, Serra is at liberty to employ assistants to create his deep, thickened blackness. Yet, for purposes unrelated to the final surface quality, he performs much of the labor himself. The issue isn't theoretical but pragmatic: "Theoretically, there is no need for me personally to surface my drawings. But in the process of covering a canvas with Paintstik, moving from the inside out, I often find the solution needed in terms of [the] weight and shape of the drawing in relation to the total field of the wall and the total volume of the space. The cutting decisions have to be based on the actual experience of the site of installation."[52] Between theory and experience, Serra emphasizes the latter. Consider a work such as *Consequence* of 2003. It consists of two large bands of Paintstik-covered linen, each 55 feet wide and 7 feet high, tacked to the parallel walls of a corridor 12 feet high. Serra placed one band low on one wall and the other band high on the opposite wall. This asymmetrical positioning causes the space to feel not only compressed but also twisted or torqued. One black element rises more than halfway from the floor while the other drops more than halfway from the ceiling. The twist activates the space: no, it activates the viewer within the space, in the moment.

Here and now

Some artists succeed in bringing the shine of the moment to works that are inherently referential, with a fictive past and future. Judd appreciated Claes Oldenburg in this respect.[53] Perhaps he would also have appreciated Mark Bradford, despite his condemning what he regarded as the major trend in the art of his time: "Art that was made to be direct is pilfered for art that is made to be indirect ... watered-down referential art."[54] Much in Bradford's art is referential, but we would hesitate to judge it "watered-down" in relation to its allusions. He often signals the cultural negotiations of people marked by race or class within contemporary society, and his own professional identity becomes an aspect of the connotative play. On at least one occasion—with a sculpture that consists of a

[51] Richard Serra, in "Richard Serra: An Interview by Mark Rosenthal," *Richard Serra: Drawings and Etchings from Iceland* (New York: Matthew Marks Gallery, 1992), n.p. (emphasis added).

[52] Richard Serra, "Notes on Drawing" (1987), *Richard Serra: Writings Interviews* (Chicago: University of Chicago Press, 1994), 178–79.

[53] See Richard Shiff in this volume, "Judd Through Oldenburg;" Richard Shiff, "To Stop the Heart," 100–108.

[54] Judd, "A Long Discussion Not About Master-pieces But Why There Are So Few of Them, Part I" (1984), *Complete Writings 1975–1986*, 59.

55
Mark Bradford
Stax, 2009
Mixed media, papier-mâché, and collage
11 ft. 8 inches × 5 ft. × 5 ft. (355.5 × 152.4 × 152.4 cm)

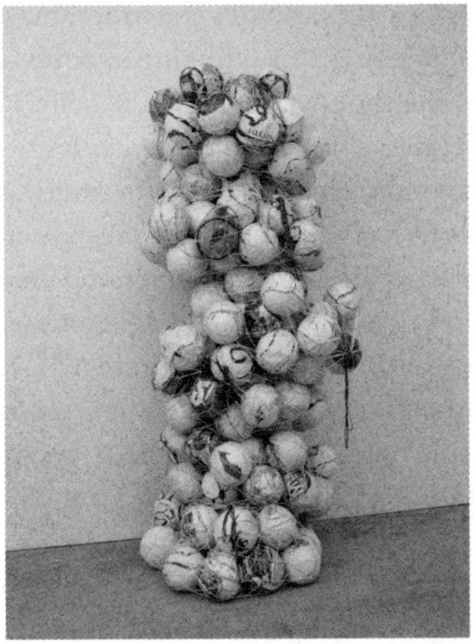

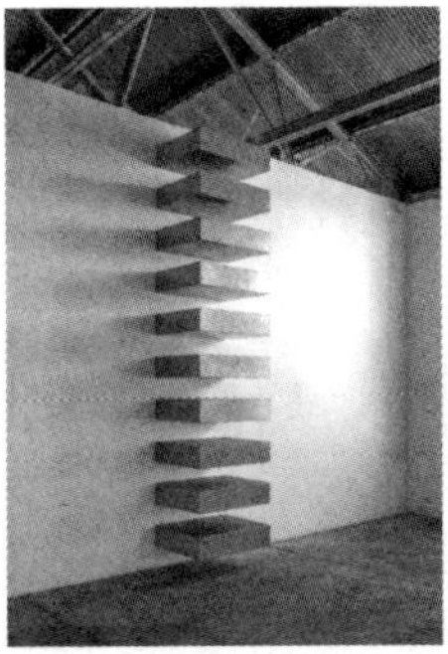

38 see page 266

stack of six mesh bags of modified children's soccer balls, supported by a wall [fig. 55]—Bradford referenced Judd's "stacks" of rectilinear box forms, also set against a wall [See fig. 38]. To conceptualize the relationship as mere pilfering would neglect the complexity of the multiple issues at stake.

Bradford didn't make Judd's art the sole allusion. As the title for his sculpture, he used *Stax*, not *Stack*; his verbal reference is to Stax Records, a company based in Memphis that promoted African American soul music during the 1960s and '70s.[55] The sculpture *Stax* mixes aesthetics and politics. Aesthetics is in the feel of the "weight of the stacking process."[56] Because this sensation must vary with each installation, it shares a quality of transience with the shine of Judd's mill aluminum or lacquered surfaces, which change by the moment. *Stax* too has the feeling of a moment, if only because of its happenstance equilibrium. Judd's and Bradford's moments are very different—isn't it the nature of a moment to be different? Physically, one sculptural installation seems fixed, though rendered fluid by light. The other seems unstable, though settled into its particular location and quite secure. A tension in aesthetic energy characterizes both: no single view proves adequate; you experience a need and a desire to continue looking.

And what of the politics? Like much of Bradford's oeuvre, *Stax* sets Los Angeles multiculturalism in play. He refers to Hispanic culture through the soccer balls while also thinking of the "layers of politics around black music." To be engaged

55 The name Stax Records combines the surnames of its two founders, Jim Stewart and Estelle Axton. On the history of the company, see Rob Bowman, *Soulsville, U.S.A.: The Story of Stax Records* (New York: Schirmer Books, 1997).
56 This and the quotation to follow are statements by Mark Bradford to the author, 23 September 2009.

with the aesthetics of Bradford's construction is to feel the "layers of politics" slipping away, slipping into the layers of paper that adhere to the spherical forms of the balls. Released from Bradford's metaphor, we return from politics to phenomenology. Yet commentary on *Stax* is likely to revert to politics, as a reference returns to a reference. References seek their likes, their semblances. This is an ordinary human response. I would rather not, I can't, resolve the situation. Some will regard *Stax* as referential (political); some will regard it as immediate (aesthetic). The evocation of a political context intrigues me; but when I empathize with the physical dynamics of *Stax*, I live in a moment without political semblance. Transformed, I have infant eyes, infant hands.

Bradford himself has particularly capacious infant hands: sensing, making, learning. In 2010, he completed *Field of Miracles*, an array of forty-four panels, each collaged with multiple layers of graphite-colored newsprint; clear acrylic medium is the adhesive [fig. 56]. By coincidence, *Field of Miracles* bears resemblance to Judd's installation at Marfa. I wouldn't think to make such a crude comparison were it not that I'm too far into the "condition" of this essay to escape it. Both works, Judd's and Bradford's, defeat attempts at discovering a pattern, an order. The defeat comes quickly because no order is needed—as you scan from unit to unit, the variation is utterly absorbing. Perhaps the nature of Bradford's process encouraged this degree of felt, intuitive variation, so he required no *theory* of variation. In this respect, he recaptured what the Romantic landscapist felt when painting the forest "straight on"—no plan, no composition needed.

Working against the rapid drying time of his acrylic medium, Bradford often tears sections of the "graphite" sheets as he flattens them against the support. His procedure also introduces inadvertent ripples, air pockets, and buckling between layers. The most critical action occurs when he sands the compound surface down through its layers in a fast-paced series of intuitive judgments. Layering, pressing, tearing, sanding: the sequence produces an unusually subtle range of grays—ink on, but also ground into, its paper ground. Like Judd, here Bradford capitalizes on effects inherent in his materials rather than forming them to refer to an outside fantasy, an existing cultural order. He doesn't bring his attitude to the condition of his materials, even though he chooses those materials. Rather, he derives his attitude from the experience. It

56
Mark Bradford
Field of Miracles, 2010
Graphite on paper on panel
12 ft. 1 inch × 22 ft. 8 inches
(358.3 × 590.9 cm)

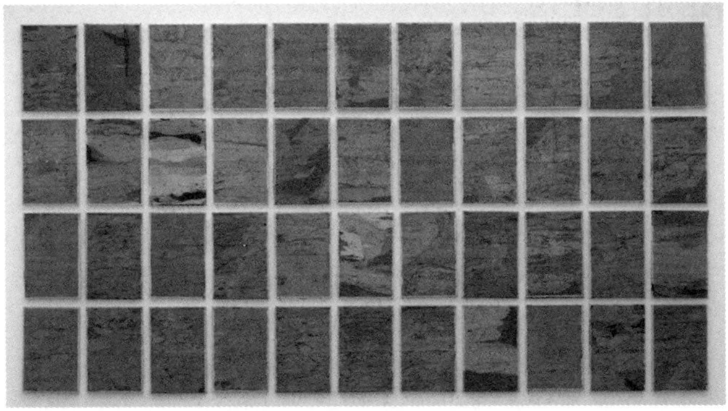

comes from the condition, of which the artist is an element (Kleist: it is the condition that knows). Metal is hard and shiny; newsprint is soft and matte. It too wants to be loved—in its way, for itself—fulfilled in the attentive gaze of an artist or viewer oblivious to all else, if only for the moment.

Field of Miracles has little shine in a literal sense, just a bit of gloss from its acrylic coating. But its range of textures – its multiple cuts, slices, scrapes, peels, and other material stresses—not only hold visual interest but also elicit an emotional response. To try to name the emotion defeats it along with the art. As with de Kooning's *Painting*, Bradford's cuts are in paper and not in skin, in matter and not in an organism. A cut can be caring as well as violent. We should be wary of anthropocentric projections and related cultural generalities that convert the artistic act into either a banality or a scandal, with a corresponding loss of material, physical, and even psychic specificity. Let at least some art exist outside our enduring cultural fantasies and outside the various fantasies of the self, coherent or divided. We will return to fantasy-land soon enough. "Here and now," Judd warned, "is little and short."[57] He seized on the possibility of canted diagonals. Attend to the sensory moment: value it; love it. Change with it.

[57] Donald Judd, "Una stanza per Panza, Part I," *Kunst Intern*, no. 4 (May 1990): 5.

As It Feels

[2014]

Philosophers often take an interest in art, just as artists often read philosophy. By profession, both are doubters, even if not always by nature. They question received ideas. To avoid relying on tradition, convention, rumor, and other indirect sources of information, artists and philosophers turn to personal experience and methods of their own devising. As doubters, they establish first principles for themselves; better still, they avoid being directed by principles.

Artists—the likes of Kasimir Malevich, Josef Albers, Ellsworth Kelly, Robert Mangold, Richard Serra—have advanced extreme forms of abstraction in order to escape existing cultural constructions. Philosophers, on their part, have long sought axiomatic statements that can be regarded as foolproof. A tautology—the notion that an entity must be the same as itself: A = A—may mean little if anything, but it has the merit of being indisputable. Well, not entirely indisputable. Some would argue that the symbolic expression of tautology is critical to its understanding and, within this expression, one A cannot equal the other. One is the first A, and the other is the second: this constitutes a difference. Analogously, one is here, while the other is there, at least as we attempt to think of the two entities (one and the same, twice over). I suspect that some would agree that A = A can be challenged in this way, whereas others would scoff at objecting to such fundamental equivalence. Even among doubters, certain positions amount to affirmations of belief, on one side of the question or the other. To claim that all facts should be doubted, even facts of logic, is to express a belief.

Charles Sanders Peirce, whose philosophical pragmatism was an inspiration to the aesthetic pragmatism of Donald Judd, understood that philosophy has to start somewhere in a real place and time; it cannot begin (all over again) at the beginning of time and evolution. Some pattern of belief needs to be acknowledged even by the most skeptical of philosophical theorists: "We cannot begin with complete doubt. We must begin with all the prejudices which we actually have."[1] In other words, we begin with everything we do not actively doubt. Peirce's thought can be rephrased: there are notions that escape doubt because it would be too risky to doubt them—in fact, unimaginable. For example, people who follow a faith cannot doubt the existence of their god. The doubt would be too much of a shock to the cultural system or way of life. Whatever we refuse to doubt must belong to our ideologically conditioned set

1 Charles Sanders Peirce, "Some Consequences of Four Incapacities" (1868), *Collected Papers*, ed. Charles Hartshorne, Paul Weiss, and Arthur W. Burks, 8 vols. (Cambridge, MA: Harvard University Press, 1958–1960), 5:156. Judd cites a related thought from Wittgenstein: "It is so difficult to find the *beginning*. Or better: it is difficult to begin at the beginning. And not try to go further back"; Ludwig Wittgenstein, *On Certainty*, ed. G. E. M. Anscombe and G. H. Von Wright, trans. Denis Paul and G. E. M. Anscombe (New York: Harper and Row, 1972), 62e (original emphasis). See Donald Judd, "Art and Architecture" (1983), *Complete Writings 1975–1986* (Eindhoven: Van Abbemuseum, 1987), 25. I thank Rob Weiner, Caitlin Murray, and Jessamine Batario for essential aid in research.

of beliefs, among the most firm and secure ("prejudices we actually have"). Doubt itself is like the shadow-puppet of a contested belief, haunting the presence of belief while dependent on it. Certain doubts can reemerge as the beliefs they question, just as beliefs can morph into doubts—but this is an odd way to put the matter, which I may soon regret.

By talking of beginning with each of our prejudices acknowledged and in place, Peirce suggests that philosophers should not delude themselves into believing that an argument can begin from the ground up, that it can start from nowhere and proceed with absolute objectivity: "Let us not pretend to doubt in philosophy what we do not doubt in our hearts."[2] Peirce's position implies that when we act with a pretense to full objectivity, we accomplish no more than proving rationally what our hearts have already caused us to believe. We will have gotten nowhere beyond where we started, having become rationally convinced of what we were already emotionally convinced. If we were to conclude otherwise, we would be internally divided, virtually schizophrenic. Reason risks failing when it doubts what emotions believe.

Peirce acknowledges the fact that feelings themselves may be unreasoned, yet this is no reason to doubt them. This is not to claim that adhering to our true feelings projects us into a better world—we may well have irrational feelings of hostility that cause harm to others. The ground of philosophy is not logical or phenomenological neutrality—a position from which we might construct a fully logical argument that would *feel* right because it would satisfy a desire for intellectual security and integrity. I have often used the figure of chiasmus as an example of a logical and rhetorical form that causes the writer, as well as the reader, to feel both intelligent and satisfied. Chiasmus is useful in wiggling out of an intellectual cul-de-sac. I succumbed already to the temptation in turning this chiasmic thought: "Certain doubts can reemerge as the beliefs they question, just as beliefs can morph into doubts." Statements about art, a difficult topic, often assume chiasmic form. In 1966, Barnett Newman said: "Just as I affect the canvas, so does the canvas affect me."[3] The symmetry of his sentence has an emotional appeal, like symmetry in the human face, even though Newman seems ambivalent about symmetry in art, sometimes featuring it and sometimes not at all. The philosopher Jean-Luc Nancy provides a more ambitious version of chiasmus in locating aesthetic emotion at the origin of

2 Peirce, "Some Consequences of Four Incapacities," *Collected Papers*, 5:157.

3 Barnett Newman, "The Fourteen Stations of the Cross, 1958–1966" (1966), *Selected Writings and Interviews*, ed. John P. O'Neill (New York: Knopf, 1990), 189.

humanity: "Man began in ... a gesture. At this [gesture], man trembled, and this trembling was him."[4] We can paraphrase to make the structure more obvious: man was the being who trembled; trembling was the essence of man. Or, still more obvious: man was trembling; trembling was man. Entity X is to entity Y, as Y is to X. It will always sound good. It will always *feel* good.

The ground of philosophy is whatever prejudiced position a person actually occupies—absolute for the individual but for no one else. Accordingly, Michael Polanyi (among his many distinctions, a philosopher of science) reached a clever conclusion in 1958: "Doubts, which we now sustain as reasonable on the grounds of our own scientific world view, have ... only our beliefs in this view to warrant them."[5] So the sense of a reasonably held doubt depends on irrational faith or belief in the tenets of modern science—the same modern science that establishes reasonable doubt as a critical method. In short, our capacity to doubt is linked to belief in the proper status of doubting, which has its reasonable limitations. Faith in reason causes reasoning, as it either leads to doubt or dispels it, to seem reasonable in doing so.

Polanyi's reference to "reasonably held doubt" opens a related line of inquiry. His phrasing evokes the legal principle of "reasonable doubt." A trial jury is not supposed to reach a guilty verdict unless the evidence indicates certainty beyond a reasonable doubt. The presumption is that doubt arises in degrees. The prosecution introduces as much scientific evidence as it can and applies logic to it. In response, the defense needs to create an atmosphere of doubt, at least a reasonable degree of doubt—doubt with some rational foundation as opposed to a mere emotional tremor of suspicion. One common strategy is to question the certainty with which any eyewitness testifies. A witness relies on sensory input, a form of feeling. Imagine that a witness saw a running shadow and judges retrospectively that it must have been the shadowy form of the person accused of the crime. The defense lawyer will probably avoid questioning the fact that the witness saw *something* shadowy, but will instill doubt with respect to the interpretation of the form. Was it really the shadow of a man? Could it not have been a woman, or even a child?

A film written and directed by Joel and Ethan Coen, *The Man Who Wasn't There* (2001), portrays the legal defense strategy of converting a tenuous fact to a tenuous feeling—that

[4] Jean-Luc Nancy, "Painting in the Grotto" (1994), *The Muses*, trans. Peggy Kamuf (Stanford: Stanford University Press, 1996), 74. In French: "silence calmement violent ... L'homme en a tremblé: et ce tremblement, c'était lui"; Jean-Luc Nancy, *Les muses* (Paris: Galilée, 1994), 127. Newman (among many others) had made the same association, tracing the tradition of art back to the emergence of humanity in a moment of emotional expression, motivated by "the terror of the unknowable"; Newman, "The Ideographic Picture" (1947), *Selected Writings and Interviews*, 108. "Man's first cry was a song ... not a request for a drink of water"; Newman, "The First Man Was an Artist" (1947), *Selected Writings and Interviews*, 158.

[5] Michael Polanyi, *Personal Knowledge: Towards a Post-Critical Philosophy* (Chicago: University of Chicago Press, 1962 [1958]), 275.

is, converting belief to doubt. The year is 1949, and an intellectually adventurous trial lawyer has just discovered the Heisenberg uncertainty principle. He ignores the qualification that it applies to particles so small that the energy or force of the light that would allow them to be observed is sufficient to cause them to change position, relative to the scale of investigation. Expanding the pragmatic scope of the principle (shifting it from the physical sciences to the human sciences), the lawyer decides that all sensory observation must change the nature of what is observed. Even everyday sights will be affected. A present-day academic involved with critical theory or, for that matter, a theorist of 1949, might agree with the lawyer. Any observational position, as well as any application of descriptive or interpretive language, alters the existing nature of the object of interest. Attention to things changes their situation. When the lawyer is explaining his discovery to the defendant, he summarizes it memorably: "Your looking changes things.... The more you look, the less you know." So the more information the prosecution introduces, the more opportunity the defense has to raise reasonable doubt. The implication for critical thought is this: the more extensive the commentary, the more doubtful the conclusion, if there ever is a conclusion. By analogy with the world of physical reality—by analogy with Werner Heisenberg's world of indeterminacy—lines of critical commentary accumulate yet fail to converge. But in the fantasy world known as society or culture, where shared ideological belief perfects social relations, lines of commentary converge in established principle. Neither objective observation nor subjective feeling can change an ideological orientation that has already determined the individual's receptiveness to observation and feeling. By invoking indeterminacy as a defense, the lawyer aims to divert the jury from an ideologically conditioned path of reason that he assumes it would otherwise follow, leading to a verdict of guilty (given the unfavorable momentum of the "facts," the hopelessness of the case).

Where is my argument headed? Bear in mind that works by Judd elicit multiple sensory observations without necessarily leading to realizations of logical structure or hierarchical order. Judd's art does not assume the form of a premise and a set of facts leading to a conclusion—we might say instead that his art consists only of facts, nothing more than facts in interaction. We normally think of a whole as constituted of elements of

42 see page 269

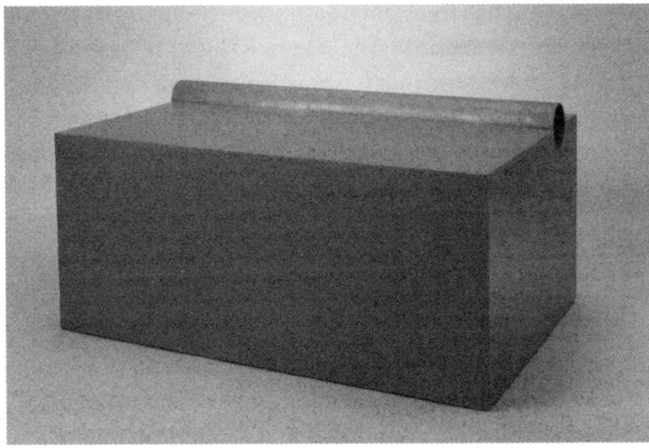

some kind. But the readily identifiable elements of a work by Judd—for instance, a red rectangular prism coupled with a gray metallic pipe, asymmetrically positioned and set into a channel (see fig. 42)—resist forming a composition of dominant and subordinate parts, even though one element may be larger than the other or one may be supporting the other. Each part will seem as present to sense as is the whole. Because Judd's constructions fail to yield to a dominant compositional order, we can perceive both the parts and the whole for what they are: they exist together, but are also unconnected, like the opposing unities of a tautology.

My experience of Judd's art encourages me to extend his aesthetic intuition. I begin to doubt conclusions based on facts, though I accept the facts that I sense and feel. It may be that the factual elements of rational discourse never form a general argument that will be coherent for analogous cases. The sensory facts remain as unconnected as the two sides of a chiasmic comparison or the particles of energy that Heisenberg was trying to observe. A stable relationship may appear but will remain on the level of appearance, no more than a tentative supposition, derived from sensation—a feeling. The ultimate relationship of entities remains anyone's guess. If this is so, where do we turn to discover genuine connections?

For an artist, this question may have an answer different from its answer for a critical interpreter. Art involves connectedness of a sort unlikely to be experienced in rational argumentation. Artistic practice is aesthetic and emotional; art appeals openly to feelings. Rational argument also appeals to feelings—it has its aesthetic attractions—but it attempts to disguise its rhetoric for the sake of its logic. If, by Polanyi's claim, we understand that the practice of science allows doubt to appear, we also know that a properly reasoned argument should not resort to appeals to feeling. We leave it to objects of art to solicit sensory appreciation. When they hold a viewer's sensory and emotional interest, we deem them successful.

Some would demand much more than interest from a work of art: a structured body of information, the support of a thesis, or a penetrating cultural gesture, whether affirming or subversive. Judd, however, became notorious for claiming that art need only be interesting.[6] In his usage, this word was not the anodyne term that it is in colloquial American English. It referred instead to a connection that a work might establish with the disposition of the viewer's psychic and emotional state, itself induced by the work. It was Judd's habit to record his thoughts as verbal notes to himself, most of which remain unpublished. In 1990, he stated that sensory perception did not lend itself to systematic analysis: "We sit and look out and see, [and] listen, and know[,] but cannot analyze doing it. If you think of it, you can't do it. One reason is that it's all very large and whole, and not discrete data. This is another gap, [a] disconnection, that cannot be directly closed. Analysis has to work around it and on little parts of the whole."[7] No obvious mathematical, compositional, or structural principle explains the positioning of Judd's gray pipe embedded in a red rectangular prism. To think of a principle would distract from the effect of the work. We see the two parts both together and separately, as if their connection—which is no proper connection at all—were established only in our act of seeing. The work requires no further connection than this existential one, because an immediate impression of the two parts as the whole is unavoidable.

In his statement, Judd makes a standard phenomenological observation: "We look … and know[,] but cannot analyze doing it. If you think of it, you can't do it." This realization is not far from "looking changes things." Judd addresses the gap between immediate sensation and its forms of cognitive reflection. In the same note, he continues with a variation on Ludwig Wittgenstein: "Art [is] a slight sound in the silence. Wittgenstein's *Tractatus* ends: 'What we cannot speak about we must consign to silence.' Well, a little [of it, we can] consign to art."[8] Judd claims that rational analysis fails to remedy the lack of connection between sensation and its description, yet art

[6] See, for example, Donald Judd, "Complaints: Part I" (1969), *Complete Writings 1959–1975* (Halifax: Nova Scotia College of Art and Design, 1975), 198.

[7] Judd, manuscript note, 18 November 1990, Judd Foundation archives, Marfa (courtesy Caitlin Murray).

[8] Judd refers here to Ludwig Wittgenstein, *Tractatus Logico-philosophicus*, trans. D. F. Pears and B. F. McGuinness (London: Routledge and Kegan Paul, 1961 [1921]), 151.

itself establishes connections in situations where language is reduced to silence.

I have invoked Peirce and Polanyi, and through Judd's statement, Wittgenstein. Like many other philosophers, including the ancients, these moderns investigated the tension between sensing and interpreting, between feeling and reasoning, between rhetoric and logic. I have also invoked the legal principle of reasonable doubt. If a prosecution team tries to establish a logical chain of events and human motivation to prove that an individual committed a crime, a lawyer for the defense works in the opposite direction, demonstrating that what looks logical amounts to a matter of personal feeling, and the implication of a feeling, the meaning of a feeling, can always be doubted. We do not doubt *that* we have a sensory experience or an emotional feeling; but we must question what any feeling signifies. A legal defense works to transform dispassionate facts ("I'm certain that I saw him") into the passionate feelings that led to such sanitized judgments ("he's a bad guy, so he must be the one I saw"). The strategy is to divide feeling from thought and convert relatively weak beliefs into strong doubts.

Peirce wrote: "Belief and doubt may be conceived to be distinguished only in degree." Why the phrase, "only in degree"? Colloquially, we commonly exchange the expression "I believe" for the expression "I think" or even the expression "I see." If all thoughts and visions amount to beliefs, doubt becomes a very weak form of belief. In other words, we experience our doubt as a nuance of the same cognitive emotion we know as belief. So if doubt and belief have a share in the same emotion, what is this feeling? How should we identify it by name? Peirce would associate this range of feeling with the experience of hypothetical thinking or what he sometimes calls abduction. In turn, abduction is linked to intuition. The situation becomes more familiar if we regard this cognitive emotion as guessing. Doubt is a form of guessing. Belief is a form of guessing. Neither a doubt nor a belief is truly secure. The nature of doubt is to be a gradation of belief and of belief to be a gradation of doubt (chiasmus again: we often conceive of dualistic relationships as reciprocal). People will say, "I believe this absolutely; I have no doubt whatever." Such a statement lies at one end of the spectrum of feelings associated with guessing. Peirce referred to hypothetical thinking or guessing as "sensuous"; it was a form of thought close to its foundation in emotion.[9]

9 "Hypothesis [guessing] produces the *sensuous* element of thought": Peirce, "Deduction, Induction, and Hypothesis" (1868), *Collected Papers*, 2:387 (original emphasis).

A diagram illustrates how the issue might be regarded as a matter of degree. Guessing occupies a range from doubt at one pole to belief at the other. If both doubt and belief are intuitions, then doubt has a negative valence and belief has a positive valence.

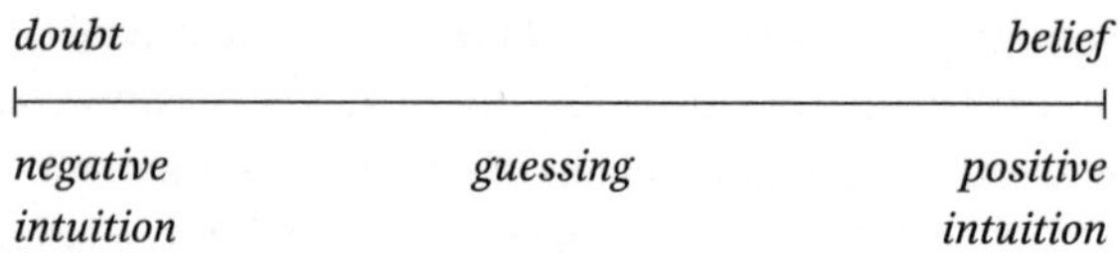

The scale of doubt and belief bears on the recent history of art. The categories currently used to define the broad lines of this history—modernism, postmodernism, the contemporary—tend to figure in polemical arguments, instilling belief in the value of one mode over another, where doubt might benefit the observer. To enter into the historical argument, we need to generalize (which ought to raise our doubt in reaction, for general categories obliterate genuine differences). Assume that the decades of the 1940s, 1950s, and 1960s were guided by a theory of modernist practice, even though this notion remains largely unexamined. If we accept the existence of an aesthetic practice specifically "modernist," a sympathetic account would acknowledge that it entailed exploring the creative potential that remained within the various traditional media.

A modernist painter active during the 1950s or early 1960s, as Judd was, would not regard as serious practice acts such as throwing a can of paint into the air or painting on the surface of a living body. So-called modernists did not intend to subvert the medium but to probe and extend it. As a painter, Judd experimented with the juxtaposition of forms that could stand against each other as equals, without relying on allusions to figure and ground, near and far, or dominant and subordinate. He would set a band of one color and texture against a field of another color and texture to intensify a viewer's awareness of both (fig. 57). His practice did not reject the value of the art of the past, but recognized the responsibility of his current generation of artists to contribute something of their independent thinking to contemporary culture (not better, but different). With similar motivation, but with her independence too, Bridget Riley devoted much of her early career to exploring what could be done with simple graphic

57
Donald Judd
Untitled, 1960
Oil on canvas
49 × 46 inches
(124.5 × 116.8 cm)

58
Bridget Riley
Shift, 1963
Emulsion on hardwood
30 × 30 inches
(76.2 × 76.2 cm)

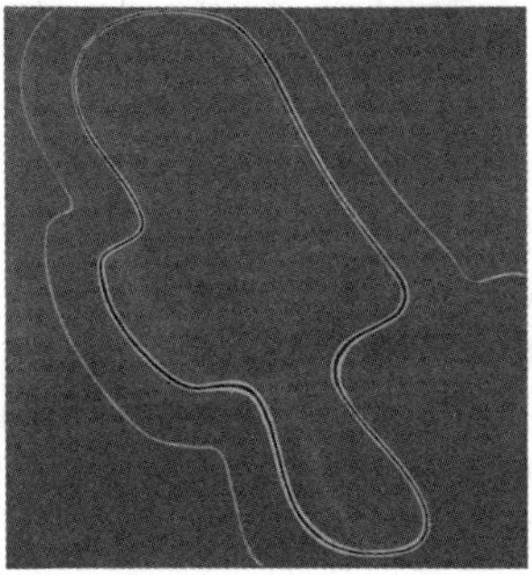

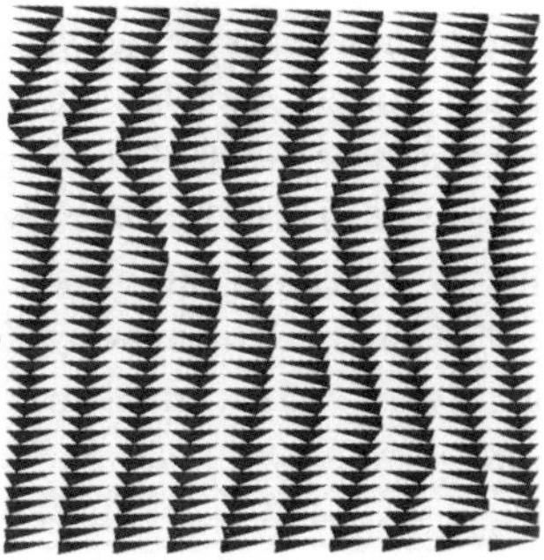

figures, such as skewed triangles. The paintings that resulted, though based on known elements of design, were radically new [fig. 58].

Analogously, for the sake of the historical argument, assume that the decades of the 1970s, 1980s, and perhaps even the 1990s were guided by a theory of postmodernist practice. This entailed mixing media, violating the boundaries of genres, flouting the protocols of authorship, and allowing the development of a narrative or literary message to dominate the materiality of the medium. Thinking about the concept of art outweighed concerns for the feeling of art, its aesthetic experience.

During the most recent decades, say, the past twenty years or so, artists and art historians have continued to *refer* to theories of modernism, postmodernism, and the like, but without themselves following any particular theory religiously. We may be living through a period of less certainty, less unanimity with respect to theoretical orientation. We are less convinced that rejecting one ideological position only to assume another (substituting postmodernism for modernism) results in more beneficial forms of art. If each of us is somewhat more tolerant of positions of doubt, then collectively we may feel free to discuss the sensory qualities of Judd's color without invoking a theory of minimalism, let alone modernism. This would represent a welcome shift in critical interest. Perhaps we can perceive that Judd, when working in three dimensions (See fig. 9), retained a painter's interest in the *sensory* fundamentals of color. We can appreciate the color without worrying whether this artist, a very political person, respected the

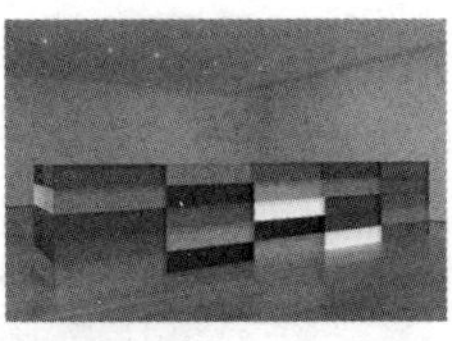

9 see page 255

political implications of his industrial fabrication process or of color itself. Such concerns would introduce a host of ideological complications, as we would need to weigh one attitude toward life against another, limited in our judgment by our preexisting personal beliefs. The critical inquiry might be engaging, but would lead us into ourselves and away from an experience Judd's object was offering—a chance to be out of ourselves.

I sometimes (not always) think that the present moment of art history and art criticism is one of theory-in-general. When I refer to "theory" in this manner, I do not mean the ideological baggage we all bring with us—specific to a time, place, and station in society—the ideological orientation that Peirce called a prejudice, informing an individual's thoughts and actions. Such ideological preconditions accompany life within a cultural order. By "theory," I mean instead certain elaborate discursive structures, the selective province of academics and public intellectuals, such as those associated with poststructuralist criticism, postmodernist art, and postcolonial politics. This theory is not enforced under threat of penalty, like a theory of allegiance to the state; an individual can take academic theory or leave it. The danger in accepting such theory is that its hypotheses may bring firm answers to vague questions. A critic begins to naturalize the constructed theoretical order, exchanging its fictions for the real chaos of experience—repositioning the scale or bar that I identify with guesswork. With a commitment to a theory, even a theory of doubt, we tend to shift the bar so it tilts toward the end labeled "belief." Adherence to a chosen theory promises to reward the loyalist with intellectual security. The obvious alternative, equally extreme, is to purge all theory, attempting to see and feel without direction or prejudice of any kind, as if to act on instinct. Noting the ironic advantage of committing less energy to conceptual thought than is customary, Heinrich von Kleist remarked two centuries ago: "The intellect cannot err where none is present."[10]

It may be that we need to accept uncritically, mindlessly, some degree of theoretical generalization, as Peirce argued. This is our prejudice. It is also fair enough to claim, as many have done, that only another blind ideology displaces a blind ideology. Surely, this is a pessimistic attitude toward cultural affairs, yet artists are often optimistic people. The three artists that have served as examples—Newman, Judd, and Riley—express pessimism about culture, but are optimistic about art. Is there something that resists the conceptual principles of a

[10] Heinrich von Kleist, "On the Puppet Theater" (1810), *An Abyss Deep Enough: Letters of Heinrich von Kleist with a Selection of Essays and Anecdotes*, ed. and trans. Philip B. Miller (New York: Dutton, 1982), 214.

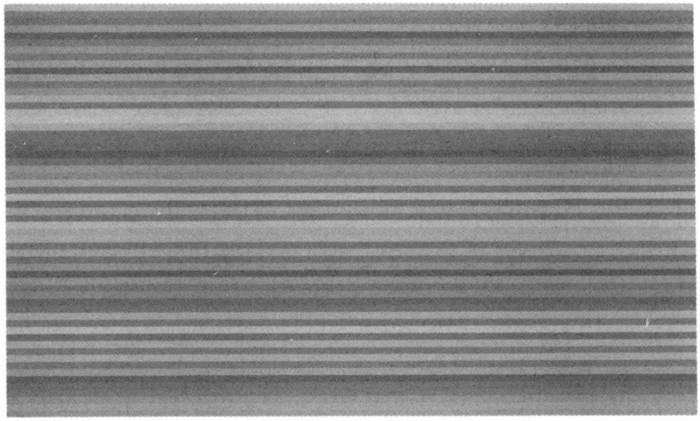

59
Bridget Riley
Arioso (Blue), 2013
Oil on linen
59⅛ × 10¼ inches
(150 × 257.2 cm)

theory without amounting to another theory? Consider returning to a moment not long ago, when postmodernists were convinced that they were theoretically justified in denying the aesthetic pretensions of modernists. Many critics who favored postmodernist practice believed that cultural communication was a matter of the dissemination of images, whereas the modernists who preceded them were said to believe that art had its foundation in personal sensation. This was one of the utopian attractions of abstract art in the postwar era—it mitigated the tyranny of representational imagery, overburdened with cultural connotations. Radically abstract art—like Newman's, Judd's, and Riley's—returned sensation to the body, to its vision and touch.

Often, artists react to cultural pressures by enhancing the sensory qualities of their work, as if to provide physical immunity to ideological mind-control. The physical has a tonic effect on the mental. Sensation clears the mind. When viewing one of Riley's new stripe paintings, completed during the past year (*Arioso (Blue)*, 2013; [fig. 59]), we might be tempted to study it analytically, to comprehend its effect through the chemistry of its pigment mixtures. According to Riley, however, the last thing we should do is worry about the idiosyncratic science of her art. It is sufficient to name the colors red, green, blue, and yellow. Forget about identifying them more precisely, she says—just look at them.[11]

Along with Riley, Judd recognized that seeing a color or a shape and naming it are incommensurable actions: "A rectangle is a shape itself; it is obviously the whole shape."[12] Seeing a rectangle reveals the obviousness to which Judd referred—the

[11] Riley, in conversation with the author, 7 March 2014.
[12] Judd, "Specific Objects" (1964-65), *Complete Writings 1959–1975*, 181-82.

recognition of a certain existence. A rectangle is rectilinear; yes, it does have right angles. But we ignore this general, theoretical definition when we *feel* the geometric form in its singularity, isolated wholeness, and actuality. We often perceive right angles as other than ninety degrees. We might doubt that a form is symmetrical or prismatic on the basis of an actual point of view. This is one of the lessons of Judd's works that consist of multiple volumetric units of equal dimensions: their placement dictates that only one among the several right-angled forms will appear "right" [see fig. 38]. Most likely, it would be the unit at eye level, which occupies a physiologically privileged position. *In experience*, no two entities are equivalent.

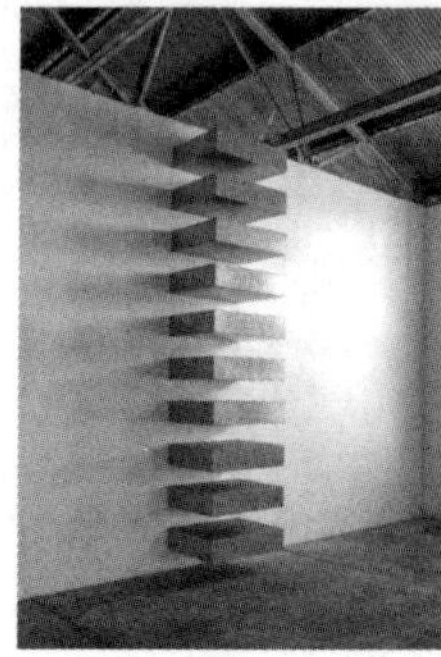

38 see page 266

Yet, some would say: the body is itself a cultural construction; no entity exists outside a conceptual system; no existence is obvious and self-sufficient; nothing stands apart from its category or type; the singularity or wholeness of experience is mythical. Furthermore, because observation is always guided by concept, we fail to observe anything that would appear to lie outside all plausible variation of the existing conceptual framework. When one experience seems equivalent to another, a concept (a generalizing category) has done its work. During the 1960s, Judd perceived that theoretical generalizations—however reasonably intentioned and formulated to debunk other, competing theories—were being pushed too far. They were threatening the specific sensory values of art.

By Judd's understanding of critical practice among his contemporaries, the problem for art became all the more aggravated subsequent to the 1960s. Just as sensation suffered depersonalization, so thought itself became unanchored, given the prevalence of challenges to traditional notions of authorship.[13] Perhaps most troubling, theorists reasoned that because thinking finds expression in a communal language, the thoughts of individuals are not their own. The self, if there is one, must differ from itself because it thinks in alien terms. It thinks as another, with the very structure of language forcing this realization on those willing to confront it.[14] Language escapes the possession of its writers and even its live speakers. This theoretical position not only removes the authority of the individual from his or her personal beliefs, but also undermines the force of an individual's experience of doubt. Those who author statements of either doubt or belief, venturing guesses, become mere vehicles of language, passive conductors

13 On the cultural refuge taken in "aesthetic integrity," see Paul de Man, "Sign and Symbol in Hegel's *Aesthetics*" (1982), *Aesthetic Ideology*, ed. Andrzej Warminski (Minneapolis: University of Minnesota Press, 1996), 92.

14 See de Man, "Sign and Symbol in Hegel's *Aesthetics*," *Aesthetic Ideology*, 98.

15 For a sophisticated form of the argument (more than a mere reversal of active and passive roles), with the authority of speech displaced by the play of graphematic writing, see Jacques Derrida, "Signature Event Context" (1971), *Margins of Philosophy*, ed. and trans. Alan Bass (Chicago: University of Chicago Press, 1982), 307-30.

of semiotic energy already in circulation.[15] The theorist who questions such a system is left in the position of introducing resistance to existing lines of cultural transmission that will remain anyway. Critical theory of the second half of the twentieth century relegated its theorist to functioning as still another participant in the system, distinguished only by being more self-aware and more troubled by the situation.

The critical trend that annoyed Judd developed in part within an area of literary study where resistance actually had a chance of being effective. Critics were challenging the long-standing practice of interpreting texts biographically and psychoanalytically. Interpretation of this sort attended to the creator far more than to the thing created. Roland Barthes's celebrated essay of 1968, "The Death of the Author," was, at its core, hardly antithetical to Judd's interests, both intellectual and aesthetic. It preserved his concern for the sensory immediacy of what he liked to call a "particular, definite object."[16] Barthes made this claim: "It is language which speaks, not the author. To write is ... to reach that point where only language acts [and] every text is eternally written *here and now*."[17] The reader's reading determines the meaning—a collaborative effect of the written text and its present reading (an effect also of intertextuality: all previous writing and all previous reading converging on a present moment). A theory of immediate sensation—the finality of the present sensory experience—was being applied to the consumption of texts. Analogous to Barthes, Judd discouraged viewers of his art from concluding that every fact related to *him*, as the personal creator of the object, must contribute to its experience. The primary meaning of a work lay in the sensation it afforded—the "here and now" of the object, as opposed to the past history of its creator, the circumstances of its creation, and the cultural connotations of its forms and materials. Recall what he noted to himself in 1990: "We look ... and know[,] but cannot analyze doing it." Because we cannot analyze, we tend to doubt the ultimate meaning of what we see, but we cannot doubt *that* we see.

Especially in the United States, critics pursued to extremes the theoretical notion of the "death of the author." The expanded concept verged on absurdity, becoming more of an indicator of an ideological position than a pragmatic realization. Any sign of the agency of an artist, especially material traces such as a painter's mark of the brush, whether associated with a particular individual or not, were interpreted as

16 Judd, "Aspects of Flavin's Work" (1969), *Complete Writings 1959–1975*, 200.

17 Roland Barthes, "The Death of the Author" (1968), *Image–Music–Text*, trans. Stephen Heath (New York: Hill and Wang, 1977), 143, 145 (original emphasis). Compare the fundamental point, often argued during Judd's lifetime, that the mode of representation, not the individual who deploys it, establishes the potential for meaning: "Instead of containing or reflecting experience, language constitutes it"; Paul de Man, "The Dead-End of Formalist Criticism" (1956), trans. Wlad Godzich, *Blindness and Insight* (Minneapolis: University of Minnesota Press, 1983), 231.

signs of an aggressive arrogation of authority. Per Kirkeby's marks of the twenty-first century would be interpreted as hardly any different from Claude Monet's marks of the nineteenth century. In 1981, Benjamin Buchloh argued that any sign of this type "confirms the hieratics of ideological domination."[18] He began with the prejudicial belief, a kind of theoretical guess, that all painting must be authoritarian since this was the dominant institutionalized medium of representation during periods of authoritarian political order. By implication, damned by association, any artist who persists in painting must be willingly adopting the pose of an authority figure. The exception would be the painter who paints only to discredit painting. As the Heisenbergian defense lawyer might say—with irony—this is a situation in which looking at something changes it. Buchloh looks at painting and sees the representation of authority. This is not what Kirkeby sees as he paints today, nor what Monet saw. But Buchloh has not founded his judgment on an assessment of the specifics of visual appearance; he initiated his critical analysis with a theoretical premise that did not require looking. The conceptual change or reorientation that he produces—equating a certain sensory engagement with an assertion of authority—occurs in the absence of visual experience. The dubious empirical reality to which Heisenberg referred—a situation forever to be doubted because it cannot be determined—has morphed into a fixed belief. Uncertainty about the status of painting has become certainty. By Buchloh's reasoning, nearly all painting becomes the same and is politically suspect.

Postmodernists argued—as many do today—that the art of the recent past, of the modern period, became modern-*ist*, as if it were determined by ideology (a set of symbolic values) rather than by experience (a set of pragmatic values). We may not be able to adjudicate whether ideology and its prejudices precede experience or the reverse, or even whether the question of precedence has validity. Being unanswerable, it probably is not an actual question. To take a side, to assume that ideology does take precedence, is a self-confirming ideological position. Once a person assumes this perspective, the equation of perception with its articulation in language becomes more of a belief than a hypothesis. Beliefs, too, are hypotheses—those that are unusually convincing. The colors and the human scale of the large floor piece that Judd created around 1990 are clear enough as sensation or feeling [fig. 65]. The fact of what we see

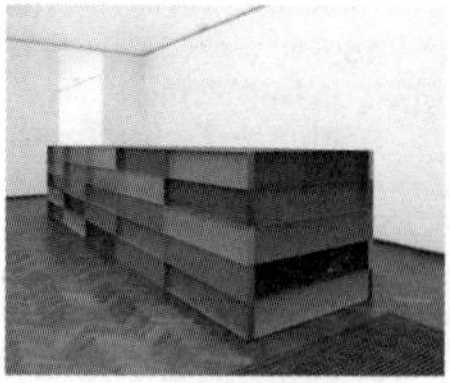

65 see page 230

[18] Benjamin Buchloh, "Figures of Authority, Ciphers of Regression: Notes on the Return of Representation in European Painting" (1981), in Brian Wallis, ed., *Art After Modernism: Rethinking Representation* (New York: The New Museum of Contemporary Art, 1984), 124.

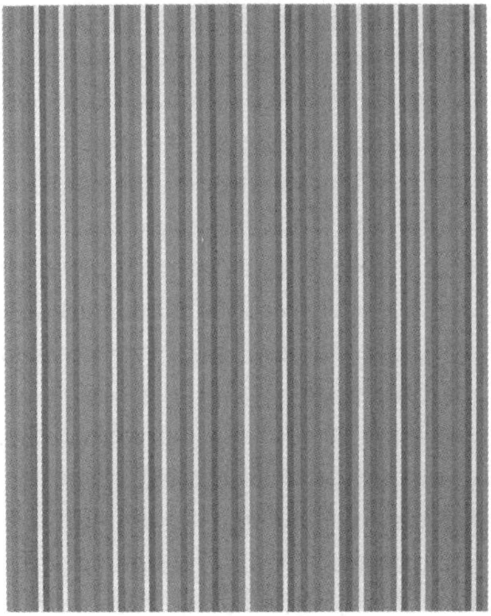

60
Bridget Riley
Lilac Painting 5, 2008/1983
Oil on linen
67.5 × 55.25 inches
(171.5 × 140.3 cm)

is certain. But what this very real construction is, what its identity might be, remains in doubt until an arbitrary linguistic equivalence substitutes for the living perception. In this instance, to be doubtful about the meaning keeps the experience alive.

An artist or author experiences the *feel* of color or of language as an intimate, immediate fact. Aesthetic invention is a flash of intuitive guesswork. It happens "here and now." This here-and-now is phrasing that both Barthes and Judd liked to use—Barthes the feeling reader, Judd the feeling viewer. If Judd's art implies a theory analogous to Barthes's sense of textuality, it is one that acknowledges the sensory materiality of temporal experience. Artists like Judd—and Riley as well—do work from a belief. They believe that an immense reserve of experience exists outside the present limits of conceptualization and intellectual understanding.[19] We may already be tapping into this reserve, but without enough sensitivity for it to affect our emotional soul. We look, yet not always with discovery or edification. Sometimes looking fails to generate change; nothing registers.

Riley explains why she continues to pursue painting despite claims that the medium has become moribund and obsolete. It offers her the opportunity to perceive color and other qualities that, despite being unconcealed, normally remain unseen. Painting and the other arts open onto realms of experience otherwise inaccessible. The painted stripes of her *Lilac Painting 5* [fig. 60]—white, yellow, green, turquoise,

19 See, for example, Bridget Riley, "Seurat as Mentor," in Jodi Hauptman, ed., *Georges Seurat: The Drawings* (New York: Museum of Modern Art, 2007), 195: "Comprehension is not everything, the unaccountable has a place in our lives ... Seurat, involuntarily perhaps, has presented us with the mysterious."

and blue—generate an optical experience of a lilac hue that appears within the bars of blue pigment, induced by the proximity of turquoise. In 1984, at a moment when postmodernists were appropriating imagery found in popular culture, Riley alluded to a different kind of finding: "In order to see one had to paint and through that activity found what could be seen."[20] Like Newman's statement about an artist being affected by his own action, this remark takes a chiasmic form, a rhetoric that troubles me, raising my doubts. But I forgive chiasmus in this instance, since Riley expresses the possibility—just a guess—of a direct connection, devoid of ideology, between the making process and the seeing process. Her statement merits repetition: "In order to see one had to paint and through that activity found what could be seen." On a different occasion, she presented the thought in a less chiasmic form, with the artist as maker assuming a more active role: "For an artist those fleeting sensations which pass unrecognized by the intellect are just as important as those which become conscious.... [An artist] looks *into* perception and shows it to be the activity which produces what it sees."[21]

Judd aimed to establish the objects he constructed within (and for) the experience of a new generation, *his* generation. Projecting abruptly from a wall or a floor, his art objects had no precedents in traditional practice. In 1987, he stated his commitment to contemporaneity: "I think that art should concern itself with the present (and not necessarily to go forward, because I don't believe in progress, but simply change)."[22] An aesthetic experience of the present moment—open to doubt as much as to belief—would bear the unique imprint of its moment ("Looking changes things," said the Heisenbergian lawyer). When Judd reflected on preparing a lecture for Yale University in 1983, he understood that it was the process of art—the looking and changing—that required discussion, rather than either the initial aims or the final results: "While writing this paper I suspected, and now realize, that what I was writing about was the process of making art, rather than about first or last principles, which should come later in a more modest form than usual.... The aestheticians are trying to draw conclusions from the process and its results, but to me the process is first and primary and in a way is the conclusion."[23]

Like Riley, Judd regarded the process as its own first principle; it justified itself in experience. To theorize art is merely to guess at principles, to hypothesize from a perspective that,

20 Riley, "The Pleasures of Sight" (1984), in Robert Kudielka, ed., *The Eye's Mind: Bridget Riley Collected Writings 1965–2009* (Ridinghouse: London, 2009), 34.

21 Riley, "The Artist's Eye: Seurat," *The Eye's Mind*, 272–73 (original emphasis).

22 Judd, in Catherine Millet, "La petite logique de Donald Judd" (interview; trans. Pascale Haas, English to French), *Art Press* 119 (November 1987): 7 (author's translation, French to English; no English original has been found).

23 Judd, "Art and Architecture," *Complete Writings 1975–1986*, 25.

rather than become rigidified in belief, should remain subject to doubt. A perspective changes with the next act of looking. Art can only be feeling; its reason is felt, not reasoned. Reaching for a suitable conclusion to his lecture, Judd set each of these matters of consideration—reason, feeling, guessing, art—into a single statement: "The function of 'reason' is [that] it estimates, understands and uses all that's known and felt, guessing sometimes, to finally help make a new kind of art." If Judd had a single aim or principle, it was to operate with "thought and feeling as one." He realized the need for this integration because he felt it. It ached, it hurt: "The division between thought and feeling is part of course of the Christian one of body and soul, an itch to be elsewhere being easier to promote than scratching at home. But when my soul aches my head hurts, so I think body and soul are right here, here and now. They are not going to leave one by one, but together for nowhere."[24] Joined in a work of art—in its making as well as in its appreciation—thought and feeling need go nowhere else.

24 Judd, "Art and Architecture," *Complete Writings 1975–1986*, 25–26, 36.

Sensuous Thoughts

[2014]

The two the same

His speech was pointed, his writing succinct, often terse. "I want a particular, definite object," Donald Judd declared in 1969, in the course of addressing the art of his friend Dan Flavin.[1] Judd was concerned to differentiate the production of objects from the production of phenomena—two approaches to art, each valid in its way. Arranging fluorescent tubes, Flavin created phenomena as volumes of chromatic light. To describe a volume of this type required more than naming its color or referring to a play of solids and voids: "There isn't any difference between the light and the color; it's one phenomenon," Judd wrote.[2] The effect distinguished Flavin's art from both painting and sculpture as generally known.

Working with metals and wood, Judd created volumes of his own, comparably problematic. They were at once in and of space. This, too, was unusual. As he explained later, in 1981, familiar objects, objects as we habitually perceive them, assume physical neutrality because they and their environment are deactivated: "They are points in space, and the space is an empty surround. Instead, what is needed is a created space, space made by someone, space that is formed as is a solid, the two the same, with the space and the solid defining each other."[3] Objects *in* and *of* space, *the two the same*: this was the crux. Judd did more than set new solids into existing voids. He formed solids and their correlative spaces as an integrated operation, as if he were establishing an architecture from the ground up, creating the entire environment, intensifying it, saturating it with its own sensation. This was his art.

Judd's various statements bore a broad implication: a sensory effect, however unstable, ought to remain fixed in the concatenation of materials, structure, and placement that generates it. Sensations are specific to their conditions. They are the lived equivalent of those conditions, experienced as continuous in time—hence, timeless—remaining wholly the same until interrupted. To the contrary, a sensation that drifts along in the meanders of cultural discourse disowns its physicality and moment. It ceases to be singular, becoming generic, distracted from itself, fragmented at its origin. It acquires many senses or meanings, none of them certain. For example, if we attach our experience of a particular color to a cultural discourse of beauty, we forfeit our full engagement with chromatic sensuousness. The effect reduces to an aspect or attribute of conceptualized beauty, a symbol, a marker of something other

1 Donald Judd, "Aspects of Flavin's Work" (1969), *Complete Writings 1959–1975* (Halifax: Nova Scotia College of Art and Design, 1975), 200. I thank Marianne Stockebrand, Caitlin Murray, Adrian Kohn, Rob Weiner, David Raskin, Jessamine Batario, Jason A. Goldstein, and D. J. McKetta for essential aid in research. For their continuing generosity in facilitating access to objects of art and primary documentation, I remain grateful to the Judd Foundation, Marfa and New York, and the Chinati Foundation, Marfa. I also acknowledge the contribution of the Pulitzer Foundation, St. Louis, sponsor in 2013 of an exhibition and scholar's meeting on Donald Judd's works in multicolored sheet aluminum.

2 Ibid., 200.

3 Donald Judd, "On Russian Art and Its Relation to My Work" (1981), *Complete Writings 1975–1986* (Eindhoven: Van Abbemuseum, 1987), 17 (punctuation added).

than itself. We confirm a certain genre of beauty, but no longer focus on the color in its aura.

In his statement of 1969, stressing specificity, Judd resorted to potentially redundant adjectives, alluding to an object not only "particular" but also "definite." Particularity refers to the unique quality of the experience; definiteness refers to its boundaries in space and time. A particular thing in a definite place yields a specific sensation. In 1981, with regard to his making "the two the same," Judd concluded: "Time and space don't exist [as idealized abstractions]; they are made by events and positions. Time and space can be made and don't have to be found like stars in the sky or rocks on a hillside."[4] Time and space are grounded in being human: they exist when someone experiences them.

The singularity of sensation as lived experience was the standard against which Judd evaluated his success in creating objects of living art, each newly born, each in its definite time and space. The capacity of objects to hold his attention amounted to their quotient of *interest*. "If you are interested in a thing it is interesting, and if you are not it is not. That isn't as obvious as it sounds."[5] In this statement of 1963, Judd referred to the interest offered by a work of art—or, alternatively, the interest projected by an artist and valorized or redeemed by an object. Either scenario would depend on a specific encounter between an artist-viewer and an object of art. Just as time needs a person to endure it and space needs a person to navigate it, a work needs to be seen or otherwise sensed in its material presence. Preferably, it would be viewed at a specific site with which it was coordinated, either within an architectural space or on the land—the site and the work, the two the same. In 1965, Judd observed that interest itself arrived whole and singular: "A work needs only to be interesting. Most works finally have one quality.... The thing as a whole, its quality as a whole, is what is interesting."[6] Like a musical composition that pervasively projects a single emotion, an object exhibiting multiple features might be sensed as "one quality." This would be the singularity that Judd identified as wholeness: an instance of the two (or the many) the same.

Division by theory

The decade of the 1980s proved extraordinarily productive for Judd. During this period, while occupying studios in West Texas as well as working at several European locations, he kept

[4] Ibid., 17.
[5] Judd, "In the Galleries: Jean Arp" (1963), *Complete Writings 1959–1975*, 92.
[6] Judd, "Specific Objects" (1964-65), *Complete Writings 1959–1975*, 184, 187.

his distance from the posturing of the New York art world and its internal bickering. Yet he found cause to complain. One of his targets was art criticism that set theory ahead of both the practice of hypothetical thought and the exercise of sensory observation. Sensation is not the cultural equal of either theory or interpretation. Acknowledging numerous associations, the interpretation of an object typically follows an established cultural route, generating interest beyond unadulterated sensation, interest of a different sort. The multiple abstractions that critics invoke to qualify and categorize an object—their strings of generalized concepts—risk overwhelming immediate experience, while never becoming its adequate substitute. When conceptual abstractions have been organized in advance as features of a theoretical system, the likelihood increases that they obscure the sensory feel of objects.

Seeing a color or a shape and naming it are incommensurable actions. "A rectangle is a shape itself; it is obviously the whole shape," Judd noted with characteristic bluntness.[7] He was unusual in perceiving the need to restate the most obvious of points, realizing that such notions were often dismissed as all too obvious and trivial, with their deeper implications remaining hidden. On the one hand, he stressed the self-fulfillment or reciprocity of the interest an individual takes in an object (this interest being specific to the situation of the particular viewer). On the other hand, he noted the singularity or compelling wholeness of interest itself, its capacity to fix a person's attention. Seeing a rectangle ("obviously the whole shape"), as opposed to naming it, reveals the obviousness to which Judd referred—the recognition of a certain existence. A rectangle is rectilinear; yes, it has right angles. But we ignore this general, theoretical definition when we *feel* the geometric form in its singularity, isolation, and actuality.[8] We often perceive right angles as other than 90 degrees. This is one of the lessons of Judd's works that consist of multiple volumetric units of equal dimensions: their placement dictates that only one among the several right-angled forms will appear "right." Judd believed that people should attend to what actually compels attention, the singular effect.

Yet, some would say: no entity exists outside a conceptual system; no existence is obvious; nothing stands alone; wholeness is mythical. Without the artifice of laws of perspective and other organizational devices—combinations of science and ideology—we would fail to explain both regularities and

[7] Ibid., 181–82.

[8] Compare Ernst Cassirer's distinction between immediate sensation and the cultural discourse: "The aim of theoretical thinking ... is primarily to deliver the contents of sensory or intuitive experience from the isolation in which they originally occur. It causes these contents to transcend their narrow limits, combines them with others, compares them, and concatenates them in a definite order, in an all-inclusive context. It proceeds 'discursively,' in that it treats the immediate content only as a point of departure ... In this system there are no more isolated points"; Ernst Cassirer, *Language and Myth*, trans. Susanne K. Langer (New York: Dover, 1953 [orig. German ed., 1925]), 32.

anomalies in what we see. Every position would remain an isolated point, unrelated to others, hence meaningless. Life itself is conflicted and fragmented, and each individual speaks with many voices, from many positions in a social network. During the 1960s, Judd perceived that theoretical generalizations of this sort—however reasonably intentioned and formulated to debunk other, competing theories—were being pushed too far. They were threatening the specific sensory values of art. A thought process directed by a bias toward multiplicity was no less pernicious than one directed by a bias toward totalization; both imposed limits, set according to select preconditions. Judd insisted: "I want a particular, definite object." He sought sensation, not a prescriptive theory of sensation.

By Judd's understanding of critical practice among his contemporaries, the problem became all the more aggravated subsequent to the 1960s. Just as sensation suffered depersonalization, just as aesthetic experience lost its presumed "aesthetic integrity," so did thought itself become unanchored, given the prevalence of challenges to traditional notions of authorship.[9] Judd's "the two the same"—despite its maintenance of duality—was facing the well-argued position that might be expressed as "no redeeming wholeness, only difference."[10] Sacred entities became targets of division: Self, Truth, Word, Being, One. Judd could have his "two" but not his "one," not his "same."

Perhaps most troubling, theorists reasoned that because thinking finds expression in a communal language, the thoughts of individuals are not their own. The self, if there is one, must differ from itself because it thinks in alien terms. It thinks as another, with the very structure of the language forcing this realization on those willing to confront it.[11] More is entailed. If the collective culture has a history, here too an alien language actively shapes it. In theory, language escapes the possession of its writers and even its live speakers. Such notions posit linguistic codes as historical agents. Those who author statements become mere vehicles, passive conductors of semiotic energy already in circulation.[12] The theorist is left in the position of introducing resistance to existing lines of cultural transmission that will remain anyway. Critical theory of the second half of the twentieth century was relegating its theorist to functioning as still another feature of the system, only more self-aware and less easy about this situation than others were.

9 On probing the cultural refuge of "aesthetic integrity," see Paul de Man, "Sign and Symbol in Hegel's *Aesthetics*" (1982), *Aesthetic Ideology*, ed. Andrzej Warminski (Minneapolis: University of Minnesota Press, 1996), 92.

10 "We provisionally give the name *differance* [sic] to this *sameness* which is not *identical*: by the silent writing of its *a*, it has the desired advantage of referring to differing, *both* as spacing/temporalizing and as the movement that structures every dissociation": Jacques Derrida, "Differance" (1968), *Speech and Phenomena and Other Essays on Husserl's Theory of Signs*, ed. and trans. David B. Allison (Evanston: Northwestern University Press, 1973), 129-30 (emphasis original).

11 See de Man, "Sign and Symbol in Hegel's *Aesthetics*," *Aesthetic Ideology*, 98.

12 For a sophisticated form of the argument (more than a mere reversal of roles), with the authority of speech displaced by the play of graphematic writing, see Jacques Derrida, "Signature Event Context" (1971), *Margins of Philosophy*, ed. and trans. Alan Bass (Chicago: University of Chicago Press, 1982), 307–30.

The critical trend that annoyed Judd developed in part within an area of literary study where resistance had a chance of being effective. Critics were challenging the long-standing practice of interpreting texts biographically and psychoanalytically. Such interpretation attended to the creator far more than to the thing created. Roland Barthes's celebrated essay of 1968, "The Death of the Author," was, at its core, hardly antithetical to Judd's interests, both intellectual and aesthetic. It preserved his concern for the sensory immediacy of a "particular, definite object." "It is language which speaks, not the author," Barthes claimed: "To write is ... to reach that point where only language acts [and] every text is eternally written *here and now*."[13] The reader's present reading would determine the meaning. Analogous to Barthes, Judd discouraged viewers of his art from concluding that every fact related to him, as the creator of the object, must be germane to its significance. The primary meaning of a work lay in the sensory experience it afforded—the "here and now" of the object, as opposed to the past history of its creator, the circumstances of its creation, and the cultural connotations of its forms and materials.

Especially in the United States, critics pursued to extremes the theoretical notion of the "death of the author." The expanded concept verged on absurdity, becoming more of an indicator of an ideological position than a pragmatic realization. Any sign of the agency of an artist, such as a painter's mark of the brush, whether associated with a particular individual or not, became an aggressive arrogation of authority, "confirm[ing] the hieratics of ideological domination" (as an influential critic claimed in 1981, the year of Judd's "the two the same").[14] Arguments of this kind allowed the arbitrary symbolic associations of common artistic methods to obliterate the practicality of their technological function. As acknowledged cultural markers subject to interpretation, the humble brush stroke and the calligraphic paraph had come a long way, perhaps too far. Certain types of marks may have signaled the active hand of the artist, but they also served a pragmatic function in allowing the artist to work quickly. The two aspects of the one method should not be divided. Imagine viewing a certain typeface as a coded reference to utopian modernity or mass industry, without also recognizing that it had been developed for ease of reading by the semi-literate. One generation's pragmatic motivation can morph into another generation's symbolic reference. In the case of the brush stroke—and more

[13] Roland Barthes, "The Death of the Author" (1968), *Image – Music – Text*, trans. Stephen Heath (New York: Hill and Wang, 1977), 143, 145 (emphasis original). Michel Foucault ("What Is an Author?" [1969], trans. Josué V. Harari, in Paul Rabinow, ed., *The Foucault Reader* [New York: Pantheon Books, 1984], 119) writes of the disappearance of the "author function" in a tempered manner, similar to Barthes: "We would no longer hear the questions that have been rehashed for so long: Who really spoke? ... With what authenticity or originality?" Compare also the fundamental point, often argued during Judd's lifetime, that the mode of representation, not the individual who deploys it, establishes the potential for meaning: "Instead of containing or reflecting experience, language constitutes it"; Paul de Man, "The Dead-End of Formalist Criticism" (1956), trans. Wlad Godzich, *Blindness and Insight* (Minneapolis: University of Minnesota Press, 1983), 231.

[14] Benjamin Buchloh, "Figures of Authority, Ciphers of Regression: Notes on the Return of Representation in European Painting" (1981), in Brian Wallis, ed., *Art After Modernism: Rethinking Representation* (New York: The New Museum of Contemporary Art, 1984), 124.

generally, any hand-oriented process—the critical commentary of the 1970s and 1980s often sundered the pragmatic from the symbolic, as if mutually exclusive concerns. At one ideological extreme was the belief that every genuine art-mark, like a sincere poetic utterance, is inherently original, an organically expressive occurrence. At the other ideological extreme was the belief that art-marks can be no more individual and original than reiterative statements formed within a communal discourse. In the first instance, the brush stroke is expressively liberating. In the second instance, it instills an illusory faith in acts of individual freedom; it furthers self-deception.

The two extremes faced off in a rhetorical fog that masked what Judd considered empirical experience. Among the originality-deniers, some advocated a radical corrective measure: "to deconstruct the Modernist claim to originality and authorship by ... appropriating someone else's work."[15] Here, the use of the upper-case *M* is revealing: the art of the recent past, the "modern" period, had become "Modernist," as if determined by ideology (symbolic value) rather than experience (pragmatic value). We may not be able to adjudicate whether ideology precedes experience or the reverse or even whether the question of precedence has validity; but to take a side, to assume that ideology does take precedence, is a self-confirming ideological position. As a critical strategy and a deconstructive gesture (though hardly a deconstruction of anything), artists of the 1980s were replicating existing imagery to demonstrate the theoretical point that every image amounts to a replication of some other. The logic of such illustration takes a potentially profound philosophical argument over the nature of language, valid in its way, and reduces it to trivial circularity. An allied move was to develop ironic pictorial allegories, as reflected in a statement from an artist prominent during the late 1980s: "The first paintings I did [were] of brick walls ... They were about the spiritual space of abstract expressionism being walled up."[16] Judd regarded strategies of this ilk as cases of parasitism: "Art that was made to be direct is pilfered for art that is made to be indirect. This watered down referential art is the academic art of this century."[17] Despite Judd's strong political beliefs that informed his attitude toward American society, ideological assertion ran counter to his aesthetic practice.[18] To liberate sensation—which, by his reasoning, constituted a political good—Judd eliminated from his fabricated objects as many conceivable ideological references as he could detect.

15 Hans-Ulrich Obrist, statement in Gerhard Richter, "Interview with Hans-Ulrich Obrist, 1993," *The Daily Practice of Painting*, ed. Hans-Ulrich Obrist, trans. David Britt (Cambridge, MA: MIT Press, 1995), 254.

16 Peter Halley, as interviewed by Trevor Fairbrother, in David A. Ross and Jürgen Harten, *The Binational* (Boston: The Institute of Contemporary Art and Museum of Fine Arts, 1988), 95.

17 Judd, "A Long Discussion Not About Master-pieces But Why There Are So Few of Them, Part I" (1984), *Complete Writings 1975–1986*, 59.

18 On Judd's politics, see David Raskin, *Donald Judd* (New Haven: Yale University Press, 2010), 87-111.

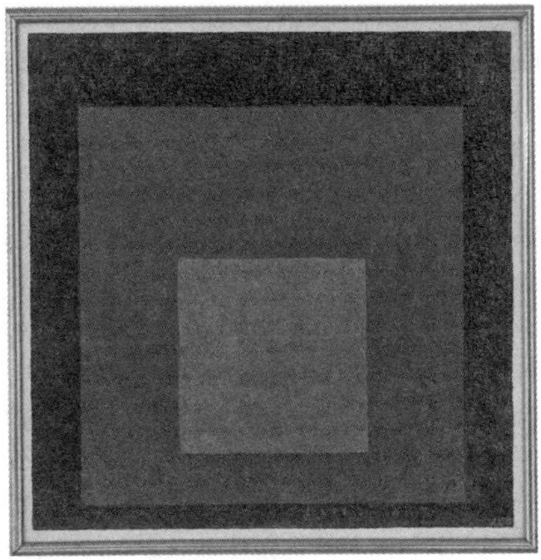

61
Josef Albers
Homage to the Square, 1958
Oil on Masonite
18 × 18 inches
(45.7 × 45.7 cm)

Principles were to be inferred from experience, not argued by illustrating them.

Did the critics' division between originality-dreamers and originality-deniers reflect the range of art actually being produced from the 1960s through the 1980s? Were so-called modernist artists exercising material claims to absolute originality by means of an authorial touch? If some were, Judd was not: "None of the three-dimensional work is meant to look handmade, including the wooden ones [from 1962 to 1964] which I made in as matter-of-fact a way as I could."[19] In matter-of-factness, he was hardly alone. Artists as diverse as Frank Stella, Bridget Riley, Robert Mangold, and Richard Serra eliminated personalized marks of the hand from their works without yielding their concern for individual inventiveness.[20] They found such marks either irrelevant to their purpose or an outright distraction. Before Judd and his contemporaries, there was Josef Albers, who spread oil paint by knife on Masonite panels in a "matter-of-fact" manner (Judd's characterization) [fig. 61]. Albers's paint quality looked "somewhat like the application in [Kasimir] Malevich's paintings."[21] So, before Albers, as Judd discovered, there was already Malevich, who avoided the fetish of precisely honed edges as much as overtly gestural strokes: "The priority of thought and the matter-of-fact execution are part of the nature of these paintings."[22] Judd described Malevich as if impatient to get the job done—a degree of precision in handling could be sacrificed.

For the most part, Judd's critical analysis of artists whom others categorized as "Modernist" ignored the factor of

[19] Judd, in John Coplans, "An Interview with Don Judd," *Artforum* 9 (June 1971): 45.
[20] On this issue, see Richard Shiff, "To Risk Not Naming," in John C. Welchman, ed., *The Aesthetics of Risk* (Los Angeles: JRP Ringier, 2008), 246–70.
[21] Donald Judd, "Josef Albers," *Josef Albers* (Cologne: Distel-Verlag, 1991), 14.
[22] Judd, "Malevich: Independent Form, Color, Surface" (1974), *Complete Writings 1975–1986*, 212.

expressive gesture and its presumed originality. These connotative qualities were not his interest. Instead, he concentrated on the material features that would account—in a practical, technical way—for the sensation he perceived. It hardly mattered whether the materiality had been fully controlled in detail or not. Judd noted the holistic perception, as opposed to speculating on its possible interpretive meanings for him or for others: "The dripped paint in most of [Jackson] Pollock's paintings is dripped paint. It's that sensation, completely immediate and specific, and nothing modifies it."[23] It was "free" in the sense of being free of the pictorial values of flatness and the "all-over" that would interest critics as diverse as Clement Greenberg and Michael Fried, just as it was independent of the symbolic values of freedom and self-expression to which critics as diverse as Harold Rosenberg and Meyer Schapiro alluded, much to the exclusion of sensation.

When Judd asserted proprietary rights to a type of object, he never suggested that precedents were inconceivable. Nor was he claiming his authorship as culturally authoritative.[24] In 1975, an interviewer asked him: "How important is it for an artist to invent something?" His reply: "It's very important, but it isn't so much to be first." He distanced invention from absolute priority and originality, and continued: "In order to do something clearly and strongly, you pretty much have to invent it. Otherwise you're not going to know what it means." Judd's sense of meaning would not be found in the referential play of an object within the cultural system, over which an artist exercises no final control (for example, the connotation of industrial efficiency or engineering that arises from the use of industrial metals). Instead, the effect that an object designed by Judd has on him—even if solely on him—becomes its meaning: "I'm the only person who knows what all those things I'm interested in really mean."[25] He was learning from experience; and his interest, and hence his meaning, was not predetermined in intention, but was in flux.[26] We imagine him reminding us that this was not as obvious a point as we might think.

Judd aimed to establish the objects he constructed within the experience of a new generation, *his* generation. If meaning was to be communicated, its natural recipient was contemporary society. In 1987, he stated his commitment to contemporaneity: "I think that art should concern itself with the present (and not necessarily to go forward, because I don't

[23] Judd, "Jackson Pollock" (1957), *Complete Writings 1975–1986*, 195.

[24] Critics who insist on linking authorship to cultural authority, or expression to self-expressiveness, take semantic shortcuts: the connections can be asserted in theory, but the terms do not entail them.

[25] Phyllis Tuchman, "An Interview with Donald Judd" (1975), *Chinati Foundation Newsletter* 12 (2007): 55.

[26] "No matter what the field of view *means*, [an artist] sees it also as it *feels*," distinguishing the general cultural meaning from the immediate, situational meaning: William James, *The Principles of Psychology* (Cambridge MA: Harvard University Press, 1981 [1890]), 874 (emphasis original).

believe in progress, but simply change)."[27] In an early review of Albers's comprehensive study of color, he had remarked: "The plain fact of color in art, the specific use of effects [or color] in art [is] contemporary ... Color can be expected to be very different in twenty years or so."[28] With his "contemporary" color, Albers may have been the best for his time, but not for all time. Color would change because experience changes with the generation. Twenty years beyond Judd's assessment of Albers's theory would take him to 1983, when he was becoming increasingly involved with work in multicolored enameled aluminum. "The motive to change," he had noted in 1965, quoting an empiricist source, "is always some uneasiness."[29]

Through the decades of Judd's career, an unchanging fact of experience persisted, uneasily: the most compelling theoretical arguments fail to accord with the pragmatics of living. Theory relates to practice as the definition of a rectangle relates to an actual rectangle: it cannot predict how the rectangle will be perceived except for viewers who allow definitions to limit perception. Is there good cause to set such limits? No, but yes. Granted, experiential generalities fail to correspond to specifics; yet societies cannot survive without entertaining the fiction that correspondence usually occurs. Take, for example, the collective investment in a general legal system, designed to cover all specific cases; individuals struggle to fit each disputed event into a format envisioned in the array of legal categories. In art, however, the situation is different. Artists need not engage in arbitration, quite the contrary. "Finally, I only believe my own work," Judd admitted in 1965: "It is necessary to make general statements, but it is impossible and not even desirable to believe most generalizations."[30] In his later comments about meaning ("I'm the only person ..."), he was saying much the same thing: allow meaning to be contingent on experience. He was an anarchist and something of a libertarian, though a very rational one, willing to compromise for the social good.

Like unforced errors among the cultural elite, instances of unnecessary submission to critical generalization plagued Judd throughout his career. "One of the many destructive assumptions now," he wrote in 1993, several months before his death, "is that all ideas have no originators; they are mutations in the public domain. The use and meaning of the ideas are vague. But someone invents ideas."[31] His reasoning requires expansion: both the "use and meaning" of an idea, process, or object are subject to cultural negotiation, which might include

27 Judd, in Catherine Millet, "La petite logique de Donald Judd" (interview; trans. Pascale Haas, English to French), *Art Press* 119 (November 1987): 7 (author's translation, French to English; no English original has been found).

28 Judd, "Books: *Interaction of Color* by Josef Albers" (1963), *Complete Writings 1959–1975*, 102.

29 Judd, "Specific Objects," *Complete Writings 1959–1975*, 181. The source is John Locke, *An Essay Concerning Human Understanding*; for the identification, see David Raskin, "Judd's Moral Art," in Nicholas Serota, ed., *Donald Judd* (London: Tate Publishing, 2004), 92 n72.

30 Judd, "Statement which appeared in 'ABC Art' by Barbara Rose" (1965), *Complete Writings 1959–1975*, 181.

31 Judd, "Some Aspects of Color in General and Red and Black in Particular" (1993), in Serota, *Donald Judd*, 148–49. For the argument against Judd's sense of invention, disassociating specific practices and images from individual artists, with the case made in terms of the "fracturing of the empirical origin ... the modernist origin," see Rosalind E. Krauss, "The Originality of the Avant-Garde" (1981), *The Originality of the Avant-Garde and Other Modernist Myths* (Cambridge MA: MIT Press, 1985), 168, 170.

appropriation and other socially recognizable actions. With all the cultural mediation, use and meaning remain ill-formed and in flux, and properly so—"vague," as Judd says, packed with the interpretive nuances, the vagaries, that Barthes and other sophisticated critics enjoyed pursuing. This degree of indeterminacy is to be expected; it is the vagueness that accompanies generality. But the artist-author experiences an act of invention as an intimate, immediate fact. The individual *feels* invention as fact, conscious of his or her realization, whether the creative thinking is singular within all history, or merely unique within the particular culture, or, perhaps more likely, neither. Invention, this flash of intuition, is analogous to having a sensation. It happens "here and now"—to invoke phrasing that Barthes and Judd could share, the two the same.

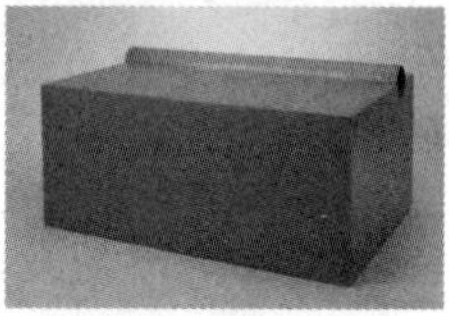

42 see page 269

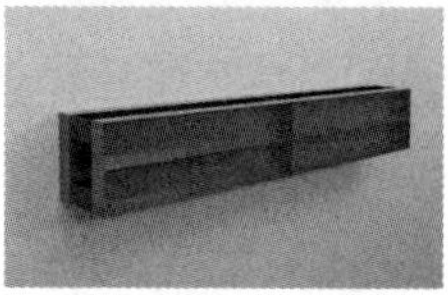

17 see page 259

Seeing red

Red is a sensation. It happens—here and now. Judd's red might be the red of a surface of wood, painted with oils [See fig. 42]. It might be the red of a surface of enameled sheet aluminum [See fig. 17]. But it cannot be the red of anger. When we sense the red of a surface, the experience is direct and constitutes an emotion in itself. To sense is to be in an emotional state.[32] The other type of red—red as in "he saw red," the metaphorical understanding of color—exists outside of sensation as an indirect linguistic production of a *category* of emotion. "As a child," Judd recalled, introducing multiple ironies, "I didn't understand why a bull should be mad at red."[33] Why would red intend or cause harm? Why would it engage in mischief, provoking anger? Judd recognized that the generality of thoughts about bulls, as well as imputations of anger, can be associated no more than circumstantially with the look of red.

From the 1960s to the 1990s, Judd articulated his pragmatic attitude in lectures, interviews, and essays, readily elaborating on matters he believed likely to be misunderstood. He was consistent. His later explanations fit what he established in earlier exchanges. He never attempted to play to shifts in the art-world audience; he remained faithful to what he knew from direct experience, from his sensations and the thoughts that accompanied them. He desired others to be as open to experience as he; but from experience itself, he knew that most others were not. They assessed experience with readymade concepts, an intellectual structure of prejudgment leading to a misdirected sense of loss. Whatever was new failed by the standard of the

32 "A purely disembodied human emotion is a nonentity": James, *The Principles of Psychology*, 1068.

33 Judd, "Some Aspects of Color in General and Red and Black in Particular," *Donald Judd*, 150.

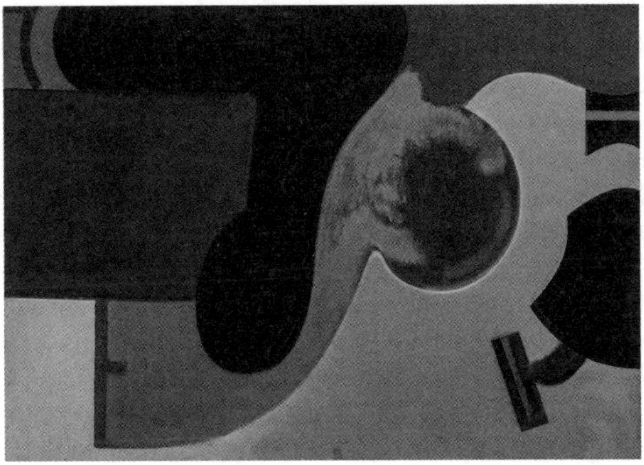

62
Donald Judd
Untitled, 1958
Oil on canvas
30 × 36 inches
(76.2 × 91.4 cm)

old: "If changes in art are compared backwards, there always seems to be a reduction, since only old attributes are counted and these are always fewer."[34] An old attribute fell into a category; a new one fell into a void. Judd's commitment to change entailed others regarding him as an agent of cultural loss. One of his best retorts came late, in the midst of commentary on Albers: "The sand on the beach is not chaotic. To call it so is to lament a kind of order which never existed anyway."[35] Sand is specific, just the way sand is: sand-like, sandy.

Judd began as a painter and retained his respect for the discipline itself, as opposed to the bulk of its contemporary products. Like manifestations of unintended surrealism, most paintings entered the realm of dreams and fictions, creating pseudo-realities beyond their material limits. Instead of a "particular, definite object," the typical painting became a referential sign or go-between, present to evoke a concept. Such painting is closer to chaos than to sand, because chaos is an abstract concept—sometimes even upper-case, like "Modernism"—whereas sand is just material. "Landscape," as a named concept, arose from abstract painting as readily as it developed within overtly representational modes. Pictorial landscape did not evoke actual land as it existed, but the dream of its atmospheric harmony. In an interview of 1976, Judd explained that painting had long ceased to serve his expressive needs.[36] Despite his effort to break the "landscape" hold on the medium, his images of the late 1950s remained landscape-like, with chromatic contrasts gradually mitigated by the affinity of one tone for another, say, muted greens relating to muted blues [fig. 62].[37]

34 Judd, "Specific Objects," *Complete Writings 1959–1975*, 189.
35 Judd, "Josef Albers," *Josef Albers*, 16.
36 Judd, in Tuchman, "An Interview with Donald Judd," 54.
37 On Judd's practice as a painter, compare Thomas Kellein, "The Whole Space: The Early Work of Donald Judd," *Donald Judd: Early Work 1955–1968*, trans. Fiona Elliott (Bielefeld: Kunsthalle Bielefeld, 2002), 21–29.

Certain of the colors within Judd's paintings of this time retained a sense of mutual opposition, but the majority of the colors merged and blended according to their similarity in hue and value. Judd achieved wholeness or integration in his early painting practice, but it came at the expense of the independent identities of the constituent elements. In this case, if "the two [became] the same," there were no longer two to distinguish. "Landscape" was the "one," an integrated image—a "one" that excludes the sense of a "two" rather than including it. An exception would be the paintings of the early 1960s, which usually set a single form or motif against a solid ground, such as a curving white line bordered by a field of deep blue [fig. 63]. A format of this kind allowed Judd to retain the independent character of the elements within an arrangement direct enough to appear whole. He had his "one," while he retained his "two." This is an instance of what Judd called "polarity," a variant of "the two the same" (to be addressed in a section to follow, "Twos"). White set against blue, a curving line opposed to a planar field—all the elements and qualities separate, yet constituting a unity. As a means of stressing contrast or polarity within his paintings of around 1960, Judd introduced differences of texture and elements set into low relief. Such oppositions, tactile as well as visual, anticipated the artist's turn to work in three dimensions, where polarities would seem to arise quite naturally (inside/outside, front/back, solid/void).

Why, in the broadest terms, does conventional painting so readily evoke landscape? A painting is physically nearly flat—as a material object, unassertive. When Judd added a degree of relief to the planarity, he enhanced by a corresponding degree the assertiveness to the medium. Still, canvas and panel paintings lack volume. Given this limitation (so Judd believed), even an abstract painting, through the interaction of its diverse colors, opens vision to an illusory realm because the object itself projects no actual space. We live in space and obey a spatial imperative, impelled to perceive spatial qualities even where they do not exist. A fantasy of space, a "landscape" composed of faded colors blending together as atmosphere, emerges from a passive canvas surface. Judd's practice of painting had been restricted by this unwanted effect, linked to the suppression of colors at their chromatic peak. Toning down the color—graying it—was the habitual way of introducing allusions to nature through painting: "If you fool around with a

63
Donald Judd
Untitled, 1961
Acrylic on canvas
67½ × 48½ inches
(171.45 × 123.19 cm)

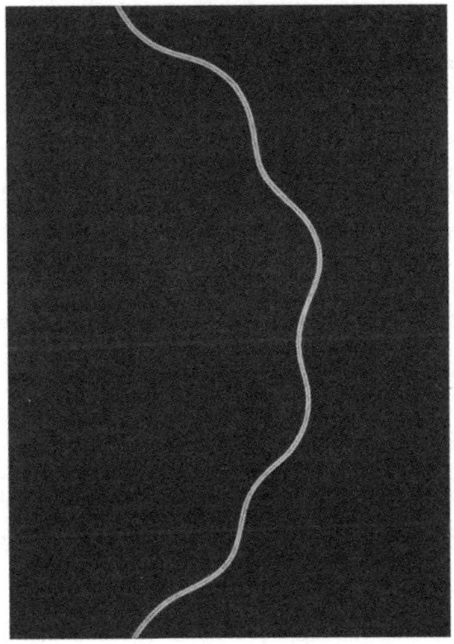

landscape scheme that's old-fashioned, gray is the color. You can't make very bright colors if there is any kind of realism in it ... After a certain point, I was certainly interested in abstraction, but it was still based on landscape."[38]

Later, Judd explained his reluctance to accept abstraction as a constructive move, having realized that the concept itself was troublesome. "I don't use the word *abstract*. I don't see how something can be more or less abstract. In general, I'm interested in making something in itself, not something abstract, something else."[39] To expand on Judd's rather compressed statement: he opposes "something in itself" to "something abstract" because abstraction converts the thing itself into a second thing that refers to the first; in this sense, an abstraction is always "something else" or "something other," something like but other than itself (in the words of the French interpreter for a bilingual publication, *quelque chose d'autre*). An abstraction becomes a referential term that divides an immediate sensation (the redness you may feel yourself feeling) into a set of interpretive propositions (a choice of associations you might consider with regard to such redness). Abstraction splits a feeling into semblances. To the contrary, as one of Judd's philosophical beacons, C. S. Peirce, had stated: "There is no resemblance at all in feeling, since feeling is whatever it is, positively and regardless of anything else, while the resemblance of anything lies in the comparison of that thing with something else."[40] Resemblance is not the meaning but a metaphoric drag on meaning.

38 Judd, in Tuchman, "An Interview with Donald Judd," 54.
39 Judd, in Millet, "La petite logique de Donald Judd," 7 (author's translation).
40 Charles Sanders Peirce, "A Definition of Feeling" (1907), *Collected Papers*, ed. Charles Hartshorne, Paul Weiss, and Arthur W. Burks, 8 vols. (Cambridge, MA: Harvard University Press, 1958–1960), 1:155.

Judd's colors are not abstract; they remain themselves rather than becoming abstractions of something else. He conceived of abstract form as the result of a process of abstraction, which amounts to a movement away from an object or a phenomenon, toward a different quality of experience. The verb *to abstract* ought to take the preposition *to* as well as the preposition *from*. If an artist were to abstract *from* a specific red *to* a general concept of redness, or *from* a set of blues and greens *to* a general concept of landscape, Judd would hardly approve.

Multiplicity all at once

In Pollock and a few others, Judd perceived an alternative mode of painting, which had little to do with abstraction even though critics classified this art within that category: "The various colors ... are more discrete than they are in most paintings, in which they are within a range or relate to an identifiable scheme. Most paintings seem harmonious in comparison."[41] Another past exception was Malevich, whose direct application of color within geometric shapes did not require a theory of abstraction to motivate it. The example of Malevich caused Judd to realize that the landscapes of Paul Cézanne, as bright as they might appear, were "grayed": "This is a real complaint of the present against the past even though the past has to be considered as itself." As an artist of the past, Cézanne was exceptional; but, for Judd at least, his glory faded in the present: "Twenty years ago [c. 1954] I liked Cézanne's paintings a great deal, and still do finally. But [now I] look through the grayed color and wonder what it would be like not gray."[42] It would be like the color Judd developed, would it not?

To keep color "discrete"—diverse yet distinct, as in Pollock or an improved version of Cézanne—to avoid generalized harmonies, atmospheric grayness, and allusions to landscape, Judd conceived of moving the surface color of his paintings into actual space. It was a way of extending the medium. Having exhausted what he believed painting in the flat might do, he turned from attaching canvases to walls, instead attaching volumetric objects to walls. As long as the objects projected abruptly from their ground, they would never be confused with painting, landscape or otherwise. This type of construction constituted a "particular, definite object." Judd could color it as red as he wished, no graying necessary.

During the final decade of his career, Judd introduced an unusually extensive chromatic range while avoiding any hint of

41 Judd, "Jackson Pollock," *Complete Writings 1975–1986*, 195.

42 Judd, "Malevich: Independent Form, Color, Surface," *Complete Writings 1975–1986*, 212.

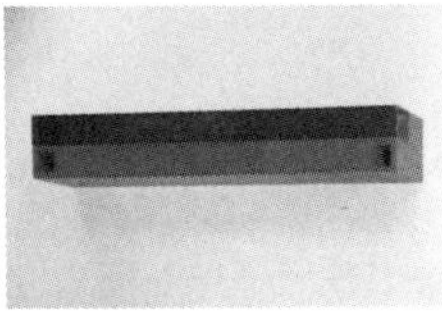

43 see page 270

conventional harmony.[43] Many of his works were comprised of elements of enameled sheet aluminum, each a specific color. He wanted to maintain the integrity of each hue, holding to a principle he established for all of his work in three dimensions: "Color is always identical with a single surface."[44] To this end, he devised a basic structural unit resembling a recessed pan. The widths of this element varied, but not its essential form, determined by folding four sides at right angles to the open interior. The ratio of height to depth remained constant at 2:1 (for example, a height of 15 cm would entail a depth of 7.5 cm; for the general configuration). Because the bent side planes reflect the color of each unit back on itself, the chromatic independence of each structural element intensifies. "I wanted all of the [distinct] colors to be present at once [as distinct]. I didn't want them to combine. I wanted a multiplicity all at once that I had not known before."[45]

When asked in 1987 why he had begun to "multiply the color," using many combinations instead of few, Judd replied with candor rather than color theory: "Maybe it's the fact of being a painter! Or the fact that I really like color!"[46] With his three-dimensional work, which he hesitated to call "sculpture," he was reinventing painting. Its individual colors—as well as their combinations—remained blatant and obvious. His combinations of hues appeared in simple juxtaposition; they neither dissolved into harmonious hierarchies, nor fell into a system of perspective, nor faded into atmosphere. "The century's development of color," Judd wrote in 1993, "could continue no further on a flat surface.... Someday, not soon, there will be another kind of painting, far from the easel, [also] far from beyond the easel, since our environment indoors is four walls, usually flat. Color to continue had to occur in space."[47] As he wrote this statement, he had already provided much of the continuity. He was building with color in space.[48]

Through trial and error, in 1963 Judd arrived at a working principle: the projection of an object from its ground—that is, its depth to the wall—should be at least as much as its height [see fig. 43]. If a box-like construction has a certain height, its projection outward should extend this far or more.[49] A second height, the height for hanging, also became critical. "There really is a standard height," Judd said in 1976: "People don't seem to know this. I would think it would be common knowledge." Why "common knowledge"? Because everyone, living within his or her body, ought to have made the relevant

43 "I especially didn't want the combinations to be harmonious": Judd, "Some Aspects of Color in General and Red and Black in Particular," *Donald Judd*, 158.

44 Judd, in Coplans, "An Interview with Don Judd," 50.

45 Judd, "Some Aspects of Color in General and Red and Black in Particular," *Donald Judd*, 158.

46 Judd, in Millet, "La petite logique de Donald Judd," 7 (author's translation).

47 Judd, "Some Aspects of Color in General and Red and Black in Particular," *Donald Judd*, 157. See also William C. Agee, "Donald Judd and the Endless Possibilities of Color," *Donald Judd: Colorist*, ed. Dietmar Elger (Ostfildern-Ruit: Hatje Cantz, 2000), 47: "[Judd] created what amount to volumes of pure color by bolting together recessed sections of varying lengths of painted sheet aluminum. In these he would work like a true painter, opening color up in ways not previously possible."

48 The same can be said of Flavin, whose materials and methods were quite different. The two artists had good cause to appreciate each other's work, as they did.

49 For more on this issue, see Richard Shiff in this volume, "What Judd Knows."

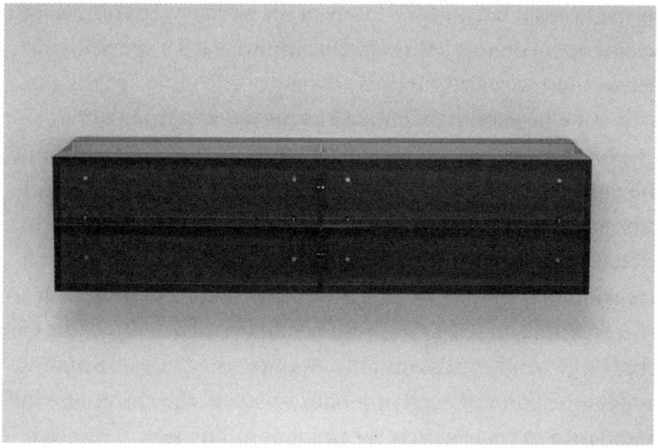

64
Donald Judd
Untitled, 1989
Painted aluminum
30 × 120 × 30 cm
(11¾ × 47¼ × 11¾ inches)

observation from experience. “The idea is to see a little bit of the top” – for Judd, a height of 62 or 63 inches suited—“because if [the object] is dead on, you can’t see either the top or the bottom and it flattens out.... If you can’t see the top, it really turns into a little bit of painting rather than a three-dimensional thing.”[50] In certain cases, only by viewing the top, side, or bottom of the projecting object would a second color appear in opposition to a first [fig. 64]. What a viewer saw had to be worth the investment of the eye—not convention-bound, shopworn painting but the planes of a substantial volume, beyond a composition of evanescent edges. This was volume with the specificity of red, or any other distinct hue, or some combination of hues in opposition—space with a presence as obvious as that of the most assertive color.

Judd had gathered this understanding from experience, from the feel of his sensation and the feel of his intuitive thought. He praised a number of artists of his generation, such as Claes Oldenburg and John Chamberlain, for having created objects unlike his own yet “absolutely thought through.”[51] These were artists in whom he perceived the process of feeling and the process of thinking as one. Sensation and thought: the two the same.

Lock / look

One of Judd’s exchanges—with Angeli Janhsen at Ruhr-Universität Bochum, Germany, in 1990—introduces to the historical record a potential misunderstanding of a kind the artist took pains to eliminate. It appears because of an error in converting the typed transcription of their discussion to the

50 First sentence: Judd, in Tuchman, “An Interview with Donald Judd,” 56–57. Second sentence: Donald Judd, Baldwin Seminar (audio recording), Oberlin College, 21 February 1976, Oberlin College Archives, Oberlin, Ohio. Compare Judd, “Some Aspects of Color in General and Red and Black in Particular,” *Donald Judd*, 149–50: “Low and high relief are basically painting ... The necessary difference was that the work not be flattened, low or high, to the wall [like a landscape projection], whether it be small or large.”

51 Judd, interview by Todd Eberle, “Der Eigensinnliche,” *Vogue* (German ed.), February 1994, 250 (author’s translation; text courtesy Adrian Kohn).

printed page, which occurred after Judd had already edited his words. Janhsen asked him whether he believed "that a circle or a proportion in itself is meaningful." To paraphrase: Can a form, such as a circle, or a relationship, such as a proportion, convey meaning on its own? Judd replied with a third consideration, linking the generalities of geometric form and mathematical proportion to the experience of a specific work as a whole, excluding any interest outside the work: "The circles, taken as part of the whole work of art, the circles or the square or whatever, is meaningful, but referring to the circle somewhere else or the square somewhere else is meaningless. I am not interested in the history of the circle, the cultural situation of the circle, the archetype of the circle."[52]

"Not interested": at a stroke, history, culture, and myth have been dismissed from Judd's aesthetic practice. Precisely where "meaning" ended for him—at the border of sensation and reference—it began for most others. He attended to immediate sensation, while others traced the residue of such sensation as it passed through the cultural language, acquiring sufficient generality to spawn numerous lines of critical inquiry. Back in 1970, Judd would have given virtually the same reply to Janhsen's question (no history, no culture, no myth), but the context of 1990 rendered his position all the more resistant to prevailing fashion, and perhaps poignant for its implications, both intellectual and aesthetic. He had just endured the 1980s, with its critical hype over postmodernism in art and architecture. Geometric and organic forms, both abstract and representational, had been commandeered for the cultural associations they might convey. Architects were developing a use of circles, squares, and classical proportions not to make space but to allude to historical prototypes. The circle had become symbolic rather than symmetrical and round. Abandoning its material presence, it passed beyond its own circumference into a cloud of cultural reference.

Janhsen followed Judd's remark about "meaning" by focusing on the appearance of proportion and arithmetic sequence in his so-called progressions. These were horizontal constructions to be placed on a wall, in which solid forms might follow a set of measures left to right, interspersed with voids following the same set, but right to left: "Someone could say that a proportion like 2:4 / 4:8 / 8:16, referring to solids, and 16:8 / 8:4 / 4:2, referring to the space between the solids, is a progression, which could show some kind of time or infinity." Judd

52 Judd, in Angeli Janhsen, "Discussion with Donald Judd," *Donald Judd*, ed. Roland Wäspe (St. Gallen: Kunstverein St. Gallen, 1990), 51–52.

responded to this introduction of time as an issue: "Time is interesting. It's a factor in the work of course, but it wouldn't be that literal. It is more visual. It is to lock the two directions together" [see fig. 2].[53] Is it too literal to associate a mathematical sequence with the passage or measure of time? It seems so, because this would render time as an abstraction, as opposed to a quality of life. Instead, Judd removes the directional sense of the numerical progression; he refers to locking the intersecting sequences together so their dual visual effect becomes single, a whole—two directions as one, the two the same (but polar opposites).

Here the typographical error appears: *look* is substituted for *lock*. A single cipher creates the difference. The published text quotes Judd this way: "It [the structural effect of a 'progression'] is more visual; it's to look the two directions together."[54] The grammatical play is curious. If *look* were the actual verb, we would expect the preposition *at* to follow, firmly associating the act of looking with its object. Lacking the preposition and hence a proper object, we sense that the looking is itself directional but without a target, that Judd's object induces its viewer to look in opposing directions simultaneously and intransitively (as in looking *around* rather than *at*). The verb has become less transitive, suspended in transit. It seems that this type of looking would resemble an intransitive sensation (the *feel* of looking) more than an act of intention. Of course, the statement is mistaken. Judd said "lock," not "look." Yet "look the two directions together" seems true to the experience of progression in Judd's art, just as "look the two colors together" might be a response suited to his work in multicolored, enameled aluminum. It would respect the independence of the colors while recognizing their collective wholeness. This *lock/look* error contains a truth—well, if not quite a truth (absolute), then a fact, a realization (contingent).

Twos

Imagine this situation: "While I am seated calmly in the dark, the lights are suddenly turned on, and at that instant I am conscious, not of a process of change, but yet of something more than can be contained in an instant. I have a sense of a saltus, of there being two sides to that instant. A consciousness of polarity would be a tolerably good phrase to describe what occurs."[55] Here, Peirce urges his reader to conceive of a single instant in lived time, immeasurably brief yet experienced as

53 Ibid., 52 (punctuation added). Here, the statement attributed to Judd follows the edited typescript (Judd Foundation, Marfa; courtesy Caitlin Murray).

54 Ibid., 52.

55 Peirce, "A Guess at the Riddle" (c. 1890), *Collected Papers*, 1:201.

2 see page 249

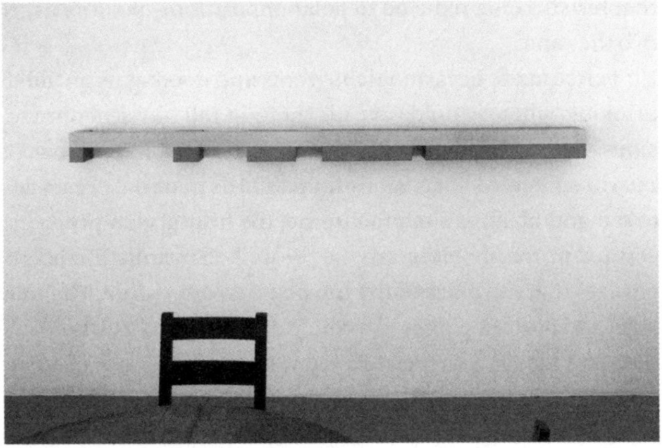

having two sides, whether linked by a common edge or separated by a gap in existence, one does not know. This is an experience of polarity, yet it lacks a context that would fix the poles into categories of opposition. We have no before and after, no positive and negative, no north and south. Such determinations of potential hierarchy would be groundless, given the immediacy of the sensation. In other words, duality is being experienced as unity: two persist, but as one. This is time without passage, which I previously called timeless—experiential time, not measurable time, not "literal" time. It is time locked in place by looking, suggesting how we might *look* Judd's two-way progressions (not *look at*, but *look*).

Imagine this possibility as well: two colors clearly in opposition, perceived as a unity—Judd's red and black, his black and red. The two colors constitute an integrated optical event despite the lack of organizational hierarchy or harmony. Red and black do not harmonize in any familiar way, as, say, red and violet might, or blue and green. This is why red and black serve so well as bold graphic signage; each color maintains its independence within a structured communication. Having observed the innovative art of his time (Pollock, Barnett Newman, Lee Bontecou, Oldenburg, Chamberlain, among others), Judd concluded in 1963: "Often power lies in a polarization of elements and qualities, or at least in a combination of dissimilar ones."[56] In 1993, a principle of polarization guided his summary thoughts about duality and the pairing of color: "In a way, side by side, the red and the black become one color. They become a two-color monochrome."[57] Here is polarity (of two sides, the red and the black) that yet becomes one—a polarity

56 Judd, "In the Galleries: Lee Bontecou" (1963), *Complete Writings 1959–1975*, 65.

57 Judd, "Some Aspects of Color in General and Red and Black in Particular," *Donald Judd*, 158 (hyphenation added).

that resists being reduced to polar opposition—polarity as "the two the same."

Peirce made occasional diagrams and doodles as an aid to thinking, whereas Judd gave his thought full physical dimen-

sions. Among his many constructions in two colors, a work of 1989 in enameled sheet aluminum affords material presence to red-and-black as a monochrome: the frontal view projects red primarily, although the prescribed installation height ensures that the black of the top plane is also visible. The top, side, and bottom planes introduce the duality in its wholeness [see fig. 17]. Like Peirce's sense of change—not a change from this to that, but just change—Judd's instance of red-and-black assumes no particular identity other than the fact of its existence. "If there were an identifiable feeling to red or to red and black together"—that is, if there were a cultural association, soliciting memory and analysis beyond sensory immediacy—"[this color] would not be usable to me."[58] Recall the problem of a bull's anger: it has nothing to do with Judd's sense of red. Red-and-black, the two-color monochrome, does have feeling. It projects feeling, but the feeling has no name, no identity other than what a given observer feels here and now in the presence of the work. This nameless feeling enters neither cultural nor historical nor critical discourse.

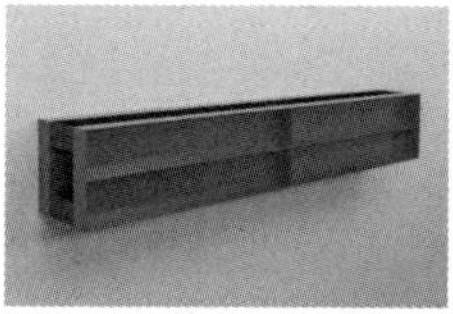

17 see page 259

If Peirce's sense of change and Judd's sense of red-and-black have no discursive implications, if they are neither effects of causes nor causes of effects, what is their meaning? With no predetermined signification attached to such experience, how much meaning, how much direction, do we receive from the characterizations of such phenomena that the likes of Peirce and Judd provide? The verbalized meaning, if there is one, will neither be self-evident, nor can it be clear. Both the two-sided instant and the two-color monochrome seem to contradict what two is and what one is. Do we need to reassess the value of our simplest numbers? Faced with explaining the immediacy of sensation and the organic flow of experience, faced with the dual instant or the dual monochrome ... we do the best we can.

To seize the quality of change in the briefest moment, Peirce resorted to language somewhat more suggestive of space than of time: *saltus* (a leap that implies a physical gap), *polarity* (a distinction of extremes implying a range between). But what might exist between Peirce's two sides of the instant? Nothing beyond the continuity of consciousness in time.[59] And what lies between Judd's red and black? Nothing again—no mediating

58 Ibid., 158.

59 Peirce, "Fallibilism, Continuity, and Evolution" (c. 1897), *Collected Papers*, 1:68–70.

values, no "landscape"—nothing other than the quality of a viewer's experience of the instant. Pondering the sensory and emotional impact of this type of situation, Judd took instruction from Peirce.[60] Polarization was of interest to both. Neither the philosopher nor the artist insisted on subjecting polar elements to resolution by synthesis. Neither sought dialectical depolarization. Nor did they attempt to validate experience by theoretical regulation: "Direct experience ... involves no error, because it testifies to nothing but its own appearance."[61] Judd made art by making it. As he said with regard to justifying his interest: "If you are interested in a thing it is interesting."[62] When one of his fabricated objects held his interest, this indicated that he had succeeded in making art.

Fallibilism

So ... we do the best we can. At times, however, the best becomes too much, when the intellectual effort outstrips its means: "Hegel's method has the defect of not working at all if you think with too great exactitude."[63] With a sly irony worthy of Judd, Peirce inserted this put-down into an otherwise technical investigation that required no side commentary. He seized on a paradox: an intelligent mind can be all too diligent in its pursuit of a method that is bound to fail if strictly applied—a method that promises more than any method can provide. The investigation proves devastating for the method and confounding for the mind that conducts it. The infallible turns fallible.

Peirce took theory to a less than perfect place, a position with which Judd sympathized: "My whole method will be found to be in profound contrast with that of Hegel [who] has committed the trifling oversight of forgetting that there is a real world with real actions and reactions."[64] "Direct experience," Peirce stated, "just is."[65] Among other considerations, he was alluding to the nature of objective facts: they resist the inertial course of intellectual order. Like sand, facts are inherently disorderly. Theories predict the place of some of them, but not all. Despite the excellence of a method, "there are three things to which we can never hope to attain by reasoning, namely, absolute certainty, absolute exactitude, absolute universality."[66] A Peircean law had to be flexible, stretching the truth: "Try to verify any law of nature and you will find that the more precise your observations, the more certain they will be to show irregular departure from the law."[67] Alluding to his preferred manner of dealing with the facts of experience, Peirce introduced

60 Judd's personal library includes Peirce's *Collected Papers* as well as other volumes of Peirce. When Flavin introduced Judd at the start of a public conversation between the two artists in 1987, he mentioned that Judd, who majored in art history at Columbia University (actually, he was enrolled in the Master's program in this field), "minored in the American pragmatics of philosopher Charles Peirce." Flavin also recalled that Judd had once made a pilgrimage to Peirce's home in New Milford, PA (from an audiotape of the event at Musée National d'Art Moderne, Paris, 1987; folder 1, box 181, Leo Castelli Gallery Records, Archives of American Art, Smithsonian Institution, Washington DC [information courtesy Adrian Kohn]). Flavin's having singled out Peirce from Judd's other philosophical sources may reflect a particular focus of the 1980s, as opposed to the 1950s, when he was engaged in a more eclectic round of academic study. On Judd's university experience, see Raskin, *Donald Judd*, 130 n29.

61 Peirce, "Fallibilism, Continuity, and Evolution," *Collected Papers*, 1:60.

62 Judd, "In the Galleries: Jean Arp," *Complete Writings 1959–1975*, 92.

63 Peirce, "Degenerate Cases: The Firstness of Firstness, Secondness, and Thirdness" (1903), *Collected Papers*, 1:286 (emphasis added).

64 Peirce, "A Guess at the Riddle," *Collected Papers*, 1:192-93.

65 Peirce, "Fallibilism, Continuity, and Evolution," *Collected Papers*, 1:60.

66 Ibid., 1:58.

67 Peirce, "The Doctrine of Necessity Examined" (1892), *Collected Papers*, 6:36–37.

additional irony: "[Even] the subtlest mind cannot get the *best* possible results from [my method]; but a mind of very moderate skill can make better analyses by this method than the same mind could obtain without it."[68] What was Peircean analysis designed to probe? Phenomena and feeling: things especially hard to define, like the two-sided instant and the two-color monochrome. Be judicious in your choice of analytical mode, the philosopher seems to advise. Then press on, to continue working against the odds of reaching any comprehensive understanding.

Judd's attitude was similar. His notion—"It's only a small order ... four things in a row.... Four units in a row are only that"—parallels Peirce's statement, "Direct experience ... just is."[69] Four units in a row do not predict the effect of six in a row, or just one. "One or four boxes in a row," Judd said, "any single thing or such a series, is local order, just an arrangement, barely order at all."[70] "[Repetition] is a small kind of order which I can deal with.... My logical order isn't the world's logical order. It's my own."[71] Do not generalize, he insists. A situation would have to be observed, thought through, tested out—in no given order. Judd was pragmatic: get some looking done; get some thinking done; get some art done. *Life is short* (as he often said), and conditions are in flux.[72] "It is obviously an ideal to pay more attention to things as they are. [This] leads to larger concerns": here Judd was referring to the politics of the first Iraq war in 1991, as much as to making art. He would strip both of any utopian ideology. His "ideal" was to acknowledge real conditions, whether in the isolated studio or the social world: "You should admit that you can't influence anything. And then do it anyway.... Art has no [practical] effect on the society ... you don't live very long anyway ... do the art."[73]

Judd persisted. Throughout his life, he engaged in political protest; and he made art. During the 1960s and 1970s, he created numerous works that induce an experience of a two-sided instant (whether he would think of it this way or not). During the 1980s, he was concentrating on two-color monochromes and their many variations. Among the earlier inventions were outdoor constructions of large scale that establish a polarity of space in relation to the land. In phenomenological terms, these early works in which Judd developed spatial polarity prefigure later works involving polarities of color. This is the case with outdoor constructions consisting of a pair of concentric wall-like surfaces, either angular or circular and closely

68 Peirce, "Degenerate Cases: The Firstness of Firstness, Secondness, and Thirdness," *Collected Papers*, 1:286 (emphasis added).

69 Judd, in Janhsen, "Discussion with Donald Judd," *Donald Judd*, 52; Judd, "Some Aspects of Color in General and Red and Black in Particular," *Donald Judd*, 156.

70 Judd, "Statement" (1968), *Complete Writings 1959–1975*, 196.

71 For the first sentence: Judd, interview by David Batchelor, "A Small Kind of Order," *Artscribe International* 78 (November/December 1989): 64. For the second sentence: Judd, in Millet, "La petite logique de Donald Judd," 7 (author's translation). Judd had made this remark in French during an interview conducted largely in English: "Ce n'est pas la logique du monde. C'est ma logique à moi."

72 "You don't live forever, so there's a little reason to hurry": Judd, in Paul Taylor, "Interview with Donald Judd," *Flash Art*, no. 134 (May 1987): 37. "Here and now is little and short": Donald Judd, "Una stanza per Panza, Part I," *Kunst Intern*, no. 4 (May 1990): 5.

73 Judd, interview by Angeli Janhsen-Vukicevic, typed transcription dated 20 February 1991, subsequently edited by Judd (Judd Foundation, Marfa; courtesy Caitlin Murray).

22 see page 67

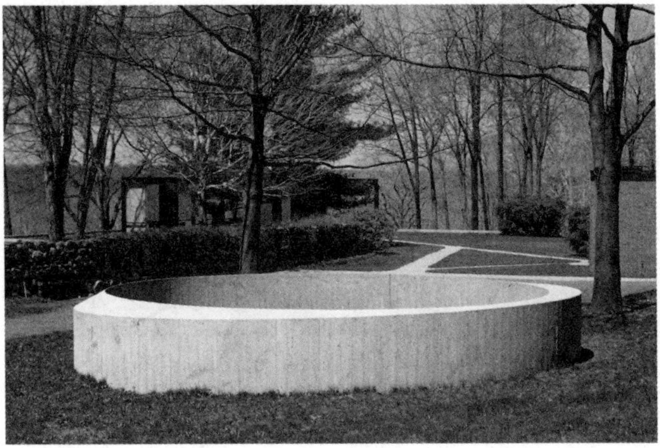

positioned, such as a rectangle within a second rectangle having dimensions slightly greater. Judd described this condition in terms of spaces rather than solids: an "enclosed narrow space enclosing a large [inner] space."[74] Aside from the opposition of inner and outer forms, these works have an additional polarizing feature: the top edge of one wall-like plane parallels the natural slope or contour of the land into which it has been set, while the top edge of the other plane remains level, at constant elevation.

For a work of this type in 1971, Judd created a single circular ring of concrete that deploys both systems—the height of the outer surface remains constant because it follows the contour of the land, whereas the height of the inner surface above the plane of the ground varies because this surface is invariant with respect to the absolute measure of elevation above sea level [see fig. 22].[75] The inner surface remains level with respect to a plumb line, as if it were designed to reflect the pull of gravity toward the center of the planet. The outer surface has regularity only with respect to the varying plane of the ground at the site; it replicates this topographical contour by retaining a height of four feet everywhere along the ring. The ring itself is eighteen inches thick and requires a complex bevel to accommodate the shifting difference between its inner and outer surfaces. Here a single object in the land—like an instant with two sides—creates two spaces of different character inside and outside its vertical surfaces. At the same time, the canted top surface of the oddly bilateral ring appears to perform two movements at once: its "power" lies in this "polarization." It is two things but one thing. Two decades later, in 1991, Judd

[74] Donald Judd, "21 February 93," *Donald Judd: Large-scale Works* (New York: The Pace Gallery, 1993), 12. On this group of works, which included one of metal installed on the ramp of the Guggenheim Museum, see William C. Agee, "Unit, Series, Site: A Judd Lexicon," *Art in America* 63 (May/June 1975): 47.

[75] Compare Judd, "21 February 93," *Donald Judd: Large-scale Works*, 12.

stated that such inventions were "almost completely meaningless to almost everyone."[76]

Judd's thinking with respect to pairs or duos escapes familiar categories. He was no boilerplate, dualistic thinker. To follow is a segment of his reasoning in 1993, quoted in condensed form; it relates in obvious ways to the concrete ring of 1971: "After a few thousand years space is so unknown that a discussion of it would have to begin with a rock. How large is it? ... If it isn't on a level surface, the tilted surface approaches a second entity.... In what way does the rock create space around itself? ... Then what if a second rock is placed nearby? ... If two objects are close together, they define the space in between.... The space between can be a single space more than the two objects are a pair."[77] Here it seems that "the two" (the pair and the space) have become "the same"—alike to the point of sharing in singularity, because the sensation of each depends on the sensation of the other. How do you determine that the rocks are sufficiently far apart to have ended their relationship? No theory answers this question. You would have to experiment with placement and observe what occurred.

By applying his reasoning about space to the problem of color, Judd arrived at his "two-color monochrome," an effect already mentioned for its convergence of duality with singularity. An investigation of color, he wrote, "would have to begin with a spot.... What color is the spot? Red. If a [black] spot is placed on the surface ... how far away is the black spot from the red spot? ... Near enough for there to be a pair of spots, red and black? Or apart enough for this to be uncertain? What if the red and black are next to each other? ... In a way, side by side, the red and the black become one color. They become a two-color monochrome. Red and black together are so familiar that they almost form a new unity"—the two the same.[78]

With regard to both space and color, a kind of sensory intuition, itself a mix of feeling and thinking, ought to determine an artist's best move in the given situation. As much as space and color would be subjected to serious thought, an equally intense component of feeling would be involved. The mix amounts to a guess, and guesses can prove mistaken. In 1984, Judd chose to quote Peirce at length on the matter of "fallibilism," including this advice: "The first step toward *finding out* is to acknowledge you do not satisfactorily know already."[79] What is the point of either philosophy or art if not to know what you do not know?—or to discover mistaken, what you

[76] Judd, interview by Angeli Janhsen-Vukicevic (Judd Foundation, Marfa; courtesy Caitlin Murray).

[77] Judd, "Some Aspects of Color in General and Red and Black in Particular," *Donald Judd*, 145-46.

[78] Judd, "Some Aspects of Color in General and Red and Black in Particular," *Donald Judd*, 158 (paragraphing eliminated, hyphenation added).

[79] Peirce, "Concerning the Author" (c. 1897), quoted by Judd, "A Long Discussion Not about Master-pieces But Why There Are So Few of Them, Part II" (1984), *Complete Writings 1975–1986*, 75 (emphasis original). Judd's probable source is Justus Buchler, ed., *Philosophical Writings of Peirce* (New York: Dover, 1955 [orig. ed., 1940]), 4.

believed you knew? Peirce reasoned that the greatest intellectual advances often depend on enlightened guesswork, which, in his terminology, was abduction: "The abductive suggestion comes to us like a flash. It is an act of *insight*, although of extremely fallible insight."[80] An intelligent guess saves the time and trouble of working systematically through all possible solutions to a problem.[81] For an artist who thrives on sensory and intellectual risk, as opposed to dreams and fantasies (which have no factor of error, hence no risk), Peircean abduction becomes an inspired method. Rather than rely on inherited certainties, Judd ventured guesses at space and color.

Thought and feeling

Judd invoked any number of emblematic ironies to illustrate the rampant insensitivity that characterized his cultural environment, shaped by the certainties he challenged and often rejected. Among his aphoristic observations was this: "The people most fond of symbols from the past are also the ones most heedless of its reality." He offered an example: "The guy in Tucson with the Spanish-Colonial TV set is the one who bulldozed the adobe houses in the old part of town." A worker's kitschy television console would signify his tacit allegiance to an established cultural aesthetic, the history of which had faded from his consciousness, if he had ever been aware of it. What results is a cultural comedy of errors with tragic overtones: the worker's daily activity is bankrupting his personal aesthetic investment. He is alienated not only from his occupation and preferred style of life but also from the aesthetic sensibility he passively acquired. His culture has instilled incompatible values and desires. The social situation exemplifies what Judd often called the "false division [of] thought and feeling."[82] The division was epitomized in the general acceptance of veneers of plastic that imitated wood. This architectural monster was not confined to the homes of the economically or culturally deprived: "Texas is paved with plastic walnut paneling, whose connotation isn't precise: all classes love it."[83] The look of this material as much as the logic of it seemed divided to Judd, like a thought that conveys ambivalent feeling or confused judgment.

Recall that Peirce's assessment of the Hegelian system reads as something of a wisecrack: a method you realize is "not working at all if you think with too great exactitude."

80 Peirce, "Pragmatism and Abduction" (1903), *Collected Papers*, 5:113 (emphasis original).

81 See the discussion of Peirce in relation to Judd in this volume, "Donald Judd: Fast Thinking."

82 Judd, "A Long Discussion Not about Master-pieces But Why There Are So Few of Them, Part I," *Complete Writings 1975–1986*, 54, 56.

83 Donald Judd, "Mansana de Chinati," *Donald Judd Architektur*, ed. Marianne Stockebrand (Münster:Westfälischer Kunstverein Münster, 1989), 48. See also Donald Judd, "Art and Internationalism: Prolegomena" (1992), *Donald Judd* (Osaka: Gallery Yamaguchi, 1992), 8.

Peirce used a relatively colloquial style to develop technical topics. Even his technical terminology had a disarming familiarity to it. In this instance, he was discussing what—if we apply his specialized language—would be the Firstness of Thirdness: the sensory feel (Firstness) of thought directed at a topic (Thirdness). We experience the sensory feel while a thought is occurring: this is feeling and thinking, the two the same. A feeling consciously felt is a sensation. An idea consciously thought is also a sensation.[84] A statement from one of Peirce's early writings helps to advance these evasive distinctions: "When our nervous system is excited in a complicated way, there being a relation between the elements of the excitation, the result is a single harmonious disturbance which I call an emotion.... This emotion is essentially the same thing as [a] hypothetic inference [later called an abduction], and every hypothetic inference involves the formation of such an emotion. We may say, therefore, that hypothesis produces the *sensuous* element of thought"—sensuous thoughts.[85] Peirce expressed the same insight in a later text: "Every operation of the mind, however complex, has its absolutely simple feeling, the emotion of the *tout ensemble*."[86] The result of Judd's creative process was a "hypothetic inference," that is, a guess or intuition as to the configuration of a work of art, which amounted to its emotional totality. By Peirce's reasoning, Judd's thinking process was "sensuous." His art presented a thought and a feeling, the two the same—separate aspects of experience, yet not to be divided.

Too much of the thinking of others seemed to Judd insensitive to emotions that should have arisen—a fault not only of ordinary people in ordinary occupations but also of art critics who ought to have known and done better. Calling forth "the guy in Tucson," Judd, like Peirce, was colloquial, as direct in language as his art was fundamental in sensation. In various interviews and essays, following the sorry implications of his observations, he often introduced supplemental ironies, exercised with a deceptively gentle touch, which nevertheless verged on utter condemnation: "Most people are not aware of this absence [of articulated architectural space].... Sometimes when traveling they enter a cathedral, recognize space, and thank God instead of the architect."[87] The observer's thought fails the sensation. On the same topic, Judd turned an amusing phrase in dismay: "The El Paso telephone directory has a list of architects and yet there's no architecture in El Paso."[88] The

84 On this point, see Peirce, "A Neglected Argument for the Reality of God" (1908), *Collected Papers*, 6:312.

85 Peirce, "Deduction, Induction, and Hypothesis" (1868), *Collected Papers*, 2:387 (emphasis original).

86 Peirce, "A Definition of Feeling," *Collected Papers*, 1:155. To be strict with respect to Peirce's terminology in this instance: what he calls "the emotion of the *tout ensemble*" is "a secondary feeling or sensation excited from within the mind." We can make a distinction between an undirected feeling (Peircean Firstness) and a sensation consciously felt (Peircean Secondness).

87 Judd, "Some Aspects of Color in General and Red and Black in Particular," *Donald Judd*, 145.

88 Judd, "Art and Architecture" (1983), *Complete Writings 1975–1986*, 28.

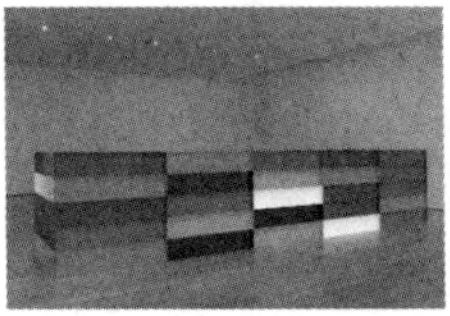

9 see page 255

local members of the profession were thinking architecture, lacking feeling.

Arguing the case for thought as sensation, Peirce marshaled his philosophical resources to identify a term that would correspond unequivocally to feeling-of-a-thought. He was forced to admit, "we have no really good word." Never reluctant to assign new uses to old words, he ventured the term *mentality* to indicate a mind active in thought in its primacy.[89] "Mentality" was something more than the mere possibility of mind or the actual existence of mind. The term alluded to the sensory experience of a mind in thought—a sensation to be savored. It was not the what (the meaning) or the how (the method) of a certain thinking. It was the feel. We think not *of* red; rather, our thought *is* red. When Peirce wanted to invoke primary experience, he nearly always chose a sensation of color to make his case; a disruption to consciousness could be imagined as "my blue life being transmuted into red life."[90] How could an artist not have an elemental interest in color to complement an elemental interest in space? All material in space has color: "All materials, gray and tan, are colored," Judd noted: "Color, like material, is what art is made from."[91]

Because Peirce's mode of speculative reasoning was mathematical—implying the factor of mathesis, or systematic calculation and ordering—he tended to graph and chart all possible variations of a concept or condition. Each of the boxes or files within one of his mental charts represented a category; but in many instances, the given position in the Peircean order had no name. Like a rhetorical form in use and yet unacknowledged, no one had previously considered its possibility, let alone addressed its presence. What had been potential at best, became in Peirce's analysis something actual. In a similar way Judd had no name for the genre of work he began to create during the early 1960s. His invention was neither painting, nor sculpture, nor architecture as he understood the extent of these categories. Any name would be as arbitrary as the name of a color. In need of a new designation for his three-dimensional non-category, Judd tried "three-dimensional work" and, in the one instance of his frequently cited essay of 1965, invoked the term "specific objects." He had approached this formulation previously—for instance, early in 1963, when he described a Bontecou relief sculpture as "actual and specific and ... experienced as an object."[92] And, of course, in 1969 he said of himself: "I want a particular, definite object."

89 Peirce, "Degenerate Cases: The Firstness of Firstness, Secondness, and Thirdness," *Collected Papers*, 1:282.
90 Peirce, "The Architecture of Theories" (1891), *Collected Papers*, 6:18. "Suppose [a] point to have any character; suppose, for instance, it is *blue*": Peirce, "Fallibilism, Continuity, and Evolution," *Collected Papers*, 1:67–68 (emphasis original).
91 Judd, "Some Aspects of Color in General and Red and Black in Particular," *Donald Judd*, 155, 158.
92 Judd, "In the Galleries: Lee Bontecou," *Complete Writings 1959–1975*, 65. See also Richard Shiff, "Specificity," in Marianne Stockebrand, ed., *The Writings of Donald Judd* (Marfa: Chinati Foundation, 2009), 78–98.

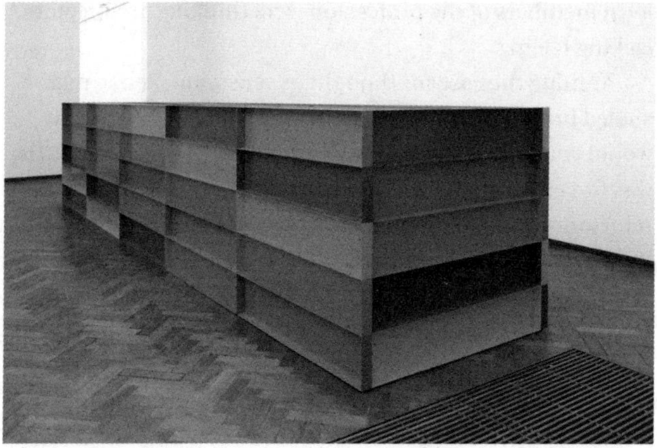

65
Donald Judd
Untitled, 1989
Painted aluminum
150 × 750 × 165 cm
(59 × 295.3 × 64 inches)

Larger pieces

In many ways, Judd's works were art as his culture knew it. They presented color as painting did, established volume and mass as sculpture did, and contained space as architecture did. In each instance, however, these sensory qualities ran afoul of conventional practice. Twenty years after Judd's death, names are still lacking. Judd always dismissed "minimalism" and "minimal art": "It was simply a derogatory publicity label [applied] to write in an easy way about art."[93] For want of better terms, we refer to Judd's freestanding multicolored, sheet aluminum works as "floor pieces" or assign them to some other, rather lame, descriptive classification. As Judd realized, it seems wrong to call them sculpture [see fig 9]. The largest of the six extant works of this type is at the Boijmans-van Beuningen Museum, Rotterdam, with a height-to-width ratio of 1:6 rather than 1:5. The prismatic, rectilinear forms of these works lack the anthropomorphism of most sculpture, even the abstract varieties, such as David Smith's or Mark di Suvero's. They are also devoid of the tectonic gestures characteristic of structurally forceful architecture. Having spent some hours with the version at the Stedelijk Museum, Amsterdam [fig. 65], I *felt* that it neither hugs the ground, nor rises to the sky, nor expresses a play of physical forces in tension, a dynamic equilibrium.[94] Its sensory qualities—whatever they are—do not evoke the usual metaphors. Yet the work has a specific feel to it, in synch with its scale, organization, and color.

The Amsterdam version of this large, floor-oriented structure is directly comparable to the ones now at Tate Modern, London, and in a private collection in Ghent. All three have

[93] Judd, in Janhsen, "Discussion with Donald Judd," *Donald Judd*, 50.

[94] "I wanted to avoid any sensation of weight. This goes back to the business of representation. I think that most of the European tradition of art represented weight"; Judd, in Batchelor, "A Small Kind of Order," 64.

9 see page 255

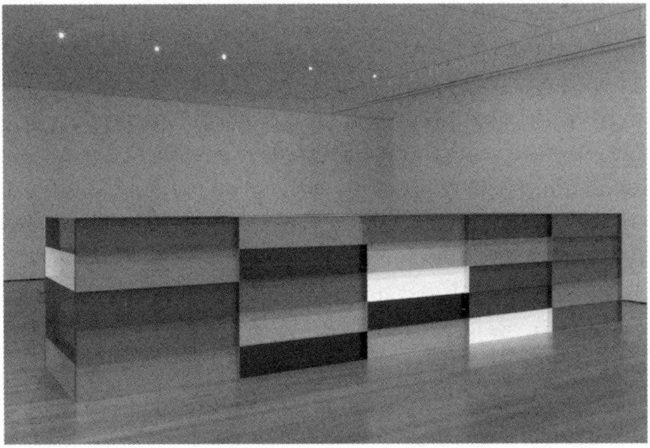

the same dimensions: 150 cm in height, 750 cm in width, 165 cm in depth. The "uncolored" metallic gray surface of the galvanized iron of the Tate version presents a very different emotional feel from the multicolored enameled surfaces of the Amsterdam and Ghent versions, which differ from each other in chromatic range (perhaps most accentuated by the presence of yellow in Amsterdam, in addition to reds and blues, the hues that dominate in Ghent). A version at Kunstsammlung Nordrhein-Westfalen, Düsseldorf, combines "clear" galvanized iron elements with enameled aluminum elements to generate another type of chromatic effect—neither a color composition nor a harmony but multiple juxtapositions of color-qualities that seem to relate in similar degrees of un-likeness (the two the same, yet two). Here it is unclear whether the galvanized elements pair most readily with the whites and the blacks, since the three are chromatic neutrals, or whether the whites and blacks pair with the reds, blues, and yellows, since all of these elements are enameled. The enameled surfaces share in reflectivity and other subtle phenomenal properties.

A version at the Museum of Modern Art, New York [see fig. 9], is similar to the Amsterdam work in deploying saturated, middle-value hues, but has a palette of eight enameled colors rather than four. Because it includes black and white, its scale of values is significantly expanded. The immediate sensory differences among the six "floor pieces" will be far more comprehensible than any logical enumeration of their various distinctions. Comprehension by looking is itself different from comprehension by logic—the thought (Peirce's "mentality") of one version in its wholeness feels different from the thought of another version in its wholeness. I refer to Judd's large floor pieces as versions of a type because they resist being seen as variations of each other. Each structure leaves the impression that it generates only one example of itself. The response is not, "I've seen something like this before," but, "This thing is something itself."[95]

What is this "something"?[96] Where do we place the thought that constitutes a work of art, if it lies somewhere between an immediate look and an extended logic? Judd was mathematical in the way that Peirce was. His notes are a mix of perspective renderings, diagrams, charts, lists, numerical computations, and verbal phrasing. He was a master of cognitive mixed media, running different modes of thought on a single track—the many the same, as it were. Referring to his working method, he stated: "It's impossible to remember the many times that red and an idea have changed precedence." Judd's feeling—*red*—brought the concept of a certain physical construct along with it, just as thoughts of a possible work would prove inseparable from the redness of its realization. "How can a feeling be stripped of the red which produces it?"[97] A form in one color is not the same form if in another color. Yet it is: the two the same, and not. In Judd's art, sameness is always under reconsideration.[98]

Peirce's effort to develop a fully inflected, philosophical language of experience, adequate to both psychic and sensory phenomena, was not Judd's concern. His far less technical remarks in writings, lectures, and interviews nevertheless sounded numerous Peircean notes, as here, in 1983: "I've always considered the distinction between thought and feeling as, at the least, exaggerated ... All thought involves feeling. All feeling is based on experience which involved thought. Emotion or feeling is simply a quick summation of experience, some of which is thought, necessarily quick so that we can act quickly ... Otherwise we could never get from A to Z, barely to C, since B would have to be always rechecked. It's a short life and a little speed is necessary."[99] In 1990, Judd argued the same point about thought and feeling, linking the notion of their integration to the wholeness of a work of art constituted from separate elements (polarities): "I don't like the division of thought and feeling ... I'm after *one* thing, one whole thing, which is the work of art. That quality of the whole ... comes from particular materials, from particular arrangements and proportions of things on the wall, of a row of things."[100]

95 Judd seems to have had this response to the monochromatic paintings of Ralph Humphrey, though he expressed it in a difficult manner, perceiving particularity in sensation and generality in meaning as (what he might have called) the two the same: "The rawest, most unique immediacy is coexistent with generality, the basic quality and meaning; sense perception is particularized into universality"; Judd, "In the Galleries: Ralph Humphrey" (1960), *Complete Writings 1959–1975*, 12.

96 On the meaning of *something*, see Richard Shiff, "Lumination," in Kristine Bell, Tiffany Bell, and Alexandra Whitney, eds., *Dan Flavin: Series and Progressions* (Göttingen: Steidl, 2010), 82–93. Many of Judd's pronouncements refer to the problem of "something": "A shape, a volume, a color, a surface is something itself. It shouldn't be concealed as part of a fairly different whole"; Judd, "Statement," *Complete Writings 1959–1975*, 196.

97 Judd, "Art and Architecture," *Complete Writings 1975–1986*, 26, 31.

98 As it was during the 1960s, with Judd's vertical stacks and horizontal box-like constructions of repeating elements. The viewer's position relative to multiple units of equal dimensions ensured that the repetitions did not *look* the same.

99 Judd, "Art and Architecture," *Complete Writings 1975–1986*, 30.

100 Judd, in Janhsen, "Discussion with Donald Judd," *Donald Judd*, 51 (emphasis original).

Bear in mind how naturally irony arises in Judd's formulations. He refers to a "distinction ... at the least, exaggerated." This apposition of terms for diminishment ("at the least") and increase ("exaggerated") converts the claim of increase to an understatement, as if exaggeration were a euphemism for utter falsehood. Judd recorded these musings over the feel of thinking, as well as his remarks on the feel of red, for a talk at Yale University in September 1983. At that time, he was engaged in plotting out the structural and chromatic orders for his initial sheet aluminum objects, with their multiple panels, each enameled with its specific color. These works included a large rectangular prism—of dimensions he later repeated, 150 × 750 × 165 cm—destined for an outdoor exhibition in Merian Park, Basel, in 1984.[101] It was soon damaged and remade the same year as a very similar work for the collector in Ghent. Horizontal panels replaced the original vertical panels of the two short ends of the prism. During the 1980s, Judd's creative thinking was in motion, somewhere in transit "from A to Z." Interviewed in 1987, he expressed his concern to keep moving: "I want to do larger pieces."[102]

Pairs

Judd liked to cite Albers, who founded his demanding study of color on the vicissitudes of personal observation: "If one says 'Red' (the name of a color) and there are 50 people listening, it can be expected that there will be 50 reds in their minds. And one can be sure that all these reds will be very different." [103] By extension, the emotional state to be associated with a specific color, perhaps aroused by it, would hardly be predictable. Accordingly, Judd noted that Albers's view "does not agree with what [he] was taught in the Bauhaus," where Johannes Itten and Wassily Kandinsky insisted that "colors always produce the same emotions." Judd demolished this bit of Bauhaus behavioral science by recalling his unresolved childhood dilemma, a point of irony already cited: "I didn't understand why a bull should be mad at red."[104] This fragment of folk wisdom implies that the emotional response to sensory stimuli is invariant. An analogous understanding of the emotional valence of colors, the position taken by Itten and Kandinsky, had been anticipated by earlier artists with expressionistic aims. "Is the sycamore sad because we place it in cemeteries," Paul Gauguin asked: "No, it's the color that's sad."[105]

[101] A note of 24 July 1983 (Judd Foundation, Marfa) relates to aspects of the work eventually placed in Basel.
[102] Judd, in Taylor, "Interview with Donald Judd," 37.
[103] Josef Albers, quoted in Judd, "Some Aspects of Color in General and Red and Black in Particular," *Donald Judd*, 150. For the Albers statement in context, see Josef Albers, *Interaction of Color* (New Haven: Yale University Press, 1975 [1963]), 3. See also Judd, "Josef Albers," *Josef Albers*, 7–25.
[104] Judd, "Some Aspects of Color in General and Red and Black in Particular," *Donald Judd*, 150.
[105] Paul Gauguin, letter to Emile Schuffenecker, 14 January 1885, *Correspondance de Paul Gauguin (1873–1888)*, ed. Victor Merlhès, (Paris: Fondation Singer-Polignac, 1984), 89.

For Judd, no harm would be done by using a certain cool, muted green, even if it risked causing a number of viewers to experience or imagine sadness. But he would avoid isolating an evocative color of this kind, for it would then be more likely to "color" the response to the object that bore it. A form would be green or red because Judd chose to make it so, not because the color somehow suited the form, as if both color and form would lead to the same universal, symbolic meaning—a case of semiotic certainty and harmony that would satisfy neither Judd nor the theoretically oriented contemporary critics whose polemics annoyed him. Both objected to universality. If a conventionally evocative color were to be used at all, Judd would pair it with another that converted the combination to a feeling of a different psychic order, one that had no ready verbal analogue. The resultant effect would be specific chromatically but vague symbolically—no acknowledged symbol, no reference to an identifiable emotion. Perhaps a green would be paired with a yellow: "All colors of the same value, such as light yellow and light green, make pairs. All values of the same color make pairs [such as a light green and a deeper green]."[106]

In notes composed around 1982 to 1984, Judd listed numerous additional classifications of pairing, which he eventually summarized in an essay written upon receiving the Sikkens Prize for research in color in 1993.[107] Two "full" colors would constitute a pair, such as a saturated red and a saturated blue. A pair could be two variants of a hue, such as a saturated red and a rose pink. Black and white form a pair, as well as any chromatic color coupled with black or white. "Acid" or "sharp" colors constitute pairs, among them cadmium red light, cerulean blue, chartreuse, and permanent green.[108] "Soft or whitish" colors form pairs, such as emerald green and cadmium yellow light. There are many other possibilities: "Dull or grayed colors, the ochres, the oxides, all form pairs, united by [lowered] value."[109] Judd also referred to "pairs [that] make 2 more pairs with outer colors"; an example might be the sequence of red, yellow, orange, and black. Within this group, red and black are an especially compelling pair, which Judd used as his prime example of a two-color monochrome. But red would also pair with yellow as saturated hues, and black would pair with orange (it pairs with any color). Judd noted that yellow and orange are "not usually seen as a pair"; presumably, the proximity to red and black could induce the effect, infectiously.[110] In fact, red and black are so compelling as a pair, as

[106] Judd, "Some Aspects of Color in General and Red and Black in Particular," *Donald Judd*, 158.

[107] Ibid., 158–59. See also, manuscript notes dated September 1982, 11 February 1984, and 15 March 1984 (Judd Foundation, Marfa). Judd's commentary on Malevich anticipated his discussion of pairs: "The two alizarins are a pair, a split color, like the two pinks, one of which is rosy and one a little orange. These sets and contrasts ... are not harmonic, do not make a further overall color or tone. The blue, black and white of the painting with the blue triangle are unchangeably themselves; they can't combine; they can only make a set of three or any two in the way that three bricks make a set. In *Supremus No. 50* the red and black make the most obvious set, a pair in this case"; Judd, "Malevich: Independent Form, Color, Surface," *Complete Writings 1975–1986*, 214.

[108] Colors in this category would often correspond to the "impure" (non-spectral) hues exploited by commerce, such as the colors of automobile paint. Compare the commentary in Agee, "Donald Judd and the Endless Possibilities of Color," *Donald Judd: Colorist*, 39–42; and David Batchelor, "Everything as Colour," in Serota, *Donald Judd*, 74.

[109] Judd, "Some Aspects of Color in General and Red and Black in Particular," *Donald Judd*, 159.

[110] Manuscript note dated 15 March 1984 (Judd Foundation, Marfa).

are red and white and also black and white, that red, black, and white form a "monochromatic triad."[111]

When Judd explained his use of color in 1993, it was precisely the symbolic, semiotic factor that his method of pairing would help him escape: "No immediate feeling can be attributed to color. Nothing can be identified." Color has *inherent* feeling and need not be interpreted. This is why attributing a secondary, "identifiable" feeling to a color only removes its experience from its reality. "If it seems otherwise, usually the association is cultural [not natural], for example, the light blue and white, supposedly the colors of peace, of the cops and the United Nations. If there were an identifiable feeling to red or to red and black together they would not be usable to me."[112] As I have noted, by Judd's reasoning (or Peirce's), red and red-and-black do each constitute a feeling, a sensation. For Judd, it was important to recognize that the sensation at issue has no discursive identity, no name. Furthermore, as a two-color monochrome, the red and the black appear as a single feeling rather than a contrast of two qualities. The feeling is red-black, not red-against-black. Nevertheless, Judd's red and black do not blend in a compound of red and black. The colors become neither a composition nor a harmony nor establish a hierarchy. They remain a pair, that is to say, the two the same.

As we know, in 1963, Judd determined that an object projecting from the wall should be at a height of 62 or 63 inches. This would extend the fact of seeing a prismatic form frontally to seeing at least some aspect of its top, with the partial view from above enhancing the holistic experience of the volumetric form. For the multicolored sheet aluminum works of the 1980s and 1990s, Judd decided that the hanging height should be somewhat lower, 140 cm, or approximately 55 inches. This measure allows the juxtapositions of color on the top plane of the structure to be all the more actively seen. The large floor pieces of the same period have a height of 150 cm, or approximately 59 inches, still low enough for the horizontal top plane to enter into an integrated experience along with one or two of the four vertical side planes, whether the viewer assumes a stationary position or circumambulates. With regard to setting colors in pairs, groupings, or sequences, the passage from one plane to another around the eight exposed right angles of the rectilinear prism was a factor in Judd's consideration. The human-scaled height of 59 inches ensures that viewers feel at ease in the presence of the floor pieces, despite their being

111 Judd, "Some Aspects of Color in General and Red and Black in Particular," *Donald Judd*, 159.
112 Ibid., 158.

unusually large by any familiar standard for indoor objects. With the exception of the Rotterdam floor piece, the long side of each prismatic object has overall proportions that match those of the basic, repeating structural element, 1:5. This factor, too, fosters a sense of ease as a viewer confronts such a grand volumetric solid. Judd's art encourages personal, even intimate, appropriation.[113]

Pairing of colors is most obvious in the distribution of hues for Judd's wall pieces. Pairs are implied by the structure itself, since each of these works juxtaposes two parallel, horizontal rows of units of enameled sheet aluminum. The most obvious pairs become the short vertical rows, each of which juxtaposes an open pan-like unit to another of equal height, width, and depth. In one of his notes, Judd referred to the pairing of two colors of related hue (two reds); these were either of dissimilar value (light red, dark red) or of dissimilar chromatic shift (a red verging on orange, a red verging on violet). Here is the thought: "the 2 reds, although so different, are like enough to run vertically through the horizontal parts."[114] Both wall pieces and floor pieces appear as horizontally disposed objects, relatively wide in relation to their height, in which pairs of colors establish counteracting verticals—horizontality and verticality, the two a whole, the two the same. The various categories of pairing result from Judd's experience with color, not from an exhaustive theory of color. Individual pairings ensure that single colors, however odd, however oppositional, do not project forward. Judd's color does not interfere with Judd's space—the two the same.

A wall piece of 1987 is an example of the smallest version of its type, with a frontal plane composed of four units of bent, enameled aluminum, each 15 × 30 × 7.5 cm [fig. 66]. Here, Judd used only three colors—orange, black-blue, and black-red. In this instance, the black-blue and black-red are not two-color monochromes, but are single colors for which the names in English correspond to terms used to designate pigments in the European system known as RAL (*Reichs-Ausschuß für Lieferbedingungen und Gütesicherung*): RAL 5004 is *Schwarzblau*, and RAL 3007 is *Schwarzrot*. The vertical row to the left consists of a black-red unit at the top and an orange unit at the bottom. The vertical row to the right consists correspondingly of a black-blue unit and a black-red unit. As Marianne Stockebrand analyzes it, "each pairing occurs both vertically and horizontally, i.e., black-red and orange make a

113 While observing the Amsterdam and New York versions for extended periods of time, I noticed that a significant number of museum visitors moved into the "personal space" of the object and touched it, despite the presence of guards and the usual prohibitions.

114 Manuscript note dated 2 June 1985 (Judd Foundation, Marfa).

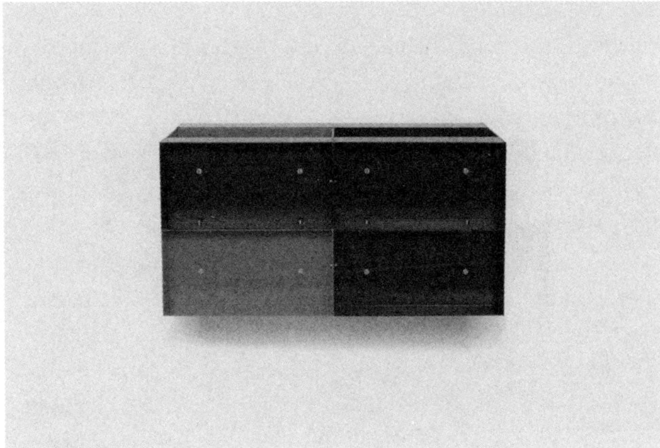

66
Donald Judd
Untitled, 1987
Painted aluminum
30 × 60 × 30 cm
(11¾ × 23⁹⁄₁₆ × 11¾ inches)

pair in both directions as does black-blue and black-red."[115] This is possible because orange is in the family of red, so the pairing of orange and black-red is analogous to a pairing of light red and dark red, contrasting values related by hue. If RAL 3007 is black-red, we can think of orange as white-red (which is not pink), a hue that Judd might have designated as "soft or whitish" in comparison with the dark color. As if the entire work were structured so that its description would result in chiasmus, the pairing of black-red and black-blue becomes analogous to a pairing of contrasting hues related by value, the inversion of contrasting values related by hue. Chromatically, this object has been "thought through," as Judd said of works by others he admired. Yet it lacks the give-and-take of conventional balance; its one light or high-value color, orange, is located only in one corner and only on the left half of the object (including the presence of orange in the top and side planes, intended to be seen).

When I view such an "unbalanced" composition of color, I sense no lack of balance; in fact, balance has ceased to be an issue, one way or another, Judd's practice having relegated it to his years as a developing painter during the early and mid-1950s. In his later work as a painter and early years exploring three-dimensional objects, his art left the question of balance to pictorialism, which was not his interest. In his view, pictorial or compositional balance reduced to a theoretical concept that need not play the sensory role theory expects of it. There is space in Judd's art, and there is color. Compositional hierarchy and balance have become superfluous concerns. The point is all the more obvious in a characteristically asymmetrical wall

115 Marianne Stockebrand, *Donald Judd: Works in Granite, Cor-Ten, Plywood, and Enamel on Aluminum* (New York: Pace Gallery, 2011), 18.

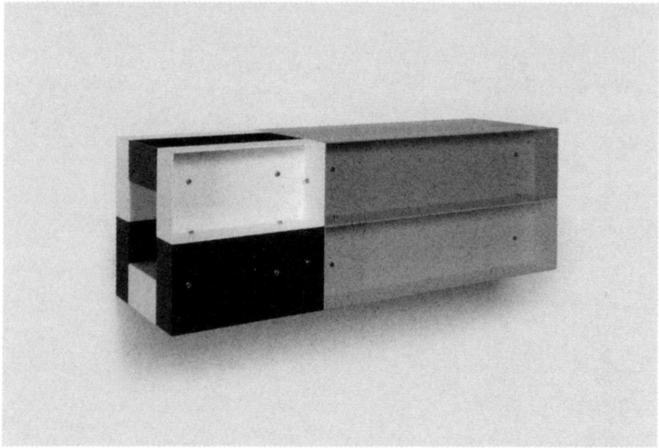

67
Donald Judd
Untitled, 1989
Painted aluminum
30 × 90 × 30 cm
(11¾ × 35⅜ × 11¾ inches)

piece of 1989, in which a left-hand vertical row of a 30 cm white unit and a 30 cm black unit are juxtaposed to a right-hand vertical row of a 60 cm deep yellow unit and a 60 cm yellow unit [fig. 67]. Just as white and black form a pair (a two-color monochrome), so do the two yellows of different values. The object distributes its hues, values, and dimensions unevenly; yet none of these factors seems to disrupt the sensory equality of the parts or the wholeness of the whole. Judd achieves sensory *equilibrium* without *balance*, as if his art were capable of opposing features that nevertheless evoke synonymous terms, the two the same. If his colors are equal, as he says they should be, would they not also balance? Like Peirce wrestling with feeling, sensation, and perception, we need new words. Or, better, we need more looking.

The distribution of pairs within the large floor pieces is more complicated because the vertical rows no longer form simple pairs in themselves but involve five elements, and these sequences also continue over the top plane of the prism and wrap around its sides. Judd did not want two elements of the same color to be juxtaposed, either vertically or horizontally—"The colors cannot touch side by side or end to end"—so planning the sequences became more difficult.[116] Because Judd believed that a color could be repeated along a diagonal without interfering with the general equality or equilibrium of sensory effects (without increasing the localized force of a single hue), a spiraling configuration would work, especially in cases for which few individual colors were being used, as in the Amsterdam floor piece, which has a red, a yellow, a blue, a turquoise, and no more.[117] Here, to prevent the juxtaposition of

[116] Judd, "Some Aspects of Color in General and Red and Black in Particular," *Donald Judd*, 159.
[117] "One above another [colors] are easy to see as a pair; diagonally they are not": ibid., 159.

two yellows around one of the right-angled corners, Judd transposed the positions that we would expect one of the reds and one of the yellows to have taken, were our eyes to trace the diagonals of the spiraling colors all around the object. As a result, the diagonals are imperfect, but no elements of the same color ever touch along a continuous edge.

Especially when working with greater numbers of individual colors, Judd could juggle the sequences or make arbitrary substitutions to introduce irregularities that would affect the emotional feel of the totality. For the floor piece in Rotterdam, which has six vertical rows to each long side rather than five, he eliminated some of the initial black, brown, and yellow units on one side, replacing them with various reds, which causes the work as a whole to appear unusually disjunctive to a circumambulating viewer. Judd thought of his general scheme as one that involved "rotating and alternating."[118] A spiraling effect could be staggered. Here, in graphic form, is the most straightforward version of a spiraling configuration, followed by a staggered version (each letter represents a unit of color):

A	E	D	C	B	A
B	A	E	D	C	B
C	B	A	E	D	C
D	C	B	A	E	D
E	D	C	B	A	E

A	D	B	E	C	A
B	E	C	A	D	B
C	A	D	B	E	C
D	B	E	C	A	D
E	C	A	D	B	E

Notice that if A and B form a pair, the duo slips down half a notch or, in the staggered version, a full notch from one vertical row to the next. In the staggered version, A and D might also be a pair, B and C might be a pair, and so on. Judd could complicate matters considerably (as he did for Rotterdam) by replacing certain elements of an initial scheme with new elements. To follow is a graph that indicates such a development, with V and X replacing D and E, along with other changes:

A	X	A	V	B	X
B	V	C	X	A	V
C	B	A	C	B	C
V	C	X	A	V	B
X	B	V	C	X	C

In the abstract, if V and X form a commutable pair (meaning that V + X is the same sensation as X + V), then it would

118 For this and the information that follows, see Judd's manuscript notes dated 12, 13, and 19 June 1984 (Judd Foundation, Marfa).

seem that A and B, A and C, and B and C would also be commutable pairs and capable of forming triads, such as A + B + A, with many other possibilities.

Thinking them out

If Judd was Peircean and Albersian, his speculations were also Nietzschean.[119] This is hardly obvious, because Friedrich Nietzsche sometimes seems to set interpretation ahead of the facts (the symbol ahead of the sensation). To the proposition, "There are only facts," he countered: "No, facts are precisely what there is not, only interpretations." An apparent affirmation of his argument, "Everything is subjective," left Nietzsche equally unsatisfied: "But even this is interpretation. The 'subject' is not something given, it is something added and invented and projected behind *what there is*."[120] We must invent the subject before matters can be subjective. Otherwise "subjective" experience is just a fact. If we see red, well, we see red—it happens. This would be the view of Judd, as it was of Peirce.[121] Whether what we see is red by some objective measure, or whether this redness might have meaning, are two points of speculation among many. Once executed, each of Judd's projective schemes of color became a fact, not a fantasy.

If things exist as a given natural order, Nietzsche implied, the human subject and the meanings it projects are not among those natural things. We construct our facts, deciding what should assume an identity in the world of experience, what should attain the status of a thing, a condition, an event. We even construct our individual being—each of us as a subject. We construct it from what? The implied source of our being, its instigation, is another realm of being, seemingly more fundamental: Nietzsche called it "what there is." The argument is circular but not illogical. Judd was adept at recognizing such non-ironical ironies of thought and experience (irony expresses a divide between one sense of a situation and another). Recall that his space was to be made, not found: someone makes space. He argued in 1983: "If the nature of art is the same as our nature and if there is no division between [projective] thought and [receptive] feeling, art is cognitive just as our experience is."[122] It must be thought as well as felt. Art becomes a fact created to be interpreted by others, an unsolicited contribution to collective subjectivity, a socializing device for communication. Its meaning (in thought) would be integral to its material form (in sensation). Judd again: "There is no form that can be

[119] And Judd also had intellectual affinities to Ludwig Wittgenstein; on this aspect of his thinking, see Shiff, "What Judd Knows," *Donald Judd*, 19–63. On the philosophical heritage directly related to Judd's education, see David Raskin, "Judd's Moral Art," in Serota, *Donald Judd*, 79–95; David Raskin, *Donald Judd* (New Haven and London: Yale University Press, 2010), 1–7. On Judd and philosophical parallels, see also Kellein, *Donald Judd: Early Work, 1955–1968*, 14–17; Rainer Crone, "Symmetry and Order: Formal Logic in the Sculptures of Donald Judd," *Donald Judd* (Eindhoven: Stedelijk Van Abbemuseum, 1987), 61–75.

[120] Friedrich Nietzsche, *The Will to Power*, ed. Walter Kaufmann, trans. Walter Kaufmann and R. J. Hollingdale (New York: Vintage, 1968), 267 (emphasis added). The quoted passage from Nietzsche's notes is dated 1883–1888. Judd's personal library includes twelve Nietzsche titles—inexpensive editions of a type usually bought personally for reading (as opposed to gifts received from others). He was probably well acquainted with Nietzsche's attitudes toward truth, fact, morality, social organization, and so on.

[121] Peirce argued for the objectivity of any visual sensation, even those that prove inconsistent with actual physical conditions: see Peirce, "Perception" (1903), *Collected Papers*, 7:368–76.

[122] Judd, "Art and Architecture," *Complete Writings 1975–1986*, 30.

form without meaning, quality and feeling. We even have feeling about a rock, about anything.... There is no pure form. And of course pure content doesn't exist."[123] This is a way of agreeing with Nietzsche that "the 'subject' is not something given." The human subject requires a situation within which it realizes itself. Its thought and its feeling are a pair.

Judd took no interest in distinguishing the objective from the subjective because their division would be analogous to a split between rational thought and emotional feeling. Like Peirce, he claimed that individual subjectivity was, for the individual, objective. How else could it be? "All experience is knowledge: subjective experience is knowledge; objective experience, which is science, is obviously knowledge. Color is knowledge. As Albers says, it is very subjective, even hard to remember. Color is also objective."[124] To demonstrate the last point, Judd cited Albers on the experience of afterimage, an illusion to which everyone is susceptible, and added this: "Allowing for everything human being subjective, this is absolutely objective."[125] The illusion is objective because everyone has it. Even if everyone did not, the experience of an afterimage would be a fact.

"I don't learn anything in the making of [a work] ... I'm interested in thinking them out."[126] This was Judd's justification for using fabricators, seasoned experts with respect to engineering the structures he needed built and handling his favored materials without introducing damage. He assigned the physical realization of his three-dimensional objects to others—objects conceived in his thinking process, acquiring initial form as notations on paper that might be mere jottings of a few numbers, a few letters, a phrase. He was inventing facts. With the RAL system of identifying available pigments, Judd had a reasonably precise sense of how a fabricator's color would look when a designed object had been built. Some of the sketches seem like decisive instructions, blueprints for action. Other notes appear as stages of an investigation in progress. "To arrive [at] the checkerboard structure, from the idea that the same color should not be adjacent" was Judd's thought in 1990, stated as an open question.[127] Does such respect for thinking things out—projecting mental forms into physical experience—imply that he should be regarded as a "conceptualist" or some sort of idealist? Hardly: "Decisions made in working result in art, not in discrete [verbal] ideas."[128] The art was a thought, one that felt like a feeling.

123 Ibid., 31.

124 Judd, "Some Aspects of Color in General and Red and Black in Particular," *Donald Judd*, 152. With regard to the point about memory, compare Peirce, "A Guess at the Riddle," *Collected Papers*, 1:200: "Memory is an articulated complex and worked-over product which differs infinitely and immeasurably from feeling. Look at a red surface, and try to feel what the sensation is, and then shut your eyes and try to remember it.... I have convinced myself that there is nothing in my memory that is in the least like the vision of red. When red is not before my eyes, I do not see it at all."

125 Judd, "Some Aspects of Color in General and Red and Black in Particular," *Donald Judd*, 152.

126 Judd, statement recorded in Marfa, Texas, fall 1975, in *The Artist's Studio: Donald Judd*, film, produced and directed by Michael Blackwood, Michael Blackwood Productions, 2010.

127 Manuscript note dated 12 January 1990 (Judd Foundation, Marfa).

128 Judd, "Art and Architecture," *Complete Writings 1975–1986*, 26.

Judd was a pragmatist, not an idealist. Objects conceived in thought were subject to negotiated adjustment in order to be conceived in physical matter. If a desired visual feature proved difficult to achieve within a reasonably economical fabrication process, then it was time to return to a sketchpad or a collage of color samples—to thinking. Imagine, by way of contrast, if Judd had chosen to work in clay or wax, with the aim of casting the form in metal after reaching a satisfactory result in the more malleable material. Clay and wax encourage immediate adjustment by touch. The majority of Judd's changes in three-dimensional design did not occur within a continuous process of tactile action and reaction with respect to a material in hand, but more in the way that architects adjust the design of a space or notations for dimensions and proportions. Each stage in the process tests a thought, a feeling.

Judd was no slave to his carefully wrought proportions and regularities. He designed his six large floor pieces of enameled sheet aluminum (and "clear" galvanized iron) to be constructed from uniform elements of 30 × 150 × 7.5 cm, yet there was an exception. He shortened by 7.5 cm the ten elements of the top surface of the structure destined to butt against the two short ends of the rectilinear prism.[129] Each of those ten exceptional panels measures 30 × 142.5 × 7.5 cm. Had Judd not made this adjustment, each of the corners would have appeared with a double lip forming a recessed angle, rather than as a projecting angle (the usual right angle, as seen in ordinary boxes). Had Judd chosen the spatial complication of the recessed angle, which both catches light and projects shadow, he would have drawn extra attention to the corners as four accented verticals. The corners are perhaps already special enough because of the narrow strip (7.5 cm) of five colors that flanks each side of the stack of five panels constituting each end of the structure.

"Color is like material," Judd stated in 1993: "It is one way or another, but it obdurately exists. Its existence *as it is* is the main fact and not what it might mean, which may be nothing."[130] Judd's sentence passes—as readily as one, two, three—from the being of color ("its existence"), to the human perception of color (its recognition as "the main fact"), to its subjective interpretation ("what it might mean"). A color of which the meaning "may be nothing" is a fact without an interpretation, a Two that never fully reaches to Three in a process of three stages: first, vague feeling; second, concrete sensation; third, discursive thought. Judd's colors were material among his materials,

[129] A manuscript note dated 19 June 1984 (Judd Foundation, Marfa) refers to "shorter top panels at ends."
[130] Judd, "Some Aspects of Color in General and Red and Black in Particular," *Donald Judd*, 158 (emphasis added).

chosen for their capacity to affect the senses and for their persistence; they would deflect or delay the urge to interpret. Like the aluminum, galvanized iron, copper, plywood, and Plexiglas that were among his favored materials, his applied colors (when he used them) were not dispensable additives but, in Nietzsche's phrase, "what there is"—or, in Judd's wording, "things that exist." His colors have sensory, phenomenal presence. For this reason, as he might also say, "everything is on their side."[131] Judd concluded: "My simple objects encourage people to think about the nature of the world we live in."[132] We see. Then we think. Then we see all the more attentively.

Two blacks (fallibilism)

The New York floor piece has eight colors, structured in terms of possibilities for pairs; its organization involves no spiraling [see fig. 9]. Most of the vertical rows, consisting of five units each, include either a black element or a white element or both. There are two rows that contain only the strongly chromatic colors from the palette of this work—two varieties of red, two of yellow, two of blue. They seem to glow, appearing bright yet relatively mellow by comparison with the ten rows in which elements of black and white punctuate the chromatic play.[133] Two of the ten rows introduce a different degree of—what to call it?—order perhaps, or disorder. I refer to the fact that two rows violate Judd's principle of avoiding the juxtaposition of units of the same color. On one of the long sides of the rectilinear prism, in adjacent positions within the grid of horizontal and vertical rows, two blacks constitute the center elements within their respective vertical rows. This doubling or repetition, or however it might be described, is unique among the five extant floor pieces.

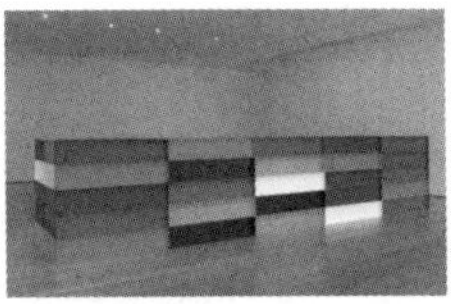

9 see page 255

Is it a mistake? We would think so, because a similar repetition in the same system was eliminated from a final working drawing of 1991 that continues to show the "error" of the two blacks surviving, apparently unnoticed.[134] According to Rob Weiner, who worked with Judd on this project, the artist had corrected a similar problem in the Düsseldorf floor piece, but may not have seen the New York piece completed.[135] His response to the juxtaposition of the blacks, if there was one, remains unknown.

For me, the curious aspect of the New York work is that its "mistake" is a feature of interest, in Judd's sense of the term. The horizontal pairing of the blacks becomes the equivalent

131 "Things that exist exist, and everything is on their side": Judd, "Black, White, and Gray" (1964), *Complete Writings 1959–1975*, 117.
132 Judd, interview by Renée Steenbergen, "Ik ben niet zo onder de indruk van Plato," *NRC Handelsblad* 23 (30 April 1993): 178 (English version: unpaginated typescript, Judd Foundation, Marfa; courtesy Caitlin Murray).
133 Two of the five rows on the top plane also include no black or white elements.
134 Letter from Rob Weiner to Joe Buguyer (representing the fabricator, Lascaux), 29 April 1991 (Museum of Modern Art, New York; courtesy Ann Temkin).
135 Rob Weiner, email to the author, 26 February 2014.

of other qualities that the work presents and an integral part of the whole. Judd's construction appears to accommodate its misstep in full stride. This could be because his art is forgiving, that is, it tolerates anomalies. The fundamental structural unit, which Judd found satisfying over a full decade of practice and showed no signs of abandoning, proved so effective a vehicle for color that not all of his cautions had to be respected. Although Judd intended the no-doubling rule primarily for the floor pieces, it seems telling that his oeuvre includes numerous wall pieces that do nothing if not double the elements of color, pairing the same, making the two the one [See fig. 64]. There is another distinct possibility: because the horizontally linked black elements pair in very different ways, each within its own vertical row, the two blacks may constitute an instance of "the two the same"—separate in their coincidental wholeness. The black to the left is bordered by chromatic primaries (blue, red), whereas the black to the right is bordered by complementary whites. If the blacks are the "same," their pairings are nevertheless entirely different—"two." We may be dealing with differentiated triads: one complete (blue, black, red), and one degenerate because it lacks a distinct third color (white, black, white).

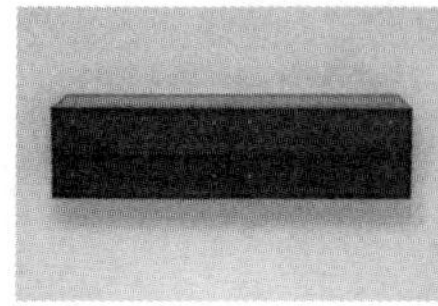

64 see page 286

deep blue	white
black	black
deep red	white

If the "mistake" causes no distress, is it the case that anything goes? No. Judd referred to wanting an order—a "small order," but more than none.[136] Among large orders that he refused to accept were comprehensive philosophical theories, cultural ideologies, and aesthetic canons. He also rejected the non-order of randomness or, more to the point, chaos (the two not quite the same). As a principle for distributing color, chaos had the failings of order. "Chaos would not achieve what I want," Judd wrote in 1993: "It [chaos] requires a greater number, which if great enough becomes order. First, the parts would touch and second, the colors would not be distributed more or less evenly. But mainly the initial selection of colors prohibits randomness. In a note of 1965 I wrote that form, which I don't like so much as a word, and color should be 'intelligent without being ordered.'"[137] In the limitless abundance that is elemental chaos, in this chaos of elements, two parts the same would

[136] See notes 69, 70, 71.
[137] Judd, "Some Aspects of Color in General and Red and Black in Particular," *Donald Judd*, 159.

touch by chance, violating a limit that Judd put on the "small order" he desired. Again, in its abundance, the variation in chaos would be so extreme that the equalizing effect of selective pairings—"the initial selection of colors"—would be lost. Equalization might exist as a collective grayness or even as a chance "landscape" harmony, but not as the uniform chromatic distinctiveness Judd was seeking. In his art in general, and in the New York floor piece in particular, effects of color equalize without evening out.

Judd seems to return, however inadvertently, to thoughts of pragmatism and its fallibilism. "Intelligence without order" is quite a claim—the less order, the more guesswork, the more fallibility. What might serve the cause of intelligence without order, or very little order? It would be spontaneity of thought and feeling—in Peirce's words, "slight tendencies to do otherwise than previously."[138] Spontaneity and its irregularity or diversion must indeed remain "slight"; if spontaneity were to evolve into a larger order of regularity, rule, or habit, it would cease to be spontaneous. A spontaneous action, one without firm precedent, is either intelligent or a mistake, perhaps both. The spontaneous tendency first appears, then eliminates its own tendency, lest it become dogma. This is the change in which Judd put his faith: "I don't believe in progress, but simply change."[139] To me, the juxtaposition of the two blacks appears as a mistake only by the precondition of its prohibition. In my sensation, spontaneously, it registers as a flash of intelligence. Yet, my thought (Judd's as well?) could be as mistaken as the two blacks. Aesthetic judgments have an objective base but are fallible. I am left to address the situation as Judd would: "Finally, I only believe my own work"—in this instance, my own thought, my own feeling.[140]

Peirce's sense of chaos is much like Judd's. Here, I cannot say that Judd found a precedent in Peirce. In thoughts, judgments, and beliefs of this kind, precedence does not matter—in sensation, it does not matter. "Every text is eternally written *here and now*."[141] The spontaneity of our thought will either set Judd in advance of Peirce or Peirce in advance of Judd. In this spirit, Peirce wrote of indefinite beginnings: "The first chaos consisted in an infinite multitude of unrelated feelings. As there was no continuity about them, it was, as it were, a powder of feelings.... Now you must not ask me what happened first.... In this chaos of feelings, bits of similitude had appeared ... A slight tendency to generalization had here and there

138 Peirce, "To Christine Ladd-Franklin, On Cosmology" (1891), *Collected Papers*, 8:214.
139 Judd, in Millet, "La petite logique de Donald Judd," 7 (author's translation).
140 Judd, "Statement which appeared in 'ABC Art' by Barbara Rose," *Complete Writings 1959–1975*, 181.
141 Barthes, "The Death of the Author," *Image–Music–Text*, 145 (emphasis original).

lighted up and been quenched. Had reappeared, had strengthened itself. Like had begun to produce like."[142] The trick to art is not to let likeness become a habit, a precondition that generalizes effects before they convey their specificity.

Two elements of the same—two feelings alike within a "powder of feelings," two blacks juxtaposed within an extensive structural grid—must remain *two*, or as Judd might say: specific, particular, definite. It seems appropriate to repeat a thought already presented, to present it twofold. It speaks of the specificity of small orders. Judd's thought bares his feeling and is as emotional as it is logical: "The sand on the beach is not chaotic. To call it so is to lament a kind of order which never existed anyway."[143] The sand needs no more order than what it manifests—more than chaos, less than culture. What holds for the sand holds for the beach and the rest of the environment, including the spaces and colors that an artist like Judd would create. Nothing is perfected; ideologies are inherently overreaching. No transcendent order exists, only small orders, which are fallible. Judd knew that the challenge as well as the interest of his art was its fallibilism.

[142] Peirce, "To Christine Ladd-Franklin, On Cosmology," *Collected Papers*, 8:215.
[143] Judd, "Josef Albers," *Josef Albers*, 16.

Plates

2
Donald Judd
Untitled, 1987
Anodized aluminum
6 × 110¾ × 6 inches
(15.2 × 281.3 × 15.2 cm)

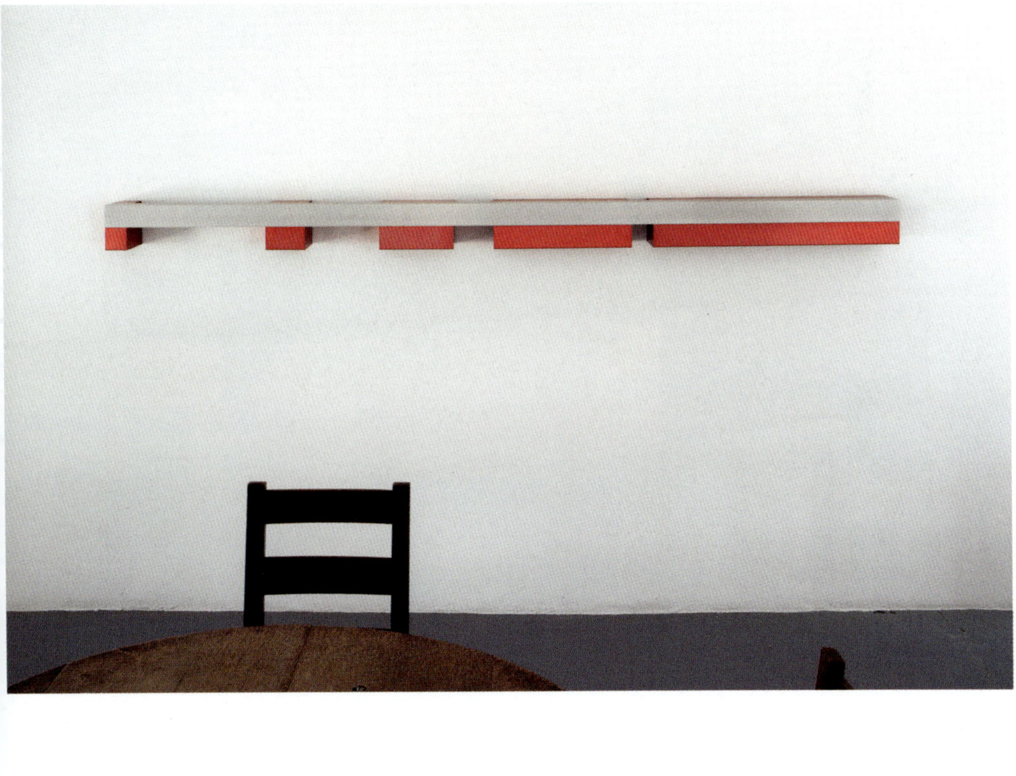

3
Donald Judd
Untitled, 1987
Painted aluminum
30 × 120 × 30 cm
(11¾ × 47¼ × 11¾ inches)

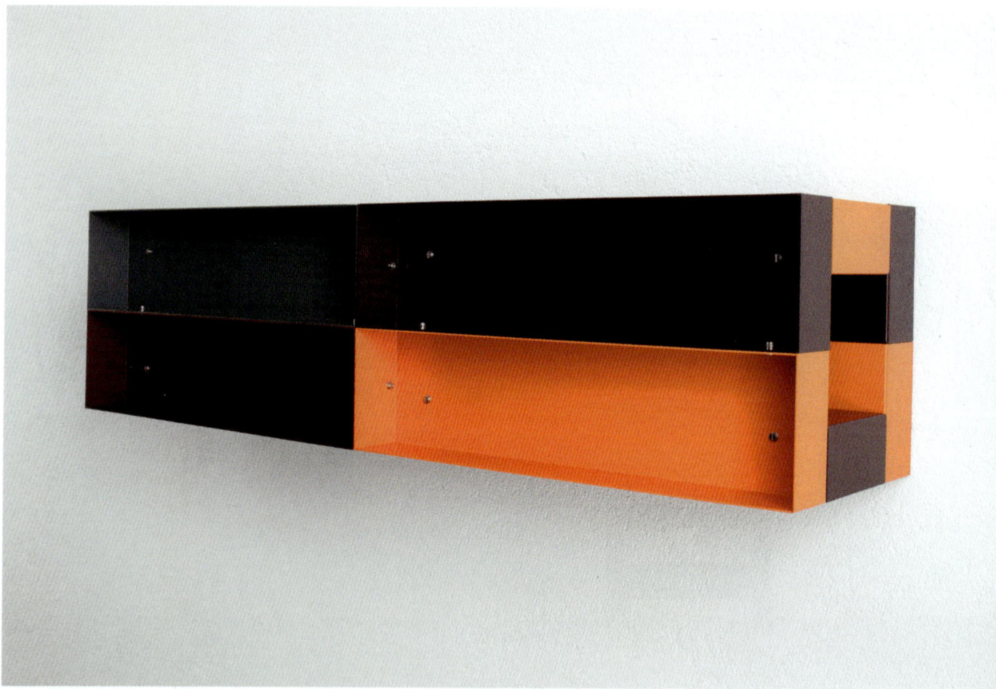

5
Donald Judd
Untitled, 1989
Clear anodized aluminum with
blue acrylic sheet
100 × 200 × 200 cm
(39.3 × 78.7 × 78.7 inches)

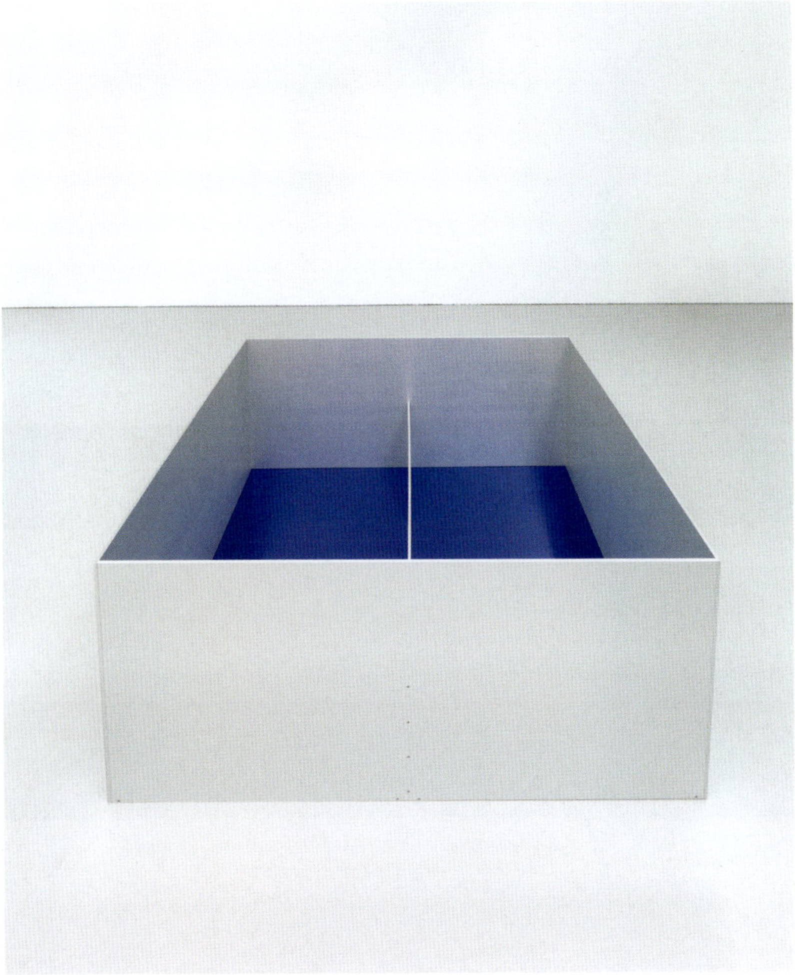

6
Donald Judd
Untitled, 1981
Brushed aluminum with blue acrylic sheets
4 units, each 50 × 100 × 50 cm
(19⅝ × 39⅜ × 19⅝ inches)

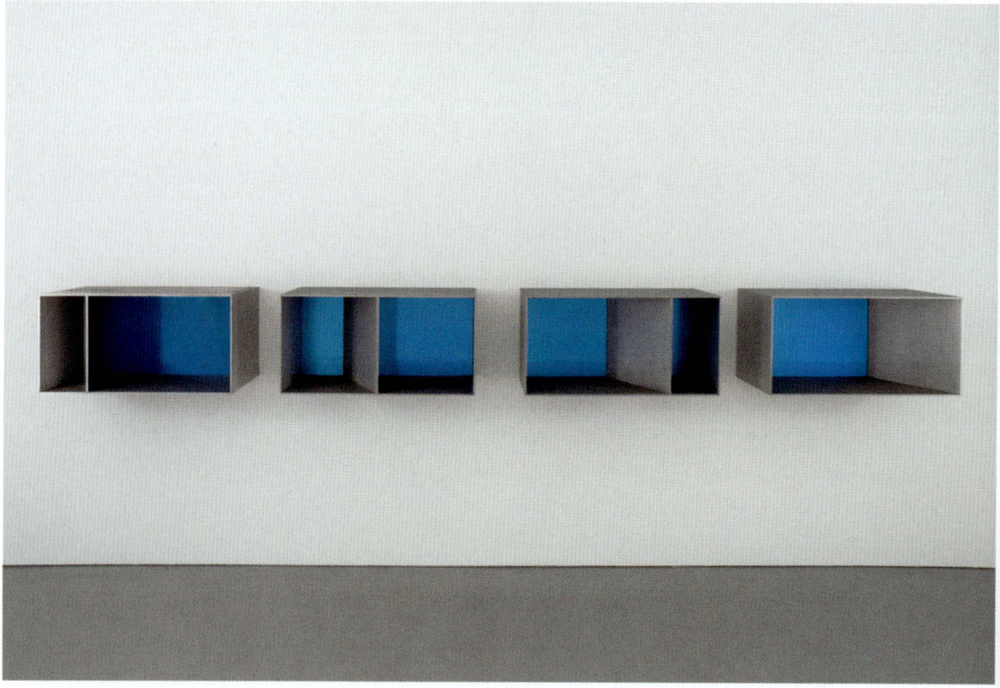

7
Donald Judd
Untitled, 1989
Cor-Ten steel with green, yellow, purple, ivory, orange, and black acrylic sheets
6 units, each 50 × 100 × 50 cm
19 5⁄8 × 39 5⁄16 × 19 5⁄8 in.

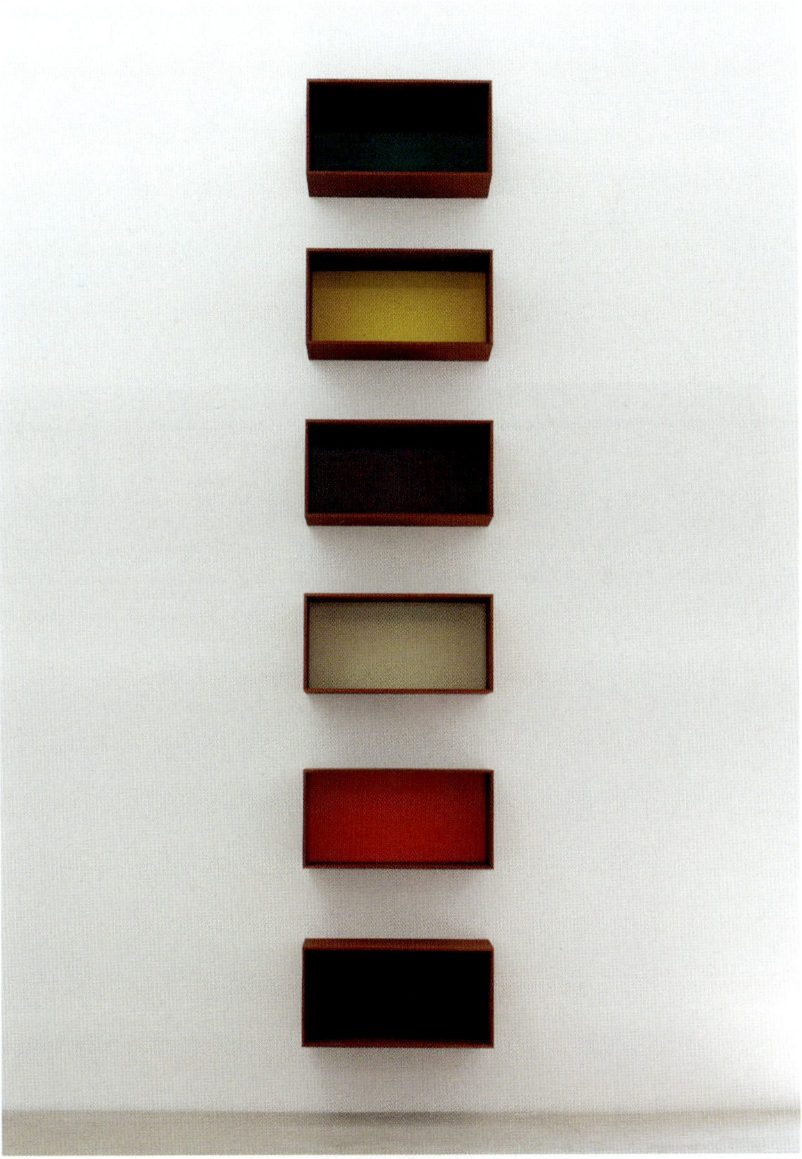

8
Donald Judd
Untitled, 1964
Red lacquer on wood
4 13⁄16 × 25 1⁄2 × 8 3⁄8 inches
(12.2 × 64.8 × 21.3 cm)

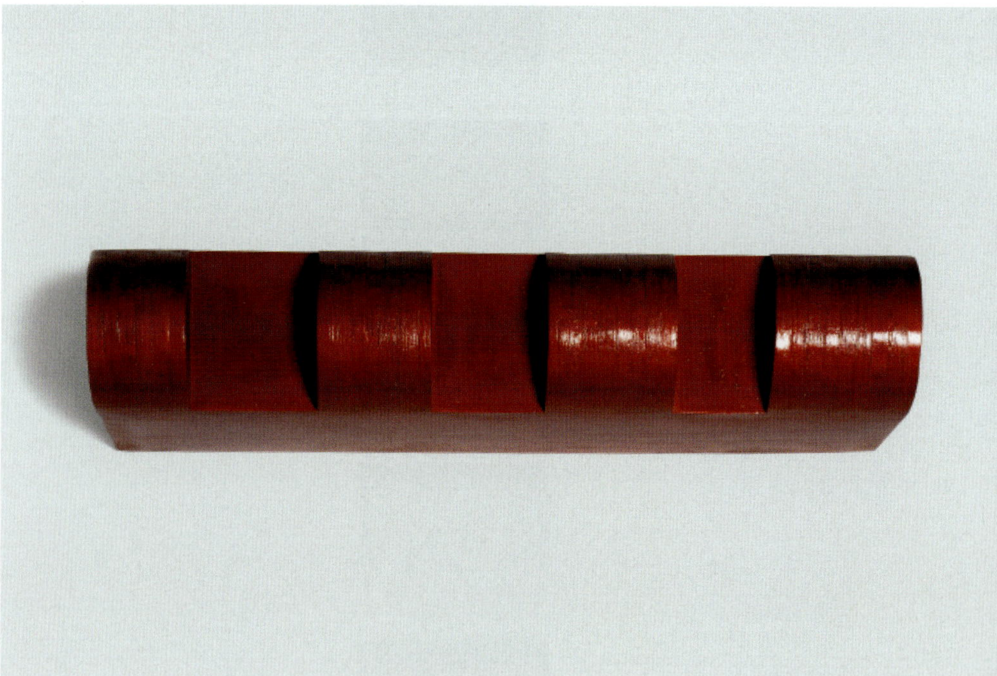

9
Donald Judd
Untitled, 1991
Enameled aluminum
150 × 750 × 165 cm
(59 × 247¼ × 65 inches)

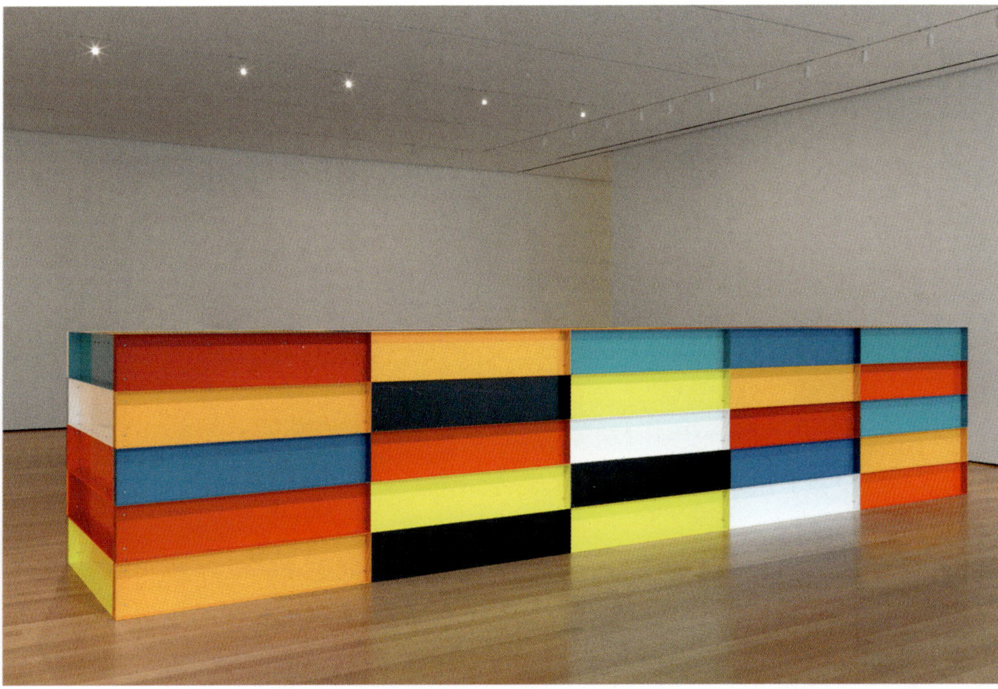

10
Donald Judd
Untitled, 1993
Plywood and yellow acrylic sheet
100 × 100 × 50 cm
(39 5/16 × 39 5/16 × 19 5/8 inches)

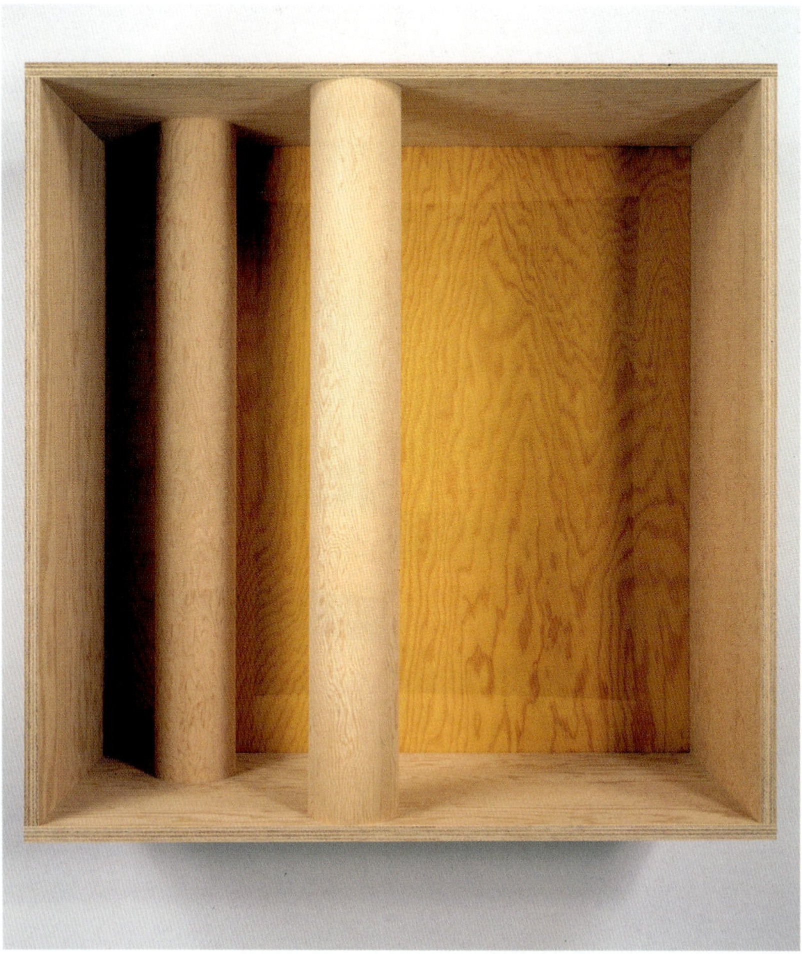

11
Donald Judd
Untitled, 1991
Cor-ten steel with painted
yellow back
4 units, each 100 × 100 × 50 cm
(39⅜ × 39⅜ ix 19⅝ inches)

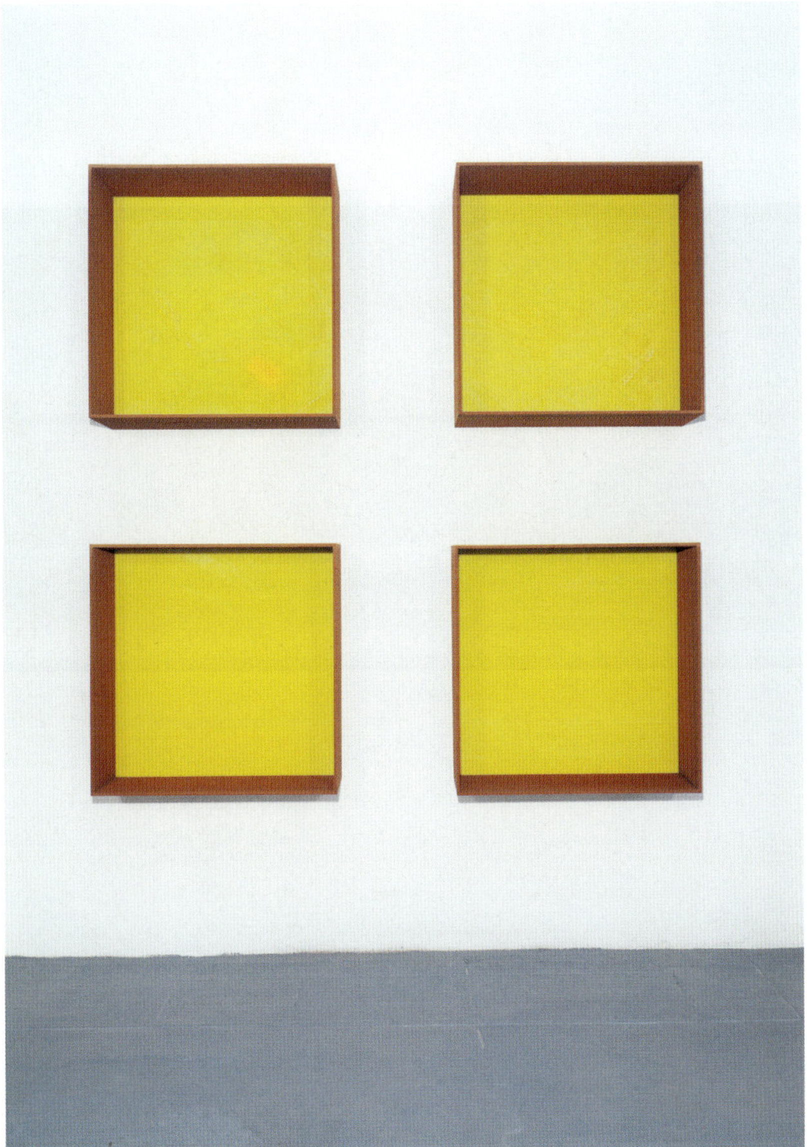

13
Lee Bontecou
Untitled, 1960
Steel, canvas, parchment, and plastic
54½ × 120 × 26 inches
(138.4 × 304.8 × 66.4 cm)

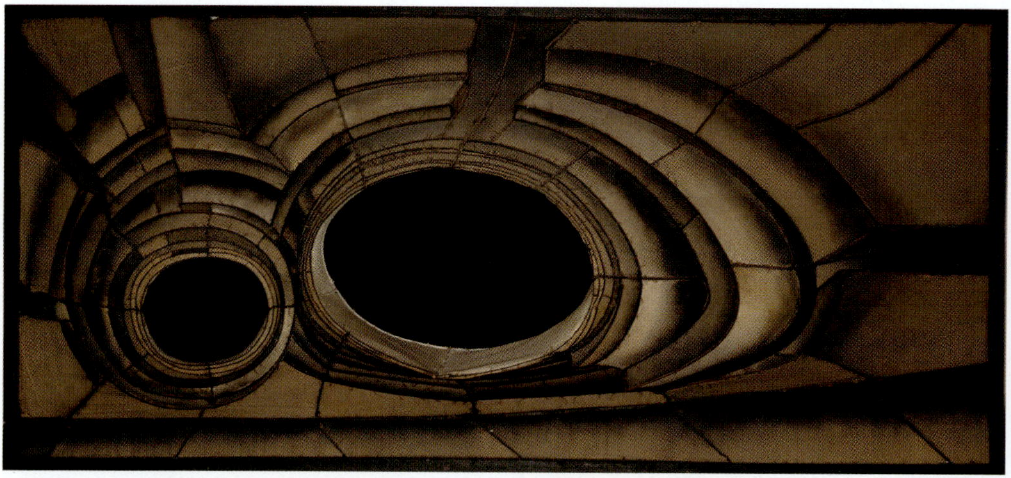

17
Donald Judd
Untitled, 1989
Painted aluminum
30 × 180 × 30 cm
(11¾ × 70 13/16 × 11¾ in.)

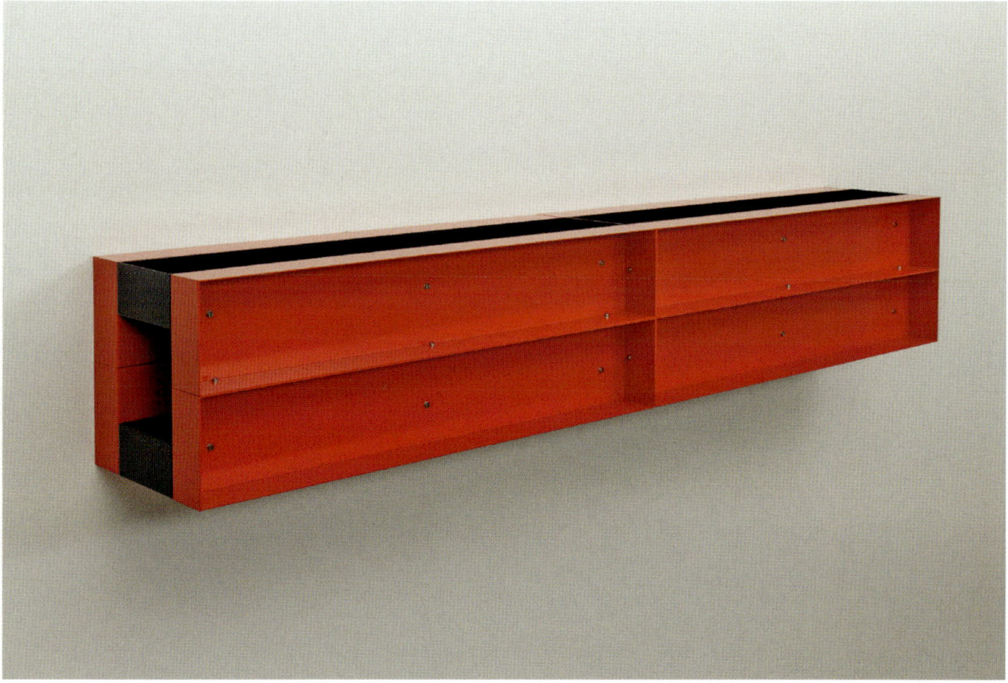

18
Donald Judd
Untitled, 1988
Anodized aluminum with brown acrylic sheets
2 units, each 50 × 100 × 50 cm
(19⅝ × 39$^{5}/_{16}$ × 19⅝ inches)

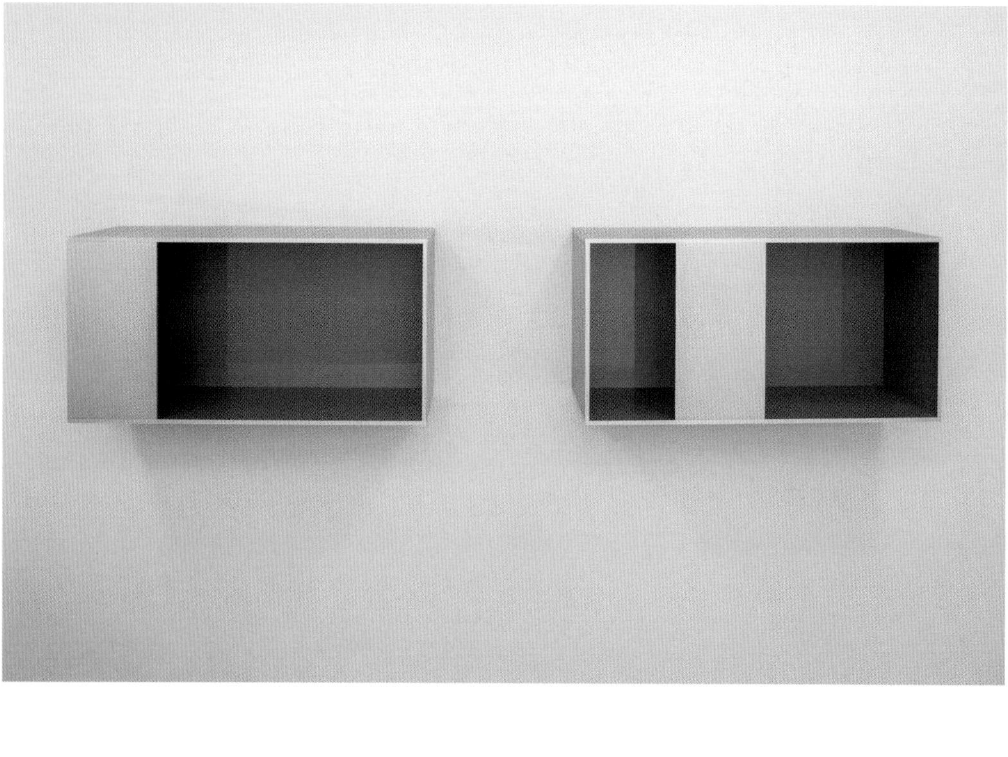

20
Donald Judd
Untitled, 1962
Cadmium red light oil on wood
and black enameled metal pipe
48 × 32½ × 21¼ inches
(121.9 × 82.6 × 54 cm)

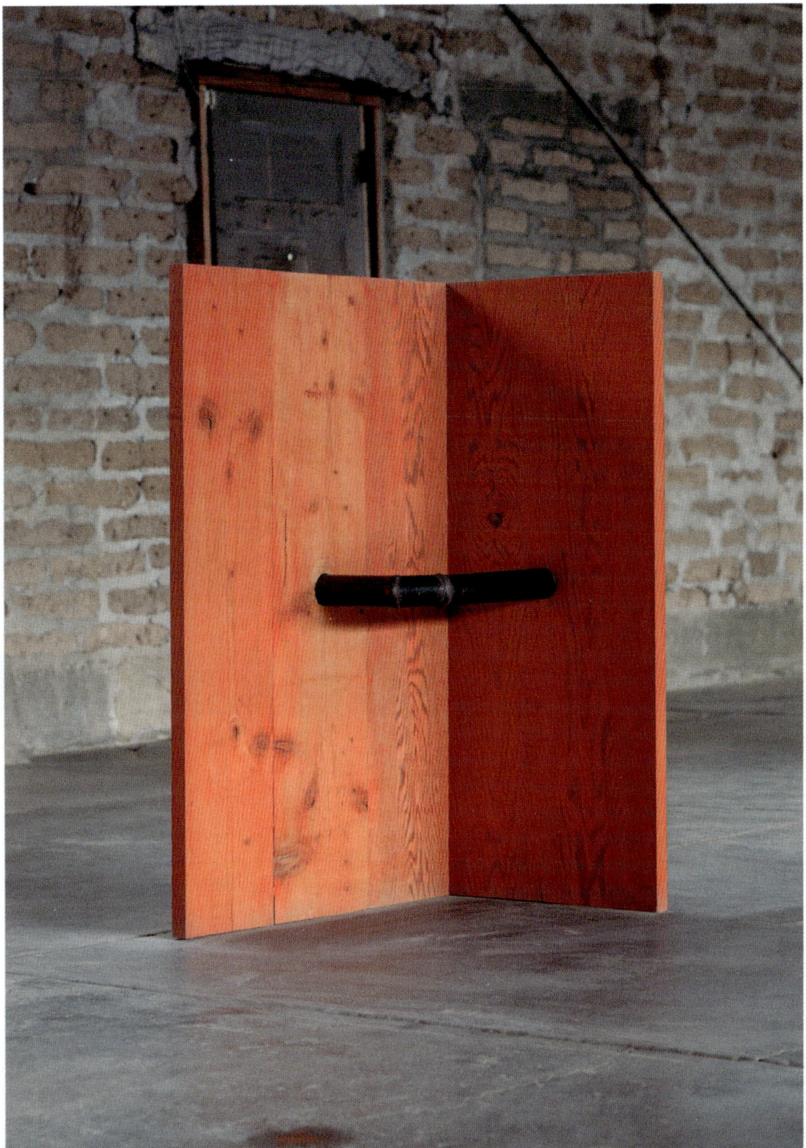

23
Donald Judd
Untitled, 1977
Copper and blue acrylic sheet
50 × 100 × 50 cm
(19 5/8 × 39 5/16 × 19 5/8 inches)

25
Donald Judd
Untitled, 1986
Cor-ten steel with purple acrylic sheet
100 × 100 × 50 cm
(39 5⁄16 × 39 5⁄16 × 19 5⁄8 inches)

27
Donald Judd
Untitled, 1992
Plywood with blue and red
acrylic sheets
50 × 100 × 25 cm
(19 5/8 × 39 5/16 × 9 13/16 inches)

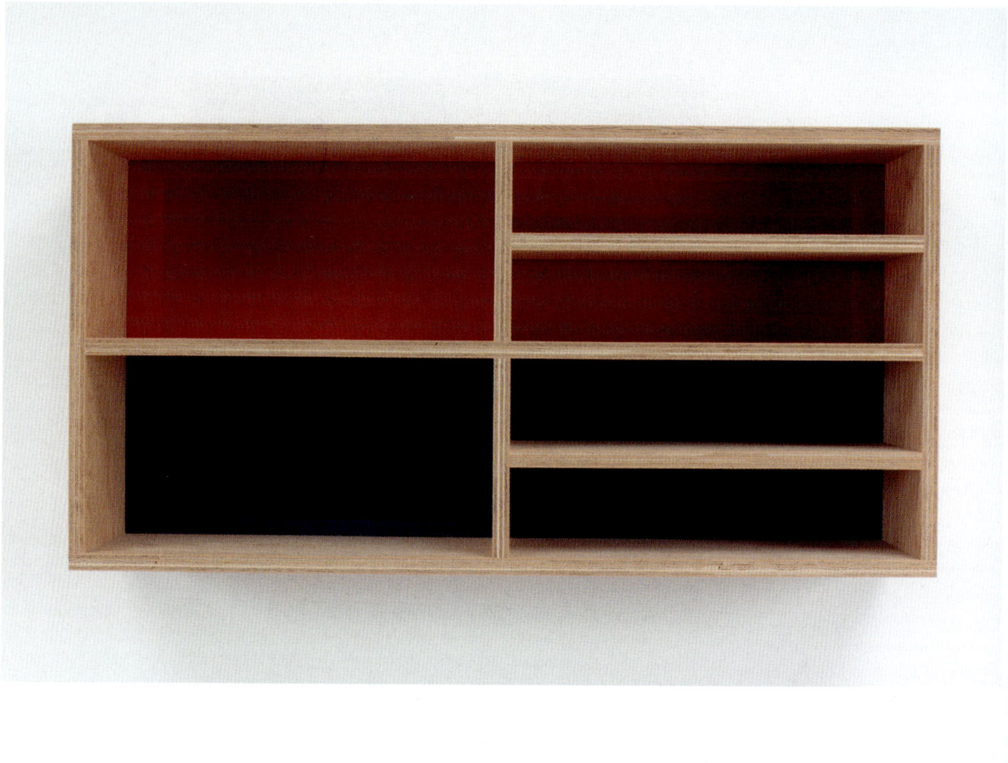

32
Donald Judd
Untitled, 1964
Red enamel on galvanized iron
over wood
6 × 27 × 24 inches
(15.2 × 68.6 × 61 cm)

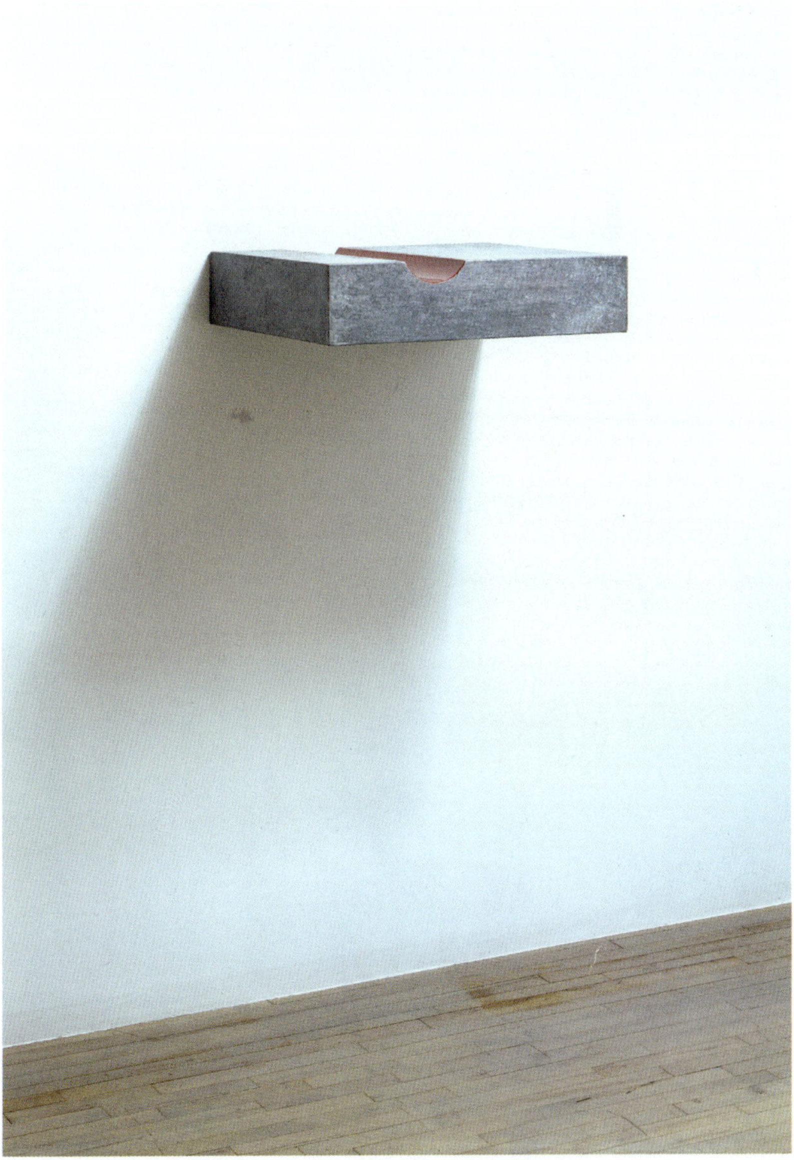

38
Donald Judd
Untitled, 1966
Galvanized iron
10 units, each 9 × 40 × 31 inches
(22.9 × 101.6 × 78.7 cm)

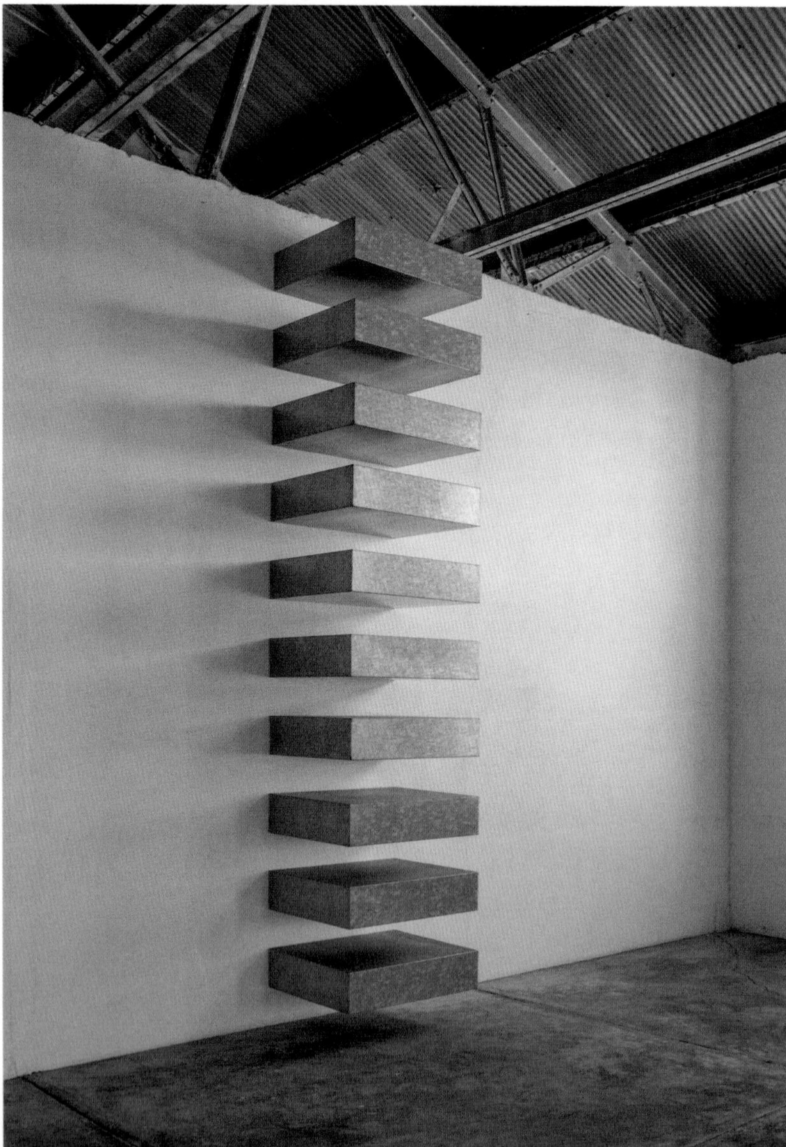

39
Donald Judd
Untitled, 1967
Galvanized iron and blue acrylic sheet
6 × 27 × 24 inches
(15.2 × 68.6 × 70 cm)

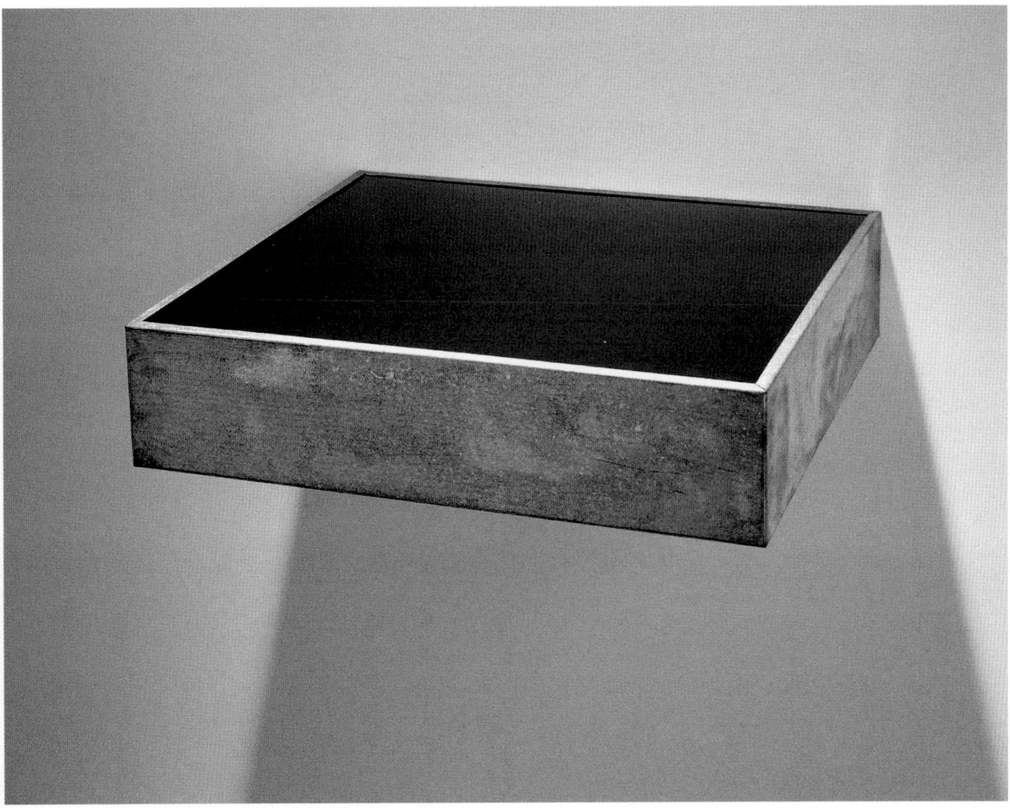

40

Donald Judd
Untitled, 1988
Clear anodized aluminum with green acrylic sheets
6 units, each 50 × 100 × 50 cm
(19⅝ × 39 5⁄16 × 19⅝ inches)

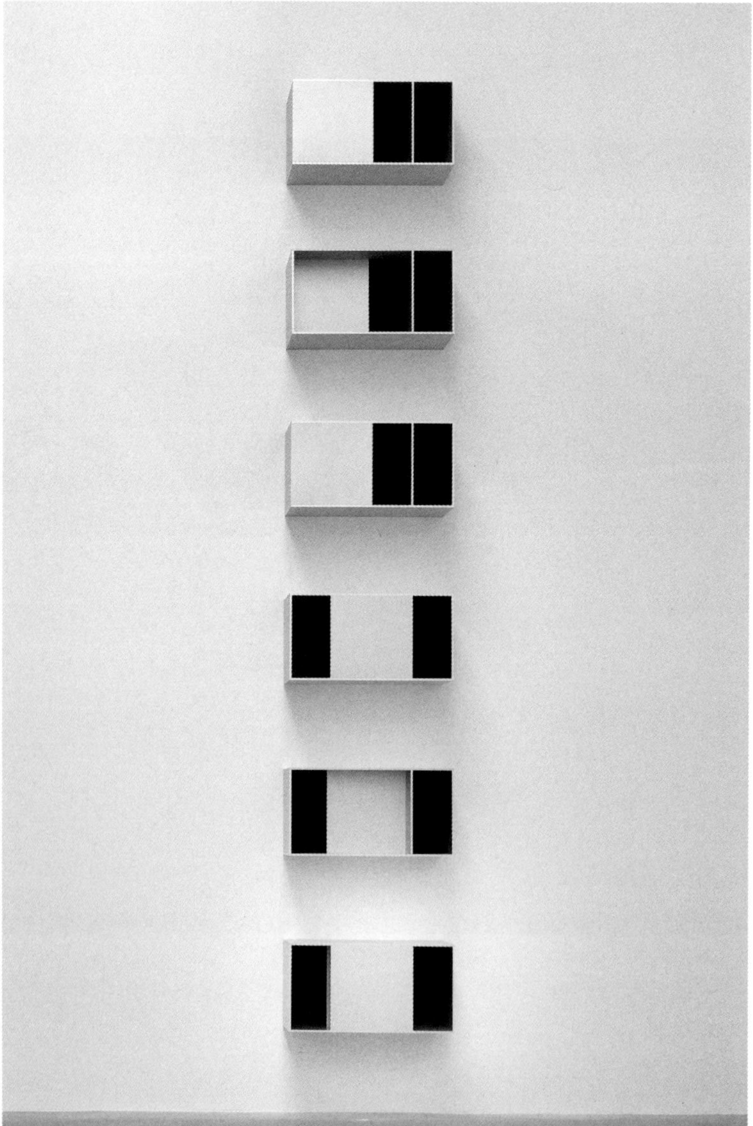

42
Donald Judd
Untitled, 1963
Cadmium red light oil on wood
with iron pipe
22⅛ × 45⅜ × 30½ inches
(56.2 × 115.3 × 77.5 cm)

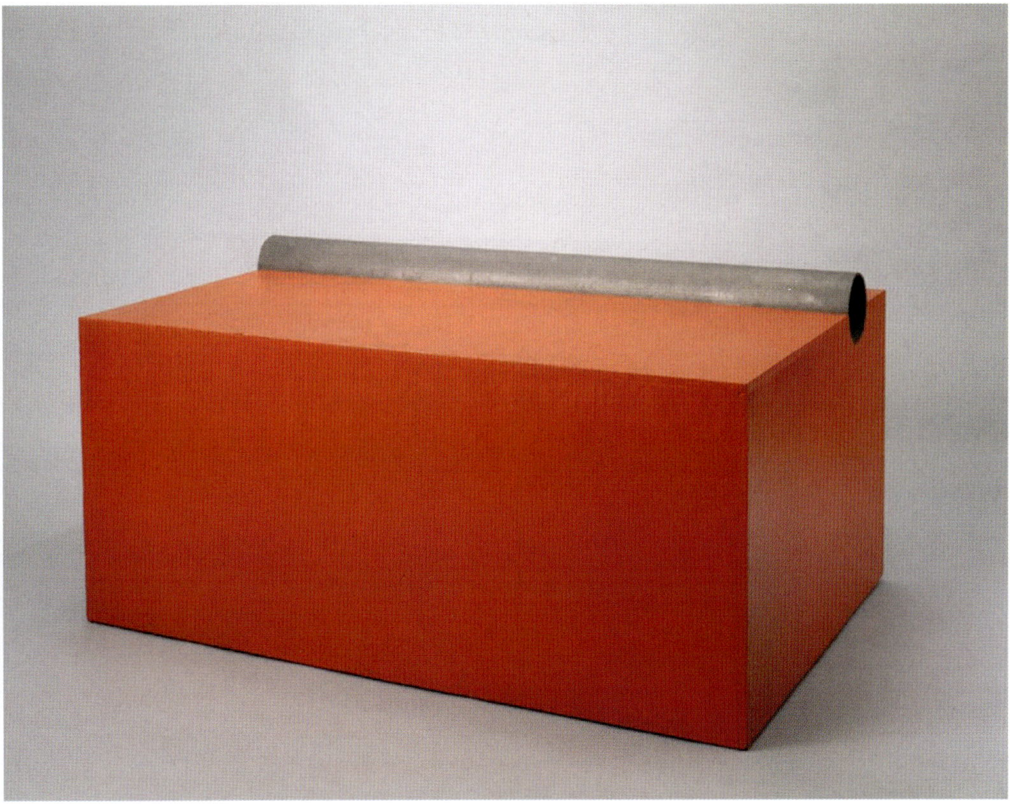

43
Donald Judd
Untitled, 1963
Purple lacquer on aluminum and cadmium red light oil on wood
5⅛ × 32⅝ × 5⅛ inches
(13 × 82.8 × 13 cm)

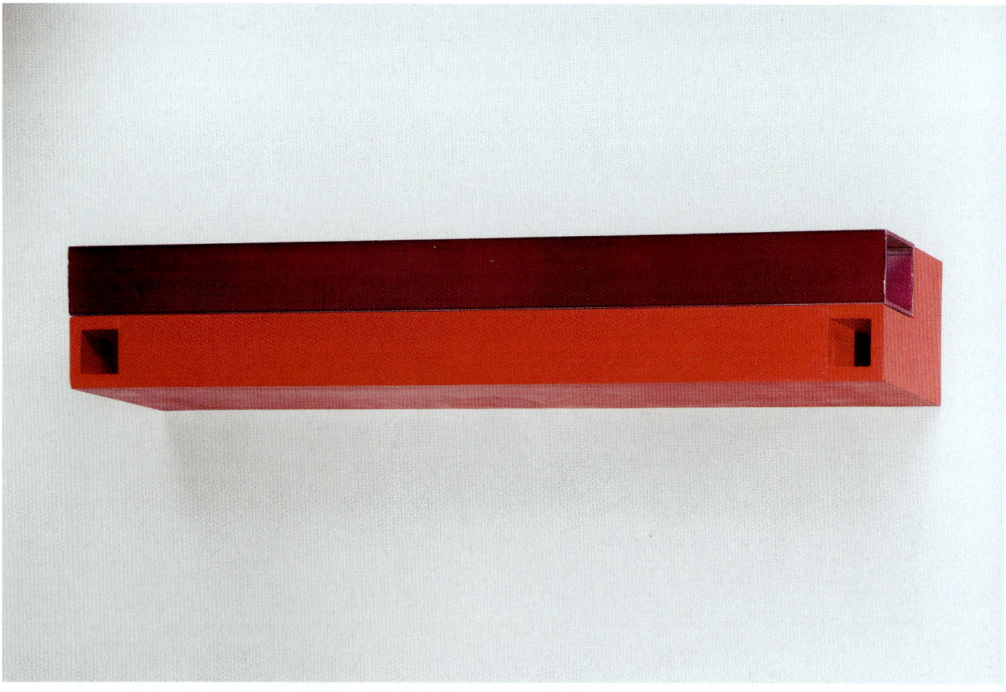

44
Donald Judd
Untitled, 1986
Aluminum with red acrylic
sheet
10 × 40 × 10 inches
(25.4 × 101.6 × 25.4 cm)

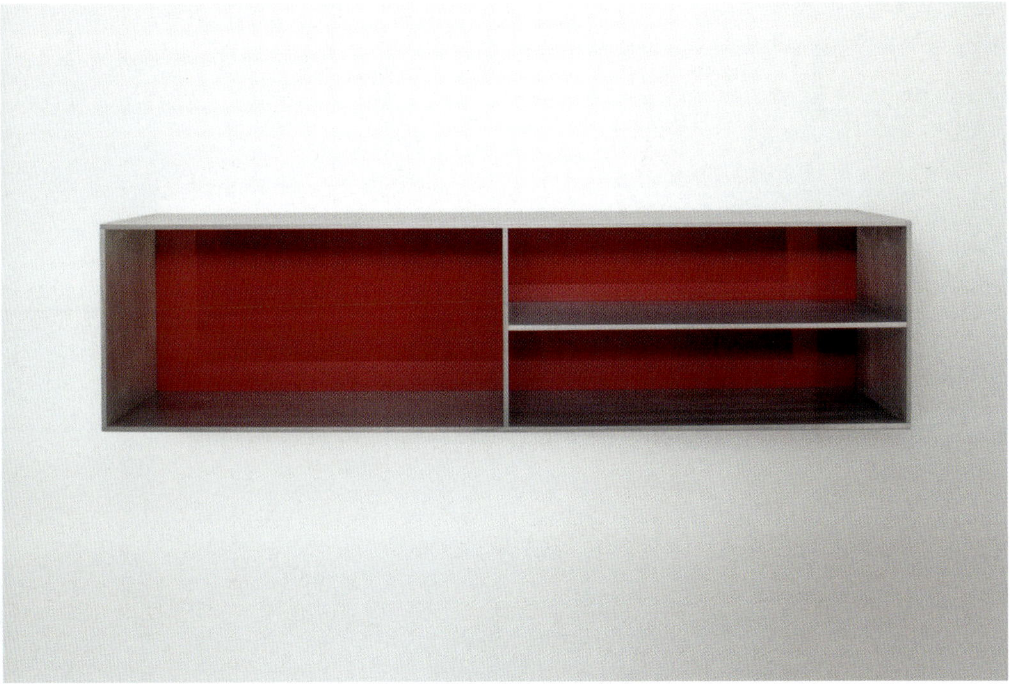

45
Donald Judd
Untitled, 1991
Plywood with aluminum found object
19½ × 45 × 30½ inches
(49.5 × 114.3 × 77.5 cm)

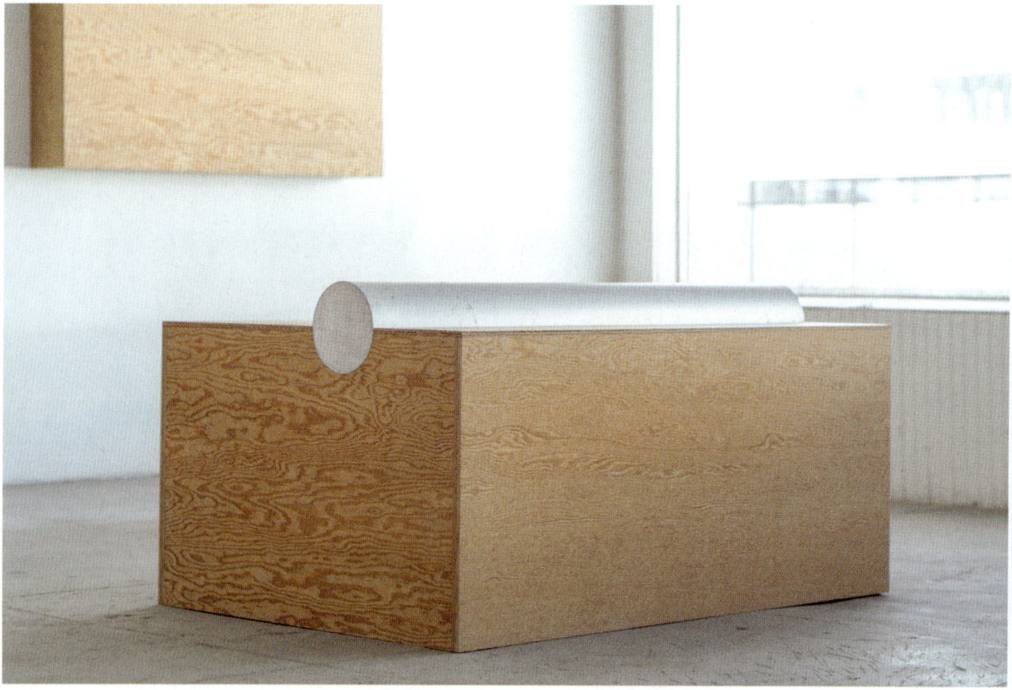

46
Donald Judd
Untitled, 1989
Clear anodized aluminum with
black acrylic sheet
100 × 200 × 200 cm
(39.3 × 78.7 × 78.7 inches)

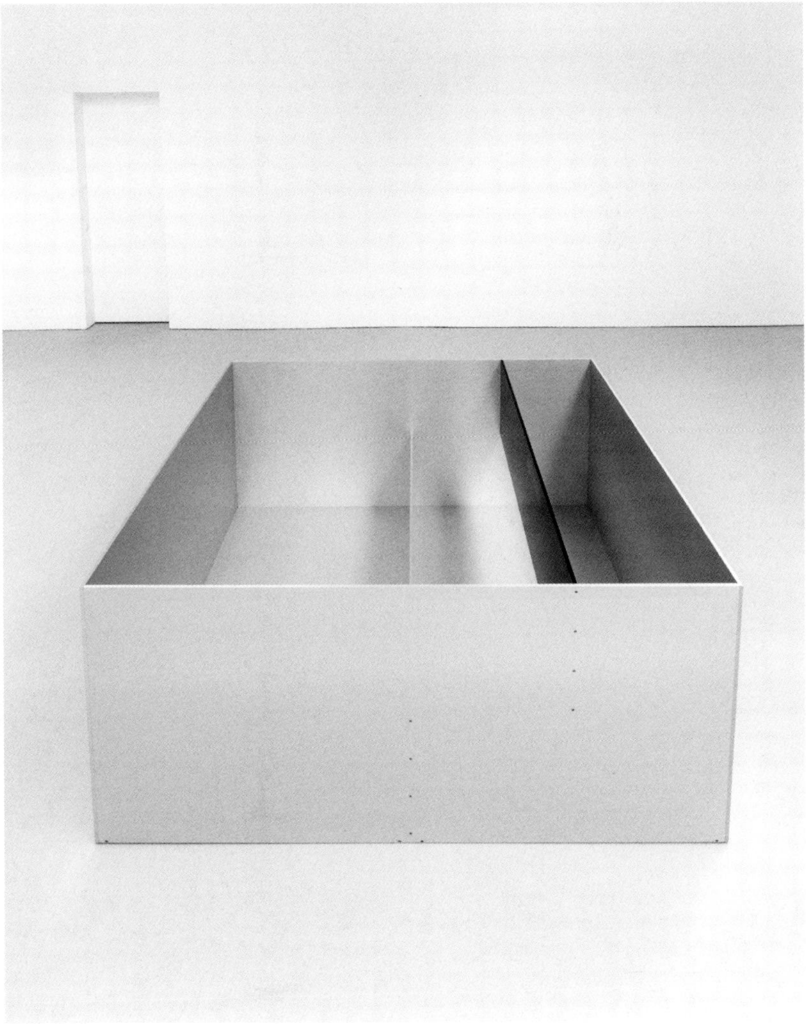

47
Donald Judd
Untitled, 1989
Clear and black anodized aluminum with amber and black acrylic sheets
100 × 200 × 200 cm
(39.3 × 78.7 × 78.7 inches)

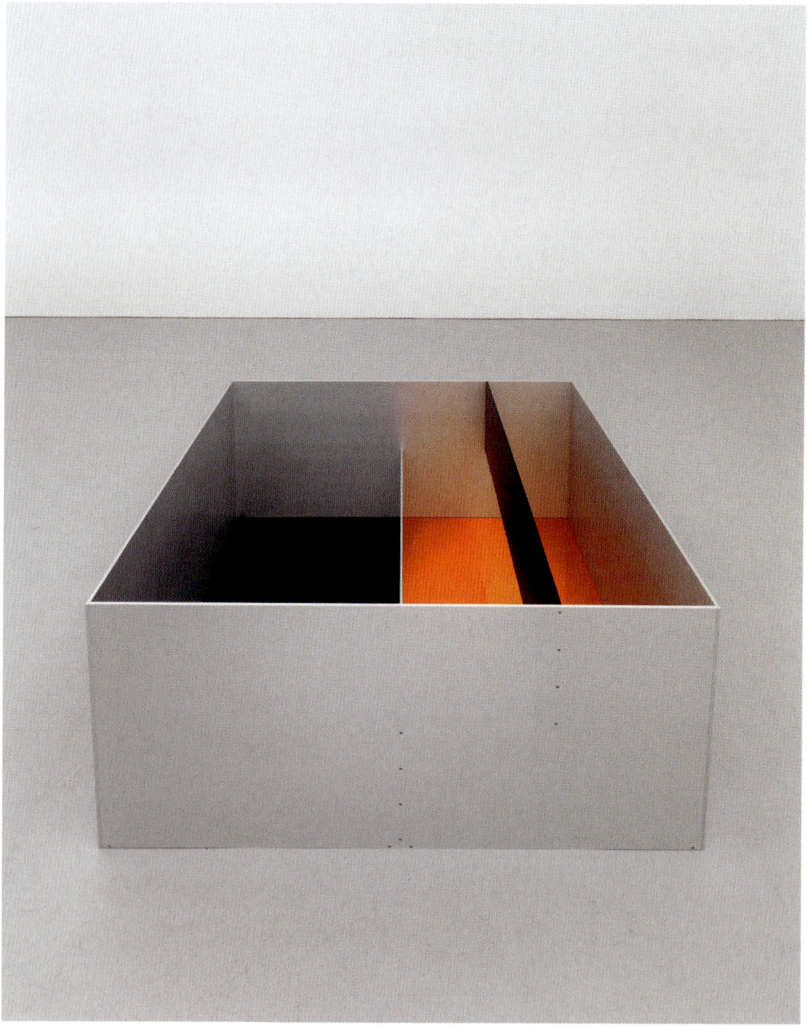

48
Donald Judd
Untitled, 1991
Clear and turquoise anodized aluminum and black acrylic sheet
25 × 100 × 25 cm
($9\frac{13}{16} \times 39\frac{5}{16} \times 9\frac{13}{16}$ inches)

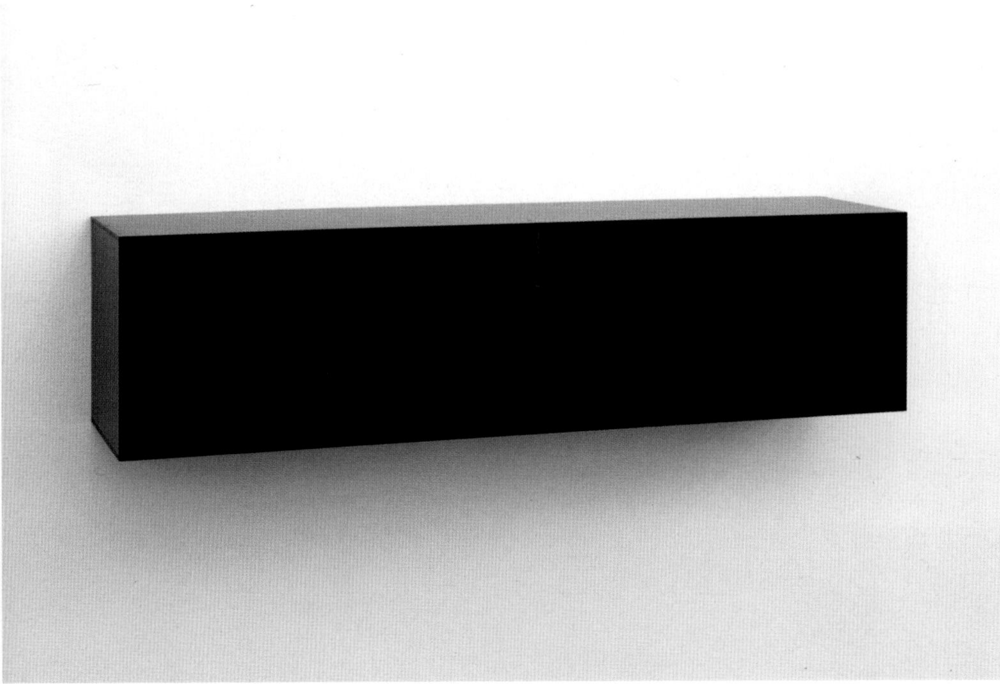

49
Donald Judd
100 untitled works in mill aluminum, 1982-1986
Chinati Foundation, Marfa, Texas

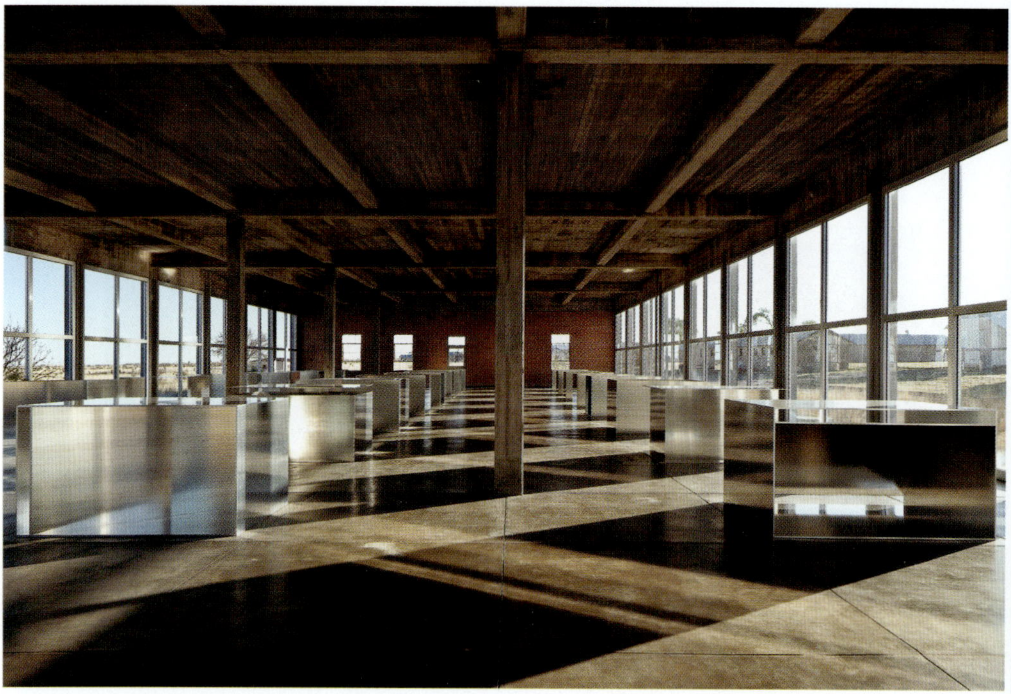

52
Willem de Kooning
Woman, 1949
Oil, enamel and charcoal on canvas
60½ × 47 ⅞ inches
(153.7 × 121.6 cm)

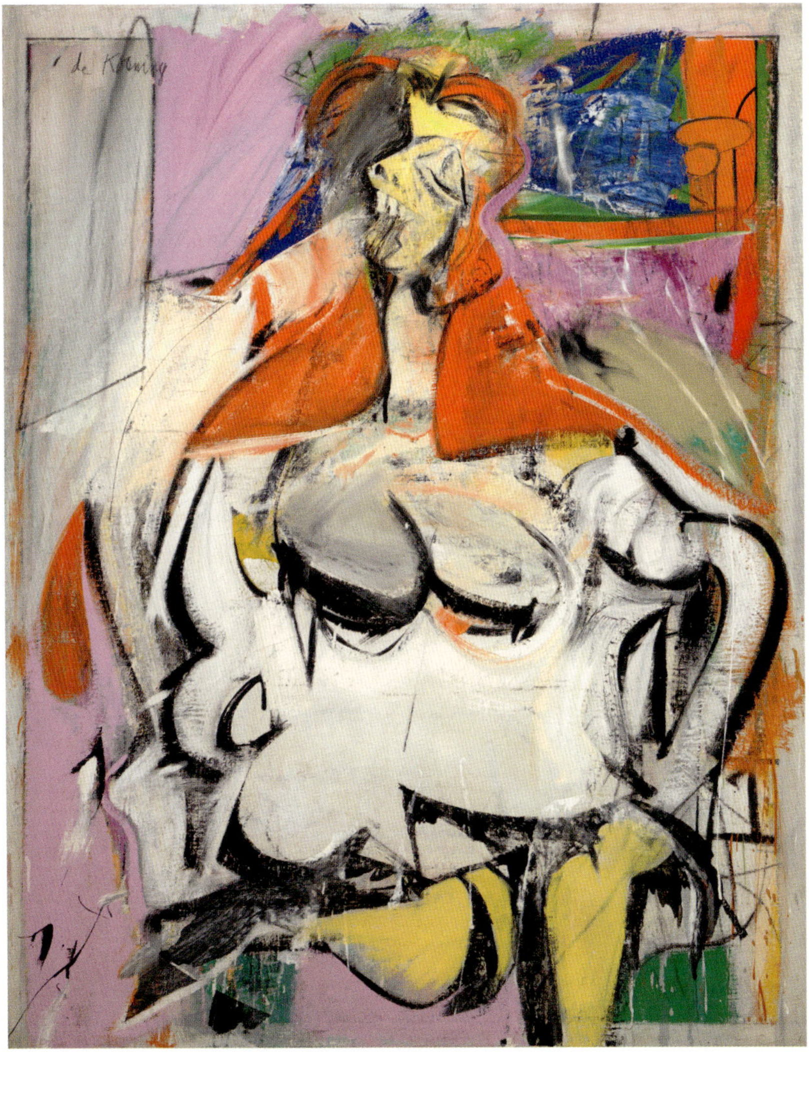

54
Bridget Riley
Evoë 3, 2003
Oil on linen
76¼ inches × 19 ft.
(193.7 × 579.8 cm)

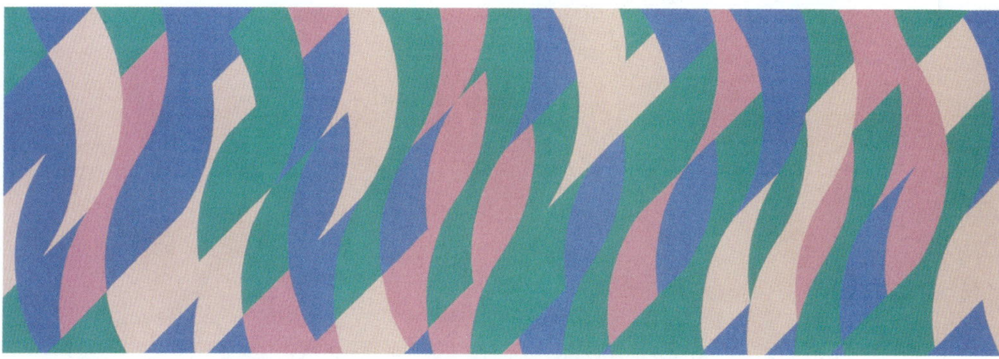

56
Mark Bradford
Field of Miracles, 2010
Graphite on paper on panel
I2 ft. 1 inch × 22 ft. 8 inches
(358.3 × 590.9 cm)

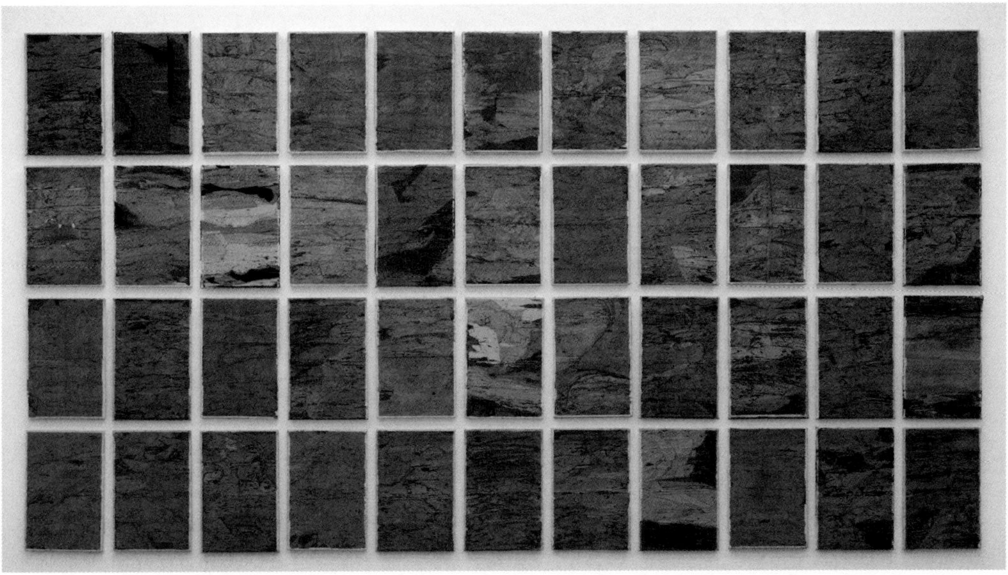

59

Bridget Riley

Arioso (Blue), 2013

Oil on linen

59⅛ × 10¼ inches

(150 × 257.2 cm)

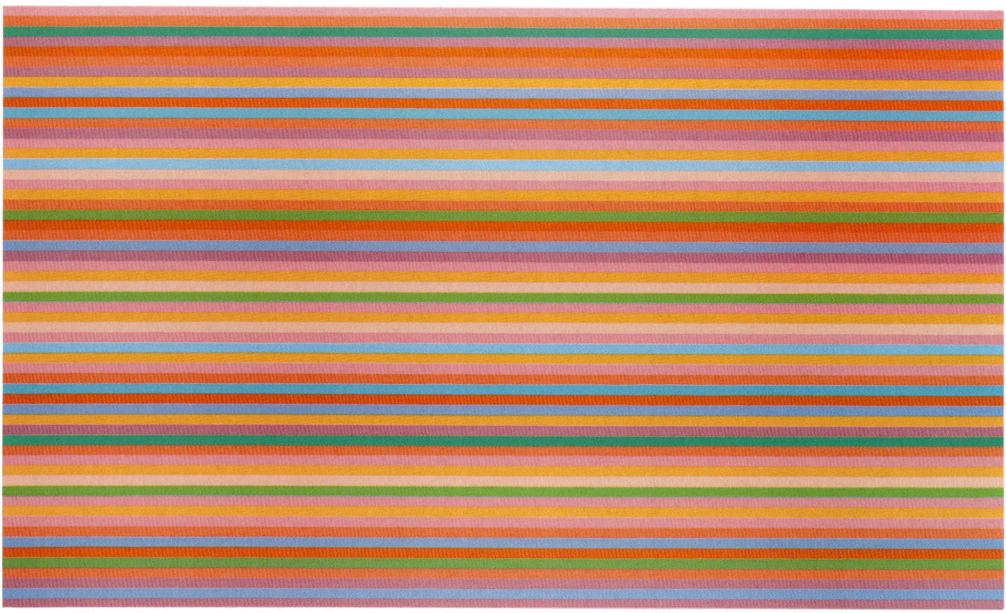

60
Bridget Riley
Lilac Painting 5, 2008/1983
Oil on linen
67.5 × 55.25 inches
(171.5 × 140.3 cm)

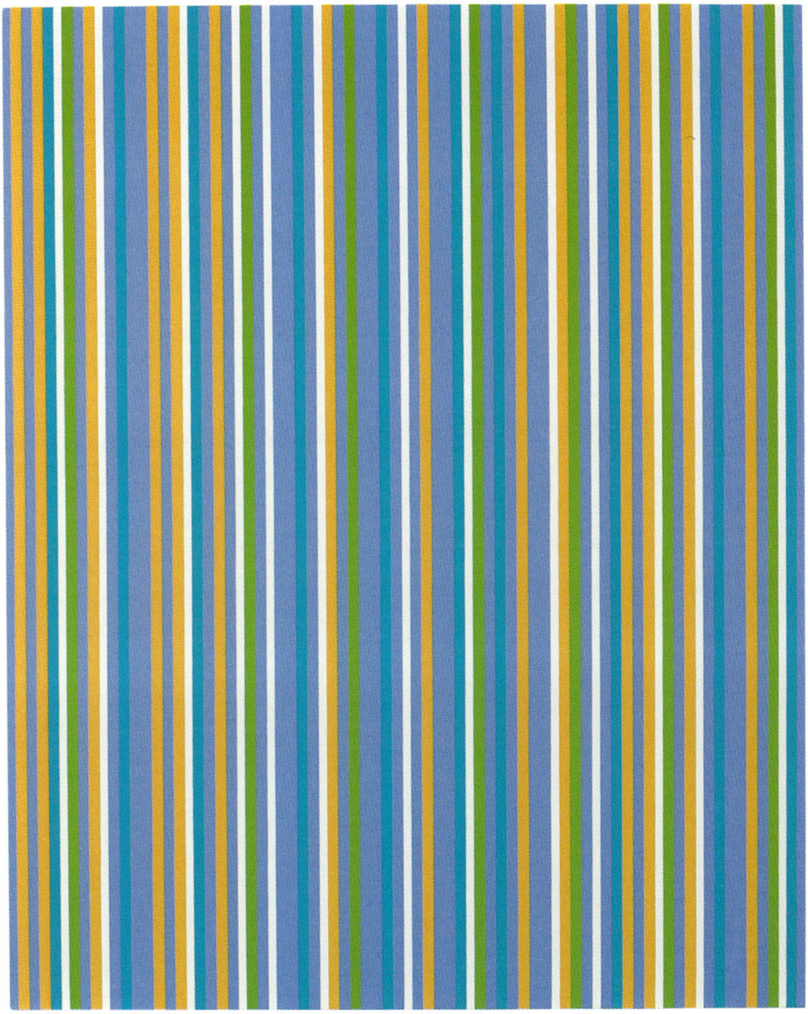

61
Josef Albers
Homage to the Square, 1958
Oil on Masonite
18 × 18 inches
(45.7 × 45.7 cm)

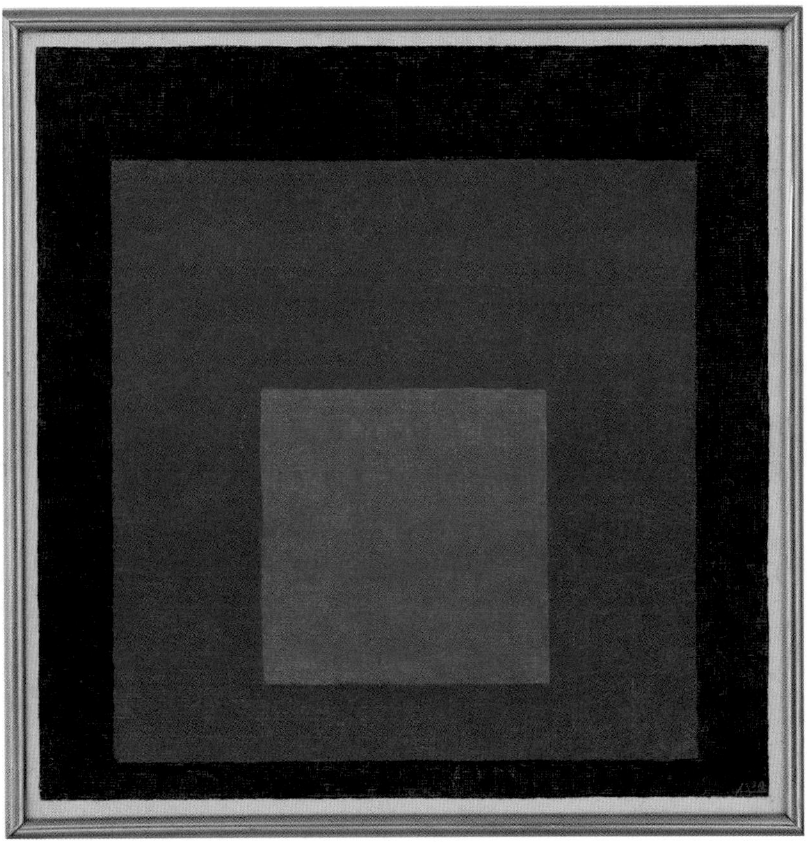

62
Donald Judd
Untitled, 1958
Oil on canvas
30 × 36 inches
(76.2 × 91.4 cm)

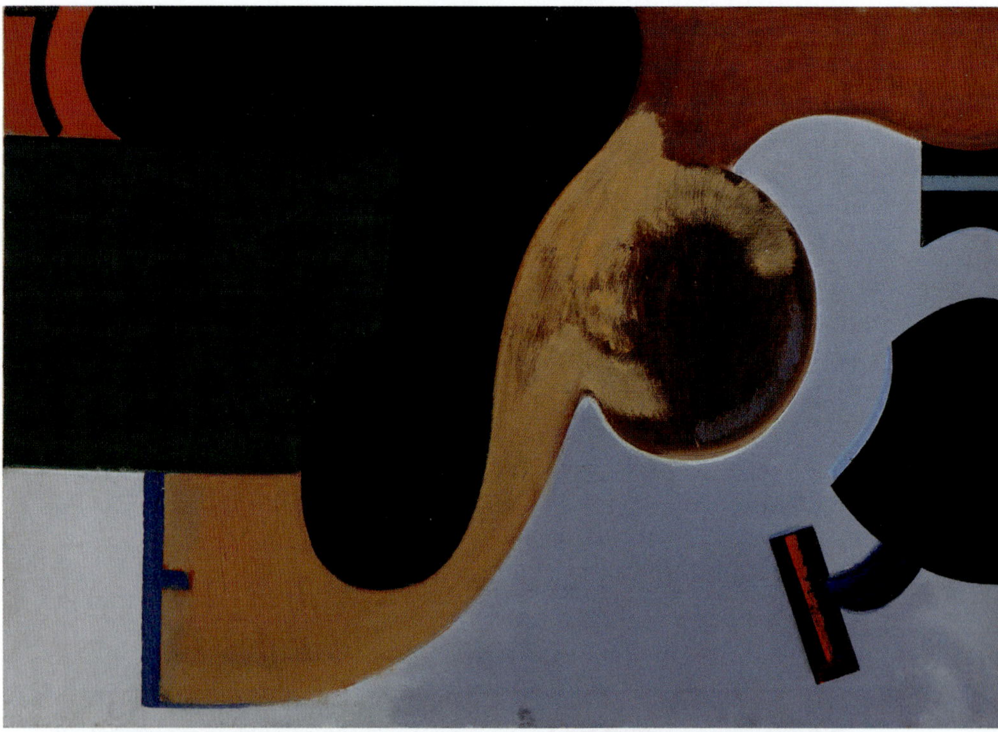

63
Donald Judd
Untitled, 1961
Acrylic on canvas
67½ × 48½ inches
(171.45 × 123.19 cm)

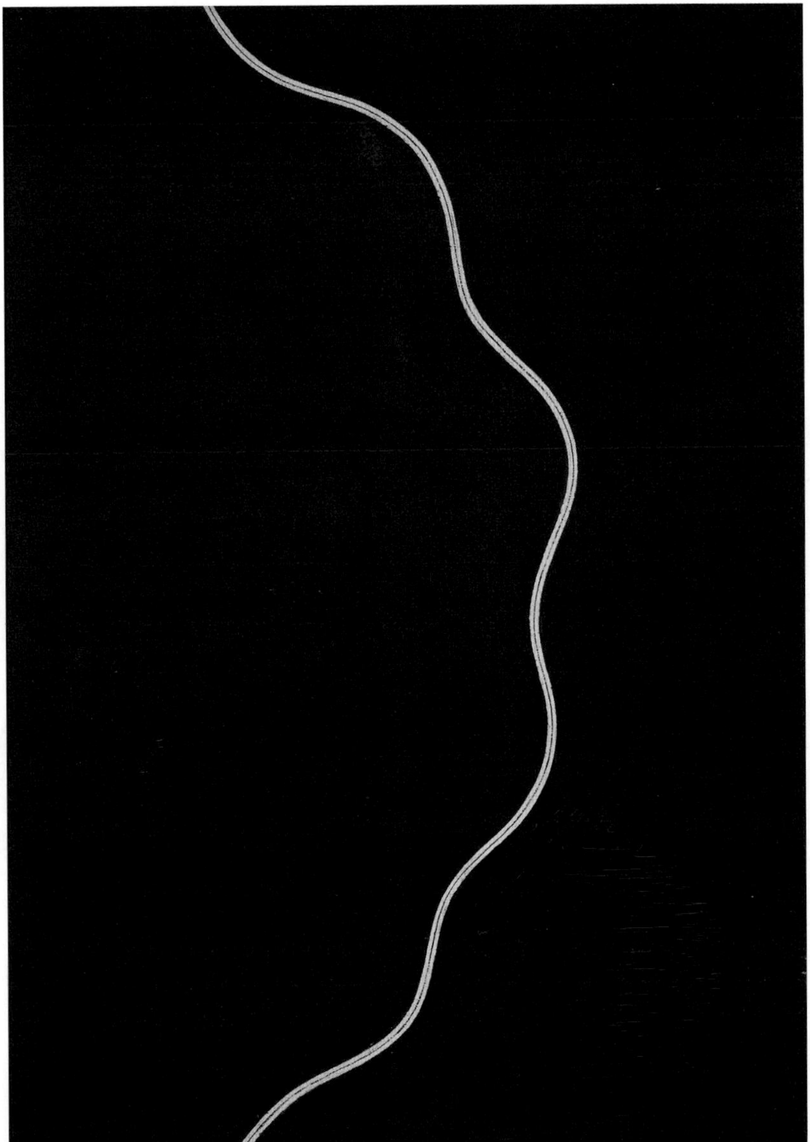

64
Donald Judd
Untitled, 1989
Painted aluminum
30 × 120 × 30 cm
(11¾ × 47¼ × 11¾ inches)

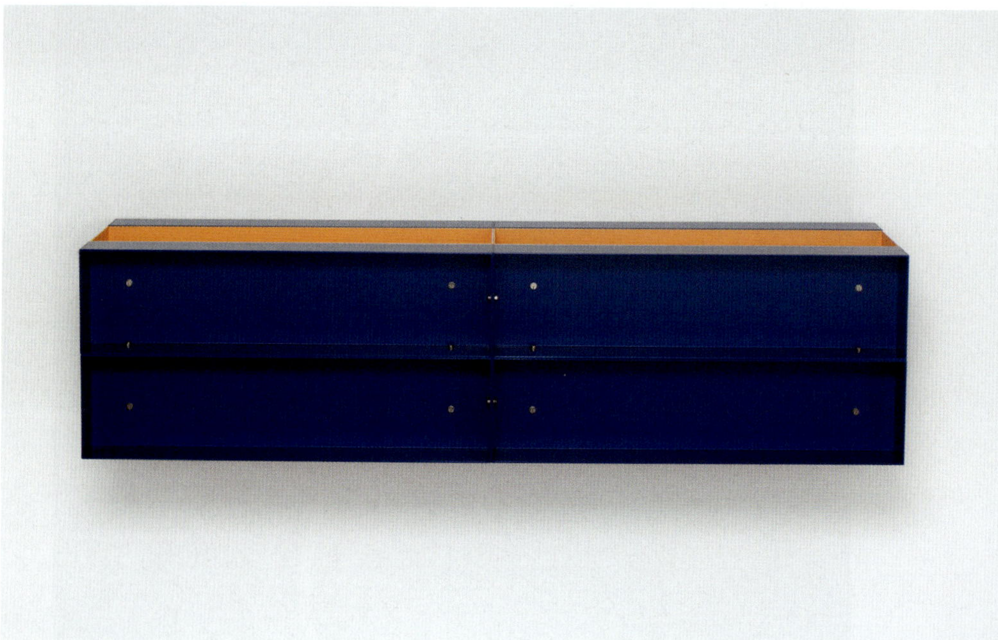

66
Donald Judd
Untitled, 1987
Painted aluminum
30 × 60 × 30 cm
(11¾ × 23 9⁄16 × 11¾ inches)

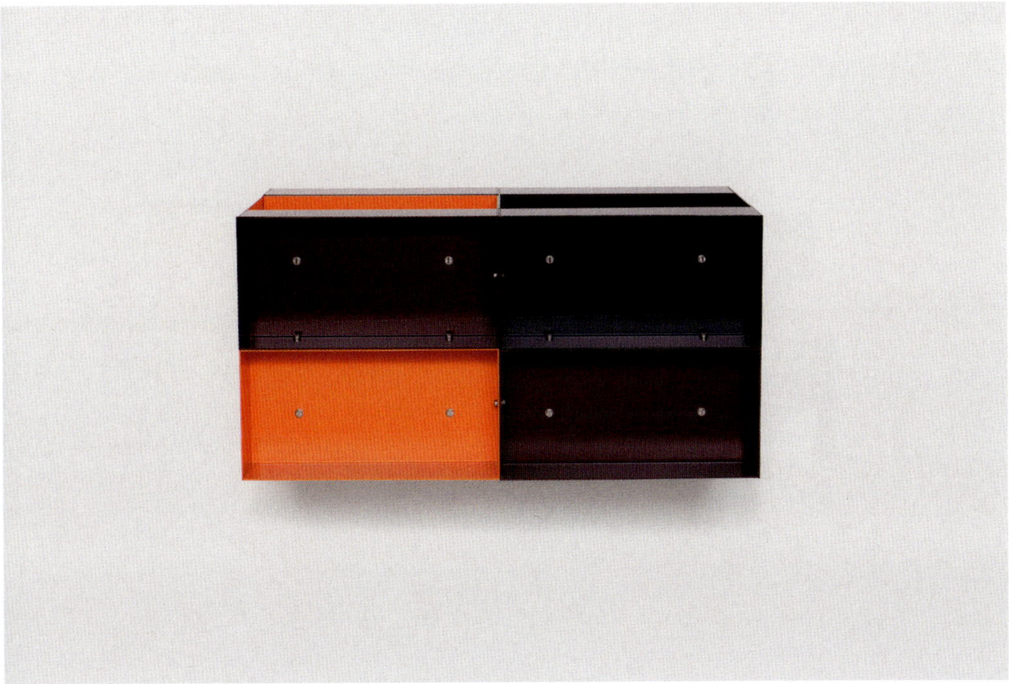

67
Donald Judd
Untitled, 1989
Painted aluminum
30 × 90 × 30 cm
(11¾ × 35⅜ × 11¾ inches)

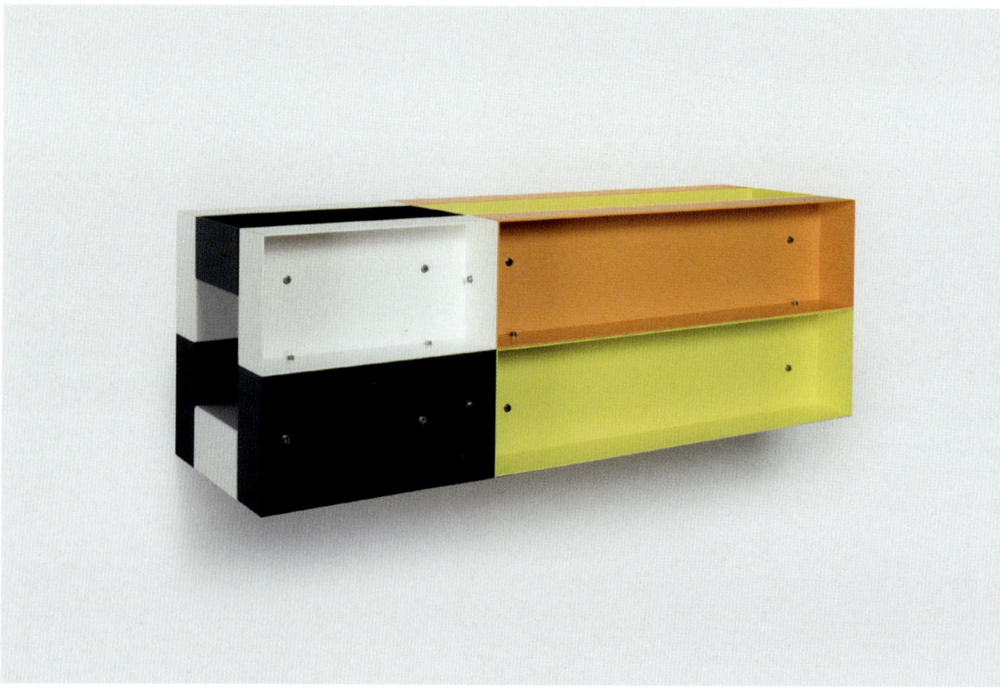

Credits

Collection and Photography Credits

Figure 1
Musée National d'Art Moderne, Centre Georges Pompidou, Paris. Photo: Philippe Migeat © CNAC/ MNAM/Dist. RMN-Grand Palais/Art Resource, NY. Art © 2020 The Barnett Newman Foundation, New York/Artists Rights Society (ARS), New York.

Figures 2, 3, 15, 18, 20, 38, 44, 45
Judd Foundation. Photo: Alex Marks © Judd Foundation.

Figure 4
Collection of Kunstmuseum Düsseldorf im Ehrenhof. Photograph courtesy of Kunstmuseum Basel. © 2020 Frank Stella/Artists Rights Society (ARS), New York.

Figures 5, 41, 46, 47
Photo: Tim Nighswander/IMAGING4ART, courtesy of David Zwirner.

Figure 6
Courtesy of David Zwirner.

Figures 7, 16, 17, 48
Photo: Keith Park, courtesy of Kukje Gallery.

Figures 8, 11, 23, 24, 26, 27, 63, 64, 66
Courtesy of Pace.

Figure 9
The Museum of Modern Art, New York. Gift of UBS
The Museum of Modern Art, New York. Bequest of Richard S. Zeisler and gift of Abby Aldrich Rockefeller (both by exchange) and gift of Kathy Fuld, Agnes Gund, Patricia Cisneros, Doris Fisher, Mimi Haas, Marie-Josée and Henry R. Kravis, and Emily Spiegel. Photograph: John Wronn.

Figures 10, 19, 40, 57, 62
Courtesy of Judd Foundation Archives, Marfa, Texas.

Figure 12
The Metropolitan Museum of Art, George A. Hearn Fund, 1957 (57.92). Photograph © 1998 The Metropolitan Museum of Art © 2020 Pollock-Krasner Foundation/Artists Rights Society (ARS), New York.

Figure 13
Staatliche Museen zu Berlin – Neue Nationalgalerie/ Art Resource, NY. Photo: bpk, Berlinches. Art © 1960 Lee Bontecou.

Figure 14
The Nelson-Atkins Museum of Art, Kansas City, Missouri. Gift of the Chapin Family in memory of Susan Chapin Buckwalter. Art © 1964 Claes Oldenburg.

Figure 21
Permanent collection, the Chinati Foundation, Marfa, Texas. Photo: Florian Holzherr, courtesy of the Chinati Foundation.

Figure 22
Collection of the Philip Johnson Glass House, National Trust for Historic Preservation, New Canaan, Connecticut. Photo: Eric Pollitzer, courtesy The Glass House, New Canaan, Connecticut.

Figure 25
Photo: Steven Probert, courtesy Paula Cooper Gallery.

Figure 28
The Museum of Modern Art, New York. Kay Sage Tanguy Fund. Art © 1961 Lee Bontecou.

Figure 31
National Gallery of Canada, Ottawa. Purchased 1974. Art © 1963 Claes Oldenburg, courtesy the Oldenburg van Bruggen Studio.

Figure 32
Collection of Jill and Peter Kraus.

Figure 35
Photo Lauretta Vinciarelli, courtesy Lauretta Vinciarelli Collection, Judd Foundation Archives, Marfa, Texas.

Figures 36, 37
Permanent collection, the Chinati Foundation, Marfa, Texas. Photo: Alex Marks, courtesy of the Chinati Foundation.

Figure 39
Collection Walker Art Center, Minneapolis. Gift of Mildred and Arnold Glimcher, 1991.

Figure 42
Hirshhorn Museum and Sculpture Garden, Smithsonian Institution, Washington, DC. Joseph H. Hirshhorn Purchase Fund, 1991. Photo: Lee Stalsworth.

Figure 43
Collection Martin Z. Margulies.

Figure 49
Permanent collection, the Chinati Foundation, Marfa, Texas. Photo by Douglas Tuck, courtesy of the Chinati Foundation.

Figures 50, 51
Permanent collection, the Chinati Foundation, Marfa, Texas. Photo by Aurora Tang.

Figures 52, 53
Photo by Tim Nighswander, Imaging4Art. Artwork © 2020 The Willem de Kooning Foundation / Artists Rights Society (ARS), New York.

Figure 54
Collection Tate Gallery © Bridget Riley 2020. Photo © Tate.
Figures 55, 56
© Mark Bradford, courtesy the artist and Hauser & Wirth.
Figures 58, 59, 60
© Bridget Riley 2020.
Figure 61
Judd Foundation. © 2020 The Josef and Anni Albers Foundation/Artists Rights Society (ARS), New York. Photo: Alex Marks © Judd Foundation
Figure 65
Photo © Stedelijk Museum, Amsterdam 2020.
Figure 67
Courtesy Paula Cooper Gallery.

Richard Shiff is the Effie Marie Cain Regents Chair in Art at The University of Texas at Austin, where he directs the Center for the Study of Modernism. His scholarly interests range broadly across the field of modern and contemporary art. His publications include *Cézanne and the End of Impressionism* (1984), *Critical Terms for Art History* (co edited, 1996, 2003), *Barnett Newman: A Catalogue Raisonné* (co authored, 2004), *Doubt* (2008), *Between Sense and de Kooning* (2011), *Ellsworth Kelly: New York Drawings 1954-1962* (2014), and *Joel Shapiro: Sculpture and Works on Paper 1969-2019* (2019).

Text Credits

Essays included in this volume were previously published in the following publications:

"Donald Judd: Fast Thinking," in *Donald Judd: Late Work*, exh. cat. PaceWildenstein, New York 2000, 4-23.

"A Space of One to One," in *Donald Judd: 50 x 100 x 50, 100 x 100 x 50*, exh. cat. PaceWildenstein, New York 2002, 56-23.

"Judd Through Oldenburg," *Chinati Foundation Newsletter* 9, October 2004: 33-44.

"Specificity," in *The Writings of Donald Judd*, ed. Marianne Stockebrand, Marfa: The Chinati Foundation, 2009, 78-98. (As published).

"To Stop the Heart," in Marianne Stockebrand, ed., *Chinati – The Vision of Donald Judd*, New Haven and London: Yale University Press, 2010, 267-71.

"Projection, Projection," *Chinati Foundation Newsletter* 15, October 2010: 64-69.

"What Judd Knows," in Kristin Bell, Anna Gray, and Alexandra Whitney, eds. *Donald Judd*, Göttingen: Steidl/David Zwirner, 2011, 19-63.

"Every Shiny Object Wants an Infant Who Will Love it," *Art Journal* 70, Spring 2011: 6-33.

"As It Feels," *Chinati Foundation Newsletter* 19, October 2014: 54-64.

"Sensuous Thoughts," in Marianne Stockebrand, ed., *Donald Judd: The Multicolored Works*, New Haven and London: Yale University Press, 2014, 106-156.

Additional essays by Richard Shiff on Donald Judd:

"Donald Judd, Safe From Birds," in Nicholas Serota, ed., *Donald Judd*, exh. cat. Tate Modern, London; K20 Kunstsammlung am Grabbeplatz, Düsseldorf; Kunstmuseum Basel and Museum für Gegenwartskunst, 2004-2005; London: Tate Publishing, 2004, 28-61.

"Space Is Made," in *Donald Judd: Single Stacks 1964-1969*, exh. cat. Van de Weghe Fine Art, New York 2006, 8-13.

"On Donald Judd's Concrete Works," *Chinati Foundation Newsletter* 15, October 2010: 16-23.

"On Knowing an Object," in Glenn Peers, ed., *Byzantine Things in the World*, exh. cat. Menil Collection, Houston 2013, 128-39.

Colophon

Editors: Tim Johnson and Caitlin Murray
Copy editor: David Tompkins
Graphic design: Rutger Fuchs
Production: Thomas Lemaître, Hatje Cantz
Reproductions: Process Graphic, Paris
Printing and binding: Livonia Print, Riga
Paper: Munken Print, Maxi Gloss, Geltex
Typeface: Arnhem

Published by:
Marfa Book Co.
105 South Highland Avenue
P.O. Box 1752
Marfa, Texas 79843
marfabookco.com

Published and distributed by:
Hatje Cantz Verlag GmbH
Mommsenstraße 27
10629 Berlin
Germany
www.hatjecantz.de
A Ganske Publishing Group Company

Library of Congress Control Number: 2020901802

ISBN: 978-3-7757-4750-9 (Hatje Cantz Verlag)
ISBN: 978-1-7923-2731-5 (Marfa Book Co.)

Printed in Latvia